Probing the Limits of Representation

D1026933

Probing the Limits of Representation

$<<<>>>$

Nazism and the "Final Solution"

Edited by

Saul Friedlander

940.5318
P962

Harvard University Press
Cambridge, Massachusetts
London, England

Alverno College
Library Media Center
Milwaukee, Wisconsin

Copyright © 1992 by the President and Fellows of Harvard College
Introduction copyright © 1992 by Saul Friedlander
All rights reserved
Printed in the United States of America
SECOND PRINTING, 1993

This book is printed on acid-free paper, and its binding materials have been chosen for
strength and durability.

Library of Congress Cataloging-in-Publication Data

Probing the limits of representation: Nazism and the "Final Solution"
edited by Saul Friedlander.
p.   cm.
Includes index.
ISBN 0–674–70765–6 (alk. paper); ISBN 0–674–70766–4 (pbk.)
1. Holocaust, Jewish (1939–1945)—Historiography.
2. Holocaust, Jewish (1939–1945)—Influence.
3. Holocaust, Jewish (1939–1945), in literature.
I. Friedländer, Saul, 1932- .
D804.3.P76   1992
940.53'18—dc20   91–29609
CIP

Acknowledgments

The conference on "Nazism and the 'Final Solution': Probing the Limits of Representation" which led to this volume was held at the University of California, Los Angeles, on April 26–29, 1990; it was organized under the auspices and with the help of the Department of History at UCLA and the "1939 Club" of Los Angeles. The conference was made possible by the generous financial assistance of the Center for Social Theory and Comparative History at UCLA; the Critical Studies and the Human Sciences Focused Research Unit (UCLA); the College of Letters and Science (UCLA); the German Academic Exchange Program; and the University of California Humanities Research Institute, Irvine.

The papers of all the commentators at the various sessions could not be included in this volume because of space constraints. Their intellectual input during the conference and in the preparation of this volume has been considerable. Their names are mentioned with gratitude: Peter Baldwin (UCLA), Edward Berenson (UCLA), Marianna Birnbaum (UCLA), Robert Boyers (Skidmore College), Philippe Burrin (Graduate Institute of International Studies, Geneva), Arnold Davidson (Chicago), Denis Donoghue (New York University), David James Fisher (UCLA), Michael Geyer (Chicago), Wulf Kansteiner (UCLA), Rudy Koshar (University of Southern California), Peter Loewenberg (UCLA), Leo Loewenthal (UC Berkeley), Charles Maier (Harvard), Peter Novick (Chicago), Froma Zeitlin (Princeton).

Finally, as convener of the conference, I would like to thank especially my two assistants, Beatrice Kansteiner (Dumin) and Wulf Kansteiner, without whose help it would have been difficult to organize the event.

Saul Friedlander

Contents

Introduction

SAUL FRIEDLANDER

> When I went into our little office this morning, it was a terrible mess; it had been requisitioned as a dressing room for the [musical] revue. The revue is taking over the whole camp. There are no overalls for people on outside duty, but the revue has an "overall ballet"—so day and night people sewed overalls with little puffed sleeves for the dancers. Wood from the synagogue in Assen has been sawed up to make a stage . . . Oh, Maria, Maria—Before the last transport, the people who were due to leave worked all day for the revue. Everything here has an indescribably clownish madness and sadness.
>
> Letter from Etty Hillesum to a friend, Westerbork camp (Holland), 2 September 1943. Hillesum died in Auschwitz on 30 November 1943.

Most of the contributors to this volume are not the usual interlocutors in discussions of the Holocaust: although a few of them are scholars who have dealt extensively with issues related to Nazism and the extermination of the Jews of Europe, the majority are not. The aim here is not to deal with a specific historical aspect of these events or with their particular expression in literature, in the arts, or in philosophy. The underlying assumption is that we are dealing with an event of a kind which demands a global approach and a general reflection on the difficulties that are raised by its representation.

This project evokes some doubts which are not easily dispelled. Can the extermination of the Jews of Europe be the object of theoretical discussions? Is it not unacceptable to debate formal and abstract issues in relation to this catastrophe? It would be if these abstract issues were not directly related to the way contemporary culture reshapes the image of this past. Present memory of Nazism and its crimes is directly influenced by global intellectual shifts intrinsically linked to the questions raised in this volume. The necessity of such discussion is thus clear; it will be evident, moreover, that none of the contributors has forgotten the horror behind the words.

The basic problem we shall be dealing with has been on the minds

< 1 >

of many since the very end of the war, and Theodor Adorno's (often misunderstood) utterance about writing poetry after Auschwitz has turned into its best-known point of reference. Nonetheless, the challenge has become more perceptible during the last two decades, as the result of an ongoing shaping and reshaping of the image of the Nazi epoch. During the seventies, film and literature opened the way to some sort of "new discourse."[1] Historiography followed and the mid-eighties witnessed heated debates about new interpretations of the "Final Solution" in history (the best-known of these debates being the German "historians' controversy") and, in more general terms, about the proper historicization of National Socialism, that is, of "Auschwitz." In these various domains new narratives about Nazism came to the fore, new forms of representation appeared. In many cases they seemed to test implicit boundaries and to raise not only aesthetic and intellectual problems, but moral issues too. The question of the limits of representation of Nazism and its crimes has become a recurrent theme in relation to various concrete subjects. Here the overall aspect of this problem is our main concern.

The immediate incentive for the conference leading to this volume was a debate which took place in 1989 on "History, Event, and Discourse," during which Hayden White and Carlo Ginzburg presented opposing views on the nature of historical truth. The echoes of such a debate were reinforced by still-lingering controversies on the historicization of Nazism. The extermination of the Jews of Europe, as the most extreme case of mass criminality, must challenge theoreticians of historical relativism to face the corollaries of positions otherwise too easily dealt with on an abstract level. Of course the basic questions asked here refer also to forms of representation other than the historical.

The very nature of this project called for the expression of a great diversity of views, some of which I have reservations about. Therefore, this introduction is not merely a traditional presentation and pulling-together of the themes raised by the contributors from the point of view of a "neutral" editor; it is equally the expression of a personal stand.

The extermination of the Jews of Europe is as accessible to both representation and interpretation as any other historical event. But we are dealing with an event which tests our traditional conceptual and representational categories, an "event at the limits."

What turns the "Final Solution" into an event at the limits is the very fact that it is the most radical form of genocide encountered in history: the willful, systematic, industrially organized, largely successful attempt totally to exterminate an entire human group within twentieth-century Western society. In Jürgen Habermas' words: "There [in Auschwitz] something happened, that up to now nobody considered as even possible. There one touched on something which represents the deep layer of solidarity among all that wears a human face; notwithstanding all the usual acts of beastliness of human history, the integrity of this common layer had been taken for granted . . . Auschwitz has changed the basis for the continuity of the conditions of life within history."[2]

It would seem self-evident that such a monstrous manifestation of human "potentialities" would not be forgotten or repressed. If one adds the fact that the perpetrators invested considerable effort not only in camouflage, but in effacement of all traces of their deeds, the obligation to bear witness and record this past seems even more compelling. Such a postulate implies, quite naturally, the imprecise but no less self-evident notion that this record should not be distorted or banalized by grossly inadequate representations. Some claim to "truth" appears particularly imperative. It suggests, in other words, that there are limits to representation *which should not be but can easily be transgressed*. What the characteristics of such a transgression are, however, is far more intractable than our definitions have so far been able to encompass.

It may be that we feel the obligation of keeping the record of this past through some sort of "master-narrative," without actually being able to define its necessary components. The reason for the sense of obligation is clear, but the difficulty in establishing the elements of such a master-narrative (except on the simplest factual level) may stem from the impression that this event, perceived in its totality, may signify more than the sum of its components. Our problem thus appears to center on intangible but nonetheless perceived boundaries. The dilemma we are identifying is *not* one of gross transgression (the denial of the Holocaust, for instance). The intractable criterion seems to be a kind of uneasiness. The problem is neither narrowly scientific nor blatantly ideological: one cannot define exactly what is wrong with a certain representation of the events, but, as Christopher Browning suggests, one senses when some interpretation or representation is wrong. Can it be that this kind of reaction is due to the sensitivity or hypersensitivity found among a specific generation—be it among Jews, Germans, or others still deeply sensitized to the Nazi epoch? I would agree with Dominick LaCapra that in this case the problem of "transference" is indeed more widespread and complex by far than for most other historical events, and is not limited to the contemporaries of those years.

I shall come back to the transference question. Our central dilemma can be defined as confronting the issues raised by historical relativism and aesthetic experimentation in the face of two possibly contrary constraints: a need for "truth," and the problems raised by the opaqueness of the events and the opaqueness of language as such. This dilemma leads us to consider some of the following points:

The implications of historical relativism in general;

The implications of the construction of any number of historical narratives about Nazism and the "Final Solution," as long as the facts are not falsified (this is the gist of various arguments regarding the historicization of Nazism and the "Final Solution");

The existence or nonexistence of limits to literary and artistic renditions of the Shoah (in general terms);

The contradictory implications of specific approaches to this last type of rendition.

Let me dwell on this last point as it is linked to contrary epistemological, aesthetic, and ideological positions: "postmodernism," as opposed to traditional and modernist modes of representation.

First, some obvious problems of limits, as understood here, have already appeared in the wake of the application of postmodern aesthetics to the rendition of Nazism and the Shoah, from Luchino Visconti and Lina Wertmüller to Hans Jürgen Syberberg in film, from Michel Tournier in literature to some of the paintings of Anselm Kiefer, among others. An argument could obviously be made for the necessity of ideological ambiguity and aesthetic experimentation in the face of events which seem to escape usual categories of representation.

Second, postmodern thought's rejection of the possibility of identifying some stable reality or truth beyond the constant polysemy and self-referentiality of linguistic constructs challenges the need to establish the realities and the truths of the Holocaust; conversely, the very openness of postmodernism to what cannot yet be formulated in decisive statements, but merely sensed, directly relates to whoever considers that even the most precise historical renditions of the Shoah contain an opaqueness at the core which confronts traditional historical narrative.

Finally, it is precisely the "Final Solution" which allows postmodernist thinking to question the validity of any totalizing view of history, of any reference to a definable metadiscourse, thus opening the way for a multiplicity of equally valid approaches. This very multiplicity, however, may lead to any aesthetic fantasy and once again runs counter to the need for establishing a stable truth as far as this past is concerned.

Jean-François Lyotard takes "Auschwitz" as reference to demonstrate the impossibility of any single, integrated discourse about history and politics. The voices of the perpetrators and those of the victims are fundamentally heterogeneous and mutually exclusive. The striving for totality and consensus is, in Lyotard's view, the very basis of the fascist enterprise. As for the indetermination, the inadequacy which assails us in the face of "Auschwitz," he succeeds in expressing it by using a particularly striking metaphor, that of an earthquake which would be so powerful as to destroy all instruments of measurement. Since no possibility would consequently exist of establishing an exact, "scientific" evaluation of this earthquake, scholars could claim that nothing was known to them about it. For the "common person," however, the "complex feeling of something indeterminate having happened would stay in memory: 'Mutatis mutandis,' the silence that the crime of Auschwitz imposes upon the historian, is a sign for the common person. Signs are not referents validatable under the cognitive regimen, they indicate that something which should be able to be put into phrases cannot be phrased in the accepted idioms . . . The silence that surrounds the phrase 'Auschwitz was the extermination camp' is not a state of mind (état d'âme), it is a sign that something remains to be phrased which is not, something which is not determined."[3] Thus on the one hand, our traditional categories of conceptualization and representation may well be insufficient, our language itself problematic. On the other hand, in the face of these events we feel the need of some stable narration; a boundless field of possible discourses raises the issue of limits with particular stringency.

In his foreword to Lyotard's *Heidegger and "the Jews,"* David Caroll phrases very precisely what is at stake:

> We are required to judge the philosophical, literary, political, historical and moral effects of the different ways of talking or not talking about "that" [the Shoah] and yet we do not have the systems of belief or knowledge, the rules, the historical certainty or the philosophical or political concepts necessary to derive or determine judgment. If for Lyotard (and Kant), the lack of determining criteria characterizes the political and the aesthetic "fields" in general, this indeterminacy has special significance when it comes to the Shoah, this limit case of knowledge and feeling, in terms of which all such systems of belief and thought, all forms of literary and artistic expression, seem irrelevant or even criminal. This does not diminish the role of the critical faculty but on the contrary makes it all the more crucial and necessary.[4]

In summation, the nature of the events we are dealing with may lead to various approaches in terms of representation, and the outright negation of most of them would not do justice to the *contradictory demands* raised by the evocation of this past.

The issue of historical knowledge, of historical "truth," which is at the origin of this debate, must be referred to at the very outset. It is at this initial point that the implications of Hayden White's positions can be confronted. White does not call into question the possibility of assessing the reality or even the exactness of historical *events*. But a mere enumeration of events leaves us at best with annals or a chronicle. In order to provide a full-fledged historical narrative, a coherent emplotment linking beginning, middle, and end within a specific *framework of interpretation* is unavoidable.

White's by now familiar position aims at systematizing a theory of historical interpretation based on a fundamental redefinition of traditional historical understanding: Language as such imposes on the historical narrative a limited choice of rhetorical forms, implying specific emplotments, explicative models, and ideological stances. These unavoidable choices determine the specificity of various interpretations of historical events. There is no "objective," outside criterion to establish that one particular interpretation is more true than another. In that sense White is close to what could be termed a postmodern approach to history.[5]

In his 1982 article, "The Politics of Historical Interpretation," White suggested that traditional historiography has repressed the indeterminacy of the "sublime." The one exception in this regard is, according to him, the fascist view of history. "The kind of perspective on history I have been implicitly praising," he wrote, "is conventionally associated with the ideologies of fascist regimes. Something like Schiller's notion of the historical sublime or Nietzsche's version of it is certainly present in the thought of such philosophers as Heidegger and Gentile and in the intuitions of Hitler and Mussolini." However, he added, "We must guard against a sentimentalism that would lead us to write off such a conception of history simply because it has been associated with fascist ideologies. *One must face the fact that when it comes to apprehending the historical record, there are no grounds to be found in the historical record itself for preferring one way of construing its meaning over another*" (my italics).[6] Although White has recognized the transparent horrors of fascism as well as the dilemma stemming from his extreme relativism, he has not offered any solution before attempting a compromise position in this volume.

For most historians a precise description of the unfolding of events is meant to carry its own interpretation, its own truth. This, for instance, is the impact of the empirical evidence presented in Christopher Browning's account of the murderous trail of *Ordnungspolizei* Unit 101 from Hamburg when transferred to the small Polish (Jewish) town of Jozefów on 13 July 1942. Browning's extremely detailed and precise description of the behavior of this unit and of individuals belonging to it, showing the passage from the "normality" of an ordinary police formation to its functioning as an instrument of mass murder, intuitively substantiates an interpretative framework which extends far beyond the history of this particular set of events. For Browning "there are no clearly distinct and separate categories of attestable fact on the one hand and pure interpretation on the other. Rather there is a spectrum or continuum": the very mass of ascertainable facts pertaining to the "Final Solution" determines the overall interpretation, not the other way around. There is still, however, the question of how one moves from the chronicle (Hayden White would probably consider Browning's harrowing account in the category of the chronicle) to levels of historiography where interpretive frameworks are determinant, notwithstanding the abundance of available material.

Whereas Christopher Browning's critique of White adopts in fact the "thick description" position, Amos Funkenstein attempts to demonstrate the paradox to which White's relativism may lead, by invoking the polemical-rhetorical genre of "counterhistory." He, too, however, has to substantiate the fact that some exercises in "worldmaking" are less arbitrary than others, by referring to an intuitive criterion not unlike Browning's. "If true," he writes, "reality, whatever its definition, must 'shine through it' [the narrative] like Heidegger's being—and, like the latter, without ever appearing directly."

Perry Anderson's critique confronts White's analytic categories directly. At the end of his analysis of one of the core texts of the "historians' debate," Andreas Hillgruber's *Zweierlei Untergang*,[7] Anderson writes:

> First, certain absolute limits are set by the evidence. Denial of the existence of either—the regime or its crimes—is plainly ruled out . . . Narrative strategies, to be credible, always operate within *exterior* limits of this kind. Second, however, such narrative strategies are in turn subject to a double *interior* limitation. On the one hand, certain kinds of evidence preclude certain sorts of emplotment: the Final Solution cannot *historically* be written as romance or as comedy. On the other hand, any generic emplotment has only a weak determinative power over the selection of evidence. Hillgruber could legitimately depict the end of East Prussia as tragic; that choice, however, permitted by the evidence, did not in itself dictate the series of particular empirical judgments that make up his account of it.

Although the criticism of White's positions mentioned thus far opts for an epistemological approach, Carlo Ginzburg's passionate plea for historical objectivity and truth is as much informed by a deeply ethical position as by analytic categories. Ginzburg quotes a letter from the French historian Pierre Vidal-Naquet referring to the controversy, launched in France by "revisionists" such as Robert Faurisson, about the existence or nonexistence of gas chambers in the Nazi camps. "I was convinced that there was an ongoing discourse on gas chambers," writes Vidal-Naquet, "that everything should necessarily go through to a discourse; but beyond this, or before this, there was something irreducible which, for better or worse, I would still call reality. Without this reality, how could we make a difference between fiction and history?" Here we are indeed—as Hayden White himself perceived—at the "irreducible" core of our discussions; here we are confronted with the unavoidable link between the ethical and the epistemological dimensions of our debate. Instead of directing his critique primarily to White's concepts as such, Ginzburg seeks to uncover the intellectual origins of White's approach and their possible consequences for our discussion.

Ginzburg underlines the intellectual influence exercised on White's thought by Italian neoidealism, particularly by Benedetto Croce and Giovanni Gentile. Gentile's radical idealism, his rejection of any truth to be derived from facts, led him, within the context of Italian fascism (of which he was the prime philosopher), to establish "effectiveness" as the only criterion for the validity of any historical-political interpretation. According to Ginzburg, in "The Politics of Historical Interpretation," White ultimately equivocates when it comes to a distinction between true interpretation and lies, and he too seems to rely on the criterion of "effectiveness" as the only compelling mode of distinction. (In my opinion, White's position could be open to different readings on this point.) For Ginzburg, the influence of the philosopher of fascism on White's theory of history is thus unambiguously established. Finally, Ginzburg rounds off his thesis by stating the most extreme counterposition to White's relativism: even the voice of *one single witness* gives us some access to the domain of historical reality, allows us to get nearer to some historical truth.

At the outset of his chapter Ginzburg discusses what may have been a *topos* of Jewish historical narration over centuries: the survival of two witnesses to tell about major catastrophes. Less than fifty years ago, *topos* and reality became one; the rhetoric of historical narration and the ascertainable facts converged. In the cases reported by Ginzburg, two witnesses survived of the forty who committed collective suicide. At the Belzec extermination site, two survived of the approximately 600,000 Jews who were massacred at this location.

Hayden White's position as expressed in the present volume appears a search for compromise, a way of escaping the most extreme corollaries or implications of his relativism. In Martin Jay's words, "In his anxiety to avoid inclusion in the ranks of those who argue for a kind of relativistic anything goes, which might provide ammunition for revisionist skeptics about the existence of the Holocaust, he undercuts what is most powerful in his celebrated critique of naive historical realism."

Saul Friedlander

< 10 >

But White's compromise position is different from that suggested by Jay, who believes in the possibility of reaching a consensus within the community of scholars on the basis of a Habermasian process of communicative reason. (Incidentally, such a position should be no less of an anathema to Carlo Ginzburg than is White's traditional stance, as truth ultimately is established by growing rational consensus, which does not necessarily mean by document and witness.) White does admit that not every form of emplotment can be used for the historical narration of every set of events: "In the case of an emplotment of the events of the Third Reich in a 'comic' or 'pastoral' mode, we would be eminently justified in appealing to 'the facts' in order to dismiss it from the lists of 'competing narratives' of the Third Reich." The hypothesis of an ironic emplotment which would allow for a metacritical comment on comic or pastoral emplotments of the events of the Third Reich would indeed not raise any specific problem, because it would cancel the validity of the comic or pastoral emplotments. The point is that pastoral or comic emplotments are excluded by "the facts" as plausible independent discourses about these events.

White's theses are, in my opinion, open to additional critique and, all in all, appear untenable when their corollaries are considered within the present context. For instance, what would have happened if the Nazis had won the war? No doubt there would have been a plethora of pastoral emplotments of life in the Third Reich and of comic emplotments of the disappearance of its victims, mainly the Jews. How, in this case, would White (who clearly rejects any revisionist version of the Holocaust) define an epistemological criterion for refuting a comic interpretation of these events, without using any reference to "political effectiveness"?

White puts considerable emphasis on the search for an adequate "voice" to represent events such as Nazism and the Holocaust, that is, for a rhetorical mode which would fit extreme occurrences in the modern epoch. Without entering here into a discussion of the "middle voice," or "intransitive writing," which White considers as the possibly adequate mode, I would suggest that the corollary of this quest is fairly apparent: *it is the reality and significance of modern catastrophes that generate the search for a new voice and not the use of a specific voice which constructs the significance of these catastrophes.*

The rather sharp dichotomy I have tried to outline repeats itself according to a somewhat more complex pattern of associations within a second set of essays. Dominick LaCapra's opening text leads in several directions: the search for new categories of historical analysis in the face of the "Final Solution" (in this sense LaCapra is close to Lyotard's overall position as well as to Hayden White's quest for a new rhetorical mode); and the centrality of the subject position of the historian in the understanding of any approach to these events (this postulate leads of necessity to the problem of German identity, through various ways of working through or repressing the Nazi past, as shown in Eric Santner's text). LaCapra's and Santner's shared concentration on the psychological dimension of the dilemmas facing postwar Germany is thoroughly opposed by those who, on critical-ideological grounds, see Western capitalism and its specific "rationality" as the matrix within which Nazism and its crimes unfolded.

In his search for new categories of historical analysis, LaCapra fundamentally calls into question any positivist approach: the historian has to rethink traditional categories when confronted with events such as the Holocaust, which in turn may lead one to a much more radical reconsideration. "I do not think," writes LaCapra, "that conventional techniques, which in certain respects are necessary, are ever sufficient, and to some extent the study of the Holocaust may help us to reconsider the requirements of historiography in general."

Although such a position seems to me highly convincing, it depends ultimately on the concrete development of new historiographical thinking and on the possibility of achieving a conceptualization of the new categories called for by events such as the Holocaust. If we set aside Hayden White's quest for a new rhetorical mode, for a new way to narrate these events, at least one of the contributors has attempted to work on a new category of historical analysis: I am referring to the notion of "counterrationality" suggested by Dan Diner.

Diner draws his concept from the form of thought of the Jewish Councils when confronted with Nazi demands and policies. This form of thought, induced by Nazi behavior, was nonetheless unable to reconstruct rationally the "logic" of this behavior: "Via the perspective of the *Judenrat* . . . ," writes Diner, "it is possible to arrive at the conclusion that if rationality was involved here at all, it could be termed 'fractured.'" Once the historian observes the events from the perspective of the *Judenräte*, "the very subject matter acts to cancel, to deactivate the connection between an assumption of rationality, or the ability to understand, and meaningful reconstruction." One could suggest, though, that "ex post" the historian can easily perceive and reconstruct the perverse rationality the Nazis used in fooling their victims and in rendering it impossible for them to understand their tormentors' "logic."

LaCapra's second line of argument refers to the unavoidable constraint imposed on the historian's study of this past by his or her subject position in relation to the past and thus by the unavoidable transferential relation to this object of inquiry. "The Holocaust," writes LaCapra, "presents the historian with transference in the most traumatic form conceivable—but in a form that will vary with the difference in subject position of the analyst. Whether the historian or analyst is a survivor, a relative of survivors, a former Nazi, a former collaborator, a relative of former Nazis or collaborators, a younger Jew or German distanced from more immediate contact with survival, participation, or collaboration, or a relative 'outsider' to these problems will make a difference even in the meaning of statements that may be formally identical." Hayden White's rhetorical "no exit" is replaced here by psychological constraints which unavoidably mold the historian's discourse but are nonetheless open to self-reflexivity and "working-through."

Following the same line of reasoning, Eric Santner considers the forms taken by "working through" or "acting out" in relation to the Nazi past, within the complex process of regaining a German identity, as illustrated in the "historians' debate" or in the production of the television series "Heimat." But Santner develops the working-through notion and, referring to Freud's *Beyond the Pleasure Principle*, suggests a form of coping with the mourning necessitated by the trauma of the Nazi experience through the ongoing retrieval of minor enactments of loss and the "redemption" of that past. According to Santner, however, this path has, all in all, not been adopted by most Germans, who prefer a "fetishization" of the narrative of the Nazi period; in other words, an avoidance of the pain through the choice of a risk-free reshaping of its most difficult sequences. What the result of this psychological development may be in terms of the future attitudes of a majority of Germans is hinted at in Santner's conclusion: "There is, perhaps, little reason to be hopeful that this crucial period of national reconstitution may become a real opportunity for reflection—not only on the issues associated with the breakdown of state socialism, which are indeed formidable, but also on a wide range of moral, political, and psychological questions that have not ceased to emanate from the traumas of Nazism and the 'Final Solution.'"

Santner's position is very close to that of Jürgen Habermas. It is part of what may be called the traditional master-narrative about a "special course" (*Sonderweg*) of German history which led to the Nazi catastrophe. This special development imposes on postwar Germany the duty of a slow working-through which would lead to a new identity tying the Germans again to the liberal tradition of the West. Such a view of German history fits within the conception of a progressing rationality and indeed posits Nazism, its explicit ideology and its crimes, as the absolute counterimage to the ideals of Western Enlightenment.

Such a position can be and has been attacked from three entirely different angles. Right-wing critics—be they German neoconservative historians or extreme anticommunists (particularly in today's Eastern Europe)—aim at undermining the notions of special historical development in the form of a German *Sonderweg* and of the specificity of the crimes of the "Final Solution." Their efforts are a result of traditional German national positions on the one hand and, on the other, are intended to push the magnitude of "Bolshevik" crimes to the foreground of a new global interpretation of world events since 1917.

The second angle of attack is that of the left, which considers the development of Western capitalism as the overall carrier of oppression and exterminatory policies in various forms and degrees. Nazism (or fascism generally) thus appears as a particularly barbaric outgrowth of the Western capitalist system. It is linked in many instances to the postmodern critique of the course (and discourse) of modernity.

Finally, a third critique stems from total despair in the face of the process of civilization, as a result of the very occurrence of "Auschwitz." The "Dialectic of Enlightenment" does not allow, in this view, for any faith in the ultimate triumph of rationality.

Some aspects of the second form of criticism have found their expression in this volume. Not surprisingly, one of the main targets of this criticism has been Jürgen Habermas, or more specifically, the way he refers to the historical place of "Auschwitz." Left-wing critics take exception to Habermas' "utilization" of "Auschwitz," to his general conception of Enlightenment and the progress of rationality, and particularly to his choice of "the West" as representing the norms of an exemplary political culture.

Vincent Pecora takes Habermas to task for his choice of a Western point of reference by indicating that the history of the West is itself a story of oppression and massacres, even genocidal policies: this history cannot serve as a point of reference to condemn Nazi barbarity. Pecora uses Max Horkheimer's and Theodor Adorno's condemnation of the Enlightenment, and their harsh judgment of a civilization that systematically eliminated and eliminates "otherness," in order to bolster his critique of Habermas' understanding of Nazism and the "Final Solution" in history. Sande Cohen starts with a similar critique of Habermas, grounding it more specifically in a critique of Western capitalism. To the Habermasian starting position, he opposes the liberating discourse of postmodernism and Jean-François Lyotard's understanding of the place of "Auschwitz" in Western civilization.

Mario Biagioli's analysis of Nazi "science" in the camps seems at first glance to belong to another set of questions. His conclusion certainly places him ideologically in the vicinity of Cohen and Pecora, however. For Biagioli, the tradition of Western science itself, and of Western medicine in particular, with its imperative of experimentation at any price as its incontrovertible raison d'être, led to the possibility of the Nazi "experiments." Thus, Nazi science and Nazi experimentation on camp inmates is not an aberration or a total reversal of the ethics and goals of Western science: it is one of its possible outcomes; it carries the very core of its tradition.

Although I am not in agreement with all the positions represented in this volume, none is so far from my own that I would wish to renounce it entirely. It is, after all, a matter of nuances within an open and complex discourse. A case in point is the convergence of left-wing critiques of Habermas. In my opinion the criticism expressed here has not sufficiently taken into account Habermas' own critique of various aspects of the dominant economic-political sphere and of the constant impingement of functional rationality on the domain of the "lifeworld," the domain of communicative reason. It is within that general context that both Habermas' critique of developments in the Federal Republic of Germany and his reference to "Auschwitz" must be understood. But even in terms of his more specific and concrete critique of present German developments, one cannot dismiss the intellectual and moral role Habermas has played within the *German* political culture with regard to the relativization of the Nazi past. In that context it is unwarranted to speak of a "utilization" of "Auschwitz"; as for the systematic reference to Western values, it seems to me essential.

My disagreement with the previous "anti-Western" theses extends to Hans Jürgen Syberberg's *Hitler: Ein Film aus Deutschland;* I am probably more critical of the film than Anton Kaes in his thorough and nuanced analysis. Syberberg launches his attack on the West from a neoconservative, neoromantic angle. For him, Hitler is the expression of the most secret wishes of Western civilization; he is the product of perverted Romanticism, but essentially of the poisoning of the romantic soul by modern rationalism and industrial civilization. Hitler the filmmaker, the stage designer who chose the world as his stage, appears, in some of Syberberg's utterances, as no more criminal than the producers of the ultimate poison of the Western mind: the Hollywood culture industry. For Syberberg, Nazism is the product and the murderous multiplicator of the all-destructive impulse of modernity. But the "Final Solution," Nazism, and modernity ultimately lose all significance from the cosmic perspective Syberberg invokes when he reaches out for the galaxies or narrates myths about the beginning and the end of the world.

Whereas the first group of texts essentially deals with issues of historical relativism and the second with ideological critique (the critique of "German ideology" and that of "Western ideology" in their relation to the Nazi epoch), the third group moves from the problems of aesthetic representation of the Shoah to the complexities of appropriation and misappropriation of this literature and art and finally to some general statements about the Shoah, its remembrance, and its place in present consciousness.

Syberberg is considered by many to be a magician of the representation of Nazism, of "Hitler," of the "Final Solution." He is indeed the creator of any number of conflicting discourses, the inventor of an almost endless chain of representations. For Anton Kaes, notwithstanding some of the sharp critical comments he makes on Syberberg's ideological premises, this constantly self-deconstructing feat of postmodernist aesthetics, this refusal of narrative closure, this relentless probing into the deepest recesses of the German, the Romantic, the Western imagination, calls for a multifaceted understanding which may confuse, but may also prove of considerable significance for approaching this past.

Kaes writes:

> The film's postmodernist multiple coding and the constantly shifting position of the author/filmmaker as *bricoleur* require an audience ready and willing to enter the slippery realm of textuality (and any recourse to statements by the filmmaker that would constrain

the potential meaning of the film does injustice to the textual multi-valence of the film's collage principle). Not surprisingly, the proliferation, disjunction, and layering of conflicting sounds and images in a *sujet* like Nazism and the Final Solution pose a danger. The sheer number of conflicting angles (including always the angle of the Nazi perpetrator) from which each event is simultaneously viewed leads inexorably to ambivalences that do not preclude readings of the film (such as the Germans in the role of victims, nostalgia for a *Heimat* and a sense of lost grandeur, etc.) that are clearly revisionist in their implication . . . The burden is placed on the spectator to engage in a dialogue with the film and create his or her own version of the Nazi story, which the film lays out in all its daunting complexity.

Syberberg's film is a prime illustration of the problem of limits with which we are dealing; the virtuosity of the aesthetic dimension is such that the viewer remains spellbound, notwithstanding the extreme ambiguity of the multiple messages conveyed almost subliminally. Anti-Western discourse blends with the overwhelming nostalgia for a German Romanticism, which constantly seeps through the representation of Nazism itself. Some of the best-known documents of the extermination of European Jewry are indeed heard and repeated, as Heinrich Himmler twists and sweats under the agile hands of his Finnish masseur, Felix Kersten. But the compelling aesthetics numb any sense of horror even when a ghostly SS figure repeatedly comes forward on the screen. In short, in this postmodern rendition of Nazism and the "Final Solution" the aesthetic dimension inevitably dominates and overwhelms a spectator lacking the necessary knowledge of the events. Incidentally, this may be a problem for any postmodern rendition of Nazism and the Shoah: the perpetrator's voice carries the full force of aesthetic enticement;[8] the victims carry only the horror and the pity.

One cannot but mention a book by Syberberg which reinforces the message of the film (with the addition of a strong dose of statements about the American-Jewish domination of postwar German culture).[9] It seems to prove that the multiple ruptures in the postmodern narrative, although they dominate the aesthetics of the film, do not convey a fundamentally complex and multiple message but cover a blatantly aggressive ideological discourse.

Syberberg's experiment would certainly have drawn much less attention were it not for its theme: Hitler, Nazism, the "Final Solution." It indicates that the problems of the limits we are examining cannot easily be considered in the abstract, but have to be faced in context. Each work creates problems of its own, but most of them seem to revolve in one way or another about some sort of "truth." It appears, for instance, that literary works which use allegoric elements to present the Shoah have to keep enough direct references to the "real" events to avoid the possibility of total disjunction, of too much allegoric distance. The novels of Aharon Appelfeld and David Grossman, for instance, seem to belong to a hybrid category which partakes both of allegory and of the realistic novel. In other words the function of realistic elements in allegories dealing with the Shoah (I am aware of the self-contradictory aspect of this formulation) appears different from their function in allegory in general.

Thus the problem of realism as presented by Berel Lang is not easily dismissible. Lang's argument is not that the challenge posed by fictionalization is insuperable, but "that it is unavoidable and that it has both unusual force and an unusual form," due to the subject we are dealing with. John Felstiner writes about Celan that he "was never too fastidious to speak about truth in connection with poetry."

It is easier to point to literary and artistic works which give a feeling of relative "adequacy" in bringing the reader and viewer to insights about the Shoah than to define the elements which convey that sense. One would readily think, among several well-known examples, of Ida Fink's stories or of Claude Lanzmann's film *Shoah*. A common denominator appears: the exclusion of straight, documentary realism, but the use of some sort of *allusive or distanced realism*. Reality is there, in its starkness, but perceived through a filter: that of memory (distance in time), that of spatial displacement, that of some sort of narrative margin which leaves the unsayable unsaid.[10]

Even when the unsayable is almost directly presented, the existence of this narrative margin appears a necessity, lest our capacity for comprehending and perceiving be entirely blunted, lest we create an internal barrier to supplement the absence of external distancing. Such an external and aesthetic distancing is clearly part of Lanzmann's *Shoah*. Consider Simon Srebnik, one of the two survivors of Chelmno, returning to the site some forty years after the events: "It is hard to recognize, but it was here. They burned people here . . . Yes, this is the place. No one ever left here again . . . It was terrible. No one can describe it . . . And no one can understand it. Even I, here, now . . . I can't believe I am here. No, I just can't believe it.

It was always this peaceful here. Always. When they burned two thousand people—Jews—every day, it was just as peaceful. No one shouted. Everyone went about his work. It was silent. Peaceful. Just as it is now." [11]

Yael Feldman's "Whose Story Is It, Anyway?", in analyzing the mechanisms of ideological appropriation of the Shoah in Israeli literature, focuses on one area where the theory of representation and the politics of memory meet. It is impossible within the framework of this book to enter into the details of Israeli literature on the Shoah and to confront Feldman's position. What she probably considers a blatant transgression is, in my mind, a much less obvious process: the multiple crosscurrents in Israeli literature about the Shoah express, it seems to me, a very wide field of ideological positions.

In any case open ideological appropriation is not the most perplexing problem. The Shoah is faced with a necessary and impossible problem of "naturalization," starkly defined by Sidra Ezrahi: "Since the 'scorched earth' which is the locus of this language cannot generate a natural audience for it, the issue of naturalization becomes crucial. Where, in our symbolic geography, do we locate Auschwitz or the Warsaw Ghetto: in Poland? In Nazi-occupied Europe? In the vast resonant spaces of Jewish memory? Or as the metonymic limit of Western civilization?" Both John Felstiner and Sidra Ezrahi attempt to unravel some of the paradoxes of this "naturalization."

Felstiner's analysis of Celan's reception and appropriation in Germany touches on one more "impossible" situation: the poem is performed vocally in high schools "to make polyphony audible" (the quotation is from a German teacher's journal) but, in Felstiner's words "not one sentence [in the meticulous analysis of the contrapuntal elements in *Todesfuge*] recognizes that the poem's very form, the rhythm and repetition so amenable to pedagogic technique, may itself—in miming German musical mastery—indict the nation that orchestrated mass murder." Ezrahi addresses both the general problem of appropriation and the specific issues of Celan's and Pagis' poetry. She evokes the existence of a "natural audience," that of the survivors, which implies a barrier against misappropriation, an immediate understanding between author and reader. But beyond this (dwindling) group, the issue becomes more intractable. Has Dan Pagis, writing in Hebrew, found in Israel the natural audience usually built by commonality of language and existential and historic references? The answer seems to me inconclusive. Ultimately Dan Pagis' verses or Aharon Appelfeld's stories are both rooted in and estranged from their Hebrew surroundings. As for Celan's German rhymes in post-Holocaust Europe, it is possibly their withdrawal into an increasingly hermetic language which ensures their inviolability against misappropriation. "The more personal or idiosyncratic the inscription . . . ," writes Ezrahi, "the more immune it is meant to be to both the debasement of metaphor and its reification in history."

The problem of the "audience," of its manipulation, appropriation, or rejection of the Shoah can, in fact, be understood in even more encompassing terms. Here, indeed, we again reach limits which belong both to the events as such and to their acceptance by the audience. As Geoffrey Hartman points out, the "incredible" aspect of the events challenges the very "credibility of redemptive thinking." "So threatening was the shoah," he adds, "that disbelief . . . touched the survivors themselves and added to the silence of the world. When speech returns, two phrases stand out in their testimony: 'I was there' and 'I could not believe what my eyes had seen.'"

Such "incredibility" runs counter to the "categorical imperative" which has dominated the existence of all those who lived through these events and of many others: to salvage the memory. It was, as has often been told, one of the most fundamental needs of the camp inmates and of those who reached the day of liberation: "The need to tell our story to 'the rest,' to make 'the rest' participate in it," as Primo Levi expresses it, "had taken on for us, before our liberation and after, the character of an immediate and violent impulse, to the point of competing with our other elementary needs."[12]

Whereas Geoffrey Hartman's closing text contains, among other themes, a meditation on memory, Peter Haidu's chapter addresses the universalization of the significance of the Shoah. In the way in which it is usually formulated, this oft-discussed problem raises, in fact, no intrinsic difficulty. Whether one considers the Shoah as an exceptional event or as belonging to a wider historical category does not impinge on the possibility of drawing a universally valid significance from it. The difficulty appears when this statement is reversed. No universal lesson requires reference to the Shoah to be fully comprehended. The Shoah carries an *excess*, and this excess cannot be defined except by some sort of general statement about something "which must be able to be put into phrases [but] cannot yet be." Each of us tries to find *some* of the phrases.

One may turn to a quasi-mystical form of rendition in the vein of what Hartman presents as "a latter-day parable" in the opening paragraphs of his chapter. One may alternatively try to find the concrete applicability of a "middle voice," along the lines of White's suggestion; or, indeed, concentrate on any number of possible modes and approaches, discussed here, with all the uncertainty they convey. Most of them are probably necessary; none appears to be sufficient. The ambiguity surrounding the more extreme attempts remains.

It has probably been apparent throughout this introduction that notwithstanding the importance one may attach to postmodern attempts at confronting what escapes, at least in part, established historical and artistic categories of representation, the equivocation of postmodernism concerning "reality" and "truth"—that is, ultimately, its fundamental relativism—confronts any discourse about Nazism and the Shoah with considerable difficulties. I cannot but adopt Pierre Vidal-Naquet's already quoted words: "I was convinced that . . . everything should necessarily go through a discourse . . . but beyond this, or before this, there was something irreducible which, for better or worse, I would still call reality. Without this reality, how could we make a difference between fiction and history?" How, indeed, can one not wish to ascertain the distinction between fiction and history when extreme events such as the Shoah are concerned? But the truth aimed at by history's, as opposed here to fiction's, specific form of discourse needs the maintaining of other convergent paths as well: "It does not kill the possibility of art—on the contrary, it requires it for its transmission, for its realization in our consciousness as witnesses."[13]

The documentary material itself often carries the story of minute incidents which seem to escape the overwhelming dimension of the overall catastrophe but which nonetheless express the excess that cannot yet be put into phrases or, differently stated, that leaves an extraordinary uncertainty in the reader's mind, notwithstanding the ultimate significance and total "concreteness" of what is being reported. Here, precisely because the events are "minute," an endless space seems to surround the facts.

Lithuania, early 1942. Einsatzkommando 3 of Einsatzgruppe A, under the command of SS Colonel Karl Jaeger, has completed the execution of approximately 137,000 Jews, among whom were 55,000 women and 34,000 children. This is the apocalyptic background. An incident among thousands is inscribed in the 14 January 1942 entry of the *Kovno Ghetto Diary.* It reads as follows: "An order to bring all dogs and cats to the small synagogue on Veliuonos Street, where they were shot." A footnote adds a complementary indication: "The bodies of the cats and dogs remained in the synagogue on Veliuonos Street for several months; the Jews were forbidden to remove them." [14]

< 1 >

German Memory, Judicial Interrogation, and Historical Reconstruction: Writing Perpetrator History from Postwar Testimony

CHRISTOPHER R. BROWNING

Shortly before dawn on 13 July 1942 a convoy of trucks carrying more than 450 men from Reserve Police Battalion 101 halted before the Polish village of Jozefów some sixty miles south of the district capital of Lublin.[1] The reserve policemen, middle-aged family men mostly of working-class background from the city of Hamburg, were considered too old to be of use to the German army—their average age was thirty-nine—and they had been drafted into reserve units of the Order Police instead. They had arrived in Poland less than three weeks earlier. This was to be their first major action, but they had not yet been told what to expect.

The battalion commander was Major Wilhelm Trapp, a fifty-three-year-old career policeman affectionately known by his men as "Papa Trapp." As daylight was breaking, he assembled the men in a half-circle. With choking voice and tears in his eyes, he visibly fought to control himself as he explained the battalion's assignment. They had to perform a frightfully unpleasant task, he said, that was not to his liking, but the orders came from the highest authorities. If it would make their task any easier, they should remember that in Germany the bombs were falling on women and children, that the Jews had instigated the American boycott against Germany, and that these Jews in the village of Jozefów supported the partisans.

Trapp proceeded to explain the assignment. The battalion was to round up the Jews in Jozefów. The males of working age were to be separated and taken to a work camp. The remaining Jews—the women, children, and elderly—were to be shot by the battalion.

Trapp then made an extraordinary offer: if any of the older men

< 22 >

among them did not feel up to the task that lay before him, he could step out. After some moments one man stepped forward from Third Company. His captain, one of only two career SS officers in the battalion, began to berate him. The major silenced the captain, and ten or twelve other men stepped forward as well. They turned in their rifles.[2]

Major Trapp, who was seen "weeping like a child" during much of the day, then met with the company commanders and gave them their respective assignments. First and Second companies were to round up the Jews, while Third Company cordoned off the village. Then First Company was to form firing squads in the woods, while Second Company was to guard the Jews assembled in the marketplace and load them on the trucks which shuttled to and from the forest. Any Jew trying to escape or hide was to be shot on the spot; anyone too sick or frail to walk to the marketplace, as well as infants, were also to be shot on the spot.

Before departing for the woods, the men of First Company were given a quick lesson in the gruesome task that awaited them. The battalion doctor traced the outline of a human figure on the ground and showed the men how to use a fixed bayonet placed between and just above the shoulder blades for aiming their carbines. Several men approached the First Company Sergeant, one of them confessing that he found the task "repugnant"; they were released from the firing squad and reassigned to accompany the trucks.

Totally inexperienced in organizing firing-squad procedures that would maximize detachment between shooter and victim, the First Company Sergeant formed two groups of about thirty-five men, which was roughly equivalent to the number of Jews loaded into each truck. In turn each squad met an arriving truck at the edge of the forest. The individual squad members paired off *face-to-face* with the individual Jews they were to shoot, then marched their victims into the forest. The Jews were forced to lie face down in a row. On signal the policemen fired their carbines at point-blank range into the necks of their victims. A noncommissioned officer had to deliver so-called mercy shots, because many of the men, some out of excitement and some intentionally, shot past their victims. By midday alcohol appeared from somewhere to "refresh" the shooters. After the shooting started, a group of men approached the First Company captain, the other career SS officer in the battalion, and pleaded that they were fathers with children and could not continue. The captain curtly refused their plea.

Subsequently, however, the First Company Sergeant released them and a number of other older men as well.

By midmorning it had become apparent that the rate of execution was too slow for the task to be completed by nightfall. Third Company was called in from its outposts around the village to take over close guard of the marketplace, and the men of Second Company were informed that they had to join the shooters in the woods. At least one sergeant once again offered his men the opportunity to report if they did not feel up to it. No one took up his offer.

Unlike First Company, Second Company received no instruction on how to carry out the shooting. Initially bayonets were not fixed as an aiming guide. Thus many of the men did not give neck shots but fired directly into the heads of their victims at point-blank range. The victims' heads exploded, and in no time the policemen's uniforms were saturated with blood and splattered with brains and splinters of bone. Though alcohol made its appearance in Second Company as well, the dropout rate among its shooters was even greater than among First Company.

As one policeman remembered: "I myself took part in some ten shootings, in which I had to shoot men and women. I simply could not shoot at people anymore, which became apparent to my sergeant . . . because at the end I repeatedly shot past. For this reason he relieved me. Also other comrades were sooner or later relieved, because they simply could no longer continue." Another recalled:

> The shooting of the men was so repugnant to me, that I missed the fourth man. It was simply no longer possible for me to aim accurately. I suddenly felt nauseous and ran away from the shooting site. I have expressed myself incorrectly just now. It was not that I could no longer aim accurately, rather that the fourth time I intentionally missed. I then ran into the woods, vomited, and sat down against a tree. To make sure that no one was nearby, I called loudly into the woods, because I wanted to be alone . . . My nerves were totally finished. I think that I remained alone in the woods for some two to three hours.

In the confusion of men coming and going around the trucks, some men evaded shooting altogether.

> It was in no way the case, that those who did not want to or could not carry out the shooting of human beings with their own hands could

not keep themselves out of this task. No strict control was being carried out here. I therefore remained by the arriving trucks and kept myself busy at the arrival point. In any case I gave my activity such an appearance. It could not be avoided that one or another of my comrades noticed that I was not going to the executions to fire away at the victims. They showered me with remarks such as "shithead" and "weakling" to express their disgust. But I suffered no consequences for my actions. I must mention here, that I was not the only one who kept himself out of participating in the executions.

Most of the men, however, continued to shoot all day. The forest was so filled with dead bodies that in the end it was difficult to find places to make the Jews lie down. Around 9:00 P.M., some twenty-nine hours after Reserve Police Battalion 101 had arrived in Józefów, the last of approximately 1,500 Jews was shot. After the men had returned to their barracks, they were given extra rations of alcohol. They were depressed, angered, embittered, and shaken. They talked little, ate almost nothing, but drank a great deal. One policeman expressed the sentiments of many, when he said: "I'd go crazy if I had to do that again." But in fact it was only the beginning of Reserve Police Battalion 101's involvement in the Final Solution, which was to stretch over many months.

I have begun my essay with this narrative of the events that took place on that one day in Józefów not only to set the basis for discussing the difficulties and limits encountered in creating such a narrative but also to remind us that the Holocaust is not an abstraction. It was a real event in which more than five million Jews were murdered, most in a manner so violent and on a scale so vast that historians and others trying to write about these events have experienced nothing in their personal lives that remotely compares. Historians of the Holocaust, in short, know nothing—in an experiential sense—about their subject. This experiential shortcoming is quite different from their not having experienced, for example, the Constitutional Convention in Philadelphia or Caesar's conquest of Gaul. Indeed, a recurring theme of witnesses is how "unbelievable" the Holocaust was to them even as they lived through it.

How have historians until now sought to cope with writing about the Holocaust? What kinds of Holocaust history have they produced? Very briefly, historians have traditionally focused on one of three groups—

perpetrators, victims, and bystanders. With the growth of Holocaust studies and the emergence of its own historiography, there is now also a fourth group, namely the historians who have written about the other three.[3] I will confine myself to the problems inherent in writing the first of these, perpetrator history.

Initially perpetrator history dominated the field. It was primarily either ideological history, focusing on antisemitism and racism among the perpetrators (Hitler in particular), or institutional history focusing on the implementation of Nazi racial policy. The evidentiary base was above all the German documents captured at the end of the war, which served not only the historian but also the prosecutors at postwar trials. The initial representation of the Holocaust perpetrators was that of criminal minds, infected with racism and antisemitism, carrying out criminal policies through criminal organizations. Only in 1961, with the appearance of Raul Hilberg's monumental work *The Destruction of the European Jews*, was this "Nuremberg view" replaced by the portrayal or representation of the Holocaust as a vast and complex administrative process carried out by a multitude of often faceless bureaucrats who were infused with an "elation" or "hubris" because they were making history.[4] Taking Adolf Eichmann as her prototype, Hannah Arendt coined her famous phrase about "the banality of evil," which has subsequently become a veritable cliché for expressing this general approach to perpetrator history and has supplanted Hilberg's own metaphor—that of the "machinery of destruction."

Hilberg's work has remained the preeminent synthesis of perpetrator history since its first appearance. Thereafter the writing of perpetrator history has basically been a typical historians' struggle between two modes of explanation which, in their caricaturish extremes, explain causality either through the actions of key individuals motivated by particular ideas (in this case, Hitler and his "program" for Lebensraum and mass murder of the Jews) or through the impersonal institutional and social structures and contradictions that create dynamics of collective behavior transcending the wills and ideologies of individual historical actors. Insofar as these two approaches have been applied to the historians of Nazi Germany, they have been dubbed the "intentionalists" and the "functionalists."[5]

This "intentionalist-functionalist" controversy was played out before a rather limited academic audience until quite recently. As long as the disputants merely quarreled over interpretations of causality in relation to policymaking but agreed upon the centrality of the Holocaust to understanding National Socialism and the centrality of National Socialism to understanding German history, the situation remained. What thrust perpetrator history into the orbit of embittered, public dispute—at least in Germany—was the *Historikerstreit:* the collapse of this consensus regarding the centrality of the Holocaust and National Socialism. Academically the *Historikerstreit* has been a sterile rather than fruitful dispute, in the sense that new questions have not been posed, new avenues of research and interpretation not opened, new methodologies not explored.[6] This has been a dispute that generates far more heat than light. The excitement has come above all from the political implications that certain questions—hitherto taboo or at least confined, by virtue of their bad taste, to neo-Nazi circles—have now been raised and indeed proudly flaunted in the form of what Charles Maier has aptly dubbed "the negative interrogative," whose practitioner par excellence is Ernst Nolte.[7]

In what directions, then, should perpetrator history develop now? I would argue that one such direction should be a renewed study of the "killers"—the "little men" at the bottom of the hierarchy of the "machinery of destruction" who personally carried out the millions of executions. Understandably the postwar trials aimed at the higher echelons of the Nazi leadership. The capture and trial of Eichmann, along with the publication of Hilberg's book, initiated many studies of the middle-echelon perpetrators.[8] Now the time has come to go beyond the ideology and policymaking of the Nazi leaders and the initiatives and organizing of the "banal" bureaucrats who made implementation of the Final Solution possible. Ultimately the Holocaust took place because at the most basic level individual human beings killed other human beings. And they did so in large numbers over an extended period of time. They became "professional killers."

Can the history of such men be written? Not just the social, organizational, and institutional history of the units they belonged to. And not just the ideological and decision-making history of the policies they carried out. Can one recapture the experiential history of these killers—the choices they faced, the emotions they felt, the coping mechanisms they employed, the changes they underwent?

Obviously, the historian attempting such an endeavor encounters numerous difficulties, only some of which are peculiar to writing about the Holocaust. The first and most basic problem is that of sources. For my case study of Reserve Police Battalion 101, for example, there are virtually no contemporary documents available. Unlike the desk-murderers the reserve policemen in the field did not leave a lengthy paper trail behind them. Unlike Heydrich's stable of intellectuals sent into Russia at the head of the Einsatzgruppen, the reserve police did not compile self-congratulatory reports to document their achievements vis-à-vis their rivals in the field. A few reports from other Order Police units, vividly documenting their participation in the murder of Jews, have survived, but not a single such "smoking pistol" document for Reserve Police Battalion 101 has been found. If one had to rely on contemporary documentation, there would quite simply be no history of Reserve Police Battalion 101 and the Final Solution.

After contemporary documents, the postwar testimony of witnesses is the historian's next resort. Those struggling to survive often felt impelled by a mission to tell their tale—to ensure that the Nazi crime would not be kept secret and that the world would henceforth "never forget." In many cases, where survivors were in prolonged contact with their immediate persecutors, such as in the camps and ghettos, their testimony has been a major contribution to our understanding of the perpetrators. But Reserve Police Battalion 101 was itinerant. Its units moved from town to town, killing Jews or driving them out of the ghettos and onto the death trains headed for Treblinka. From Józefów, we do not know of a single survivor. From survivors of other towns that lay in the battalion's destructive wake, we learn nothing about the unit. Unknown men arrived, carried out their murderous task, and left. Seldom, in fact, can the survivors even remember the peculiar green uniforms of Order Police to identify what kind of unit was involved. Thus there can be no history of Reserve Police Battalion 101 from survivor testimony.

Unlike the survivors, of course, the perpetrators did not rush to write their memoirs after the war. They felt no mission to "never forget." On the contrary, they hoped to forget and be forgotten as quickly and totally as possible. Again there is no history of Reserve Police Battalion 101 through voluntary testimony of the perpetrators.

In 1960, however, the Zentralstelle der Landesjustizverwaltungen in Ludwigsburg, West Germany, began an investigation of the battalion. Once the Zentralstelle was convinced the case should be pursued further, it was assigned to the state prosecutor's office in Hamburg. Over the course of more than five years, the investigators there were able to identify, locate, and interrogate 210 former members of the battalion. Almost everything we know about the men of Reserve Police Battalion 101 and their role in the murder of Polish Jews is based upon the testimony contained in roughly 125 of these 210 interrogations (the others being useful only for compiling statistics about average age, occupation, and social background).

To read about the same events experienced by a single unit as filtered through the memories of 125 different men more than twenty years later is disconcerting for a historian looking for certainties. Each of these men played a different role that day. Each saw and did different things. Each subsequently repressed or forgot certain aspects of that experience or reshaped his memory of it in a different way. Thus one inevitably encounters the *Rashomon* effect of multiple perspectives and multiple memories gone berserk. Paradoxically, one would have the illusion of being more certain about what happened in Jozefów that day with one detailed recollection instead of 125!

Beyond the differing perspectives and memories, there is also the interference caused by the circumstances in which the testimony was given. Quite simply, some men deliberately lied about what they remembered, for they feared the judicial consequences of telling "the truth" as they remembered it. For instance, former rank-and-file policemen who admitted having the choice and not shooting, along with those who admitted shooting but denied having had a choice, were not indicted. Those who admitted both having a choice and shooting stood a much greater chance of being put on trial. Thus not only repression and distortion but conscious mendacity shaped the accounts of the witnesses. Furthermore, the interrogators asked questions pertinent to their task of collecting evidence for specific, indictable crimes committed by particular people, but did not systematically investigate other broader, often more impressionistic and subjective facets of the policemen's experience that are important to the historian, if not to the lawyer.

As historians have increasingly recognized over the past half-century, there is no clean distinction between "facts" and "interpretation," in which the latter emerges as self-evident or is constructed out of the undisputed raw materials of the former.[9] For instance, probably the only "facts" of the opening narrative that are beyond contention are that Reserve Police Battalion 101 arrived in Jozefów on the morning of 13 July 1942 and shot many hundreds of Jews in the nearby forest. Such "facts" quite simply allow no interpretation, no meaning of the event at all, at least in terms of the questions to which I am seeking answers.

Virtually no other element of the narrative at the beginning of the chapter was simply a building block of "historical fact" out of which I reconstructed the events in a way that corresponded to the "reality" of what occurred in that place on that day. For the history of one day in Jozefów, as for all history, virtually every "fact" was an act of interpretation in itself, which is to say that it resulted from a judgment on the part of the historian. The many accounts and perspectives had to be sifted and weighed. The reliability of each witness had to be assessed. Much of the testimony had to be partially or totally dismissed in favor of other conflicting testimony that was accepted. Many of these judgments are both straightforward and obvious. For instance, when one man states that his company was merely assigned to guard duty, but many others in the company admit that their unit was sent to the woods to shoot and can recall the shooting in the most vivid and graphic detail, and in so doing potentially expose themselves to criminal prosecution, the first witness can easily be dismissed. But not all matters of "fact" can be settled so easily, and historians must often make more difficult judgments when working through such diffuse materials. As self-conscious as historians try to be, at times they undoubtedly make purely instinctive judgments without even being aware of it. Quite simply, different historians reading the same set of interrogations would not produce or agree upon an identical set of "facts"— beyond an elementary minimum—out of which a narrative of the events of that day could be created.

Even if different historians did agree on a long list of basic facts or particular events which occurred that day in Jozefów, they would produce neither the same narrative nor the same interpretation. They would not structure their retelling of those events in the same way; they would not find identical meaning and importance in those events.

Hayden White has argued that inherent in historical narrative is the "impulse to moralize reality." The "plot" of the narrative imposes a meaning on what in reality is a chaotic, incoherent, meaningless series of events. But this plot, which produces the "moral" of the story, he continues, is an "embarrassment" which must seem to be found in the story rather than put there by narrative technique.[10]

I would disagree only with certain aspects of this assessment. First,

I do not find the moral dimension an "embarrassment" that must seem immanent in the story. Quite clearly, what organizes and drives my narrative of Jozefów is a series of moral concerns. What choice did the policemen have? How did they react when faced with this choice? What happened to them subsequently, depending on the choice they made? What are the implications of the policemen's behavior for previous explanations or interpretations of the perpetrators? If other kinds of questions had been asked, other aspects of the testimony would have seemed more important and been selected instead; a different story would have been told.

Second, although I would not disagree that it is the plot that determines the narrative, I would add that the questions being posed shape the plot and narrative together. It is the concerns and unanswered questions of historians that from the beginning will cause them to screen out some testimony as irrelevant, ponder and weigh other testimony for its importance, and immediately seize upon yet other testimony as obviously crucial. These questions will set the parameters within which any plot and narrative can be constructed, but the full dimensions of the plot or "moral of the story" are not known before the research begins. Furthermore, even if the moral stance and concerns of the historian undertaking the research are already shaped, they too can change under the impact of the research itself. There is a constant dialectical interaction between what the historian brings to the research and how the research affects the historian.

These kinds of historiographical issues are relevant to the writing of any history, not just that of the Holocaust. But they become particularly crucial when the writing of Holocaust history is at stake. Quite simply, if a number of "valid" histories of that one day in Jozefów (or any other aspect of the Holocaust) can be written, is any version of events of that day (or any other Holocaust event) valid? The standard refrain of one lawyer for the neo-Nazi revisionists is that all history is mere opinion, and there is no such thing as even a bare minimum of uncontrovertible historical fact. [11]

If the offensive thrust of such neo-Nazi revisionists is that the Holocaust never happened, their first line of legal defense is more sophisticated, namely that this denial is as historically valid as any account that states the opposite. It would be, in the "logic" of this position, no less valid to write a history of Jozefów based on the testimony of the few members of the battalion who claim to remember nothing about it, and to conclude that the massacre never took place, than to write any number of possible histories of Jozefów based on the "incontestable" fact that a massacre occurred. Since the testimony of the other witnesses is inconsistent and in conflict on so many points, virtually all of the witnesses must be telling something other than the truth much of the time.[12] Why, then, should any of their testimony have any preferred value? Where, in short, does one draw the line between differing but valid histories and invalid or pseudohistories?

Hayden White broaches the question and denounces the very notion of the denial of the Holocaust to be "as morally offensive as it is intellectually bewildering."[13] The grounds on which this judgment was made remain unclear, however, for his main concern in this regard seems to be to prevent this self-evident concession from being extended too broadly. Thus in the same article he subsequently rejects the notion of an "objective" historical methodology, opposes the notion of invalidating history on the basis of ideological deformation, and ultimately declares that the study of history is "never innocent." At best, if I read him correctly, he accepts a theoretical distinction between interpretations that deny the very reality of events they treat and those that draw different conclusions from reflection on events whose reality is "attestable on the level of 'positive' historical inquiry." I, at least, remain puzzled as to how "'positive' historical inquiry" differs from the "objective historical methodology" that White elsewhere chides others, such as Pierre Vidal-Naquet or Lucy Dawidowicz, for invoking.

In my view there are no distinct and separate categories of attestable fact on the one hand and pure interpretation on the other. Rather there is a spectrum or continuum. No one, not even the neo-Nazis, doubts that Adolf Hitler headed a Nazi government in Germany from 1933 to 1945 and that World War II occurred. They do not doubt that the Japanese navy attacked the American naval base at Pearl Harbor on 7 December 1941 or that the British carried out nighttime area bombing of German cities. The neo-Nazis and their fellow travelers claim only to doubt that millions of Jews lost their lives during the war and that gas chambers were constructed in extermination camps as part of the Nazi program to destroy European Jewry. In fact at least one historian, Arno Mayer, has claimed that certainly in Auschwitz and probably in all of Europe as well, more Jews perished from so-called natural causes of disease, starvation, and exhaustion that were inherent in the terrible living conditions the Nazis inflicted upon them than from so-called unnatural causes like gassing and shooting.[14]

The mixing of "fact" and "interpretation" becomes even more apparent in the debate over a Hitler decision and order for the Final Solution. Many historians have argued for different interpretations about when such a decision or series of decisions was made and the order or series of orders given, and in what way the very concepts of a Hitler decision or order should be understood. Two historians—Martin Broszat and Hans Mommsen—have argued that there was "in fact" no Hitler order or decision at all. [15] This is an interpretive argument partly about the meaning of concepts (what is meant by a *Führerbefehl*, or Hitler order) and partly about a disputed or contested "historical fact"—a time- and place-specific event—that could conceivably be definitively resolved if the evidentiary basis were less incomplete. More purely interpretive are disputes about the relative importance of causal factors—antisemitism, the authoritarian habits of German political culture, the "banality of evil," and so on—in "explaining" the Holocaust. More purely interpretive still would be statements about the "significance" or "meaning" of the Holocaust, and what it tells us about Western civilization or the modern industrial/bureaucratic society or human nature. Virtually no one would claim that statements of this nature are "factual."

Is there some scientific or positivist methodology that can delineate absolute boundaries along this continuum, that can say here is where bedrock, indisputable fact ends; here is where transparent, politically motivated falsification begins; here is a clear case of obvious neglect of readily available evidence that any "open-minded" and careful scholar should have taken into consideration, given the structure of the argument and the nature of the evidence which is referred to; here is a question of fact that theoretically could be resolved if evidence were not missing but in the present circumstances cannot be established as bedrock fact, and thus can be argued only in terms of degree of plausibility; and here are interpretive assertions that can give insight, that can be more or less coherent and persuasive in their presentation, but that cannot be proved or claimed as fact? I can sympathize with the judge who remarked of pornography: "I can't define it, but I know it when I see it." The archetypal cases seem obvious. But if there is a clear-cut method to decide the borderline cases, I do not know it.

The legal profession has, of course, also wrestled with the issue of establishing or proving "facts," and since World War II events of the Holocaust have been the subject of numerous legal proceedings. The so-called war crimes trials conducted by the Allies in the late 1940s were followed by numerous German trials of so-called NS crimes in the 1960s and 1970s. Extradition proceedings in the United States have added another chapter in the 1980s. In all these cases eyewitness testimony, documents, physical evidence, and circumstantial evidence—the same materials that historians use—have regularly been invoked to prove "beyond a reasonable doubt" that certain time- and place-specific criminal acts were committed by particular people. The historian and lawyer often ask different questions and meet different levels of proof (the historian often has the luxury of settling for "preponderance of evidence" as opposed to "beyond reasonable doubt"). Nonetheless, the historical study and judicial investigation of the Holocaust have been inextricably intertwined, as historians and lawyers have used the fruits of one another's labors.

A different kind of legal case, focusing directly on the issue of writing about the Holocaust, was that of the neo-Nazi publisher Ernst Zundel, who was tried twice, in 1985 and 1986, before a court in Toronto, Canada.[16] The ultimate resort was to the "reasonable man" embodied in a jury of twelve people, who were persuaded "beyond a reasonable doubt" that the neo-Nazi denial of the Holocaust contained in a particular pamphlet was both false and known to be so by its author and publisher, and furthermore constituted a potential danger to the public interest in the form of inciting racial hatred. Some subsequent pamphlet, embodying the same denial of the Holocaust but less clumsy in its construction, which successfully concealed the obvious intent of the author and publisher to falsify, would be in a different legal category, subject to public denunciation or refutation but not to successful legal prosecution under present Canadian law. Moreover, a different jury in a different, nazified culture could find in the same pamphlet the praiseworthy harnessing of history to the higher political goal of Nazi resurgence. The "intent" of the author is all too slippery, and the "reasonable man" judging historical disputes is obviously culture-bound. The individual problem of a particular pamphlet may have been solved by the combined clumsiness of neo-Nazi author and publisher, the always abrasive and frequently counterproductive behavior of defense counsel, and the "common sense" of a Canadian jury, but the wider theoretical question is not.

If my history of Reserve Police Battalion 101 in Jozefów is one among a number of valid histories that could be written, and if the issue of drawing a borderline for an "invalid" or pseudohistory remains uncomfortably unresolved, another and quite different question is whether my history, shaped by the particular questions I have posed, should be written. Two kinds of issues have recently been raised in this regard. The first concerns the merits and dangers of so-called *Alltags-geschichte* (history of everyday life). The second concerns the desirability of empathy in writing this or any kind of perpetrator history.

Some of my Israeli colleagues writing Holocaust history have felt considerable unease about the emergence of *Alltagsgeschichte* in Germany. They fear that it will normalize the image of the Nazi regime by concentrating on the mundane, everyday aspects of life that continued relatively undisturbed. They also fear that it will turn attention away from the most significant—the so-called world-historical—features of the Nazi regime, in particular the genocidal mass murder of European Jewry.

My own view is that the issue is not in fact a methodological one. Traditional diplomatic and military histories of Nazi Germany can and indeed have all too easily ignored the Holocaust as well. No methodology guarantees the inclusion or exclusion of certain subject matter. My study is, I would argue, the *Alltagsgeschichte* of a particular police unit in Nazi-occupied Poland. Rather than turning attention from the Holocaust, it demonstrates that for Germans in occupied Poland the mass murder of the Jews was incorporated into the very fabric of their everyday life—to the point that tracking down and killing individual Jews who had escaped to the forest before the clearing of the ghettos (the so-called Jew hunt, or *Judenjagd*) was routine—in the words of one policeman "our daily bread." In short, there is nothing inherent in the methodology of *Alltagsgeschichte* that necessarily diminishes the centrality of the Holocaust in the history of Nazi Germany. On the contrary, I would argue, it is the best method for revealing how deeply mass murder was embedded in the lives of German personnel stationed in occupied eastern Europe.

As for the issue of empathy, Bruno Bettelheim, in a review of Robert Lifton's *Nazi Doctors,* expresses regret about the subject and approach of that book which would equally apply to my history of Reserve Police Battalion 101. He notes: "I restricted myself to trying to understand the psychology of the prisoners and I shied away from trying to understand the psychology of the SS—because of the ever-present danger that understanding fully may come close to forgiving . . . I believe there are acts so vile that our task is to reject and prevent them, not to try to understand them empathetically . . ."[17] Certainly, the writing of my history of Reserve Police Battalion 101 requires a rejection of demonization. The men who carried out these massacres, like those who refused or evaded, were human beings. I must recognize that in such a situation I could have been either a killer or an evader—both were human—if I want to understand and explain the behavior of both as best I can. This recognition does indeed mean an attempt to empathize. What I do not accept, however, are the old clichés that to explain is to excuse, that to understand is to forgive. Explaining is not excusing; understanding is not forgiving. The notion that one must simply reject the acts of the perpetrators and not try to understand them would make impossible not only my history but any perpetrator history that sought to go beyond one-dimensional caricature.[18]

Even if the empathy necessary to writing perpetrator history is desirable, is it possible? Elie Wiesel has argued that the core of the Holocaust is beyond the human comprehension of anyone but the survivors. These survivors suffered an experience within the universe of the camps that is beyond communicability even by the "messengers," and certainly cannot be re-created, represented, or understood by those who were not there. Is an understanding, representation, and communicability of the perpetrators' experience as impossible as Wiesel thinks it is of the survivors' experience? Saul Friedlander suggested as much at a 1990 conference at Northwestern University, when he argued that the historian's attempt to find a "psychological common denominator" with the perpetrators resulted in an "intractable unease." An "intuitive *Verstehen*" of the perpetrator was not possible in the face of an "immorality beyond evil" that had been brought forth in an ethos of *Führer-Bindung* and "elation."[19]

If I understand him correctly, the terms of Friedlander's eloquent argument were addressed to the top Nazi leadership. I do not see how they can apply to the reserve policemen who carried out the massacre at Jozefów. I find no *Führer-Bindung* in a situation in which the commanding officer, openly before his men, disassociated himself from the orders he had received from above. I find no "elation" in a situation in which the overwhelmingly predominant reaction of the men—both those who killed all day and those who refused, evaded, or stopped—was sheer horror and physical revulsion at what they had been asked to do. Eventually, of course, they got used to the killing. But in that too, they were all too human.

< 2 >

Historical Emplotment and the Problem of Truth

HAYDEN WHITE

There is an inexpungeable relativity in every representation of historical phenomena. The relativity of the representation is a function of the language used to describe and thereby constitute past events as possible objects of explanation and understanding. This is obvious when, as in the social sciences, a technical language is so used. Scientific explanations openly purport to bear upon only those aspects of events—for example, quantitative and therefore measurable aspects—which can be denoted by the linguistic protocols used to describe them. It is less obvious in traditional narrative accounts of historical phenomena: first, narrative is regarded as a neutral "container" of historical fact, a mode of discourse "naturally" suited to representing historical events directly; second, narrative histories usually employ so-called natural or ordinary, rather than technical, languages, both to describe their subjects and to tell their story; and third, historical events are supposed to consist of or manifest a congeries of "real" or "lived" stories, which have only to be uncovered or extracted from the evidence and displayed before the reader to have their truth recognized immediately and intuitively.

Obviously I regard this view of the relation between historical storytelling and historical reality as mistaken or at best misconceived. Stories, like factual statements, are linguistic entities and belong to the order of discourse.

The question that arises with respect to "historical emplotments" in a study of Nazism and the Final Solution is this: Are there any limits on the *kind* of story that can responsibly be told about these phenomena? *Can* these events be responsibly emplotted in *any* of the modes, symbols, plot types, and genres our culture provides for "making sense" of such extreme events in our past? Or do Nazism and the Final Solution belong to a special class of events, such that, unlike even the

< 37 >

French Revolution, the American Civil War, the Russian Revolution, or the Chinese Great Leap Forward, they must be viewed as manifesting only one story, as being emplottable in one way only, and as signifying only one kind of meaning? In a word, do the natures of Nazism and the Final Solution set absolute limits on what can be truthfully said about them? Do they set limits on the uses that can be made of them by writers of fiction or poetry? Do they lend themselves to emplotment in a set number of ways, or is their specific meaning, like that of other historical events, infinitely interpretable and ultimately undecidable?

Saul Friedlander has elsewhere distinguished between two kinds of questions that might arise in the consideration of historical emplotments and the problem of "truth": epistemological questions raised by the fact of "*competing* narratives about the Nazi epoch and the 'Final Solution'" and ethical questions raised by the rise of "representations of Nazism . . . based on what used to be [regarded as] *unacceptable* modes of emplotment." Obviously, considered as accounts of events already established as facts, "competing narratives" can be assessed, criticized, and ranked on the basis of their fidelity to the factual record, their comprehensiveness, and the coherence of whatever arguments they may contain. But narrative accounts do not consist only of factual statements (singular existential propositions) and arguments; they consist as well of poetic and rhetorical elements by which what would otherwise be a list of facts is transformed into a story.[1] Among these elements are those generic story patterns we recognize as providing the "plots." Thus, one narrative account may represent a set of events as having the form and meaning of an epic or tragic story, and another may represent the same set of events—with equal plausibility and without doing any violence to the factual record—as describing a farce.[2] Here the conflict between "competing narratives" has less to do with the facts of the matter in question than with the different story-meanings with which the facts can be endowed by emplotment. This raises the question of the relation of the various generic plot types that can be used to endow events with different kinds of meaning—tragic, epic, comic, romance, pastoral, farcical, and the like—to the events themselves. Is this relationship between a given story told about a given set of events the same as that obtaining between a factual statement and its referent? Can it be said that sets of real events *are* intrinsically tragic, comic, or epic, such that the representation of those events as a tragic, comic, or epic story can be assessed as to its *factual* accuracy? Or does it all have to do with the perspective from which the events are viewed?

Of course, most theorists of narrative history take the view that emplotment produces not so much another, more comprehensive and synthetic factual statement as, rather, an *interpretation* of the facts. But the distinction between factual statements (considered as a product of object-language) and interpretations of them (considered as a product of one or more metalanguages) does not help us when it is a matter of interpretations produced by the modes of emplotment used to represent the facts as displaying the form and meaning of different kinds of stories. We are not helped by the suggestion that "competing narratives" are a result of "the facts" having been *interpreted* by one historian as a "tragedy" and *interpreted* by another as a "farce."[3] This is especially the case in traditional historical discourse in which "the facts" are always given precedence over any "interpretation" of them.

Thus for traditional historical discourse there is presumed to be a crucial difference between an "interpretation" of "the facts" and a "story" told about them. This difference is indicated by the currency of the notions of a "real" (as against an "imaginary") story and a "true" (as against a "false") story. Whereas interpretations are typically thought of as commentaries on "the facts," the stories told in narrative histories are presumed to inhere either in the events themselves (whence the notion of a "real story") or in the facts derived from the critical study of evidence bearing upon those events (which yields the notion of the "true" story).

Considerations such as these provide some insight into the problems both of competing narratives and of unacceptable modes of emplotment in considering a period such as the Nazi epoch and events such as the Final Solution. We can confidently presume that the facts of the matter set limits on the *kinds* of stories that can be *properly* (in the sense of both veraciously and appropriately) told about them only if we believe that the events themselves possess a "story" kind of form and a "plot" kind of meaning. We may then dismiss a "comic" or "pastoral" story, with an upbeat "tone" and a humorous "point of view," from the ranks of competing narratives as manifestly false to the facts— or at least to the facts that *matter*—of the Nazi era. But we could dismiss such a story from the ranks of competing narratives only if (1) it were presented as a *literal* (rather than *figurative*) representation of the events and (2) the plot type used to transform the facts into a specific kind of story were presented as inherent in (rather than imposed upon) the facts. For unless a historical story is presented as a literal representation of real events, we cannot criticize it as being either true or untrue to the facts of the matter. If it were presented as a figurative representation of real events, then the question of its truthfulness would fall under the principles governing our assessment of the truth of fictions. And if it did not suggest that the plot type chosen to render the facts into a story of a specific kind had been found to inhere in the facts themselves, then we would have no basis for comparing this particular account to other kinds of narrative accounts, informed by other kinds of plot types, and for assessing their relative adequacy to the representation, not so much of the facts as of what the facts *mean*.

For the differences among competing *narratives* are differences among the "modes of emplotment" which predominate in them. It is because narratives are always emplotted that they are meaningfully comparable; it is because narratives are differently emplotted that discriminations among the kinds of plot types can be made. In the case of an emplotment of the events of the Third Reich in a "comic" or "pastoral" mode, we would be eminently justified in appealing to "the facts" in order to dismiss it from the lists of "competing narratives" of the Third Reich. But what if a story of this kind had been set forth in a pointedly ironic way and in the interest of making a metacritical comment, not so much on the facts as on versions of the facts emplotted in a comic or pastoral way? Surely it would be beside the point to dismiss *this* kind of narrative from the competition on the basis of its infidelity to the facts. For even if it were not positively faithful to the facts, it would at least be negatively so—in the fun it poked at narratives of the Third Reich emplotted in the mode of comedy or pastoral.

On the other hand, we might wish to regard such an ironic emplotment as "unacceptable" in the manner suggested by Friedlander in his indictment of histories, novels, and films which, under the guise of seeming to portray faithfully the most horrible facts of life in Hitler's Germany, actually aestheticize the whole scene and translate its contents into fetish objects and the stuff of sadomasochistic fantasies.[4] As Friedlander has pointed out, such "glamorizing" representations of the phenomena of the Third Reich used to be "unacceptable," whatever the accuracy or veracity of their factual contents, because they offended against morality or taste. The fact that such representations have become increasingly common and therefore obviously more "acceptable" over the last twenty years or so indicates profound changes in socially sanctioned standards of morality and taste. But what does *this* circumstance suggest about the grounds on which we might wish to judge a narrative account of the Third Reich and the Final Solution to be "unacceptable" even though its factual content is both accurate and ample?

It seems to be a matter of distinguishing between a specific body of factual "contents" and a specific "form" of narrative and of applying the kind of rule which stipulates that a serious theme—such as mass murder or genocide—demands a noble genre—such as epic or tragedy—for its proper representation. This is the kind of issue posed by Art Spiegelman's *Maus: A Survivor's Tale*,[5] which presents the events of the Holocaust in the medium of the (black-and-white) comic book and in a mode of bitter satire, with Germans portrayed as cats, Jews as mice, and Poles as pigs. The manifest content of Spiegelman's comic book is the story of the artist's effort to extract from his father the story of his parents' experience of the events of the Holocaust. Thus, the story of the Holocaust that is told in the book is framed by a story of how this story came to be told. But the manifest contents of both the frame story and the framed story are, as it were, compromised as fact by their allegorization as a game of cat-and-mouse-and-pig in which everyone—perpetrators, victims, and bystanders in the story of the Holocaust and both Spiegelman and his father in the story of *their* relationship—comes out looking more like a beast than like a human being. *Maus* presents a particularly ironic and bewildered view of the Holocaust, but it is at the same time one of the most moving narrative accounts of it that I know, and not least because it makes the difficulty of discovering and telling the whole truth about even a small part of it as much a part of the story as the events whose meaning it is seeking to discover.

To be sure, *Maus* is not a conventional history, but it is a representation of past real events or at least of events that are represented as having actually occurred. There is nothing of that aestheticization of which Friedlander complains in his assessments of many recent filmic and novelistic treatments of the Nazi epoch and the Final Solution. At the same time, this comic book is a masterpiece of stylization, figuration, and allegorization. It assimilates the events of the Holocaust to the conventions of comic book representation, and in this absurd mixture of a "low" genre with events of the most momentous significance, *Maus* manages to raise all of the crucial issues regarding the "limits of representation" in general.

Indeed, *Maus* is much more critically self-conscious than Andreas Hillgruber's *Zweierlei Untergang: Die Zerschlagung des Deutschen Reiches und das Ende des europäischen Judentums* (Two kinds of ruin: the shattering of the German Reich and the end of European Jewry).[6] In the first of the two essays included in the book, Hillgruber suggests that, even though the Third Reich lacked the nobility of purpose to permit its "shattering" to be called a "tragedy," the defense of the eastern front by the Wehrmacht in 1944–45 could appropriately be emplotted—and without any violence to the facts—as a "tragic" story. Hillgruber's manifest purpose was to salvage the moral dignity of a part of the Nazi epoch in German history by splitting the whole of it into two discrete stories and emplotting them differently—the one as a tragedy, the other as an incomprehensible enigma.[7]

Critics of Hillgruber immediately pointed out: (1) that even to cast the account in the mode of a narrative was to subordinate any analysis of the events to their aestheticization; (2) that one could confer the morally ennobling epithet *tragic* on these events only at the cost of ignoring the extent to which the "heroic" actions of the Wehrmacht had made possible the destruction of many Jews who might have been saved had the army surrendered earlier; and (3) that the attempt to ennoble one part of the history of the "German Empire" by dissociating it from the Final Solution was as morally offensive as it was scientifically untenable.[8] Yet Hillgruber's suggestion for emplotting the story of the defense of the eastern front did not violate any of the conventions governing the writing of professionally respectable narrative history. He simply suggested narrowing the focus to a particular domain of the historical continuum, casting the agents and agencies occupying that scene as characters in a dramatic conflict, and emplotting this drama in terms of the familiar conventions of the genre of tragedy.

Hillgruber's suggestion for the emplotment of the history of the eastern front during the winter of 1944–45 indicates the ways in which a specific plot type (tragedy) can simultaneously determine the kinds of events to be featured in any story that can be told about them and provide a pattern for the assignment of the roles that can possibly be played by the agents and agencies inhabiting the scene thus constituted.[9] At the same time, Hillgruber's suggestion also indicates how the choice of a mode of emplotment can justify ignoring certain kinds of events, agents, actions, agencies, and patients that may inhabit a given historical scene or its context. There is no place for any form of low or ignoble life in a tragedy; in tragedies even villains are noble or, rather, villainy can be shown to have its noble incarnations. Asked once why he had not included a treatment of Joan of Arc in his *Waning of the Middle Ages,* Huizinga is said to have replied: "Because I did not want my story to have a heroine." Hillgruber's recommendation to emplot the story of the Wehrmacht's defense of the eastern front as a tragedy indicates that he wants the story told about it to have a hero, to be heroic, and thereby to redeem at least a remnant of the Nazi epoch in the history of Germany.

Hillgruber may not have considered the fact that his division of one epoch of German history into two stories—one of the shattering of an empire, the other of the end of a people—sets up an oppositional structure constitutive of a semantic field in which the naming of the plot type of one story determines the semantic domain within which the name of the plot type of the other is to be found. Hillgruber does not name the plot type which might provide the meaning of the story of "the end of European Jewry." But if the plot type of the tragedy is reserved for the telling of the story of the Wehrmacht on the eastern front in 1944–45, it follows that *some other* plot type must be used for the end of European Jewry.

In forgoing the impulse to name the kind of story that should be told about the Jews in Hitler's Reich, Hillgruber approaches the position of a number of scholars and writers who view the Holocaust as virtually unrepresentable in language. The most extreme version of this idea takes the form of the commonplace that this event ("Auschwitz," "the Final Solution," and so on) is of such a nature as to escape the grasp of any language to describe it or any medium to represent it. Thus, for example, George Steiner's famous remark: "The world of Auschwitz lies outside speech as it lies outside reason."[10] Or Alice and A. R. Eckhardt's question: "How is the unspeakable to be spoken about? Certainly, we ought to speak about it, but how can we ever do so?"[11] Berel Lang suggests that expressions such as these must be understood figuratively, as indicating the difficulty of writing about the Holocaust and the extent to which any representation of it must be judged against the criterion of respectful silence that should be our first response to it.[12]

Nonetheless, Lang himself argues against any use of the genocide as a subject of fictional or poetic writing. According to him, only the most literalist *chronicle* of the facts of the genocide comes close to passing the test of "authenticity and truthfulness" by which both literary and scientific accounts of this event must be judged. *Only the facts* must be recounted, because otherwise one lapses into figurative speech and stylization (aestheticism). And *only a chronicle* of the facts is warranted, because otherwise one opens up oneself to the dangers of narrativization and the relativization of emplotment.

Lang's analysis of the limitations of *any* literary representation of the genocide and its *moral* inferiority to a sparse or denarrativized historical account is worth considering in detail, because it raises the question of the limits of representation in the matter of the Holocaust in the most extreme terms. The analysis hinges on a radical opposition between literal and figurative speech, the identification of literary language with figurative language, a particular view of the peculiar effects produced by any figurative characterization of real events, and a notion of "morally extreme" events of which the Holocaust is considered to be a rare, if not historically unique, instantiation. Lang argues that the genocide, quite apart from being a *real* event, an event that really happened, is also a *literal* event, that is, an event the nature of which permits it to serve as a paradigm of the kind of event about which we can be permitted to speak only in a "literal" manner.

Lang holds that figurative language not only turns or swerves away from literalness of expression, but also deflects attention from the states of affairs about which it pretends to speak. Any figurative expression, he argues, *adds* to the representation of the object to which it refers. First, it adds itself (that is, the specific figure used) and the decision it presupposes (that is, the choice to use one figure rather than another). Figuration produces stylization, which directs attention to the author and his or her creative talent. Next, figuration produces a "perspective" on the referent of the utterance, but in featuring one particular perspective it necessarily closes off others. Thus it reduces or obscures certain aspects of events.[13] Third, the kind of figuration needed to transform what would otherwise be only a chronicle of real events into a story at once personalizes (humanizes) and generalizes the agents and agencies involved in those events. Such figuration personalizes by transforming those agents into the kind of intending, feeling, and thinking subjects with whom the reader can identify and empathize, in the way one does with characters in fictional stories. It generalizes them by representing them as instantiations of the types of agents, agencies, events, and so on met with in the genres of literature and myth.

On this view of the matter the impropriety of any literary representation of the genocide derives from the distortions of the facts of the matter effected by the use of figurative language. Over against any merely literary representation of the events comprising the genocide Lang sets the ideal of what a literalist representation of the facts of the matter reveals to be their *true* nature. And it is worth quoting a longish passage from Lang's book in which he sets up this opposition between figurative and literalist speech as being homologous with the opposition between false and truthful discourse:

> If . . . the act of genocide is directed against individuals who do not motivate that act *as* individuals; and if the evil represented by genocide also reflects a deliberate intent for evil in principle, in conceptualizing [a] group and in the decision to annihilate it, then the intrinsic limitations of figurative discourse for the representation of genocide come into view. On the account given, imaginative representation would personalize even events that are impersonal and corporate; it would dehistoricize and generalize events that occur specifically and contingently.
>
> And the unavoidable dissonance here is evident. For a subject which historically combines the feature of impersonality with a challenge to the conception of moral boundaries, the attempt to personalize it—or, for that matter, only to *add* to it—appears at once gratuitous and inconsistent: gratuitous because it individualizes where the subject by its nature is corporate; inconsistent because it sets limits when the subject itself has denied them. The effect of the additions is then to *misrepresent* the subject and thus—where the aspects misrepresented are essential—to *diminish* it. In asserting the possibility of alternate figurative perspectives, furthermore, the writer asserts the process of representation and his own persona as parts of the representation—a further diminution of what (for a subject like the Nazi genocide) is its essential core; beside this, an "individual" perspective is at most irrelevant. For certain subjects, it seems, their significance may be too broad or deep to be chanced by

an individual point of view, [and the significance may be] morally more compelling—and actual—than the concept of possibility can sustain. Under this pressure, the presumption of illumination, usually conceded *prima facie* to the act of writing (*any* writing), begins to lose its force.[14]

But literary writing and the kind of historical writing that aspires to the status of literary writing are especially objectionable to Lang, because in them the figure of the author obtrudes itself between the thing to be represented and the representation of it. The figure of the author must obtrude itself into the discourse as the agent of that act of figuration without which the subject of the discourse would remain unpersonalized. Since literary writing unfolds under the delusion that it is only by figuration that individuals can be personalized, "the implication is unavoidable," Lang says, that "a subject . . . could be represented in many different ways and as having no *necessary* and perhaps not even an *actual* basis. The assertion of alternate possibilities [of figuration] . . . suggests a denial of limitation: *no* possibilities are excluded," neither the possibility of figuring a real person as an imaginary or nonperson nor that of figuring a real event as a nonevent.[15]

It is considerations such as these that lead Lang to advance the notion that the events of the Nazi genocide are intrinsically "antirepresentational," by which he apparently means, not that they cannot be represented, but that they are paradigmatic of the kind of event that can be spoken about only in a factual and literalist manner. Indeed, the genocide consists of occurrences in which the very distinction between "event" and "fact" is dissolved.[16] Lang writes, "If there ever was a 'literal' fact, beyond the possibility of alternate formulations among which reversal or denial must always be one, it is here in the act of the Nazi genocide; and if the moral implication of the role of facts needed proof, it is also to be found here, again in the phenomena of the Nazi genocide."[17] It is the overriding actuality and literalness of this event which, in Lang's view, *warrant* the effort on the part of historians to represent real events "direct[ly] . . . immediately and unaltered" in a language purged of all metaphor, trope, and figuration. Indeed, it is the literalness of this event which indexes the difference between "historical discourse" on the one hand and "imaginative representation and its figurative space" on the other: "However it may be conceived beyond [the distinction between history and fiction] the *fact* of the Nazi genocide is a crux that separates historical discourse from the process of imaginative representation, perhaps not uniquely, but as certainly as any fact might be required or is able to do."[18]

I have lingered on Lang's argument because I think that it carries us to the crux of many current discussions regarding both the possibility of representing the Holocaust and the relative value of different ways of representing it. His objection to the use of this event as an occasion for a *merely* literary performance is directed at novels and poetry, and it can easily be extended to cover both the kind of belletristic historiography which features literary flourish and what the book clubs identify as "fine writing." But it must, by implication, be extended also to include any kind of narrative history, which is to say, any attempt to represent the Holocaust *as a story*. And this is because, if every story must be said to have a plot, and if every emplotment is a kind of figuration, then it follows that every narrative account of the Holocaust, whatever its mode of emplotment, stands condemned on the same grounds that any merely literary representation of it must be condemned.

To be sure, Lang argues that, although historical representation may "make use of narrative and figurative means," it is not "essentially dependent on those means." Indeed, in his view, historical discourse is posited on "the possibility of representation that stands in direct relation to its object—in effect, if not in principle, immediate and unaltered."[19] This is not to suggest that historians can or should try to occupy the position of the naive realist or mere seeker after information. The matter is more complex than that. For Lang indicates that what is needed for anyone writing about the Holocaust is an attitude, position, or posture which is neither subjective nor objective, neither that of the social scientist with a methodology and a theory nor that of the poet intent upon expressing a "personal" reaction.[20] Indeed, in the introduction to *Act and Idea*, Lang invokes Roland Barthes's notion of "intransitive writing" as a model of the kind of discourse appropriate to discussion of the philosophical and theoretical issues raised by reflection on the Holocaust. Unlike the kind of writing that is intended to be "read *through*, . . . designed to enable readers to see what they would otherwise see differently or perhaps not at all," intransitive writing "denies the distances among the writer, text, what is written about, and, finally, the reader." In intransitive writing "an author does not write to provide access to something independent of both author and reader, but 'writes himself' . . . In the traditional account [of writing], the writer is conceived as first looking at an object with eyes already expectant, patterned, and then, having seen, as representing it in his own writing. For the writer who writes-himself, writing becomes itself the means of vision or comprehension, not a mirror of something independent, but an act and commitment—a doing or making rather than a reflection or description."[21] Lang explicitly commends intransitive writing (and speech) as appropriate to individual Jews who, as in the recounting of the story of the Exodus at Passover, "should tell the story of the genocide as though he or she had passed through it" and in an exercise of self-identification specifically Jewish in nature.[22] But the further suggestion is that the product of intransitive writing, which is to say a distance-denying discourse, might serve as a model for *any* representation of the Holocaust, historical or fictional. And it is with a consideration of the ways in which the notion of intransitive writing might serve as a way of resolving many of the issues raised by the representation of the Holocaust that I would like to conclude.

First, I would note that Berel Lang invokes the idea of intransitive writing without remarking that Barthes himself used it to characterize the differences between the dominant style of modernist writing and that of classical realism. In the essay entitled "To Write: An Intransitive Verb?" Barthes asks if and when the verb "to write" became an intransitive verb. The question is asked within the context of a discussion of "diathesis" ("voice") in order to focus attention on the different kinds of relationship that an agent can be represented as bearing to an action. He points out that although modern Indo-European languages offer two possibilities for expressing this relationship, the active and the passive voices, other languages have offered a third possibility, that expressed, for example, in the ancient Greek "middle voice." Whereas in the active and passive voices the subject of the verb is presumed to be external to the action, as either agent or patient, in the middle voice the subject is presumed to be *interior* to the action.[23] He then goes on to conclude that, in literary modernism, the verb "to write" connotes neither an active nor a passive relationship, but rather a middle one. "Thus," Barthes says,

> in the middle voice of *to write*, the distance between scriptor and language diminishes asymptotically. We could even say that it is the writings of subjectivity, such as romantic writing, which are active, for in them the agent is not interior but *anterior* to the process of writing: here the one who writes does not write for himself, but as if by proxy, for an exterior and antecedent person (even if both bear

the same name), while, in the modern verb of middle voice *to write,* the subject is constituted as immediately contemporary with the writing, being effected and affected by it: this is the exemplary case of the Proustean narrator, who exists only by writing, despite the references to a pseudo-memory.[24]

This is, of course, only one of the many differences that distinguish modernist writing from its nineteenth-century realist counterpart. But this difference indicates a new and distinctive way of imagining, describing, and conceptualizing the relationships obtaining between agents and acts, subjects and objects, a statement and its referent— between the literal and figurative levels of speech and, indeed, therefore, between factual and fictional discourse. What modernism envisions, in Barthes' account, is nothing less than an order of experience beyond (or prior to) that expressible in the kinds of *oppositions* we are forced to draw (between agency and patiency, subjectivity and objectivity, literalness and figurativeness, fact and fiction, history and myth, and so forth) in any version of realism. This does not imply that such oppositions cannot be used to represent some real relationships, only that the relationships between the entities designated by the polar terms may not be oppositional ones in some experiences of the world.

What I am getting at is expressed very well in Jacques Derrida's explication of his notion of *différance,* which also uses the idea of the middle voice to express what he means to convey. Derrida writes:

> *Différance* is not simply active (any more than it is a subjective accomplishment); it rather indicates the middle voice, it precedes and sets up the opposition between passivity and activity . . . And we shall see why what is designated by *différance* is neither simply active nor simply passive, that it announces or rather recalls something like the middle voice, that it speaks of an operation that is not an operation, which cannot be thought of either as a passion or as an action of a subject on an object, as starting from an agent or a patient, or on the basis of, or in view of, any of these *terms.* And philosophy has perhaps commenced by distributing the middle voice, expressing a certain intransitiveness, into the active and the passive voice, and has itself been constituted by this repression.[25]

I cite Derrida as representing a modernist conception of the project of philosophy, founded on the recognition of the differences between a distinctively modernist experience of the world (or is it the experience of a distinctively modernist world?) and the notions of representation, knowledge, and meaning prevailing in the inherited "realist" cultural endowment. And I do so in order to suggest that the kind of anomalies, enigmas, and dead ends met with in discussions of the representation of the Holocaust are the result of a conception of discourse that owes too much to a realism that is inadequate to the representation of events, such as the Holocaust, which are themselves "modernist" in nature.[26] The concept of cultural modernism is relevant to the discussion inasmuch as it reflects a reaction to (if not a rejection of) the great efforts of nineteenth-century writers—both historians and fictioneers—to represent reality "realistically"—where *reality* is understood to mean *history* and *realistically* to mean the treatment, not only of the past but also of the present, *as* history. Thus, for example, in *Mimesis*, a study of the history of the idea of realistic representation in Western culture, Erich Auerbach characterizes "the foundations of modern realism" in the following terms: "The serious treatment of everyday reality, the rise of more extensive and socially inferior human groups to the position of subject matter for problematic-existential representation, on the one hand; on the other, the embedding of random persons and events in the general course of contemporary history, the fluid background—these, we believe, are the foundations of modern realism."[27]

On this view, the modernist version of the realist project could be seen as consisting of a radical rejection of *history*, of *reality as history*, and of *historical consciousness* itself. But Auerbach was concerned to show the continuities as well as the differences between realism and modernism. Thus, in a famous exegesis of a passage from Virginia Woolf's *To the Lighthouse*, Auerbach identifies among the "distinguishing stylistic characteristics" of that "modernism" which the passage has been chosen to exemplify:

1. The disappearance of the "writer as narrator of objective facts; almost everything stated appears by way of reflection in the consciousness of the *dramatis personae*";
2. The dissolution of any "viewpoint . . . outside the novel from which the people and events within it are observed . . .";
3. The predominance of a "tone of doubt and questioning" in the narrator's interpretation of those events seemingly described in an "objective" manner;
4. The employment of such devices as "*erlebte Rede*, stream of con-

sciousness, *monologue interieur*" for "aesthetic purposes" that "obscure and obliterate the impression of an objective reality completely known to the author . . .";

5. The use of new techniques for the representation of the experience of time and temporality, e.g., use of the "chance occasion" to release "processes of consciousness" which remain unconnected to a "specific subject of thought"; obliteration of the distinction between "exterior" and "interior" time; and representation of "events," not as "successive episodes of [a] story," but as random occurrences.[28]

This is as good a characterization as any we might find of what Barthes and Derrida might have called the style of "middle voicedness." Auerbach's characterization of literary modernism indicates, not that history is no longer represented realistically, but rather that the conceptions of both history and realism have changed. Modernism is still concerned to represent reality "realistically," and it still identifies reality with history. But the history which modernism confronts is not the history envisaged by nineteenth-century realism. And this is because the social order which is the subject of this history has undergone a radical transformation—a change which permitted the crystallization of the totalitarian form that Western society assumed in the twentieth century.

As thus envisaged, cultural modernism must be seen as both a reflection of and a response to this new actuality. Accordingly the affinities of form and content between literary modernism and social totalitarianism can be granted—but without necessarily implying that modernism is a cultural expression of the fascist form of social totalitarianism.[29] Indeed, another view of the relation between modernism and fascism is possible: literary modernism was a product of an effort to represent a historical reality for which the older, classical realist modes of representation were inadequate, based as they were on different experiences of history or, rather, on experiences of a different "history."

Modernism was no doubt immanent in classical realism—in the way in which Nazism and the Final Solution were immanent in the structures and practices of the nineteenth-century nation-state and the social relations of production of which *it* was a political expression. Looked at in this way, however, modernism appears, less as a rejection of the realist project and a denial of history, than as an anticipation of a new form of historical reality, a reality that included, among its supposedly unimaginable, unthinkable, and unspeakable aspects, the phenomena of Hitlerism, the Final Solution, total war, nuclear contamination, mass starvation, and ecological suicide; a profound sense of the incapacity of our sciences to *explain*, let alone control or contain these; and a growing awareness of the incapacity of our traditional modes of representation even to *describe* them adequately.

What all this suggests is that modernist modes of representation may offer possibilities of representing the reality of both the Holocaust and the experience of it that no other version of realism could do. Indeed, we can follow out Lang's suggestion that the best way to represent the Holocaust and the experience of it may well be by a kind of "intransitive writing" which lays no claim to the kind of realism aspired to by nineteenth-century historians and writers. But we may want to consider that by intransitive writing we must intend something like the relationship to that event expressed in the middle voice. This is not to suggest that we will give up the effort to represent the Holocaust realistically, but rather that our notion of what constitutes realistic representation must be revised to take account of experiences that are unique to our century and for which older modes of representation have proven inadequate.

In point of fact I do not think that the Holocaust, Final Solution, Shoah, Churban, or German genocide of the Jews is any more unrepresentable than any other event in human history. It is only that its representation, whether in history or in fiction, requires the kind of style, the modernist style, that was developed in order to represent the kind of experiences which social modernism made possible, the kind of style met with in any number of modernist writers but of which Primo Levi must be invoked as an example.

In *Il Sistema periodico* (The periodic table), Levi begins the chapter entitled "Carbon" by writing:

> The reader, at this point, will have realized for some time now that this is not a chemical treatise: my presumption does not reach so far—"ma voix est faible, et même un peu profane." Nor is it an autobiography, save in the partial and symbolic limits in which every piece of writing is autobiographical, indeed every human work; but it is in some fashion a history.
>
> It is—or would have liked to be—a micro-history, the history of a

trade and its defects, victories, and miseries, such as everyone wants to tell when he feels close to concluding the arc of his career and art ceases to be long.

Levi then goes on to tell the story of a "particular" atom of "carbon" which becomes an allegory (what he calls "this completely arbitrary story" that is "nonetheless true"). "I will tell just one more story," he says, "the most secret, and I will tell it with the humility and restraint of him who knows from the start that this theme is desperate, the means feeble, and the trade of clothing facts in words is bound by its very nature to fail."

The story he tells is of how an atom of carbon that turns up in a glass of milk which he, Levi, drinks, migrates into a cell in his own brain— "the brain of *me* who is writing, and [how] the cell in question, and within it the atom in question, is in charge of my writing, in a gigantic minuscule game which nobody has yet described." This "game" he then proceeds to describe in the following terms: "It is that which at this instant, issuing out of a labyrinthine tangle of yeses and nos, makes my hand run along a certain path on a paper, marks it with these volutes that are signs: a double snap, up and down, between two levels of energy, guides this hand of mine to impress on this paper this dot, here, this one."

< 3 >

On Emplotment: Two Kinds of Ruin

PERRY ANDERSON

Of the literature involved in the historical dispute that broke out in West Germany four years ago, one work stands out in retrospect. Andreas Hillgruber's *Two Kinds of Ruin* not only poses what is likely to be the most persistent substantive problem, it also raises the most significant formal issue to emerge from that debate. The text comprises two essays, whose respective subjects are designated by the subtitle, *The Shattering of the German Reich and the End of European Jewry.*[1] In their original versions these were written separately; the latter, much shorter than the former, concluding a colloquium on "The Murder of European Jews in the Second World War." But both essays are terse, their economy not unusual in this historian.

The first question presented by the text is an obvious one. The two accounts that make up the work are not interwoven, but remain at a distance from each other. What, then, is the force of their juxtaposition? A dissociate double narrative is a rare form of historical composition. Plutarch's *Lives*, a biographical undertaking, is perhaps the only sustained use of it. What is its function here? If we adopt the vocabulary of *Metahistory*, the figural ground of the text is the trope termed in classical rhetoric *collatio*[2]—two objects are set in parallel, without being identified, by means of a metaphorical projection across them. Hayden White does not discuss this particular device, but his claim that tropes typically govern the narrative strategies of historians[3]— whatever its general validity—undoubtedly holds good here. In this case the initiating trope commands the emplotment in a quite precise sense. The conventional narrative of World War II represents it as a gigantic ordeal that nevertheless ends with the reconciliation of a fortunate victory—that is, in the technical terms used by Frye and White, plots it as comedy. Hillgruber's figure reverses this representation, by the gesture of an apposition which draws the fate of Germany into the orbit of that of Jewry, an area of incontestable tragedy.

< 54 >

He insists on the category of tragedy, expressly, in a significant passage on the German beginning and ending of the war. "Whether the concept of the tragic can be applied to the events that culminated in the Second World War, may be left open; guilt and fate, legitimate demand and blatant injustice, tyranny and entanglement, were here inextricably mixed. But in the case of the German East in 1944–45 we ought indeed to speak of tragic processes, for there it is clear that there was no way out for the soldiers and inhabitants of those provinces."[4]

In *The Content of the Form* White has argued that narrativity always involves moralization—historical emplotments invariably embodying ethical judgments.[5] Plutarchian parallelism is certainly a case in point. What is the moral effect of Hillgruber's construction? In the historians' controversy it was assimilated by his critics to the effects of Ernst Nolte. Both were charged with relativizing the Nazi extermination of the Jews, by extenuating comparison—in other words, a banalization of evil. The procedures of the two were nevertheless distinct. Nolte's work fully meets the charge. Its direct effect is to diminish the enormity of the Judeocide, in two arguments: that it was typologically—in quantity and quality—no worse than other great massacres of the twentieth century; and that it was causally precipitated by the fear and example of Communist terror, within a European civil war. Hillgruber's text makes neither of these claims. His essay on the Final Solution asserts it to be historically unique, and ascribes it essentially to Nazi racial doctrine.[6] Within the spectrum of scholarly interpretations of the extermination program (as of the war aims) of the Third Reich, Hillgruber, who died in May 1989, was an intentionalist. He stressed Hitler's fanatical pursuit of biological purification and territorial expansion in the East, as the central goals—the nucleus—of Nazi ambitions at large.[7] A certain intentionalism, by concentrating overwhelmingly on the demonic figure of the Führer himself, can tacitly exonerate any wider sections, or longer traditions, of German society from responsibility for the crimes of the regime. Hillgruber, who went out of his way to reject any view that would put Nazism into a realm of pathology outside history, was not of this kind. He dates the origins of both the turn to virulent antisemitism and the drive for an immense empire in the east to the year 1916, when Hindenburg and Ludendorff took command of the Third Army on the Russian front.[8] When the fatal opportunity of limitless conquest and killing came twenty-five years later, he stresses, responsibility for them was very widely shared. In the party and state apparatus, apolitical functionaries as well as zealots organized the extermination of the Jews; much larger numbers carried out their deportation; while "the mass of the German population," preoccupied with the pressures and hardships of the war, predictably accepted the *unvermeidlicherweise nur unzulänglich verschleierten Vorgang* (a process that could never be more than inadequately concealed).[9] It would be difficult to find a stronger statement of far-ranging moral responsibility than this. The officer corps too, Hillgruber argues, was deeply implicated in the practices of exterminism unleashed by Operation Barbarossa. From the Wilhelmine epoch on, the traditional tension within it between an ethos of corporate honor and a duty of strict obedience had shifted steadily toward unconditional fulfillment of orders; and when the operation ended, freebooters outside the service knew no law but violence anyway. Since 1918 German soldiers had been able to take the path of the Freikorps or that of the Reichswehr under Seeckt. "These roads seem to have divided," Hillgruber grimly observes, but in the collaboration of the SS and Wehrmacht elites in the Russian campaign of the forties, "they ran more or less closely back together again."[10] Without the active or passive collaboration of a large part of the traditional military leadership of the country, in whom all moral substance had been lost, Hitler could never have waged his unprecedented war of annihilation in the East, which from the start had combined territorial expansion and racial extermination.

It cannot therefore be said that the purpose of Hillgruber's dual narrative is to normalize the Final Solution, by assimilating it to other mass killings. Its function is rather to solemnize the German Expulsion as a tragedy, too, albeit of another kind, historically adjacent to it. The distinction is not mere artifice. It corresponds, as we have seen, to two quite different treatments of the Judeocide. Nevertheless, it remains to be asked: within the generic category of tragedy, which in principle might allow any number of illustrations, what is Hillgruber's specific justification for associating the fate of the Germans in the east with that of the Jews? His foreword asserts more than the formal characterization of both as national catastrophes, of which there have been many. It argues that this particular pair "belong together."[11] What reasons does Hillgruber give for this commonality? He stresses, in the same sentences, that the prehistory of and responsibility for each differed. "The murder of the Jews was exclusively a consequence of the radical racial doctrine that in 1933 became the ideology of the state in Hitler's Germany."[12] The expulsion of the Germans, on the other hand, was not simply a response to the crimes of the Nazi dictatorship; it also answered to independent war aims of the Allies, formulated in ignorance of the full measure of these crimes. Later in the text Hillgruber argues that in a longer-term historical perspective, the fatal idea of *völkische Feld- und Flurbereinigung*—ethnic clean sweeps—can be seen to have spread practices of organized mass killing and forcible population transfer from the European periphery, when Armenians and Greeks were their principal victims, to the whole of Europe under Nazi domination, not leaving even the British or American record intact by the end of the war.[13] Critics have objected to this contextualization, but it is difficult to deny it all validity. Hillgruber does not here equate the Judeocide with the massacres and deportations that preceded it, but views it rather as the finalized absolute of an inhumanity of which they were initial or relative versions. The argument, however, is not pressed. Hillgruber's linkage of the destiny of the Germans of the east with that of the Jews does not essentially depend on either the proximate causes or precise character of the disasters which overtook them; it rests instead on the ultimate *consequence* that issued from them. They belong together, above all, for their common effect, which was to destroy the so-called Europe of the center. Once the middle of the continent was broken to pieces in the cataclysm of war, Europe as a whole was the loser. Division and subordination to the two great powers on its wings inevitably followed.[14]

How is this construction to be assessed? Much of the discussion of it has treated Hillgruber's text as if it were more homogeneous than it is. In fact, it contains a number of different arguments, which require a more discriminating response. Let us look at four of them. The first is in a sense the most obvious. Because Hillgruber never directly compares the two processes of which his title speaks, but simply juxtaposes them under a runic adjective *zweierlei* (two kinds), the parallel narrative cannot accord them their due disproportionate weight. The result is inevitably to scale down, however inadvertently and *indirectly*, the nature of the Judeocide. The effect of this oblique reduction is then aggravated by the register in which the end of the German east is described. Notoriously, Hillgruber declares that the presumptively German historian is obliged to "identify" with "the concrete fate of the

German population in the East" and therefore also with "the desperate and sacrificial efforts" of the German armed forces to protect it from the vengeful advance of the Red Army, with its train of savageries and deportations.[15] The notion of identification, often at work in the practice of historians, but rarely so ingenuously professed, belongs to a certain traditional canon of tragedy. Hillgruber's appeal to it has been emphatically and rightly dismissed by Wehler and Maier, in particular.[16] Behind it, almost certainly, lies biographical experience. Hillgruber grew up in Königsberg, where his father was a schoolteacher dismissed by the Nazis, and as a young man he fought in the Wehrmacht's defensive campaign in East Prussia in the winter of 1945, an event he describes as allowing two million refugees to escape across the Baltic to Denmark or Schleswig-Holstein. Had Hillgruber simply noted this personal background as a subjective basis for his account of the situation confronting German civilians and troops in the eastern provinces, rather than declaring identification with them objectively mandatory, few could have quarreled. But with this false move Hillgruber slipped in one step from the understandable to the indefensible. His construction is immediately compromised. For identification with the fate of the Jews is not demanded of the historian in the companion essay. Perhaps he thought that otiose.

The procedural fallacy of Hillgruber's plea for identification, nevertheless, does not in itself dispose of the substance of his analysis of the collapse of the German east. Hillgruber makes three fundamental claims here. The first concerns the final year of the German military effort against Russia. In June 1944 the Wehrmacht had suffered its decisive defeat of the war, when the strongest of its forces, Army Group Center, was suddenly overwhelmed and broken by a Soviet offensive in Belorussia that cost it 350,000 casualties—four times the number at Stalingrad—and drove a huge breach through the German front, exposing East Prussia to immediate attack. A month later the military opposition led by Von Stauffenberg attempted to kill Hitler and overthrow the Nazi regime. How does Hillgruber judge the *attentat* of July 20? He argues that by that date, after so many previous opportunities had been missed, the conspiracy was too late. The war was by now lost anyway, and even if the coup had been successful, it would only have led to strife and chaos in the German leadership, accelerating the debacle on the eastern front. The motive of the Resistance plotters was an ethic of expressive intention, designed to show the world that a

Germany other than that of the regime existed. By contrast, he suggests, many of those soldiers and officials who fought on did so out of an ethic of responsibility, seeking to lessen the consequences of looming Soviet conquest and vengeance for the German population in the east. Hillgruber in effect validates their choice. The continued resistance of the Wehrmacht permitted, he argues, the escape of two million people across the Baltic, and the eventual surrender of some 60 percent of the troops in the east—close to another two million—to the western Allies rather than to the USSR, so saving large numbers of further lives. From a strictly German standpoint, then, the prolongation of the war for another ten months appears from Hillgruber's account to have been the lesser evil. It is this suggestion, more than any other in *Zweierlei Untergang*, which lacks any historical warrant. Here the full strength of the moral reaction against Hillgruber expressed by Habermas and Wehler is justified.[17] For in those months German military and civilian casualties alone amounted to between one and a half and two million dead—half the total killed in the fighting of the entire war—not to mention the continuing victims of Nazi terror and the Allied casualties on the other side. If a counterfactual calculation is to be made, the overthrow of Hitler in July 1944, by shortening the war, would without question have saved far more lives than the continuation of the fighting hypothetically saved before Germany surrendered. Moreover, the surrender itself would all but certainly have been partially negotiated—as, despite the principle of unconditional surrender, was in practice that of Japan, in a far weaker position vis-à-vis the Allies in August 1945 than a Goerdeler government would have been in August 1944; to say nothing of the peace concluded by Finland in September. Postwar suffering and loss for Germany would thus also have been curtailed.

For the terms of the peace in turn play a central role in Hillgruber's second argument. One of the major themes of his text is that the truncation of Germany, by the transfer of East Prussian, Pomeranian, and Silesian lands to Poland in 1945, cannot be regarded simply as geopolitical retribution for Nazi criminality in the east. It had already been projected as a strategic goal by leading Polish politicians in the interwar period, and was then adopted by Britain and the United States during the war, with the aim of eradicating what was widely supposed to be the driving force of Prussian militarism and thus putting an end to Germany as a major European power. These plans, Hillgruber argues, envisaged the expulsion of up to six million people from their homes, in the name of raison d'état, not of commutative justice. In the event, the number of those expelled at the end of the war was eleven million, of whom probably two million perished in the process. These deportations were—Hillgruber's account is so powerful that he does not even need to say so—unjustifiable. Herein lay the final German tragedy of the war.

The most extended attempt to rebut this case has been undertaken by the English historian Richard Evans, in his general review of the German controversy entitled *In Hitler's Shadow.* Evans argues that the role of the German minorities in Poland, Czechoslovakia, and elsewhere before the war had revealed their subversive potential, convincing the western Allies of the need to remove them; that Poland had to be compensated in the west for its loss of territories to Russia in the east; and that in any case, however they were brought about, "forty years of uninterrupted peace add up to an unanswerable defense of the arrangements reached in 1945." Evans concedes that the expulsions were accomplished with "appalling harshness," but maintains that "the wholly unacceptable means by which the expulsions were effected can and must be distinguished from the end sought by the expulsions themselves."[18]

The distinction, however, does not convince. What are the acceptable means of forcibly dispossessing millions of people from their homes and driving them from their native lands? Sudeten irredentism did provide the pretext for Hitler's aggression against Czechoslovakia; but did it therefore warrant the wholesale deportation of the German communities of the area after the war? On the authority of the current Czech president himself, it did not. Was Poland's extension to the Oder-Neisse Line in the west a compensation of equivalent nature to its contraction behind the Curzon line in the east? In the territories lost, Poles were a minority of perhaps 30 percent of the population—which was why the Entente had originally awarded them to Russia after World War I; in the territories gained, Germans were a majority of nearly 90 percent of the population.[19] Is the fact of subsequent peace in itself justification of these events? Both ethically and logically it is quite insufficient. Peace has reigned for seventy years along Turkey's eastern frontier, over the graves of the Armenian community: is that a defense of them? The population of the German east was expelled, not massacred; but is it really the case that peace depended on such expulsions—that no alternative settlement was conceivable? Allied calculations precluded any other outcome, it may be said; that, however, is to confirm the force of Hillgruber's observation that not only universal values but traditional imperial interests, capable of overriding such values, determined the fate of Germany in 1945.[20] The violences committed then were in no way commensurate with those inflicted by the Nazi state. But for the millions who lived through them, they were suffering enough.[21]

When Hillgruber was asked in a questionnaire what was his fondest dream, and ironically replied, to live a life in Königsberg, his answer commands respect. It does not mean he thought the disappearance of his native province reversible; but he recalled for explanation, and criticized, the expulsions which had brought it about. Although Hillgruber's reflection is here at its most nationally self-absorbed, the issues it raises are paradoxically of most contemporary concern to Jews too—as Israeli historians recover, against official legends, the complex and painful realities of the mass flights involved in the birth of their country, at a time when some voices envisage their repetition in the West Bank of today.

Finally, beyond the dilemmas of German soldiers or the expulsions of German farmers, there was in Hillgruber's view a third tragic element in the collapse of 1945. The obliteration of the German east, he argued, broke Europe itself in two; for it had historically been Germany, the "Land of the Middle," which had been the principal bridge between the western and eastern halves of the continent—mediating, in innumerable economic, cultural, and political as well as military ways, influences from beyond the Rhine into the vast area between the Baltic and the Black seas. Once this bridge was destroyed, Europe's center could not hold, and the continent was doomed to scission and subjection by the rival great powers on its flanks. The dismemberment of Germany thus also spelled the overthrow of Europe as a whole in world politics. It remained to be seen whether a common German nationality and a Europe of the center could be reconstructed anew.[22] These reflections were bitterly attacked by Habermas, who charged them with threatening "the only reliable basis of our connexion to the West," and by Wehler, who declared that they subverted loyalty to the West "far more effectively even than the foolish talk of the Greens."[23] For Habermas and Wehler the very idea of Germany as a "Land of the

Middle," indeed of a Europe of the center, was to be rejected as incompatible with the anchorage of the Federal Republic in the west—not just Western Europe, but the Western world headed by the United States. Modern German national identity, Habermas maintained, could take only one legitimate form: a constitutional patriotism centered on Bonn. Anything else was a dangerous lure.

How are we to judge this exchange? Strangely, in their haste to repudiate Hillgruber's whole problematic, such critics overlooked what is in fact the main reproach to be made against his treatment of it. Hillgruber starts by linking—programmatically—the Jewish and German catastrophes as dimensions of the collapse of Central Europe. But in what follows, whereas the role played by Germans in the history of the region is directly touched upon more than once, that of the Jews is not. Logically Hillgruber's argument requires some rendered account of the contribution of European Jewry to the binding of the two halves of the continent. That role merits the term *mediation* much less ambiguously than the German, since it was always essentially economic and intellectual, free of the stains of political and military domination that marked the latter. The consequences of its removal are evident enough—there are few more vivid illustrations of the disappearance of what a Europe of the center once meant than the culture of, say, postwar Austria. Hillgruber finds no words for this. Yet to register it is not to deny, but to accept, the validity of the notion of peoples and places located in the middle of Europe, on whose fate the linkages between its western and its eastern ends historically depended. Hillgruber's own concern with this theme was, of course, not simply a scholarly but also an avowedly political one. Despite the catastrophe of World War II, he maintains, Germany's role in the center of Europe has not been inevitably canceled for all time. German national identity cannot be divorced from the spatial setting of an undivided nation. Replying to his critics, Hillgruber wrote that it was necessary always to keep in mind the prospect—the hope—that one day Germany would be reunited again on the basis of self-determination.[24] In however unforeseeable a way, the possibility of a reconstruction of Central Europe was still open.

In November 1989 the Berlin Wall was breached, and less than a year later German unification was at hand. Hillgruber, a conservative, saw things here more lucidly than his liberal critics. One might say that his equations are taking shape before our eyes. The reunion of

Germany will indeed involve the reemergence of a Central Europe—already *in statu nascendi;* and the reconstruction of Central Europe will all but certainly restore independence to Europe as a whole, in the wider theater of the world. To have asserted these connections so clearly on the eve of their historical realization was a not inconsiderable achievement.

In 1989 Charles Maier described Hillgruber's emphasis on Germany's mediating role between western and eastern Europe as "the geopolitics of nostalgia."[25] The phrase looks less appropriate now. Maier's discussion of the problems of national identity raised in the course of the German historians' debate nevertheless remains the most interesting exploration of the issues at stake. Criticizing conceptions of the "land of the middle," he argues that national identity should in any case not be viewed simply as a deposit of successive historical experiences. It ought perhaps to be rethought as something closer to the old idea of national character—an idea especially strong, he notes, in America, from the time of Crèvecoeur onward: a character in good part amenable to nonhistorical, quasi-anthropological analysis. To this end Maier invokes Lévi-Strauss's well-known scouting of any special value in history.[26] The character or identity of an individual is, of course, always something relatively plural and unstable—how much more so is that of a nation? But if the concept of a national identity is at all negotiable, and its elements can be held to exceed the imprints of historical time, what are the most plausible further constituents? Surely not the biological substrata of race detected by Gobineau nor the involuntary uniformities of the human mind divined by Lévi-Strauss, but the coordinates of geographical space. These are durable and material enough, in most cases, to possess an obvious specific efficacy. The logic of Maier's argument paradoxically points back to the very thematic he initially discounts. German national identity, if it exists, must in part be a function of German territorial position. It is because the idea of the "land of the middle" corresponds to certain objective realities that it was a polemical mistake of the liberal left in Germany to allow conservatives to make it their own. There the Greens showed better sense.

Scrutiny of *Zweierlei Untergang* reveals, then, a series of complexities. Hillgruber was a nationalist historian, but he was not an apologist of national socialism. The device of *collatio* does not in itself dictate a diminution of the Final Solution. Nor does Hillgruber's treatment of the destruction of European Jewry as such contribute to one. But any juxtaposition of Jewish and German fates demands an exceptional—moral and empirical—delicacy that was beyond the compass of this historian. In its absence, the laconic cannot but seem the insensible. For its part, colored by personal memory, Hillgruber's obituary of the German east is of divided validity too—its counterfactual assessment of the conspiracy of July 1944 groundless, its factual verdict on the expulsions of 1945–1947 well grounded. Finally, Hillgruber's projection of Central Europe as the common scene, and victim, of the tragedies he related signally fails to situate the Jews historically within it; but, political in impulse, his projection captures the current position of the Germans, and some of the possible consequences of that position, remarkably well. All of this, in its mixture of acuteness and obtuseness, fallacies and foresights, is quite normal for a historian.

Abnormal, however, is the subject. If we ask what are the limits of a historical representation of Nazism and the Final Solution, through the prism of Hillgruber's work the answer is surely this. First, certain absolute limits are set by the evidence. Denial of the existence of either—the regime or its crimes—is plainly ruled out. No such issue arises in this case. Counterfactuals are also subject to control by the rules of evidence, which will eliminate some of them, as they do in this case: narrative strategies, to be credible, always operate within *exterior* limits of this kind. Second, however, such narrative strategies are in turn subject to a double *interior* limitation. On the one hand, certain kinds of evidence preclude certain sorts of emplotment—the Final Solution cannot *historically* be written as romance or as comedy. On the other hand, any generic emplotment has only a weak determinative power over the selection of evidence. Hillgruber could legitimately depict the end of East Prussia as tragic; that choice, however, permitted by the evidence, did not in itself dictate the series of particular empirical judgments that make up his account of it. There is a large gap between genre and script. Other divergent, tragic accounts could be written of the same events—and these would not be aesthetically incommensurable forms, or so many fictions, but epistemologically discriminable attempts to reach the truth. The typical measure of such discrimination is not the presence of *suggestio falsi*, very rare in modern historiography, but the degree of *suppressio veri*—that is, representation omitted rather than misrepresentation committed. In history, as in the sciences, the depth of a truth is usually a function of its width—how much of the evidence it engages and explains.

Narratives, then, are never plenipotentiaries over the past. The modern skepticism that would reduce history to rhetoric has a number of sources. It would be a mistake to read these selectively—as if, for example, one could trace in them principally a fascist ancestry or a leftist progeny. That would be to satisfy oneself too easily. American pragmatism, a liberal philosophy, was earlier and more influential than Italian activism in diffusing the notion of what today are sometimes called "truth-effects." It was Claude Lévi-Strauss, on the moderate right, who was the first theorist of the incommensurability of historical codes, each of them arbitrary in relation to the others.[27] There is good sense in Gramsci's remark that in intellectual battles, the only lasting victories are those won over the adversary at his strongest. For those who conceive representation as a responsibility, rather than a velleity or (as in the successor doctrine of Michel Foucault) an impossibility, the advice remains sound.

< 4 >

History, Counterhistory, and Narrative

Amos Funkenstein

History and Narrative

It is one thing to call to mind the basically narrative character of history writing as an antidote against the hypertrophy of analysis. "Historia scribitur ad narrandum, non ad probandum," Burckhardt said in one of his letters, quoting Quintilian, and added: "aber wenn sie dann durch ihre blosse Wahrheit der Darstellung beweist, so hat sie um so grösseren wert."[1]

But it is another matter altogether to claim that there is nothing to history but narrative; that history as *res gestae* collapses completely into history as *narratio rerum gestarum*. Now, there is one sense in which this claim is true—namely, in that the distinction between events and the narrative reflecting them is an untenable distinction, or at least not an absolute one. There is another sense in which this claim, taken to the extreme, is preposterously false: namely, if we take it to mean that there is no criterion by which to discern a true from a false narrative, or a precise from a sloppy one; that only literary or social categories are applicable in judging historical narratives. Hayden White, whose work I admire, has more or less taken this position.[2] I want to take some time, before introducing my theme proper, to argue against it.

There is, indeed, a sense in which history, beginning even with personal history, is *eo ipso* narrative. My acting in the world—be it the social world or the world of nature which always is "humanized nature"[3]—is the continuous plotting of a narrative. Acting in the world involves and construes my identity continuously, and my identity is a narrative. In the very same sense in which telling my narrative is a speech act, my actions, my involvement with the world, are an act of speech, a building up of a continuous story. "Ich wünschte ich wäre eine Beethovensche Symphonie oder sonst etwas, was geschrieben

< 66 >

ist," said the young Rosenzweig in one of his letters; "das geschrieben werden tut weh."[4] It is this dialectic of memory and history, self-identity and purposeful action, which Hegel had in mind in a famous passage in his "Philosophy of History," in which he said that the word *history* has both a subjective and an objective meaning. "It means both the *res gestae* and the *historia rerum gestarum*, and it is no coincidence," because there is no history without historical memory.

Are the narratives we tell—by word or act—arbitrary? Neurologists such as Oliver Sacks tell us that some patients with Korsakov disease exhibit an uncanny fabulatory ingenuity. In rapid succession, the patient changes identities from a butcher to a pastor to a scientist; every identity is narrated with convincing details, a "thick description" of sorts.

> But Mr. Thompson, only just out of the hospital—his Korsakov had exploded just three weeks before, when he developed a high fever, raved, and ceased to recognize all his family—was still on the boil, was still in an almost frenzied confabulatory delirium (of the sort sometimes called "Korsakov psychosis," though it is not really a psychosis at all), continually creating a world and self, to replace what was continually forgotten and lost. Such a frenzy may call forth quite brilliant powers of invention and fancy—a veritable confabulatory genius—for such a patient must literally make himself (and his world) up every moment. We have, each of us, a life-story, an inner narrative—whose continuity, whose sense, is our lives. It might be said that each of us constructs and lives a "narrative," and that this narrative is us, our identities.[5]

You may object that Sacks's Mr. Thompson, like similar cases discussed by Luria, was deficient precisely because he could not stick to one narrative. If he could have, who could have told whether it was authentic? Yet schizophrenics often do stick to a false identity. It is false because it does not allow them an orientation within our world, or even within theirs. Reality is absent both from the confabulated narrative sequences of Korsakov patients and from the continuous false identities of schizophrenics. In the first case reality leads to indifference ("equation"), in the second to anxiety; in both it is a contrived, false meaning imposed on the world. Narratives are historical in that they are not arbitrary, inasmuch as they are true, that is to say, historical. The "truth" or authenticity of a historical narrative—if we strip off the subjective categories and points of view of the narrator—is, like the *je ne sais quoi* of eighteenth-century aesthetic theoreticians, or like Kant's "intuition" (*Anschauung*), evasive, incapable of isolation, yet ever present, triggered—we do not know how—by "things in themselves" we cannot define except to say that they are, and are of necessity. Troeltsch still spoke of the *unvertilgbarer Rest der Anschaulichkeit* without which no historical narrative is authentic.[6] Beyond the modes of narrative, the mythopoeic intensity of the narrator, the intervening subconsciousness and superego, there is also that which can never be isolated yet is all-pervasive: the constraints of reality.

At this point you may accuse me of confusing form with content. Historical accounts do indeed choose a certain mode of narrative— romance, tragedy, comedy, satire—which is sustained by certain tropes (metaphor, metonomy, synecdoche, irony) that correspond to a quaternity of ideological stands or of "world hypotheses." But all of this, you will argue, has nothing to do with the *quaestio facti*—only with the categories by which we perceive and order the facts. For "unlike literary fictions . . . , historical works are made up of events that exist outside the consciousness of the writer."[7] This would be, on your part, an illicit turn in the argument. Form and content, imposed categories and received facts, cannot easily—cannot at all—be separated. White's *Metahistory* has had such a wide echo precisely because our choice of a "form of narrative" dictates the facts we select to fit into it. Indeed, in a sense it creates the facts. Facts are not atomic entities out there which declare their own importance; such was the medieval view of historical facts which, I will show, led to the conviction that the eyewitness is the best historian. This naive view of historical facts was replaced, starting in the seventeenth century, with the growing insight that "facts" gain their meaning and even their very factuality from the context in which they are embedded, a context reconstructed solely by the historian, whose narrative makes and shapes the fact. "Historical events" have no unequivocal referent or *denotatum*—unlike tables, crocodiles, or even the number two (which refers to the set of all sets of two numbers). Herein lies the core of the celebrated hermeneutical circle: The narrative does not simply "represent" facts, it participates in their making. Its form matters.

Let me explicate what I mean by reality. I do not advocate naive realism, nor a theory of truth as *adequatio rei ad intellectum.* "The real" is spoken of in two contradictory yet complementary senses. In one sense, real is that which escapes our control, which forces itself upon us whether or not we welcome it; in another, real is only that which we make relevant, which we construct, manipulate: *verum et factum convertuntur.* It is this dual, dialectical nature of the real which Fichte tried to capture and tame in his "original insight" into the nature of the self-setting "I." What we call a "fact" is, inasmuch as it is independent of us, made by us—and first and foremost among these facts is the self. Our memory, our narrative of the self (and hence of all that is nonself) is both given and constructed, both already constructed and constructing. Its authenticity is not arbitrary, nor does it reside in mere formal consistency or, alternately, in the mere narrative. Only because I recognize the constraint of "reality" can I manipulate "it."

I do not think that the metahistorical debate between "realists" and "narratologists" differs in principle from similar debates in philosophy of science between "realists" and "conventionalists" (or instrumentalists) or, in general, from epistemological debates that intend to clarify the constraints and the freedom of the interpreter of nature, of history, of texts. It is wholesome to call into question the absolute dividing line between "facts" and "hypotheses," "text" and "context," set by positivists old and new. It is also wholesome to realize that this process does not make facts into arbitrary fictions of the mind, even if you are an instrumentalist or a neo-Kantian.[8]

But rather than losing myself in epistemological distinctions, let me try to exemplify the issue by drawing your attention to a form of historical narrative (and, *eo ipso*, action) which is more often than not an inauthentic narrative and a pernicious action, destructive and self-destructive. I shall call it, for the sake of brevity, the *counterhistory*.[9]

Counterhistory: Ancient to Early Modern

Counterhistories form a specific genre of history written since antiquity; it is curious that they have not sooner been identified as such in treatises on historiography. Their function is polemical. Their method consists of the systematic exploitation of the adversary's most trusted sources against their grain—*die Geschichte gegen den Strich kämmen.*[10] Their aim is the distortion of the adversary's self-image, of his identity, through the deconstruction of his memory.

A counterhistory in this precise sense was once Manetho's hostile account of Jewish history, based largely on an inverted reading of Biblical passages: Manetho had, so to speak, turned the Bible on its

head.[11] Does not the Bible admit that the people of Israel lived secluded in the Egyptian province of Goshen, because "breaking bread
with them was an abomination in the eyes of Egyptians"? And that
Moses grew up an Egyptian nobleman; that a riffraff (*asafsuf*)—a
"mixed multitude" (*erev rav*)—accompanied the Hebrews on the flight
out of Egypt; that they conquered Canaan by brute force, driving out
its indigenous inhabitants? Indeed, the Bible admits that much, because—here begins Manetho's deconstruction—the Hebrews started
as an Egyptian leper colony, secluded and despised, until they called
to their aid the (Semitic) tribe of the Hyksos, and established an absolute reign of terror (Joseph's?) for over a century. Expelled by Iachmes
I, the Hyksos, together with those outcasts, were led by a renegade
Egyptian priest named Ossaersiph (Joseph? Moses? or both?). He gave
them a constitution that was, in all respects, a plagiarized, inverted
mirror image of Egyptian mores.[12]

The last point was one of the most repeated *topoi* in the ancient anti-
Jewish polemics. The Jews in antiquity enjoyed religious and political
autonomy—to the point of exemption from the cult of *divus Caesar*—
because they were regarded and esteemed as an ancient people with
an old, venerable, home-grown constitution. The Romans did not seek
to destroy what was old and venerable: they loathed *homines rerum
novarum cupidi*. This is why Jewish communities remained *collegia
licita*[13] while Christianity, by its own admission not only Jewish (which
was bad enough, though a tolerable evil) but on top of that Judaism
with a *new* dispensation, was persecuted. Manetho's propaganda was
the archetype of many similar claims that the Jews are neither a genuine nation (*gens*) nor is their constitution original: "Moses . . . introduced new laws contrary to those of the rest of mankind. Whatever is
sacred to us, is profane to them; and what they concede, we negate as
sacrilege." A millennium and a half later, John Spencer, whose *De legibus et moribus Iudaeorum* is often praised as a first antecedent to a
modern, historical-comparative science of religion, still wanted to
show the same thing—that nothing in Jewish law is original, that all of
it is an inverted mirror image of Egyptian law.[14] There was again,
among humanists and puritans, too much admiration for the ancient
res publica iudaeorum, manifested by the proliferation of seven-
teenth-century treatises with this title.

Back to Manetho's counterhistory, which continues with its narrative of the Hebrews' conquest of Canaan by force (again, an appropria-

tion of the biblical narrative) and establishment there of a common-wealth worthy of former lepers and outcasts, a constitution calculated to perpetuate the law of their origin—a rebellious spirit nourished by the hatred of the human race (*misanthropia, odium humani generis*). Indeed, Manetho's description of the way in which outcasts preserve their sense of value by constructing a (sometimes pathological) counterideology, interpreting their discrimination as a sign of special chosenness, is strongly reminiscent of what some modern sociologists of knowledge describe as the formation of a "counteridentity." The hypothetical case discussed by Berger and Luckmann is, by curious coincidence, a leper colony.[15]

Other examples of counterhistory come to mind. That Roman history, read in *malam partem*, was not a story of justice and world pacification, was a point not lost on Roman authors. They knew of accusations that Romans "create a desert and call it peace" (*solitudinem faciunt, pacem appellant*).[16] Augustine's *De Civitate Dei* wove many such traditions into a veritable counterhistory of Rome. Cicero had once written his *De Republica* with the intent to show (against his better knowledge) that the history of Rome is the history of the gradual enfoldment of *iustitia*. Augustine used the same and other Roman sources to show, on the contrary, that it is the history of greed, of lust for power (*libido dominandi*). Lust for power may be necessary if a semblance of peace is to be established among humans *post lapsum;* but it is neither just nor ever stable. *Remota iustitia, quid sunt imperia nisi magna latrocinia?*[17] Justice exists only in the *Civitas Dei*—both the one in heaven and its projected counterpart on earth, the *civitas Dei peregrinans in terris.* There is no bridge or link between the latter and the earthly city, the *civitas terrenea:* there is only a coincidence of important events in both (Abraham/Ninus = Nimrod; Jesus/Augustus), which heightens the sense of contrast between them. Augustine, in other words, not only *wrote* a counterhistory (in the sense of *historia rerum gestarum*): he also perceived the progress (*processus*) of the city of God as a counterhistory (in the sense of *res gestae*) to the history of the worldly city (*civitas terrena*).[18]

A counterhistory was also the seventh-century(?) Jewish "Narrative of the History of Jesus" (*Sefer Toldot Yeshu*).[19] Again, it employed the sources of the adversary—in this case, the Gospels—in order to turn Christian memory on its head. Jesus, it tells us, was the son of an illicit affair. He became a magician, having acquired by ruse possession of the explicit divine names (*shem hameforash*); and thus he turned into a powerful seducer of the unlearned multitude (*mesit umediah*). The Jewish legal establishment (the Sanhedrin), at the end of its wits, knew no better remedy than to have one of its own ranks volunteer to infiltrate the heretical movement in disguise and destroy it. The name of this hero was Judas Iscariot. The Gospels' heroes turn into villains, its villains into heroes.

A later continuation of the *Sefer Toldot Yeshu* attends to the early history of the Church. Again the Jewish establishment, it tells us, was searching for a strategy to separate unequivocally Christians and Jews. A heroic rabbi, Petrus by name, volunteered to pretend to be a Christian. Once he became a leader, he persuaded Christians that separation from Judaism was in the best interest of their new religion. It seems that the fabulator confused the roles of Peter and Paul.

There are counterimages, both ancient and modern, that avoid the negative. In Herodotus' image of Egypt, everything is done the opposite way from that among the Hellenes; Tacitus' image of the Germans was written as a critique of his own society.[20] Neither seeks to destroy the self-identity of its adversarial narrative. But Manetho, Augustine, and the author of the *Sefer Toldot Yeshu* did. What was the methodical rationale, the self-justification, for such an inversion of the adversary's account (*eversio*)?

Changes in Early Modern Times

Elsewhere I have tried to show in what sense the ancient or medieval notion of "historical fact" differs from ours. The premodern perception of historical fact was atomic: facts of history—such that are *digna memoria*—are immediately recognizable, distinct, and accessible to the truthful eyewitness, without need of interpretation; wherefore the eyewitness, if only truthful, is the best historian ("apud veteres nemo conscribebat historiam nisi interfuisset et ea quae conscribenda sunt vidisset," said Isidor of Seville).[21] "Literal" and "historical" meanings of a text were synonymous to the medieval exegete, who recognized a deeper sense only in the theological perspective (*spiritualis intelligentia*).[22] And since events *digna memoria* were evident and always recorded, world history is a continuous claim of eyewitness reports.[23]

What if the eyewitness lies? Why then, only then, it is the *officium* of the later historian to debunk the narrative—indeed, to create a counterhistory out of the falsified narrative, guided by the assumption that every good lie contains a germ of truth. Ancient and medieval historiography—or rather, historical methodology—obeyed strictly the principle of the excluded middle: a story is either true or false; *tertium non datur.* To say (as we do) that an account, either of an eyewitness or of a remote narrator, is subjectively true yet objectively distorted, that everyone is a captive of his individual, local, or temporal "point of view" and preconception[24]—to say all that, as we do, is to recognize that the "historical fact" is not at all self-evident, that it needs interpretation, that it obtains its meaning from a context which the historian, always caught in a hermeneutical circle, must reconstruct. History has ceased, for us, to be a *simplex narratio gestarum:* it has become *eo ipso* interpretation subject to time, place, and the point of view of the interpreter. Such has been the insight advanced by humanists since the sixteenth century, when it induced a veritable revolution in philology, biblical studies, legal interpretation (the *mos gallicus*)[25] and, finally, historical studies proper.

The genre of counterhistory that we have identified as a well-defined, literary-polemical genre in antiquity and in the Middle Ages likewise changed with the "historical revolution" of the sixteenth century. It focused on an explicit reinterpretation, rather than an inverted exploitation, of sources. Consider, for example, the pietist Gottfried Arnold's counterhistory of the Church, first published in 1698.[26]

Protestant historiography was driven, from its beginning, toward the construction of a counterhistory of the Church. It called to its aid the new art of philological–historical criticism cultivated already by generations of humanists. Gottfried Arnold's history of Christianity was such a critical counterhistory, examining the sources directly rather than, as in our earlier examples, referring to them obliquely and surreptitiously. He called it an *Unparteyische Kirchen und Ketzergeschichte,* but he is hardly impartial when it comes to deciding between Church and deviants. Paul's words, "Heresies are necessary" (*opertet ut haereses esse*),[27] acquired even in the Middle Ages historical-providential connotations: heresies were seen as a providential challenge to which the Church, inspired by the Holy Spirit, answered by the development of dogmas and rejuvenation through new orders. Heresies, like Goethe's Mephisto, are "ein teil von jenem Geist, der stets das Böse will doch stets das Gute schafft." Gottfried Arnold turned this evaluation on its head. Sectarians and so-called heretics were the only historical vestiges of Christianity during the long night of its decay, of the eclipse of truth. Examining the sources, he could show that, whenever the corrupt establishment defined a movement as heretical, it did so because it abhorred being reminded of the true, spiritual, nondogmatic, and nonceremonial origins of Christianity, that Christianity was internal and apolitical by the very "scandalous" paradigm of its founder. Arnold, then, went back *ad fontes* both in the historiographic and in the religious sense of the word, and he meant his "history" to be an incentive for all Christians to do the same. He did not seek reason in history: rather, he put his trust in the continuous, subterranean instances of true *Innerlichkeit*, of defiance of the world and its wisdom, which always was the trademark of martyrs and sectarians alike. Jesus himself stood trial as a heretic.[28] The "true" sacred history of Christianity was a secret private history—even after the age of Luther. The public history of Christianity was, by contrast, a secular history—a history of involvement with this world (*saeculum*), of entanglement with power and greed: hence, a history of a falsification.

Counterhistory in Marx

Arnold expressed, as did most early Protestant thinkers, a disdain of history, seen basically as a history of human deprivation and error. Still, his use of history is critical. Historical thought during the Enlightenment was far more optimistic, but history still served basically as a foundation of ahistorical arguments about human nature. With the triumph of the historical dimension of discourse in the nineteenth century came also a different mode of counterhistory, of which Marx is an excellent example.

Every aspect of Marx's thinking and planning is dominated by the now all-pervasive historical discourse. At the very core of his economic theory lies the realization that the "laws of the market" are historical, rather than natural, laws. There exists no natural drive to barter in humans, nor do commodities own a "nature" dictating their (exchange) value (the "fetishization of the ware"). Both reflect historical conditions of social relations shaped by modes of production. If Hobbes changed the course of modern political theory by systematically denaturalizing the state—it is a human artifact, not a result of social inclinations—

Marx did the same to the *homo economicus*, except that his interpretation presupposes a coherent historical narrative.

Marx's interpretation of history is in a sense a protracted exercise in counterhistory. Bourgeois historians (seen from the Marxist—even from Marx's—perspective) tell the history of modern times, since the rise of the bourgeoisie, as a history of growing freedom, human rights, equality before the law. The driving force of this progress is the pursuit of economic self-interest, whereby "private vices" generate of themselves "public virtues."[29] The French Revolution, with its declaration of the *droits de l'homme* and equality before the law, legitimized the achievements of the third estate; the modern national state is its fortunate outcome. Standing above all parties and interest groups, the state only watches that individual; healthy antagonisms do not grow out of the rules of the game.[30]

But this "political emancipation," the liberal ideal of the bourgeoisie, only appears to be also a human emancipation; in reality even the celebrated *droits humains* epitomize the opposite. They guarantee the maximal exploitation of the dispossessed, they strip the individual of all bondages—feudal or corporative—so as to make him free to sell himself, that is to say his labor, everywhere as a commodity in the market. The modern state just appears to stand above the parties: in reality, it ensures maximal antagonization, the atomization of society. The civil society is indeed a society in which everything, including human labor, has become a commodity obeying the "laws of the market"; the logic of capitalism demands that this commodity be there in superabundance, forming "the reserve army of capital" out of these atomized, seemingly free individuals. The social paradox latent in every commodity—that if it purports to represent abstract labor, then it cannot represent abstract labor—becomes transparent, explosively so, when labor itself turns into a commodity.[31] "Private vices" lead to catastrophe rather than to a stable, uniform increase of wealth. The dialectic of *Wesen* and *Erscheinung*, the theme of Hegel's *Wesenslogik*, dominates Marx's analysis of the state, of commodity, of history.[32] Essence turns *eo ipso* into appearance, and vice versa. This saves Marx's counterhistory from being merely the revision of history from the point of view of the oppressed, a revision worthy of utopian socialists. Rather his is the account of the "slave" inevitably becoming, through his labor, the true "master"—and of his revolutionizing history simply by knowing it. Marx truly turned the bourgeois vision of state and history on its head—or back on its feet.

Nazism and Revisionism

Let me move to my last examples of counterhistory, *cum ira et cum studio*. All antisemitic ideologies since the end of the nineteenth century have this in common, that they are directed less against traditional, orthodox Jews who can be recognized as Jews, and much more against Jews who are well acculturated and assimilated. Assuming, as antisemitic ideologues do, that being Jewish is an unobliterable, indelible, innate character, the assimilated Jew deceives, in the best case, both himself and others; or, in the worst case, his assimilation is a conspiratorial pretense, whose purpose is to undermine the healthy texture of society from within. Even extreme antisemites until the 1930s did not go beyond the suggestion to undo the emancipation, to return the Jews from the status of citizen to the former status of mere subjects. This program was thoroughly implemented during the first seven years following the Nazi *Machtergreifung* in Germany.

But the National Socialist ideology contained the germ of a much more ruthless "solution of the Jewish question." In its dramatic-apocalyptic reading of world history, Jews were the hypostatized negation of sanity, creativity, health, and order, a secularized antichrist described in hygienic-pseudobiological terms. If other "races," say the Slavs (or, indeed, the Semites), were subhuman (*Untermenschen*), the Jews throughout history were unhuman (*Unmenschen*), a counterrace to the *Herrenrasse*, a vermin, a bacillus. To have exterminated them would even be worthy of a German catastrophic defeat, Hitler said at the end of the war.

Now, observe how this constructed counteridentity of Jews was made into a reality in the concentration camps. The Jews, themselves lice in the Nazi terminology, had to be deliced (*entlaust*) entering the camp; they were made into vermin, deprived of identity, dehumanized even in their own eyes, and finally exterminated as lice. Symbolism and reality become almost one, exactly as in Kafka's *Metamorphosis*.

Indeed, although many of Kafka's texts deal with the dissolution of identity, none addresses it so explicitly as the *Metamorphosis*, in which Gregor Samsa wakes up one day to find himself "ein riesen Ungeziefer."[33] At first, his physical and mental behavior is still more human:

slowly, gradually, through a subtle interaction between his family and himself, he acquires more and more the mentality of a bug, and he dies like one. At the end of the story we discover that, in a sense, he was always a bug, even before the narrative commenced: the family, seemingly once dependent on him totally, gets along splendidly without him. He always was superfluous; "becoming" a bug was no coincidence after all, but rather the continuous translation of a symbol or metaphor into reality.

Earlier we attended to the sense in which history (as *res gestae*) is *ipso facto* narrative: namely, inasmuch as deeds, no less than words, are the continuous construction of the self-identity of agents—be the agents individuals or collectives.[34] The systematic destruction of self-identity of inmates in concentration camps was also the attempt to destroy their narrative of themselves. Inasmuch as the history of a period ultimately depends on the identity of its agents, the reconstruction of a coherent narrative of the experience of the victims, individual and collective, is an almost insurmountable task, much harder than the refutation of the collective counterhistory that Nazi ideology tried to reify.

An offshoot of the Nazi counterhistory still lives in the various apologetic-polemical exercises known as "revisionist" literature. It is a name given (inter alia) to a distinct group of writings—books, articles, pamphlets—that deny the facticity of the Nazi genocide of the Jews.[35] Of the various examples of counterhistories, this denial is the most recent and vicious. The writings qualify as counterhistories par excellence, not only because the revisionists deny that the victim is a victim, but because most of them also accuse—explicitly or implicitly—the victim of being the perpetrator, and this in two ways.

1. Some authors, while denying the existence of extermination camps, do not deny the existence of KZ camps: now in those, they say, Jews (Kapos) did kill other Jews in large numbers. This is all there is to the legend of mass killings. If there were any, they were perpetrated by the Jews themselves (the assumption being that they were given genuine autonomy). Of course there have also been accidental civilian casualties—among Jews just as among every population. Why had the Jews to be "concentrated" to begin with? Because they declared war on Germany (rather than vice versa), be it with the general economic boycott of the thirties, be it in a letter of Weizmann of 1939 in which he said that Jews are at war with Germany.

2. The victims become perpetrators also ex post facto: the legend of genocide was a world conspiracy of Jews—some revisionists add—in order to enable them to gain a state after the war. The world conspiracy of Jews is a motif that has continued in anti-Jewish European literature, as I have shown elsewhere, since the twelfth century. Then and there, I believe I have proven, Judaism lost the image it had hitherto in Christian eyes of an anachronistic yet transparent religion—"noluerunt ipsi Judaei mutari cum tempore"[36]—and acquired, instead, the image of a religion adhering to the Old Testament only seemingly, while in fact committed in secret to a new, satanic law ("pugnasti tanto tempore diabolicis libris divinos libros"—Peter the Venerable).[37] Some added, a religion committed also to the shedding of Christian blood—every year their rabbis convened in secret and chose another community to shed Christian blood on Passover, for otherwise they believed they would not be redeemed (Thomas of Monmouth).[38] It is one continuous tradition which leads from here to the *Protocols of the Elders of Zion*; its latest version is the revisionist account of the Jewish anti-German character assassination—a spiritual genocide, as it were.

How does one deny a fact? By arguing it away. Argument (rather than narrative) is the preferred discourse of revisionists. Two modes of argument prevail in particular, and Pierre Vidal-Naquet has exposed them brilliantly. It is either a *reductio ad impossibile* or an argument from analogy. The KZ camps, we are told, could not have been death camps; the alleged gassing chambers, for example, were so constructed that, had they contained poison gas, it would have poisoned everything for miles around. Analogy is used, for example, when we are admonished to remember that already once, during World War I, rumors of German atrocities were cultivated which proved after the war to have been widely exaggerated for propaganda purposes.

Almost every facet of this revisionist literature is present in another recent brand of revisionist literature, the attempt to deny the genocide of Armenians during World War I. It is hard (and redundant) to establish who influenced whom; minds intent at similar tasks argue alike. Again we are told that at best there were a few local pogroms blown out of proportion. The deportations were understandable in view of the Armenian insurrection at Van; besides, they were ordered for the Armenians' own benefit, for they lived along the exposed shores of Syria. The myth of genocide is kept alive by hopes that it will prompt the bad conscience of the nations of the world to grant independence to the Armenians; they evidently were encouraged by the success of the Jews to turn their national catastrophe into an instrument to gain independence. (It is this latter argument which George Steiner made into a fictitious last speech of Hitler's in *The Portage to St. Cristobal of A.H.*)[39]

At one crucial point, the revisionists' counterhistories are prompted and aided by a genuine paradox of the subject matter. Many of us say that the Nazi crimes were "incomprehensible," that the sheer limitless inventiveness in degradation of that regime defies all of our historical explanatory schemes: it certainly did not spring out of self-interest or raison d'état.[40] Precisely this incomprehensibility of the crimes makes their denial into a much more rational account of a possible world (better than ours) in which people act out of rational, or at least predictable, motivations. *Aber die Wirklichkeit, die ist nicht so.*

Which brings us back to our initial question—what makes one story more "real" than another? Or, in another variation, what distinguishes a legitimate revision from a revisionist confabulation? Some counterhistories—by no means all of them—present us with a limit case; from the limit case something may be learned for less clear-cut cases. They are inauthentic, unreal, not because their authors lie consciously— this may or may not be the case—but rather because they are through-and-through derivative, altogether dependent in every detail on the story they intend to overthrow. Reality is an elusive notion, perhaps even a paradoxical one. No historiographical endeavor may presume to "represent" reality—if by representation we mean a corresponding system of things and their signs. Every narrative is, in its way, an exercise in "worldmaking." But it is not arbitrary. If the narrative is true, reality, whatever its definition, must "shine through it" like Heidegger's being—and, like the latter, without ever appearing directly. Nothing in the counterhistories of Manetho, of the *Sefer Toldot Yeshu*, of the revisionists "shines through": everything in them is a reflexive mirror image. (Augustine, Arnold, Marx are different.) Closeness to reality can be neither measured nor proven by a waterproof algorithm. It must be decided from case to case without universal criteria. Everything in a narrative—factual content, form, images, language—may serve as indicators.

Moralité

This, then, is the final lesson I want to draw from our long preoccupation with counterhistories, ancient or modern. In their most vicious forms, they deprive the adversary of his positive identity, of his self-image, and substitute for it a pejorative counterimage. But how could we discriminate between a genuine narrative and a counternarrative unless by a criterion outside the narrative? You are not an old nation with ancient, venerable institutions, but rather lepers imitating our institutions, said Manetho to the Jews; you and your history are not a paradigm of justice and virtue, but rather of greed and *libido dominandi*, said Augustine to the pagan Romans; you and the founders of your religion were and are magicians, said the Jews to the Christians; you are not real Jews, said medieval Christians to the Jews; you are not Christians, said Arnold to the Catholics; you are not the protagonists of freedom, but of its opposite, of exploitation and dehumanization, said Marx to the liberals of his time; you are not human at all, said the Nazi ideologues to the Jews, and tried as much as they could actually to dehumanize them even in their own eyes before killing them. You are not even victims of atrocities, say the revisionists to the Jews.

In both the case of some mental diseases which I discussed at the beginning and the more vicious case of counterhistories, identities are destroyed: but it may seem as if the schizophrenic, or the one who suffers from Korsakov psychosis, has his own identity destroyed, while in the case of counterhistories, personal or collective, it is the self-identity of the *other* which is under attack. Yet both lose contact with reality—both reveal aspects of that involuntary constraint which allows effective manipulations of our world. Because of that, every serious counterhistory that will try to become reality turns at the end to destroy not only the identity of the other, but also the self-identity of the destroyer. And it is self-destructive of necessity, if only because the forger of a counteridentity of the other renders his own identity dependent on it. In this *Kampf um Leben und Tod*[41] both identities are inevitably destroyed if the counteridentity succeeds in its aim to destroy the self-identity of the other. This self-destruction is no solace: because while it is going on, the guilty and the unguilty alike suffer.

"To the threshold lies sin" (Gen. 4:7). In the beginning, Zionist ideology labored hard to construct a new, positive Jewish self-image, to restore a Jewish "self-respect" (Pinsker) so as to achieve "autoemancipation." It was a noble and timely endeavor, which at its worst could be blamed for disregarding the fact that the land of Israel was not empty and barren, that it was already populated by indigenous Arabs. By now, however, the collective self-identification of many Israelis—

not of all—is inextricably tied to a downright negation of the national identity of the Palestinians. "There is no Palestinian nation," Golda Meir once said. A standing political argument has it that the Palestinian—or even Arab-national—movements are not authentic, that they are a mere mirror image of the emergence of a Jewish national consciousness and a reaction thereto; as if the genesis of a national identity really matters. Another political argument has it that Arab immigration to Palestine swelled only after the Zionist efforts made the land attractive. Depersonalization of the Palestinians, denial of their personal and political self-identity, has become an oppressive political reality. As a Zionist and as a historian, I fear these developments and abhor their consequences. By destroying the identity of the other we will destroy our own. It need not happen: it is incumbent on us not to let it happen.

< 5 >

Just One Witness

CARLO GINZBURG

For Primo Levi

On 16 May 1348, the Jewish community of La Baume, a small Provençal village, was exterminated. This event was only a link in a long chain of violence which had started in southern France with the first eruption of the Black Death just one month before. The hostilities against the Jews, who were widely believed to have spread the plague by poisoning wells, fountains, and rivers, had first crystallized in Toulon during Holy Week. The local ghetto had been assaulted; men, women, and children had been killed. In the following weeks similar violence had taken place in other Provençal towns like Riez, Digne, Manosque, and Forcalquier. In La Baume there were no survivors except one—a man who ten days before had left for Avignon, summoned by Queen Jeanne. He left a painful memory of the episode in a few lines inscribed on a Torah, now preserved at the Oesterreichische Nationalbibliothek in Vienna. In a very fine essay Joseph Shatzmiller has succeeded, by combining a new reading of the lines inscribed on the Torah with a document extracted from a fiscal register, in identifying the survivor's name: Dayas Quinoni.[1] In 1349 Quinoni was settled in Aix, where he received his Torah. We do not know whether he ever came back to La Baume after the massacre.

Let us now briefly discuss a different, though not unrelated, case. The accusations that the Jews had spread the plague in 1348 closely followed a pattern which had been established a generation before. In 1321, during Holy Week, a rumor suddenly spread throughout France and some neighboring regions (western Switzerland, northern Spain). According to the different versions, lepers, or lepers inspired by Jews, or lepers inspired by Jews inspired by the Muslim kings of Tunis and Granada, had built up a conspiracy to poison sane Christians. The Muslim kings were obviously out of reach, but for two years lepers and

< 82 >

Jews became the targets of a series of violent acts performed by mobs and by religious and political authorities as well. I have tried else-where to disentangle this complex series of events.[2] Here I would like to analyze a passage from a Latin chronicle written in the early four-teenth century by the so-called continuator of William of Nangis, an anonymous monk who, like his predecessor, lived in the abbey of Saint-Denis.

After the discovery of the alleged conspiracy many Jews, mostly in northern France, were killed. Near Vitry-le-François, the chronicler says, approximately forty Jews were jailed in a tower. In order to avoid being put to death by the Christians they decided, after some discus-sion, to kill one another. The deed was performed by an old, highly respected man, with the help of a young man. The older man then asked the younger man to kill him. The young man reluctantly ac-cepted. But instead of committing suicide, he grabbed some gold and silver from the corpses on the ground. He then tried to escape from the tower using a rope made of sheets tied together. But the rope was not long enough. The young man fell to the ground, breaking his leg, and was then put to death.[3]

The episode is not implausible. However, it presents some undeni-able affinities with two passages from Flavius Josephus' *Jewish War*: (1) the hiding of *forty people* in a grotto near Jotapata, in Galilea, in C.E. 67, followed by the collective suicide of all of them, with only two exceptions—Josephus himself and a fellow soldier who accepted his proposal not to kill him (III,8); and (2) the siege of Masada, the desper-ate resistance of the Jews assembled within the fortress, followed by a collective suicide with two exceptions, both women (VII, 8–9).[4] How should we interpret the analogies between Josephus' texts and the al-ready mentioned passage in the chronicle written by the continuator of William of Nangis? Should we assume a factual convergence or rather the presence of a historiographical *topos* (including, in this ver-sion, an additional element—the allusion to Jewish greed)? We must recall in this context that the latter suggestion has already been raised, at least as a possibility, in order to explain Josephus' account of the events of Masada.[5] Flavius Josephus' work, either in Greek or in the famous Latin version prepared under Cassiodorus' direction, was widely circulated in the Middle Ages, especially in northern France and Flanders (as far as we can judge from the extant manuscripts).[6] Although we know that Flavius Josephus was mandatory reading during Lent at the monastery of Corbie around 1050, Josephus' works are not included in a fourteenth-century list of readings for the monks of Saint-Denis—among whom, as has been recalled before, was the continuator of William of Nangis.[7] Moreover, we have no direct proof that manuscripts of Josephus' *Jewish War* existed in the library of Saint-Denis.[8] Still, they would have been easily available to the anonymous chronicler. The Bibliothèque Nationale in Paris owns many of them, including one (a twelfth-century copy) from the library of Saint-Germain-des-Prés.[9] We can conclude that the continuator of William of Nangis may have been familiar with Flavius Josephus' *Jewish War* (or with the late fourth-century adaptation of it, known as "Hegesippus").[10] This does not necessarily imply, however, that the collective suicide near Vitry-le-François never took place. More work is needed on this issue, although a clear-cut conclusion is perhaps unattainable.

A multiple relationship connects these stories from a distant, half-forgotten past to the topic of this book. A poignant awareness of this connection can be detected in Pierre Vidal-Naquet's decision to republish in the same volume (*Les Juifs, la mémoire et le présent*, Paris, 1981) his essay on "Flavius Josephus and Masada" and "A Paper Eichmann," a long piece on the so-called revisionist school which claims that Nazi extermination camps were just a hoax.[11] I believe, however, that the similarity of content—the persecution of Jews in the Middle Ages, the extermination of Jews in the twentieth century—is less important than the similarity of the theoretical issues involved in both cases. Let me explain why.

The analogies between the two passages from Josephus, describing the Jotapata and Masada episodes, include, in addition to the collective suicide, the survival of two people: Josephus and his fellow soldier in the first case, two women in the second.[12] We may say that the survival of at least one person was logically required by the necessity to provide an account of each episode, but why two? I think that the well-known rejection of a single witness in court, shared by the Jewish and Latin juridical traditions, explains the choice of two witnesses.[13] Both traditions were familiar, of course, to Flavius Josephus, a Jew who became a Roman citizen. Later on, Constantine, the Roman emperor, made the exclusion of a single witness a formal law, which was subsequently included in the Justinian Code.[14] In the Middle Ages the implicit reference to Deuteronomy 19, verse 15 (*Non stabit testis unus contra aliquem*) became *testis unus, testis nullus* (one witness, no witness): a maxim referred to, either implicitly or explicitly, in trials and legal literature.[15]

Let us now imagine for a moment what would happen if such a criterion were applied to the field of historical research. Our knowledge of the events which took place in La Baume in May 1348, near Vitry-le-François sometime during the summer of 1321, and in the grotto near Jotapata in July C.E. 67, is based, in each case, on a single, more or less direct witness. That is, respectively, the person (identified as Dayas Quinoni) who wrote the lines on the Torah now in the National-bibliothek in Vienna; the continuator of William of Nangis; and Flavius Josephus. No sensible historian would dismiss this evidence as intrinsically unacceptable. According to normal historiographical practice, the value of each document will be tested by way of comparison—that is, by constructing a series including at least two documents. But let us assume for a moment that the continuator of William of Nangis, in his account of the collective suicide near Vitry-le-François, was merely echoing Josephus' *Jewish War*. Even if the supposed collective suicide would finally evaporate as a fact, the account itself would still give us a valuable piece of evidence about the reception of Josephus' work (which is also, except for hard-nosed positivists, a "fact") in early fourteenth-century Ile-de-France.

Law and history, it seems, have different rules and different epistemological foundations. This is the reason why legal principles cannot be safely transferred into historical research.[16] Such a conclusion would contradict the close contiguity stressed by sixteenth-century scholars like François Baudouin, the legal historian who solemnly declared that "historical studies must be placed upon a solid foundation of law, and jurisprudence must be joined to history."[17] In a different perspective, related to antiquarian research, the Jesuit Henri Griffet, in his *Traité des différentes sortes de preuves qui servent à établir la vérité de l'histoire* (Treatise on the various types of proofs by which it is possible to obtain historical truth) (1769) compared the historian to a judge in court, testing the reliability of different witnesses.[18]

Such an analogy today has a definitely unfashionable ring. Many contemporary historians would probably react with a certain embarrassment to the crucial word *preuves* (proofs). But some recent discussions show that the connection among proofs, truth, and history emphasized by Griffet cannot be easily dismissed.

I have already mentioned "A Paper Eichmann," the essay written by Pierre Vidal-Naquet to refute the notorious thesis advanced by Robert Faurisson and others, according to which Nazi extermination camps never existed.[19] The same essay has recently been republished in a small volume, *Les assassins de la mémoire* (The killers of memory), which Vidal-Naquet has dedicated to his mother, who died at Auschwitz in 1944. We can easily imagine the moral and political motives which urged Vidal-Naquet to engage himself in a detailed discussion, involving among other things a punctilious analysis of the evidence (witnesses, technological possibilities, and so on) concerning the existence of gas chambers. Other, more theoretical implications have been spelled out by Vidal-Naquet in a letter to Luce Giard, which was published a few years ago in a memorial for Michel de Certeau. Vidal-Naquet writes that the collection of essays *L'écriture de l'histoire* (The writing of history) published by de Certeau in 1975 was an important book which contributed to the dismantling of the historians' proud innocence. "Since then, we have become aware that the historian *writes;* that he produces space and time, being himself intrinsically embedded into a specific space and time." But we should not dismiss, Vidal-Naquet goes on, that old notion of "reality," meaning "precisely what happened," as evoked by Ranke one century ago.

> I became very conscious of all this when the *affaire Faurisson*—which unfortunately is still going on—began. Faurisson's attitude is, of course, totally different from de Certeau's. The former is a crude materialist, who, in the name of the most tangible reality, transforms everything he deals with—pain, death, the instruments of death—into something unreal. De Certeau was deeply affected by this perverse folly, and wrote me a letter about it . . . I was convinced that there was an ongoing discourse on gas chambers; that everything should necessarily go through to a discourse [*mon sentiment était qu'il y avait un discours sur les chambres à gaz, que tout devait passer par le dire*]; but beyond this, or before this, there was something irreducible which, for better or worse, I would still call reality. Without this reality, how could we make a difference between fiction and history?[20]

On this side of the ocean this question about the difference between
fiction and history is usually associated with (or elicited by) the work of
Hayden White. Notwithstanding the difference between White's and
de Certeau's historiographical practice, some convergence between,
let us say, *Metahistory* (1973) and *L'écriture de l'histoire* (1975, but
including essays published some years earlier) is undeniable. I will try
to show, however, that White's contribution can be fully understood
only in the framework of his intellectual development.[21]

In 1959, introducing the American edition of *Dallo storicismo alla sociologia* (From historicism to sociology) by Carlo Antoni (one of Benedetto Croce's closest followers), Hayden White labeled Croce's youth-
ful essay *La storia ridotta sotto il concetto generale dell'arte* (History
subsumed under a general concept of the arts) as "revolutionary."[22]
The relevance of this essay, published by Croce in 1893 when he was
twenty-seven years old, had already been emphasized by Croce himself in his intellectual autobiography (*Contributo alla critica di me
stesso*), as well as later on by R. G. Collingwood (*The Idea of History*).[23] Not surprisingly, the chapter on Croce in *Metahistory* includes
a detailed discussion of *La storia ridotta*.[24] But White's appreciation of
this essay had become, after sixteen years, remarkably colder. He still
shared some relevant points, such as the sharp distinction between
historical research (regarded as merely propaedeutic work) and proper
history, and the identification between the latter and historical narrative. But then he concluded:

> It is difficult not to think of Croce's "revolution" in historical sen-
> sibility as a retrogression, since its effect was to sever historiography
> from any participation in the effort—just beginning to make some
> headway as sociology at the time—to construct a general science of
> society. But it had even more deleterious implications for historians'
> thinking about the artistic side of their work. For, while Croce was
> correct in his perception that art is a way of knowing the world, and
> not merely a physical response to it or an immediate experience of
> it, his conception of art as literal *representation* of the real effectively
> isolated the historian as artist from the most recent—and increas-
> ingly dominant—advances made in representing the different levels
> of consciousness by the Symbolists and Post-Impressionists all over
> Europe.[25]

This passage already points to some elements of Hayden White's later work. Since *Metahistory* he has become less and less interested in the construction of a "general science of society," and more and more in "the artistic side of the historian's work," a shift not remote from Croce's long battle against positivism, which inspired, among other things, his scornful attitude toward social sciences. But by the time of *Metahistory* Croce had already ceased to be the crucial influence he had been in the early stages of White's intellectual career. Undoubtedly Croce still scored some very high points: on the one hand, he is labeled "the most talented *historian* of all the philosophers of history of the century," and on the other, his allegedly "ironical" attitude is warmly praised in the very last page of the book.[26] But the global evaluation quoted above reveals also a significant disagreement with Croce's theoretical perspective.

White's dissatisfaction with Croce's thought focuses, as we have seen, on "his conception of art as a literal *representation* of the real": in other words, on his "realistic" attitude.[27] Such a word, which in this context has a cognitive, not purely aesthetic meaning, may sound a bit paradoxical, when referring to a neoidealist philosopher like Croce. But Croce's idealism was rather peculiar: a label like "critical positivism," suggested by one of his most intelligent critics, seems more appropriate.[28] The most definitely idealistic stage in Croce's thought was related to the strong impact exerted on him, especially in the crucial years 1897–1900, by Giovanni Gentile, who for two decades was his closest intellectual associate.[29] In a note added to the second edition of his *Logica come scienza del concetto puro* (1909) Croce provided a retrospective reconstruction of his own intellectual development, starting from *La storia ridotta,* in which he had put history within the larger category of art, to the recent recognition, made under the impact of Giovanni Gentile ("my dearest friend . . . whose work had been so influential on my own"), of the identity between history and philosophy.[30] Some years later, however, the intrinsic ambiguities of this identity (as well as, on a general level, of the alleged theoretical convergence between Croce and Gentile) fully emerged.[31] Croce, by interpreting philosophy as the "methodology of history," seemed to dissolve the former within the latter. Gentile went in the opposite direction. "Ideas without facts," he wrote, "are empty; philosophy which is not history is the vainest abstraction. But facts are simply the life of the objective side of self-consciousness, outside which there is no real constructive thought." He emphasized that historical facts [*res gestae*] "are not presupposed by history [*historia rerum gestarum*]." He strongly rejected, therefore, "the metaphysical theory of history (that is, historicism) based directly on the idea that historical writing presupposes historical fact, an idea as absurd as those of other metaphysics, and pregnant with worse consequences; for no enemy is so dangerous as one who has managed to creep into your house and hide there."[32]

By identifying that unnamed "metaphysical theory of history" with historicism Gentile was reacting to a polemical antifascist essay by Croce, "Antistoricismo," which had just been published.[33] The theoretical core of Gentile's essay went back to his *Teoria generale dello spirito come atto puro* (1918), a response to Croce's *Teoria e storia della storiografia* (1915).[34] But by 1924 the philosophical dispute between the two former friends had transformed itself into a bitter political and personal feud.

This apparent digression was required in order to make the following points.

1. Hayden White's intellectual development can be understood only by taking into account his exposure, at an early stage of his career, to Italian philosophical neoidealism.[35]

2. White's "tropological" approach, suggested in *Tropics of Discourse,* his collection of essays first published in 1978, still showed the impact of Croce's thought. "Croce," he wrote in 1972, "moved from his study of the epistemological bases of historical knowledge to a position in which he sought to subsume history under a general concept of art. His theory of art, in turn, was construed as a 'science of expression and general linguistics' (the subtitle of his *Aesthetics*). In his analysis of the bases of speech of all possible modes of comprehending reality, he came closest to grasping the essentially tropological nature of interpretation in general. He was kept from formulating this near perception, most probably, by his own 'ironic' suspicion of system in any human science."[36]

Such an approach starts with Croce but goes beyond him. When we read that "tropics is the process by which all discourse *constitutes* [my italics] the objects which it pretends only to describe realistically and to analyze objectively" (a passage from the introduction to *Tropics of Discourse* [1978]),[37] we recognize the aforementioned criticism addressed to Croce's "realism."

3. This subjectivist stand was emphasized by the encounter with the work of Foucault. But it is significant that White tried to "decode" Foucault through Vico, the alleged founding father of Italian philosophical neoidealism.[38] In fact, White's statement about discourse creating its own objects seems to be echoing—with a major difference to be discussed soon—Croce's emphasis on expression and general linguistics combined with Gentile's extreme subjectivism implying that historiography (*historia rerum gestarum*) creates its own object: history (*res gestae*). "Le fait n'a jamais qu'une éxistence linguistique": these words by Barthes, used as a motto for *The Content of the Form* (1987), could be ascribed to this imaginary combination of Croce and Gentile. Even White's reading of Barthes in the early eighties (he was still barely mentioned in *Tropics of Discourse*[39]) reinforced a preexisting pattern.

The most questionable element in this reconstruction is Gentile's role. As far as I know, White has never discussed his writings or even mentioned him (with one relevant exception, as we shall see). But familiarity with Gentile's work can be safely assumed in a scholar who, through Antoni, became deeply involved in the philosophical tradition initiated by Croce and Gentile. (On the other hand, a direct knowledge of Gentile's work must be ruled out for Barthes. The crucial role played by Barthes in de Certeau's work can explain—but only in part—the partial convergence between the latter and Hayden White.)

Gentile's close association with fascism, through his life and his violent death, has somewhat obscured, at least outside Italy, the first stage of his philosophical career. His adhesion to Hegelian idealism came through an original reading of Marx's early philosophical writings (*La filosofia di Marx*, 1899).[40] In his analysis of Marx's *Theses on Feuerbach*, Gentile interpreted Marxian praxis through Vico's famous dictum *verum ipsum factum*, or rather through the idealistic interpretation of it. Praxis, therefore, was regarded as a concept implying the identity between subject and object, insofar as the Spirit (the transcendental subject) creates reality.[41] Even Gentile's late statement on historiography creating history was just a corollary of this principle. This presentation of Marx as a fundamentally idealistic philosopher had a lasting impact on Italian intellectual and political life. For instance, there is no doubt that Antonio Gramsci, by using in his *Prison Notebooks* an expression like "philosophy of praxis" instead of "historical materialism," was obviously trying to fool fascist censorship. But he was also echoing the title of Gentile's second essay on Marx ("La filosofia della praxis") as well as, more significantly, Gentile's emphasis on "praxis" as a concept which diminished (not to say rejected altogether) materialism as a crucial element in Marxian thought. Echoes of Gentile's interpretation of Marx have been detected in Gramsci's early idealistic Marxism.[42] It has even been suggested that the well-known passage in *Prison Notebooks,* on Gentile's philosophy's being closer than Croce's to the futurist movement, implies a favorable evaluation of Gentile: had not futurism been regarded by Gramsci in 1921 as a revolutionary movement which had been able to respond to a need for "new forms of art, of philosophy, of behavior, of language"?[43] A similar closeness between Gentile's philosophy and futurism, as negative examples of "antihistoricism," was implicitly suggested by Croce in a liberal-conservative antifascist perspective.[44]

In light of a left-wing reading of Gentile's work (or at least of part of it) the quasi-Gentilian flavor detectable in Hayden White's writings since *The Burden of History*—his 1966 plea for a new historiography written in a modernist key—sounds less paradoxical.[45] One can easily understand the impact (as well as the intrinsic weakness) of this attack launched against liberal and Marxist orthodoxies. In the late sixties and early seventies subjectivism, even extreme subjectivism, had a definitely radical flavor. But if one regarded *desire* as a left-wing slogan, then *reality* (including the emphasis on "real facts") would have looked definitely right-wing. Such a simplistic, not to say self-defeating, view has been largely superseded—in the sense that attitudes implying a basic flight from reality are certainly not restricted today to some factions of the left. This fact should be taken into account by any attempt to explain today's rather extraordinary appeal of skeptical ideologies, even outside the academic world. In the meantime Hayden White has declared that he is "against revolutions, whether launched from 'above' or 'below' in the social hierarchy."[46] This statement was elicited, he explains in a footnote, by the fact that "the relativism with which I am usually charged is conceived by many theorists to imply the kind of nihilism which invites revolutionary activism of a particularly irresponsible sort. In my view, relativism is the moral equivalent of epistemological skepticism; moreover, I conceive relativism to be the basis of social tolerance, not a license to 'do as you please.' "[47]

Skepticism, relativism, tolerance: At first sight the distance between this self-presentation of White's thought and Gentile's theoretical perspective could not be wider. Gentile's attacks against positivist historians ("Historical science, priding itself on the 'facts', the positive and solid realities, which it contrasts with mere ideas or theories without objective validity, is living in a childish world of illusion")[48] have no skeptical implications, insofar as the theoretical reality he was concerned with implied one transcendental Spirit, not a multiplicity of empirical subjects. Therefore he never was a relativist; on the contrary, he strongly advocated a religious, intransigent commitment in both theoretical and political matters.[49] And of course he never theorized tolerance, as his support of fascism—including *squadrismo*, the most violent aspect of it—shows.[50] The notorious statement describing the *squadristi*'s blackjack as a "moral force" comparable to preaching— a remark made by Gentile during a speech for the 1924 electoral campaign[51]—was consistent with his strictly monistic theory: in a reality created by Spirit there is no place for a real distinction between facts and values.

These are not minor theoretical divergences. Any argument suggesting a theoretical contiguity between Gentile's and White's perspectives must take these major differences into account. So we may wonder on what ground does White stress, in his article "The Politics of Historical Interpretation," that his own historical perspective shares something with "the kind of perspective on history . . . conventionally associated with the ideologies of fascist regimes," whose "social and political policies" he simultaneously rejects as "undeniably horrible."

This contradiction, so clearly perceived, leads us to the moral dilemma involved in White's approach. "We must guard," he says, "against a sentimentalism that would lead us to write off such a conception of history simply because it has been associated with fascist ideologies. One must face the fact that when it comes to apprehending the historical record, there are no grounds to be found in the historical record itself for preferring one way of construing its meaning over another."[52] No grounds? In fact, in discussing Faurisson's interpretation of the extermination of Jews, White does suggest a criterion according to which we must judge the validity of different historical interpretations. Let us follow his argument.

White's aforementioned statement is based (1) on the distinction (better to say disjunction) between "'positive' historical inquiry" and "proper history," that is, narrative, advocated by Croce in *La storia ridotta;* (2) on a skeptical interpretation of this distinction, converging in many ways with Gentile's transcendental subjectivism. Both elements can be detected in White's reaction to the refutation provided by Vidal-Naquet "on the terrain of positive history," of Faurisson's "lies" about the extermination of Jews. Faurisson's claim is as "morally offensive as intellectually bewildering"; but the notion of a "lie," insofar as it implies concepts like "reality" or "proof," is clearly a source of embarrassment for White, as this remarkably twisted sentence shows: "The distinction between a lie and an error or a mistake in interpretation may be more difficult to draw with respect to historical events less amply documented than the Holocaust." In fact, even in this latter case White is unable to accept Vidal-Naquet's conclusion, suggesting that there is a big difference "between an interpretation that would 'have profoundly transformed the *reality* of the massacre' and one that would not. The Israeli interpretation leaves the 'reality' of the events intact, whereas the revisionist interpretation de-realizes it by redescribing it in such a way as to make it something other than what the victims know the Holocaust to have been."[53] The Zionist historical interpretation of the Holocaust, White says, is not a *contre-vérité* (as has been suggested by Vidal-Naquet) but a truth: "its truth, as a historical interpretation, consists precisely in its *effectiveness* [my italics] in justifying a wide range of current Israeli political policies that, from the standpoint of those who articulate them, are crucial to the security and indeed the very existence of the Jewish people." In the same way, "the effort of the Palestinian people to mount a politically *effective* [my italics] response to Israeli policies entails the production of a similarly *effective* [my italics] ideology, complete with an interpretation of their history capable of endowing it with a meaning that it has hitherto lacked."[54] We can conclude that if Faurisson's narrative were ever to prove *effective*, it would be regarded by White as true as well.

Is this conclusion the result of a tolerant attitude? As we have seen, White argues that his skepticism and relativism can provide the epistemological and moral foundations for tolerance.[55] But this claim is historically and logically untenable. Historically, because tolerance has been theorized by people who had strong theoretical and moral convictions (Voltaire's sentence "I will fight in order to defend my opponent's freedom of speech" is typical). Logically, because absolute skepticism would contradict itself if it were not extended also to tolerance as a regulating principle. Moreover, when moral and theoretical differences are not ultimately related to truth, there is nothing to *tolerate*.[56] In fact, White's argument connecting truth and effectiveness inevitably reminds us not of tolerance but of its opposite—Gentile's evaluation of a blackjack as a moral force. In the same essay, as we have seen, White invites us to consider without "sentimentalism" the association between a conception of history which he has implicitly praised and the "ideologies of fascist regimes." He calls this association "conventional." But the mention of Gentile's name (with Heidegger's) in this context does not seem to be conventional.[57]

Since the late sixties the skeptical attitudes we are speaking about have become more and more influential in the humanities and social sciences. This pervasive diffusion is only partially related to their alleged novelty. Only eulogy could suggest to Pierre Vidal-Naquet that "since then [the publication of Michel de Certeau's *L'écriture de l'histoire* in 1975] we have become aware that the historian *writes;* that he produces space and time, being himself intrinsically embedded in a specific space and time." As Vidal-Naquet knows perfectly well, the same point (leading sometimes to skeptical conclusions) was strongly emphasized, for instance, in a not particularly bold methodological 1961 essay by E. H. Carr (*What Is History?*)—as well as, at a much earlier date, by Croce.

By looking at these issues in historical perspective, we can have a better grasp of their theoretical implications. As a starting point I would suggest a short piece written by Renato Serra in 1912 but published only in 1927, after his untimely death (1915). The piece's title— *Partenza di un gruppo di soldati per la Libia* (A soldiers' group leaving for Libya)[58]—gives only a vague idea of its content. It starts with a description, written in a dazzling experimental style reminiscent of Boccioni's futurist paintings from the same era, of a railway station full of departing soldiers surrounded by a huge crowd;[59] then there are some antisocialist remarks; then a reflection on history and historical writing, which ends abruptly in a solemn metaphysical tone, full of Nietzschean echoes. This unfinished essay, which certainly deserves a longer and deeper analysis, reflects the complex personality of a man who, besides being the best Italian critic of his generation, was a person of erudition with strong philosophical interests. In his correspondence with Croce (to whom he was personally very close, without ever being a follower) he first explained the genesis of the pages we are speaking about.[60] They had been elicited by *Storia, cronaca e false storie* (1912), an essay by Croce which later on was included, in a revised form, in the latter's *Teoria e storia della storiografia*. Croce had mentioned the gap, emphasized by Tolstoy in *War and Peace*, between a real event, like a battle, and the fragmentary and distorted recollections of it on which historical accounts are based. Tolstoy's view is well known: the gap could be overcome only by collecting the memories of every individual (even the humblest soldier) who had been directly or indirectly involved in the battle. Croce dismissed this suggestion and the agnosticism which it seemed to involve as absurd: "At every moment we know all the history we need," therefore the history we don't know is identical with the "eternal ghost of the thing in itself."[61] Serra, ironically defining himself as "a slave of the thing in itself," wrote to Croce that he felt much closer to Tolstoy; however, he added, "the difficulties I am confronted with are—or at least seem to be—much more complicated."[62] They were indeed.

There are some naive people, Serra observed, who believe that "a document can express reality . . . But a document can express only itself . . . A document is a fact. The battle is another fact (a myriad of other facts). Those two entities cannot become a unity. They cannot be identical, they cannot mirror each other . . . The individual who acts is *a fact*. The individual who tells a story is *another fact* . . . Every testimony is only a testimony of itself; of its immediate context (*momento*), of its origin, of its purpose—that's all."[63]

These were not reflections by a pure theoretician. Serra knew what erudition was. His cutting criticism did not artificially oppose historical narratives to the stuff they are made of. He mentioned all kinds of narrative: clumsy letters sent by soldiers to their families, newspaper articles written to please a distant audience, reports of war actions scribbled in haste by an impatient captain, historians' accounts full of superstitious deference toward all these documents. Serra was deeply aware that these narratives, regardless of the directness of their character, have always a highly problematic relationship with reality. But reality ("the things in themselves") exists.[64]

Serra explicitly rejected simple positivist attitudes. But his remarks help us to reject also a perspective which piles up positivism and relativism: "'positive' historical inquiry" based on a literal reading of the evidence, on the one hand, and "historical narratives" based on figurative, uncomparable and unrefutable interpretations, on the other.[65]

In fact, the narratives based on one witness that are discussed earlier in this chapter can be regarded as experimental cases which deny such a clear-cut distinction: a different reading of the available evidence immediately affects the resulting narrative. A similar although usually less visible relationship can be assumed on a general level. An unlimited skeptical attitude toward historical narratives is therefore groundless.

On Auschwitz, Jean-François Lyotard has written:

> Suppose that an earthquake destroys not only lives, buildings, and objects but also the instruments used to measure earthquakes, directly and indirectly. The impossibility of quantitatively measuring it does not prohibit, but rather inspires in the minds of the survivors the idea of a very great seismic force . . . With Auschwitz, something new has happened in history (which can only be a sign and not a fact), which is that the facts, the testimonies which bore the traces of *here*'s and *now*'s, the documents which indicated the sense or senses of the facts, and the names, finally the possibility of various kinds of phrases whose conjunction makes reality, all this has been destroyed as much as possible. Is it up to the historian to take into account not only the damages, but also the wrong? Not only the reality, but also the meta-reality that is the destruction of reality? . . . Its name marks the confines wherein historical knowledge sees its competence impugned.[66]

Is this last remark true? I am not fully convinced. Memory and the destruction of memory are recurrent elements in history. "The need to tell our story to 'the rest,' to make 'the rest' participate in it," the late Primo Levi wrote, "had taken on for us, before our liberation and after, the character of an immediate and violent impulse, to the point of competing with our other elementary needs."[67] As Benveniste has shown, among the Latin words which mean "witness" there is *superstes*—survivor.[68]

< 6 >

Of Plots, Witnesses, and Judgments

MARTIN JAY

Hayden White has so often scandalized his fellow historians that I hope he will find it refreshing to be reproached for not being scandalous enough in "Historical Emplotment and the Problem of Truth." That is, in his anxiety to avoid inclusion in the ranks of those who argue for a kind of relativistic "anything goes," which might provide ammunition for revisionist skeptics about the existence of the Holocaust, he undercuts what is most powerful in his celebrated critique of naive historical realism. His chapter offers two distinct and not fully integrated arguments about the relation between the past and its representation as narrated history. The first will be well known to readers of his pathbreaking analyses of the forms of historical emplotment, *Metahistory*, *Tropics of Discourse*, and *The Content of the Form*. The second, although less familiar, draws on his well-known injunction to jettison realist modes of historical writing in favor of modernist alternatives, a directive he made as early as his 1966 essay, "The Burden of History." Let me take the two arguments in order.

White's contention that written history is inevitably beholden to formal reconstructions that cannot be perfectly mapped onto the historical reality they purport to represent is based on a tripartite division of the process of history writing. Although this is a division he construes only to deny, it remains operative in the position he defends, at least in the initial portion of his chapter. First, he posits facts or events, which he identifies with the "content" of history as it happened. These are understood to be prelinguistic phenomena, which include, to repeat his list, wars, revolutions, earthquakes, and tidal waves. He then suggests these become the stuff of stories, which are emplotted narrations about their significance. Finally, he suggests that interpretations about the *meaning* of these stories is a higher level of historical analysis, at least for traditional historians.

White, of course, wants to subvert tradition by collapsing the sec-

< 97 >

ond and third stages of the process into one, so that all stories are to be understood as always already meaningful interpretations. Here I think he has made a powerful and indisputable case. But oddly, he remains unwilling to efface the boundary between the first category, the facts or events of history, and the second, their narrative representation. He does so, I think, for one basic reason. If the stuff of prenarrated history, or at least a significant chunk of it, were to be acknowledged as no less discursive and emplotted than the historian's reconstruction, then the cry would arise for congruence between the two as the measure of good or bad history. That is, if the content of history were experienced by sufficiently large numbers of the participants at the time as formal emplotments, then the historian might be expected only to reproduce that original formed content, rather than imposing one of his or her own on it. He or she would, in other words, be beholden to Dilthey's unconvincing contention that history writing is the imaginative re-experiencing (*nacherleben*) of the original actors' meaning-laden *Erlebnis*. White, anxious to maintain the undecidability of narrative reconstructions, thus attempts to build as firm a barrier as he can between the content and the form. Accordingly he claims that any given set of events can be "emplotted" in a variety of ways, which is to say, endowed with a variety of "meanings" or significance . . . without violating the order of "facts" in any way whatsoever.

As a result of this distinction, White implicitly suggests another, which his chapter never adequately develops: that is, the contrast between the "truth" of facts whose order cannot be violated, and the "meaning" of their narrative/interpretative reconstruction. Here we have the traditional opposition of mere chronicle and genuine history. Occasionally, to be sure, he seems to assume that the truth of facts and the meanings of stories are synonymous—for instance, when he claims that "stories, like factual statements, are linguistic entities." More typically—for example, when he writes that two different narratives may represent the past "with equal plausibility and without doing any violence to the factual record"—he keeps them apart. The latter assumption, which undergirds the argument in the first part of the paper, seems to me a failure of nerve and prevents White from being as scandalous as he might or indeed should be.

For the factual record is not, I want to argue, entirely prior to its linguistic mediation, or indeed its figural signification. What distinguishes the events and facts that later historians reconstruct is precisely their being often already inflected with narrative meaning for those who initiate or suffer them in their own lives. It is for this reason that White's list of nonlinguistic entities—wars, revolutions, earthquakes, and tidal waves—is problematic. For it puts in one pot phenomena that are indeed linguistically charged and humanly meaningful, wars and revolutions, with natural events, earthquakes and tidal waves, that only become so if they impinge on human experience. Wars, after all, are normally declared by a performative speech act, and revolutions are at least in part deliberate challenges to the linguistic order that sustains the old regime.

There is, in other words, virtually no historical content that is linguistically unmediated and utterly bereft of meaning, waiting around for the later historian to emplot it in arbitrary ways. White himself, to be sure, seems to acknowledge this conclusion in his critique of Berel Lang's problematic distinction between literal events and figural expressions. But he retreats from it in his own evocation of the "same set of events" that can be narrated or interpreted in different ways. In so doing, he reinstates the untenable contrast between the truth of nonnarrated events (the putative chroniclelike "content" of history) and the meaning of their formal reconstruction that runs throughout the first part of the paper.

There are, it seems to me, several ways out of this dilemma. First, one might follow Nietzsche and boldly deny the very existence of an ontological realm of events or facts prior to their reconstruction, thus frankly embracing the radical relativism that haunts White's project and which he wants to exorcise. Second, one might acknowledge the existence of formed content in the narrations the historical actors or victims themselves have produced, and use them as a check on the absolute license of the historian to emplot the past in an entirely capricious way. This alternative does not, however, mean arguing for a perfect fit between the two, as Dilthey at times may have thought possible, nor does it even entail a harmonious fusion of horizons in Gadamer's sense between past and present. It is rather an injunction to take seriously the found narratives—not merely prelinguistic facts or events—that historians must themselves somehow fashion into one of their own. I take Carlo Ginzburg's stress on the importance of honoring the testimony of witnesses, which may already be filtered through previous historiographical *topoi*, to reflect this alternative. Although it has problems of its own, which I will briefly address when I turn to his essay, it is at least a useful corrective to the radical Nietz-schean collapse of object and subject of inquiry into nothing but the subject's projection.

In the second part of his chapter, however, White opts for a third solution, which he derives from Lang's notion of intransitive writing and identifies with the modernist attempt to go beyond the very di-chotomy of subject and object, thus making an end-run around the challenge of epistemology. Here he sheds his neo-Italian idealist cap and puts on one that he labels Derridean, but which sounds even more characteristically Heideggerian. That is, he posits a modernism in which the external narrator describing events external to him or her is replaced by a subjectless "middle voice" like the *"erlebte Rede"* of some modernist fiction. Here the vision of pure immanence, a point of indifference between polarities such as subject and object, is claimed to be the way out of the dilemmas of representation that bedevil the realist project. No less overcome, at least implicitly, is the hegemony of the ironic mode of writing history, which White ever since *Metahis-tory* has implored us to transcend.

Putting aside the issue of how exclusively modernist this alternative actually is—Flaubert, after all, got into trouble when he sought the same effect in *Madame Bovary*—White is right to claim that one of the most typical modernist dreams was to find a third way beyond the tired dichotomies of the Cartesian, Kantian or positivist traditions. The search for a pure linguisticality in Mallarmé was matched by a similar yearning for a pure visuality in the high modernist art celebrated by Clement Greenberg. Philosophically, it was echoed in those attempts, most notably Heidegger's and his phenomenological and poststructur-alist progeny, to allow Being, the flesh of the world or *différance* to emerge from the rubble of epistemological dualisms and reveal itself as their ground. In all of these cases, realism is not so much abandoned as redefined in terms of submission to an imperative that comes from elsewhere. White's citation from Primo Levi makes this affiliation very clear, as the atom of carbon somehow becomes "in charge of my writ-ing, in a gigantic minuscule game which nobody has yet described."

If indeed such an imperative compels us as historians to write real-istically, in the modernist sense of the term suggested by White, then the dilemma of relativism can be overcome. And so too can the dichot-omy between the truth of found content and the meaning of imposed form. Writing intransitively, listening for the middle voice that speaks through us, we can serve as the vessels of the historically real, just as Heidegger thought Dasein could act as the shepherd of a Being that unconceals itself to those who patiently wait for it to do so.

But, alas, there is precious little evidence to warrant such a conclusion. First, the high modernist search for a third way beyond subject and object, a linguistic or visual realm of purity in which reality will shine forth, has itself come a cropper. If postmodernism means anything, it implies the abandonment of precisely the dream of submitting to the exigencies of pure language or pure vision. Discourse and figurality, knowledge and power, the chiasmic intertwining of desire and its objects—all this calls into question the possibility of a middle voice that overcomes all dichotomies and, like Levi's atom of carbon, takes charge of our writing.

But perhaps even more damaging is the admission that White himself both makes and then attempts to withdraw: that the dream of this new realism links cultural modernism and political totalitarianism in an unexpected way. Although he wants to salvage his argument from the negative aspersions cast by Jameson's linkage of the two by claiming that modernism was not an "expression" of fascism, but merely an attempt to represent it, the suspicion lingers that there is a disturbing fit between a method that waits for reality to manifest itself and the authoritarianism of a political ideology that also wants to close the gap between subject and object by heeding the commands of a higher truth.

No less troubling are the implications of White's argument that the overcoming of the distinction between active and passive voice in intransitive writing is appropriate for representing "modernist" events like the Holocaust. For it is precisely the distinction between those who acted and their victims that must be scrupulously retained in any responsible account of the horror of those years. Thus, although I would agree that older, more objectivist notions of realism are outmoded, the alternative of writing in the "middle voice" seems even more deeply flawed.

The political uneasiness honestly evoked in Hayden White's essay is especially worthy of emphasis, because of the astonishing political claims made in Carlo Ginzburg's critique in Chapter 5 of White's earlier work. Shining through Croce's acknowledged influence on White, he contends, is the figure of Giovanni Gentile, whose fascist politics were intimately connected to his antihistoricist philosophy of pure action. For Ginzburg, despite all the obvious differences, White's radical subjectivism and skepticism about historical truth echo Gentile's sinister position. Rather than leading to tolerance, it betrays a tacit concession that might makes right, which in historical terms means accepting Faurisson's version of the Holocaust if it ever becomes "effective." Thus White's warning to guard against a sentimental rejection of certain positions because of their adventitious association with fascism becomes for Ginzburg a self-serving excuse to avoid confronting the sinister political implications of White's own position.

These are very serious charges indeed and should be left to Hayden White to address directly. In some ways his chapter has already provided a kind of answer in its implicit rejection of a voluntarist philosophy of pure action, historiographical or political, and its turn toward intransitive writing and the middle voice as an antidote. There is very little Gentilean transcendental subjectivism in this alternative, although as noted above, there may ironically be other links via Heidegger with a problematic politics. White loosely links Gentile and Heidegger in the passage Ginzburg cites, but I think the differences between them are more important than the similarities. However, I do not wish to belabor this point. I would rather focus on the alternative presented in Carlo Ginzburg's chapter to the crisis of historical relativism.

Here, alas, he gives us only fragmentary guidance. Rejecting Lyotard's contention that for phenomena like the Holocaust we have only signs and no facts, he invokes the example of Renato Serra, who believed that the things themselves stubbornly exist and are somehow preserved in the memories of witnesses. Thus, he implies a certain sympathy for Tolstoy's utopian project of collecting the memories of everyone involved in an event, testimonials which might provide the only proof for a subsequent historical interpretation. Here the power relationship between the form-giving historian in the present and the residues of the past preserved by survivors is rendered more nearly in balance than it is in the Gentilean historiography he attributes to White.

As indicated earlier, I share Ginzburg's qualms about an artificial opposition between historical narratives and the allegedly nonnarrativized stuff of which they are made. I also would accept his contention that mere effectiveness in terms of winning agreement is insufficient as a criterion of truth or plausibility, especially if we have no further criteria for deciding what constitutes a rational or irrational process of achieving that agreement. But I am uncertain about precisely how he proposes to bridge the gap between the remembered or preserved narratives of witnesses and the historical reconstructions we fashion from them. For there are some obvious problems with the process as he has left it.

First, the tantalizing issue of the legal demand for at least two witnesses to establish proof is not really adequately dealt with in his argument. Historians can certainly get useful information about the past from only one witness, but that information may be more about the mindset of the witness than about the event itself. Just one witness simply won't suffice as an antidote to a historian's emplotting the story in other terms. What, after all, would the Holocaust be in our reconstructions if the only witness were, say, Adolf Eichmann? Second, even if we have a multiplicity of witnesses, there is always the problem of how we make our way through conflicting testimony and with which witnesses we choose to identify. From Ginzburg's account, I see no way to reproach the notorious decision of Andreas Hillgruber to identify with the German "witnesses" fighting on the Eastern front against the Russians instead of with the Jewish "witnesses" whose agony was prolonged by that fight.

Third and finally, there is a basic problem with the assumption, expressed in Serra's Tolstoyan answer to Croce—which is also Ginzburg's to White—that our macronarratives can be ideally construed as the sum total of all the micronarratives of the historical actors. As one of the lucky survivors of the Holocaust, Siegfried Kracauer, pointed out long ago in his remarkable book *History—The Last Things before the Last*,[1] it is impossible to go so smoothly from micro to macro levels of interpretation. The historical universe, he pointed out, is heterogeneous, and no amount of accumulation of detail will provide guidance for how the macro level could be constructed. No better example of this caution can be given than the Holocaust itself, a post facto conceptual entity not in use at the time, which no one individual ever witnessed and whose truth or meaning, however we fashion the relation between those two very different concepts, cannot be proved by stitching together all of the individual testimonies.

Although I have insufficient space to develop my own alternative solution to those proposed by White and Ginzburg, let me suggest a few indications of where I would begin. I would start by retaining the tension between the two levels in White's argument instead of trying to collapse them in the name of a middle way. But rather than characterize the first level as nonnarrativized chronicle and the second as the historian's formal imposition of plot and meaning, I would call them, at least as an initial approximation, first and second order narratives. For although not absolutely everything that historians fashion into their own stories is already emplotted by the actors, enough is to make it more than unformed raw material available as mere fodder for the historian's imagination. There is instead a process of negotiation that goes on between the two narrative orders, which prevents historical representation from being an utterly arbitrary concoction. Even when historians ask questions that seem far removed from anyone's conscious experience, probing, say, deep-seated structural transformations occurring beneath the surface of specific events, there are always narrativized records that bear on the plausibility of the answers they give.

The *telos* of the process of negotiation is not, however, perfect congruence between the two narratives, that of the actors and that of the historian, for such a goal is impossible to obtain. No uniform meaning can be assumed to have existed for all the participants in historical events, even in the most harmonious society, let alone one in which the conflicts were as radical as in Nazi Germany. In addition, the narrative expectations of historians will be shaped by later outcomes, which no protagonist in the events themselves can know. Thus, even if we identify with one group in the past, such as the victims of the Holocaust, our narrative reconstruction of their experience and the meaning they give to it will always be incongruent, which is why the testimony of witnesses, although necessary, cannot be sufficient to provide guidance for our historical accounts.

The negotiation between the two narrative orders may be especially complicated in the case of the Holocaust, where *post facto* reconstruction cannot begin to do justice, in both epistemological and ethical senses, to the events it emplots. For there will always be an unavoidable tension between the first order narratives of the victims, which must approach a kind of incoherence because of the fundamental unintelligibility of what happened to them, and the second order narrative of the historian trying nonetheless to make sense out of their experience and the hidden structures underlying it.[2] Indeed, it is perhaps for this reason that Hayden White's call for a modernist historiography sensitive to the flaws in realistic representation can be granted a certain amount of power. Or rather, it can if it is understood in the terms of his argument before the "intransitive writing" move in his present paper, for such a modernism would foreground the tension between the historian's reconstruction and what is being reconstructed, rather than smooth it over in the name of an impersonal middle voice. In so doing it would paradoxically acknowledge the limitations on the historian's capacity to refashion the past on his or her own terms, thus avoiding the Gentilean subjectivism Ginzburg finds so troubling in White's work.

Another consideration also militates against the unfettered freedom of historians to narrativize arbitrarily, and this concerns the community of others that reads and judges their work. Historical accounts are, after all, only as persuasive as they are deemed to be by those who read them. In this sense another negotiation can be said to take place besides that between first-order narratives (or their imperfectly narrativizable surrogates) and second-order reconstructions. This is the never-ending negotiation that we might call the art of historical judgment exercised in communal terms. "History" in this sense is not a single historian emplotting the past, but rather the institution of historians, now more often credentialed than not, trying to convince each other about the plausibility of their reconstructions. It is not so much the subjective *imposition* of meaning, but rather the intersubjective *judgment* of meanings that matters.

In the struggle to win assent for one interpretation or another, historians both adduce evidence—the testimony of Ginzburg's witnesses, first-order narratives, and other residues of the past—and pattern that evidence into second-order stories. The relationship between the two can be assumed to be more or less harmonious or, as I have argued in the case of Holocaust victims' experience, in some tension, but in both cases what gains common, if not universal, acceptance depends on the intersubjective judgment of the community rather than on any congruence with the "truth" of what really happened. That this judgment is more than the mere "effectiveness" against which Ginzburg prudently warns is likely if we take seriously the arguments for communicative reason made by theorists like Karl-Otto Apel and Jürgen Habermas.

Although this is not the place to rehearse those arguments in full, it may be useful to recall some of their main features. Contrary to thinkers such as Nietzsche or Foucault, who want to reduce knowledge to a function of power, or to those such as Wittgenstein and Winch, who

want to turn reason into an expression of a local language game, Apel
and Habermas are concerned with the ways in which rational criteria
of judgment transcend their contextual origins. That is, by raising discursive claims for truth and rightness, anyone who enters a critical
discussion tacitly presupposes the power of the better argument rather
than coercion or authority as the ground for conviction. The criterion
of effectiveness is thus not merely winning assent by any means possible, but rather winning it by redeeming validity claims through procedures that satisfy conditions of rationality.

Although a cultural relativist will always reply that those conditions
are different in different contexts, Apel and Habermas have, I think,
been able to show that rational arguments are also able to transcend
their original point of origin and bridge the gap between cultures.
Whether or not one accepts the more strongly transcendental version
of this claim held by Apel, who posits a species-wide competence to
reason, even in a weaker form, it suggests that there exist discursive
communities, sharing standards and procedures of communicative rationality, that are more inclusive than the communities from which
their members come. To use Alvin Gouldner's terminology, the "community of critical discourse" extends beyond any one local group
trapped in its own local language game. People in Los Angeles as well
as in Frankfurt possess a similar competence to argue about Apel and
Habermas' position, even though they may not come from precisely
the same cultural background.

Similarly, historians all over the world have been able to engage in a
debate about the *Historikerstreit,* introducing criteria of logic, evidence, and interpretation that are not completely specific to their contexts. Although it would be foolish to assume that the uncoerced consensus of opinion, which is the *telos* of the discursive process, can be
more than a regulative ideal never to be fully realized, it is still the
case that scholars striving to convince each other live by it. However
complicated the process may be made by the interference of nondis-
cursive elements, however inconclusive the outcome always is, the
professional institutionalization of communicative rationality means
that "effectiveness" can be more than merely a neutral description of
what the majority believes is true or right. It may, to be sure, sometimes be little more than that, but there is no reason to despair of a
more compelling alternative. Indeed, otherwise the entire raison
d'être of scholarly discourse is undone.

There are two final conclusions to be drawn from all this. First, the Holocaust like all other historical phenomena can never be made absolutely safe from either oblivion or distortion. No memory can ever survive the death of its original holder without the collective will to keep it alive. No story can permanently resist being refashioned or even forgotten. But if this conclusion may be troubling, its corollary should be a bit more encouraging. For what it suggests is that the task of maintaining historical memory is an ongoing collective or at least intersubjective project. So long as an institutional framework, however imperfect, exists for critically judging our reconstructions, no individual historian can impose his or her will on the past. Single historians, like single witnesses, gain credibility through a process of corroboration. If witnessing history and writing it are never perfectly congruous, the same must be said of writing and judging historical accounts. Acknowledging the give-and-take among all of these moments prevents us from succumbing to the opposing temptations of thinking history is mimetic reproduction and thinking it is subjective imposition. Recognizing that there is no way to overcome the tensions, keeping them apart provides a no less salutary warning against the search for an intransitive mode of writing, in which something powerful but undefined guides our tremulous hand.

< 7 >

Representing the Holocaust:
Reflections on the Historians' Debate

Dominick LaCapra

The *Historikerstreit* or German historians' debate erupted in the summer of 1986. It was occasioned by an article published in the *Frankfurter Allgemeine Zeitung* by the historian Ernst Nolte.[1] Its promotion to the status of a heated public controversy if not a *cause célèbre* was provoked by two articles in *Die Zeit* by Jürgen Habermas.[2] As Habermas recognized, the *Historikerstreit* evoked many basic issues ranging from the nature of historical understanding to the self-conception of the Federal Republic of Germany. Whatever their personal motives or agendas, the views of revisionist historians were, for Habermas, symptomatic of a neonationalist resurgence that was most prominent on the part of conservative forces that wanted to rewrite the Nazi past in order to provide a "positive" or affirmative German identity in the present. This larger context of the debate among historians provided the crucial code or subtext for arguments that might otherwise seem to be purely methodological and run-of-the-mill.

The *Historikerstreit* should not be conflated with the issue of "historicization" (*Historisierung*) in general. But a close examination of the historians' debate does help to accentuate the question of precisely how "historicization" takes place and the functions it fulfills in specific contexts. The neoconservative idea that history as a secular surrogate for religion provides satisfying meaning (*Sinnstiftung*) for those who have been uprooted by modernizing processes serves to divert attention not only from negative aspects of the past but from modern problems that are not totally dissociated from earlier difficulties and dilemmas. As Nietzsche saw long ago, history as a surrogate for religion is clearly ideological in its dubiously providential role as provider of unearned, compensatory meaning.

In his 1988 book, Charles Maier formulates a prevalent conception

< 108 >

of the more specifically historiographical issues in the *Historiker-streit*—a conception with which Maier basically agrees:

> The central issue has been whether Nazi crimes were unique, a leg-acy of evil in a class by themselves, irreparably burdening any con-cept of German nationhood, or whether they are comparable to other national atrocities, especially Stalinist terror. Uniqueness, it has been pointed out, should not be so important an issue; the killing remains horrendous whether or not other regimes committed mass murder. Comparability cannot really exculpate. In fact, however, uniqueness is rightly perceived as a crucial issue. If Auschwitz is admittedly dreadful, but dreadful as only one specimen of geno-cide—as the so-called revisionists have implied—then Germany can still aspire to reclaim a national acceptance that no one denies to perpetrators of other massacres, such as Soviet Russia. But if the Final Solution remains noncomparable—as the opposing historians have insisted—the past may never be "worked through," the future never normalized, and German nationhood may remain forever tainted, like some well forever poisoned.[3]

Maier's insightful and balanced account provides an excellent place to begin any contemporary discussion of the *Historikerstreit*. It is noteworthy that Maier invokes the binary opposition between the unique and the comparable (or the general)—one of the oldest such oppositions in historical thought. Yet this opposition takes on a spe-cific—albeit debatable—significance in the context of the *Historiker-streit*. Maier's initial paragraph has a manifestly contradictory struc-ture: uniqueness is not the issue; uniqueness is the issue. I think this contradiction is not debilitating, but the aporia it conceals must be subjected to further analysis. For it may indicate that the point is both to deconstruct the binary opposition and to see precisely how it func-tions historically and ideologically. Seeing how the opposition func-tions is necessary in the analysis of how uniqueness and comparability are coded in a historically and ideologically specific situation. Decon-structing the opposition is necessary in the attempt to elaborate a dif-ferent way of posing the problem and even of defining the "central" issue.

I would like to argue that one crucial—perhaps *the* crucial—histor-ical issue is whether (and how) the Holocaust[4] is attended to or whether attention is diverted from it in a manner that decreases chances that it will be worked through to any conceivable extent. The

attempt to provide a historical account of the Holocaust offers a limiting case of a problem that confronts historians in general. This problem
is perhaps best formulated in psychoanalytic terms: how should one
negotiate transferential relations to the object of study whereby processes active in that object are repeated with more or less significant
variations in the account of the historian?[5] The Holocaust presents the
historian with transference in the most traumatic form conceivable—
but in a form that will vary with the difference in subject position of
the analyst. Whether the historian or analyst is a survivor, a relative of
survivors, a former Nazi, a former collaborator, a relative of former
Nazis or collaborators, a younger Jew or German distanced from more
immediate contact with survival, participation, or collaboration, or a
relative "outsider" to these problems will make a difference even in
the meaning of statements that may be formally identical. Certain
statements or even entire orientations may seem appropriate for someone in a given subject position but not in others. (It would, for example, be ridiculous if I tried to assume the voice of Elie Wiesel or of
Saul Friedlander. There is a sense in which I have no right to these
voices. There is also a sense in which, experiencing a lack of a viable
voice, I am constrained to resort to quotation and commentary more
often than I otherwise might be.) Thus although any historian must be
"invested" in a distinctive way in the events of the Holocaust, not all
investments (or cathexes) are the same and not all statements, rhetorics, or orientations are equally available to different historians.

How language is used is thus critical for the way in which a transferential relation is negotiated. It is also decisive in determining the manner in which subject-positions are defined and redefined. Certain
voices would seem unavailable for certain historians and more possible
for others. But no historian should be content with a conventional
voice that levels or routinizes problems that make particular demands
and pose special challenges. I do not think that conventional techniques, which in certain respects are necessary, are ever sufficient, and
to some extent the study of the Holocaust may help us to reconsider
the requirements of historiography in general. Conventional techniques are particularly inadequate with respect to events that are indeed limiting. With respect to these events language may break down,
and the most appropriate form of representation may be minimalist.
Still, I would contend that it is more possible to indicate what has not
worked than to legislate what approach must be taken in trying to

write or speak about the Holocaust. In addition, silence here is not identical with simple muteness, and the way language breaks down is itself a significant and even telling process. In any event, the language user—including the historian—is under special constraints and obligations which he or she avoids through a reliance on standard operating procedures. Positivism in general may be seen as an abuse of scientific method through an autonomization of the constative or empirical-analytic dimension of discourse in a way that denies the problem of transference. (Indeed one way to define positivism is as a denial of transference.) Nowhere more than with reference to the Holocaust do positivism and standard techniques of narrowly empirical-analytic inquiry seem wanting. How historians should use language with reference to the subject positions that they occupy and are attempting to forge is a pressing issue with no prefabricated or pat solutions; it cannot be obviated through a reversion to type. To make this point is not to deny an important role for objectivity. Objectivity does, however, become a more difficult and problematic undertaking redefined in terms of the attempt to counteract modes of projection, self-indulgence, and narrow partisanship in an exchange with the past. (Here one has the possibility of a "postdeconstructive" notion of objectivity that resists absolutization or foundational status but has its valid uses in conjunction with the socially sensitive, psychoanalytically informed concept of subject positions.)

In view of what I have been arguing, there is a sense in which the Nazi crimes are both unique and comparable. They are unique not only in that they have a distinctive effect on people who have a specific "lived" relation to them and occupy different subject positions; they are also unique in that they are so extreme that they seem unclassifiable and threaten or tempt one with silence. But they will be compared to other events insofar as comparison is essential for any attempt to understand. The problem is how this process of comparison takes place and the functions it serves. To see the Holocaust in terms of transference is to some extent to make it comparable, but the value of the concept of transference is to enable one to stress the differences in traumatizing potential of events and to situate the Holocaust as a limiting case that tests and may even unsettle categories and comparisons. When employed in a certain fashion, comparisons may serve manifestly levelling functions.

I would propose that the greatest danger at the present time (at least in the context of the historians' debate) is that certain comparisons may function as mechanisms of denial that do not enable one to "work through" problems. Indeed they may misleadingly conflate normality with a levelling normalization. The seemingly balanced account of an unbalanced situation—particularly the appeal to comparisons that even-handedly show the distribution of horror in history—may well be coded in a specific manner as mechanisms of denial that seek normalization and a "positive" identity through an avoidance or disavowal of the critical and self-critical requirements of both historical understanding and anything approximating "normality." The emphasis upon uniqueness has the virtue of opposing normalization and may be contextually effective as a limited strategy of reversal. But it may also be conducive to "acting out" problems rather than working them through. With respect to any extremely traumatic situation—and clearly with respect to the Holocaust—some "acting out" may be unavoidable and even necessary. In fact critiques of "acting out"—critiques that may at times have a partial validity (notably when they address the problem of the self-legitimating or self-righteous use of the Holocaust as "symbolic capital")—may themselves function to reinforce tendencies toward denial. Still, a historical and critical account should attempt to provide a measure of distance toward events that is required in order to hold a degree of objectivity and self-critical perspective.[6]

One critical role of comparisons in history is to bring out not only similarities but significant differences. Comparisons that accentuate only similarity are *ipso facto* dubious. Despite certain of his disagreements with Habermas, Eberhard Jäckel has offered a succinct and justifiably oft-quoted statement of the manner in which the Holocaust was unique in this sense: "The Nazi extermination of the Jews was unique because never before had a state, under the responsible authority of its leader, decided and announced that a specific group of human beings, including the old, the women, the children, and the infants, would be killed to the very last one, and implemented this decision with all the means at its disposal."[7] Jäckel here underscores the significance of official, political antisemitism involving a systematic, state-sponsored policy of extermination directed against an entire people for the express scapegoating purpose of eliminating a putative source of pollution.

In the course of my discussion, I shall try to give more substance to the schema I have suggested. I should like to begin with a brief discussion of two foremost revisionist historians: Ernst Nolte and Andreas Hillgruber. (I shall not address complications introduced by the consideration of other revisionists such as Michael Stürmer.)

The larger philosophical premise of Nolte's analysis is his peculiar concept of transcendence, by which he means the radical emancipation of the individual from tradition. The transcendent individual becomes atomized and deracinated and requires history as the replacement of lost tradition, particularly lost religious tradition. The daunting task facing the historian in Germany is to furnish a binding answer to anomie through a conception of tradition that may be taken up and affirmed by the individual in quest of roots and a feeling of being at home in the world. The comparative method is one key means of making one's nation more available as an object of sustaining commitment and a bulwark against communist threats to the West.

Through rhetorical questions, Nolte takes comparison in the dubiously metaphysical (perhaps magical) direction of making Nazi crimes derivative or mimetic of a more basic original, and he even suggests that they were preemptive with respect to the archetypical Bolshevik menace. He thereby resuscitates the hackneyed apologetic claim that at least the Nazis opposed the Bolsheviks and thereby defended the interests of Western civilization. In Nolte's "Vergangenheit": "Did the National Socialists, did Hitler carry out an 'Asiatic' action perhaps only because they regarded themselves and their kind as potential or real victims of an 'Asiatic' action? Was not the Gulag Archipelago more original [*ursprünglicher*] than Auschwitz? Was not the 'class murder' of the Bolsheviks the logical and factual *prius* of the 'racial murder' of the National Socialists? Was it not a scientific mistake to focus on the latter and neglect the former, although a causal nexus is probable?"

Thus, for Nolte, the Gulag may have "caused" Auschwitz: the Nazis did it because the Russians did it first, and the Nazis were afraid that the Russians would do it to them. The identification of the Holocaust as an "Asiatic" action performs the astonishing feat of projecting guilt away from the Germans in an act of racial slander that is particularly offensive in view of its context. The concluding invocation to science is a sheer propaganda ploy in the attempt to lend credibility to an outlandishly speculative and implausible causal imputation; it too is reminiscent of Nazi tactics. With consummate insensitivity, Nolte also asserts that the "Final Solution" was itself not substantively different from other pogroms of mass annihilation "but for the sole exception of the technical procedure of gassing." In an earlier essay, Nolte even went to the absurd extreme of suggesting that the "Final Solution" could be understood as a preemptive strike against the Jews themselves and that it was prompted by Chaim Weizmann's "official declaration in the first days of September 1939, according to which Jews in the whole world would fight on the side of England."[8]

Nolte is nonetheless to the point in warning against indiscriminate conceptions of German "guilt" that unconsciously replicate the kind of thinking by which the Nazis convinced themselves of the "guilt" of the Jews. Nor would one want to deny the prevalence of atrocity in the twentieth century. But Nolte insists on this prevalence not so much to emphasize its importance as to mitigate if not evade that of specifically Nazi behavior. In light of his premise (or fixation) whereby communism is the ultimate cause of all modern evil, Nolte's argument takes on a circular, paranoid structure which makes it impermeable to counterevidence. His argument also has the earmark of uncontrolled transference in its uncritical repetition of features of his object of study.

Habermas himself recognized that one could not simply amalgamate the views of Nolte and Andreas Hillgruber. In the two essays he published together in book form in 1986, however, Hillgruber did to some extent relativize the Holocaust, especially through comparisons, for example, with Stalin's "extermination and resettlement practices [*Ausrottungs- und Umsiedlungspraktiken*]."[9] The ill-chosen subtitle of Hillgruber's book is itself telltale in its opposition of "the shattering of the German Reich" and "the end of European Jewry." Both the euphemism of "the end" (in contrast to the decidedly emphatic "shattering") and the impersonality of "Jewry" (creating a false parallelism with the Reich) attest to a process of normalization and routinization.

Hillgruber traces the roots of antisemitism in Germany, and he notes (p. 96) the priority of the destruction of the Jews in Nazi policy even in the later portion of the war. He even at one point (p. 98) refers to the historical uniqueness of events (*historische Einmaligkeit des Vorgangs*). But he insists that, while others went along and might even be culpable in their indifference, the "Final Solution" was Hitler's distinctive venture. Indeed, within the compass of a relatively short essay, Hillgruber devotes a disproportionate amount of space to the question of Hitler's role in the "Final Solution." Hillgruber moreover argues that the Allies were not moved by Nazi crimes but prompted by power politics and misled by a crude image of Prussian militarism in their presumably longstanding ambition to dismember Germany and destroy its heartland, Prussia. In this sense, Germany was victimized. The events on the eastern front during the final phase of the war were themselves aspects of a normal struggle for dominance and of a heroic yet desperate attempt to save as much of German culture and as many German lives as possible from the atrocity-mongering Russian army. For Hillgruber, the historian must empathize with the Germans in the east, notably including German soldiers fighting against overwhelming odds on the eastern front—soldiers who were victims in their own right as fighters for a cause that had been sacrificed to power politics. Hillgruber's plea for empathy is remarkably one-sided, especially in view of the fact that the continuance of the war on the eastern front prolonged the operation of the death camps. It is facilitated by the generalizing and essentializing nature of his account of the plight of German soldiers and—at least in this book—the limitations of his inquiry into the degree of the military's complicity in Nazi policy and the extent of their own atrocities against both Russian soldiers and civilians on the eastern front. Making a distorted use of a distinction drawn by Max Weber, Hillgruber also contrasts what he sees as the commendably realistic ethic of individual responsibility upheld by German party, state, and military leaders in the east with the unrealistic ethic of inner conviction that motivated those who plotted against Hitler's life.

I have treated Hillgruber's account selectively by singling out some of its features without addressing the important rhetorical issue of the way in which they are embedded in the erudite and at times intricate analysis of a historian with a strong and solid professional reputation. It is nonetheless important to recognize that Hillgruber's account is at times questionable even though, when compared to Nolte's, it is apparently more historical, less philosophical, more securely authorized by previous publications, and hence more professionally reputable. (Most historians would probably agree with Habermas in thinking that Nolte's status is not enhanced by the fact that he was Heidegger's student.) Indeed, at least for certain audiences, Hillgruber's approach may be more effective than Nolte's in legitimating a more guarded and sophisticated relativization. In fact it is very tempting to be taken in by Hillgruber and to begin playing his game. In understanding Hillgruber's role in the historians' debate, it is, however, insufficient to isolate and evaluate the truth value of his claims one by one; it is necessary also to analyze how these claims function in his account. Otherwise one runs the risk of displacing normalization onto one's understanding of Hillgruber's text and perhaps unintentionally participating in a larger process of relativization.

Nolte's conception of transcendence is in certain respects the photographic negative of the notion of emancipation and Enlightenment of which Jürgen Habermas has made himself the champion.[10] At times Habermas' own self-image and his understanding of the tradition of critical rationality he wishes to defend induce him to caricature more substantial questioners of that tradition (such as Jacques Derrida, whom Habermas often interprets misleadingly as a mere mystical, anarchistic opponent of reason); they also lead him to make allowance in his own approach only for rather reduced variants of notions that disorient rationality without simply denying it (such as Freud's notion of the unconscious). But Habermas' intervention in the *Historikerstreit* enabled him to put his best foot forward and even to elaborate in more telling fashion certain of his basic arguments.

In one of his interventions, Habermas puts forth a striking formulation of the relationship between collective responsibility and the public role of memory:

> There is the obligation we in Germany have—even if no one else is prepared to take it upon themselves any longer—to keep alive the memory of the suffering of those murdered at the hands of Germans, and we must keep this memory alive quite openly and not just in our own minds. These dead have above all a claim to the weak anamnestic power of a solidarity which those born later can now only practice through the medium of memory which is always being renewed, which may often be desperate, but which is at any rate active and circulating. If we disregard this Benjaminian legacy, Jewish fellow citizens and certainly the sons, the daughters and the grandchildren of the murdered victims would no longer be able to breathe in our country. ("Concerning the Public Use of History," p. 44)

Habermas also argues for a critical rather than a blind appropriation of traditions—a critical appropriation that would validate only traditions that "stand up to the suspicious gaze made wise by the moral catastrophe" (p. 44). Instead of a particularistic nationalism, Habermas calls for a "postconventional identity" based on universal norms and a constitutional patriotism. In themselves these ideals may seem rather ineffective and overly indebted to the abstract aspirations of the Enlightenment and German idealism. But the passages I have quoted indicate that the larger project may be to join these ideals to the selective appropriation of traditions, including those of the Enlightenment, that in their own way also carry historical sedimentation and concrete commitments. In another intervention in the debate—an address delivered in Denmark—Habermas inquires further into the complex transformations of embeddedness in a traditional life-world. While insisting on a complementary rather than an analogical relation between individual and collective identity, he stresses the postconventional implications of Kierkegaard's notion of a conversionlike existential choice that consciously and responsibly transforms one's life-history. This choice puts the individual in the ethical position of an editor deciding what should be considered essential and worth passing on in his or her past. The counterpart in the life of a people would be the decision, conscious of the ambivalence in every tradition, that publicly and critically determines which traditions or aspects of traditions one wants to continue and which one does not.[11] The reference to Kierkegaard might itself be read to indicate that, with respect to the tense conjunction of universalizing constitutional principles and more specific—to some extent nonreflective—bonds, there is a need for continual rethinking and renegotiation rather than speculative synthesis of *Aufhebung*.

One obvious problem is the use made of any notion of unquestioned or nonreflective attachments as well as the manner in which it interacts with a critical approach to problems. Indeed, any justifiable sense of responsibility for the past would not rest on passive acceptance of a burden; it would require both a nonreflective involvement in a shared history and a critical and self-critical attempt to come to terms with that history. In this sense, there is still much of value in Habermas' earlier critique of the kind of uncritical, customary identity that seeks an affirmative conception of the past and a self-confirming normalization or national identity even at the price of denial and distortion. Contrasting the following questions with the earlier quoted questions rhetorically raised by Ernst Nolte enhances their power:

> Can one assume the legal succession of the German Reich, can one continue the traditions of German culture without also assuming historical liability for the form of existence in which Auschwitz was possible? Is it possible to remain liable for the context in which such

crimes had their origins and with which one's existence is interwoven, in any way other than through the solidarity of the memory
of that which cannot be made good, in any way other than through
a reflective and keenly scrutinizing attitude towards one's own
identity-creating traditions? Is it not possible to say in general terms:
the less communality such a life-context allowed internally and the
more it maintained itself by usurping and destroying the lives of
others, the greater then is the burden of reconciliation, task of
mourning, and the self-critical scrutiny of subsequent generations.
Moreover, doesn't this very sentence forbid us to use levelling comparisons to minimize the non-transferability of the shared responsibility imposed on us? This is the question concerning the singularity
of Nazi crimes. ("Concerning the Public Use of History," p. 47)

Habermas sees no simple dichotomy between memory and history,
and his concept of conventional identity is more probing than a stereotypical idea of "mythical memory" at times tendentiously opposed to
"authentic" history. (Indeed, as we shall see, those who put forth this
idea of mythical memory only to reject it are themselves at times close
to a conventional identity, at least in their conception of "authentic"
historiography.) It would be mistaken, moreover, to identify Habermas' specific and limited notions of historical liability and solidarity of
memory with an indiscriminate conception of German guilt that is visited on each and every German as irrational fate or pathogenic stain,
even though those "born later" may at times feel unjustifiably guilty
about the past.

Yet Habermas himself lends too much credence to the standard opposition between the citizen and the expert, and he is thus unable to
elaborate a conception of the validly mixed or hybridized role of the
historian both as a professional scholar and as a critical intellectual engaged in dialogic exchange with a past that he or she attempts to reconstitute as "scientifically" as possible. Habermas is led to make an argument that underwrites a very conventional identity for the historian
and that seems particularly inappropriate for a field that is not formalized but instead remains in many significant ways very close to public
discourse in its own protocols of explanation and interpretation:

We are addressing the dispute about the right answer from the perspective of the first person. One should not confuse this arena, in
which it is not possible to be a disinterested party, with discussions
between scientists who, in the course of their work, must adopt the

perspective of the third person. The political culture of the Federal Republic is without doubt affected by the comparative work of historians and other academics within the humanities; but it was only through the sluice gates of publishers and the mass media that the results of academic work, with its return to the perspective of the participants, reached the public channels for the appropriation of traditions. Only in this context can accounts be squared by using comparisons. The pompous outrage over an alleged mixing of politics and science shunts the issue onto a completely wrong track. (Ibid.)

Habermas is of course well advised in noting his lack of special expertise in the historiography of the Nazi period and in taking exception to the reaction of certain members of the historical profession to his articles. But he concedes too much to those historians who took offense at his intervention rather than seeing it as a stimulus to public discourse and a prod for them to assume certain responsibilities not excluded by professional expertise but, on the contrary, demanded by it. One may even raise the question of whether Habermas' own general conception of the division of modern society into rather neat spheres or areas obviates critical thought about the more difficult problem of the nature of valid combinations or hybridizations of roles in different fields such as history, philosophy, literary criticism, social theory, and at times even journalism.

There are other questionable aspects of Habermas' argument, including a tendency to conflate or at least implicitly to correlate a normative conception of Western democratic values with the existing Western political alliance. Moreover, in view of his defense of modernity as an uncompleted project of enlightenment, Habermas has strategic as well as more deepseated philosophical reasons for not placing too much emphasis on the ambivalence of Western traditions and the possibly dubious role of a critique of revisionism in lessening awareness of the implication of other Western countries in massively destructive or even genocidal processes. Given the history of the United States, this danger is clear and present for an American, and identification with Habermas' position may be facilitated by the narcissistic and self-justificatory gains it brings. It would nonetheless be a mistake simply to process all of Habermas' arguments in the historians' debate in terms of a preset conception of his politics or philosophy. Such a response to Habermas is itself rather leveling and leads one to miss or underplay significant, contextually important features of his interventions, not least of which was his role in triggering the historians' debate itself.

Not addressed in Habermas' critique but bearing on the question of at least limited relations between the *Historikerstreit* and the general issue of historicization (*Historisierung*) of the Holocaust is the representation of the Nazi period in and through the social history of everyday life (*Alltagsgeschichte*). Here the exchange of letters between Martin Broszat and Saul Friedlander is particularly illuminating.[12]

Broszat is upset by the fact that, for a long time after the war, Germans were able to write German history only by way of extreme distancing, as if they were treating the history of a foreign people. "We wrote about this history only in the third person, and not in the first person plural; we were no longer able to feel that this history was somehow dealing with ourselves, and was 'our thing'" (p. 100). For Broszat "historicization" contributes to lifting this barrier by putting Germans in touch with their past. As Friedlander notes, however, the problem is the relation between intention and result. Broszat construes historicization in terms of the insertion of the Nazis into the larger context of everyday life, which at times went on relatively undisturbed by what was happening in the concentration and death camps. For Friedlander, both leveling comparisons and the integration of events into everyday life may induce "some kind of overall relativization of the moral problems *specifically raised by Nazism*" (p. 104).[13] He elaborates his point in this manner:

> For the historian, the widening and nuancing of the picture [i]s of the essence. But the "historicization" . . . could mean not so much a widening of the picture, as a *shift of focus*. From *that* perspective, the insistence on *Alltag* or on long-range social trends could indeed strongly relativize what I still consider as the decisive historiographical approach to that period, an approach which considers these twelve years as a definable historical unit dominated, first of all, by the "primacy of politics." (p. 104)

Friedlander would seem to allow for an *Alltagsgeschichte* that would widen the picture without shifting the focus, perhaps one that would stress the tense and complex interaction between the role of everyday life and that of larger issues that are of crucial concern to Friedlander.[14] Still, Friedlander's notion of the primacy of politics includes the centrality of Auschwitz—and everything it stands for—in focusing one's picture of the Third Reich. Here I would note that centering in this case need not be conceived as a mere metaphysical residue; it may be understood as a functional necessity that is most responsibly under-taken when it is self-conscious and critically related to an explicit eval-uation of priorities in the representation of historical events. Indeed a central focus is least subject to control when its role and determinants are not posed as an explicit problem and thereby problematized. Any central focus cannot, however, be essentialized or presented as eter-nal, and the open question is whether and how an account may be justifiably decentered insofar as Auschwitz is indeed "worked through" in an acceptable manner—a question that may arise more for future than present generations. At present it may be enough to observe that Auschwitz as a central focus need not serve to provide the false comfort and unearned security that critics of "centering" contest.

That Broszat's defense of *Alltagsgeschichte* may indeed involve a du-bious shift of focus and even possibly apologetic tendencies is indicated by other features of his argument. For example, he relies on a contrast between mythical memory and scientific history. He asserts that the former is not "simply the negative opposite pole to scholarship and scientific method" (p. 101). But he wants to keep the two clear, dis-tinct, and sharply separated, and the very terms he employs convey a negative connotation with respect to what he terms mythical. He also relegates the mythical to Jews with special needs in representation that are nonetheless beyond the bounds of "authentic" historiography: "Precisely when confronted with the inexpressible events of the Holo-caust, many Jews have indeed come to regard as indispensable a ritu-alized, almost historical theological remembrance, interwoven with other elements of Jewish fundamental world-historical experience, alongside the mere dry historical reconstruction of facts—because the incommensurability of Auschwitz cannot be dealt with in any other way" (ibid.). I shall later touch on the manner in which Broszat's con-cerns may be related to the problem of "acting-out" in contrast to "working-through." But I have already intimated that acting-out is probably unavoidable with respect to extremely traumatizing events, and one has to be especially careful about possible functions of any seeming critique of it. Indeed those who criticize it may combine de-nial with their own form of acting-out. In any case, it is not helpful to oppose "dry historical reconstruction of facts" to "ritualized, almost theological remembrance," for such an opposition repeats in displaced form the seemingly averted opposition between history and mythical memory. It also avoids the crucial problem of the demands placed upon the historical use of language in attempting to account for phenomena such as Auschwitz, and it facilitates a return to conventional if not narrowly positivistic historiography. I have already argued that the basic problem is best posed in terms of transference and the need to work through rather than deny it or act it out. This problem in different ways confronts not only Jews but those in various subject positions, including Germans, and it is arguable that certain ritualized aspects of language may be essential to processes of mourning that are bound up with working-through transference in certain cases. This issue should not be prejudged, and the precise manner in which historiography is or is not compatible with ritualized uses of language is certainly intricate and controversial. Neither should the issue be foreclosed through overly simple oppositions between history and "mythical memory" or between dry reconstruction of facts and ritualization.

The questionable nature of Broszat's argument is even more pronounced when he appeals to the experience of people living under the Third Reich. In a crucial passage, Broszat asserts that

> the liquidation of the Jews was only feasible during the period of time in which it actually was carried out specifically because that liquidation was not in the limelight of events, but rather could largely be concealed and kept quiet. Such concealment was possible because this destruction involved a minority which even many years before had been systematically removed from the field of vision of the surrounding non-Jewish world as a result of social ghettoization. The ease with which the centrality of the "Final Solution" was carried out became a possibility because the fate of the Jews constituted a little-noticed matter of secondary importance for the majority of Germans during the war; and because for the allied enemies of Germany, it was likewise only one among a multitude of problems they had to deal with during the war, and by no means the most important one.

It is evident that the role of Auschwitz in the original historical context of action is one that is significantly different from its subsequent importance in terms of later historical perspective. The German historian too will certainly accept that Auschwitz—due to its singular significance—functions in retrospection as the central event of the Nazi period. Yet qua scientist and scholar, he cannot readily accept that Auschwitz also be made, after the fact, into the cardinal point, the hinge on which the entire factual complex of historical events of the Nazi period turns. He cannot simply accept without further ado that this entire complex of history be moved into the shadow of Auschwitz—yes, that Auschwitz even be made into the decisive measuring-rod for the historical perception of this period. (pp. 102–103)

Once again the structure of contradiction is apparent: Auschwitz is/ is not the central event/cardinal point of the Nazi period. Here one may observe that even if one accepts all factual elements of Broszat's account as accurate, his argument may still be seen as faulty. The historian should certainly note whatever corresponds to the experience of the time, although the construction of this experience may be more difficult than Broszat's account intimates. But this experience does not simply dictate the perspective of the historian. The centrality of focus may be determined by a priority in values even if this priority is not shared by participants or, more precisely, by participants exercising—or more or less actively accepting—hegemony. (With respect to Jews and other oppressed groups such as gypsies and homosexuals living under the Nazi regime, it would be a euphemistic understatement to speak of the "centrality" of Auschwitz.) But even if the Nazi period does indeed move under the shadow of Auschwitz, this does not mean, as Broszat later intimates, that one must "force totally under [Auschwitz's] usurped domination those non–National Socialist German traditions which extended into the Nazi period and, due to their being 'appropriated' by the regime, to a certain extent themselves fell prey to National Socialism" (p. 103). Instead the problem would be to determine how—and precisely to what extent—such traditions fell prey to, or even facilitated the emergence of, National Socialism, and the attempt to extricate them from their Nazi uses and abuses would require, as Habermas has intimated, an explicit reckoning with the ways they were or were not involved in Auschwitz.

In his response to Broszat, Saul Friedlander provides grounds to question the factual premises as well as the formal argumentation of Broszat's account. Relying on such recent studies as Ian Kershaw's revised English edition of *The "Hitler Myth": Image and Reality in the Third Reich*[15] and H. and S. Obernaus' *"Schreiben, wie es wirklich war!" Aufzeichnungen Karl Duerkefaeldens aus den Jahren 1933–1945*,[16] Friedlander states:

In short, although the destruction of the Jews may have been a minor point in the perceptions and policies of the Allies during the war, it seems, more and more, that it loomed as a hidden but perceived fact in many German minds during the war itself.

If my point is correct, it has considerable importance in relation to the core thesis of [Broszat's] "Plea." Indeed, normal life with the knowledge of ongoing massive crimes committed by one's own nation and one's own society is not so normal after all. (p. 108)

Friedlander's comment of course raises the issue of suppression and repression versus simple ignorance. Its force is heightened by another set of observations he makes:

Nobody denies the "banality of evil" at many levels within this annihilation process, but it possibly is not the only explanation at all levels.

In my opinion, part of the leadership and part of the followers, too, had the feeling of accomplishing something truly, historically, metahistorically exceptional . . . Himmler's Posen speech [was] the expression of a *Rausch*, the feeling of an almost superhuman enterprise. That is why I would tend to consider some important aspects of the Nazi movement in terms of "political religion" in the sense used by Eric Voegelin, Norman Cohn, Karl Dietrich Bracher, James Rhodes, Uriel Tal and many others. (p. 109)[17]

Broszat himself touches upon suppression with respect not to Germans under the Third Reich but to historians, and his comment brings out some of the dubious possibilities of the critique of acting-out:

As I see it, the danger of suppressing the period consists not only in the customary practice of forgetting, but rather, in this instance—almost in paradoxical fashion—likewise in the fact that one is too overly "concerned," for didactic reasons, about this chapter in history . . . The gigantic dictatorial and criminal dimension of the Nazi period also harbors within it the danger that the authenticity of this segment of history may end up being buried beneath monumental sites for the Resistance—and indeed perhaps also beneath memorials for the Holocaust. (p. 118)

The reminder that the Holocaust may serve as "symbolic capital" or as a pretext for self-serving monumentalization is apposite. Still, the very concept of "authenticity" is of questionable usefulness, particularly when it is employed as a misleading synonym for accurate reconstruction. And one may well resist the degeneration of concern or even commitment into propaganda and partisan advocacy but nonetheless insist that there are valid didactic purposes in historiography, especially for those who are teachers as well as scholars. There is also a problem in the appeal to normalized methods or balanced accounts in the representation of rather abnormal and unbalanced phenomena that make distinctive demands upon the historian. But the most basic point is that the critique of acting-out may, if undertaken in a certain way, facilitate denial or even the inclination to blame the victim. Indeed it may not be entirely beside the point to observe that a concern for memorials as necessary acts of memory is quite understandable in light of the fact that the Nazis wanted the destruction of Jews to be total and to include their elimination from memory itself at least in the form of Jewish self-representation. (In this specific context, a Jewish public act of memory might function as an act of resistance.) Hitler planned to substitute Nazi memories of Jews for Jewish ones through monuments that commemorated his acts of destruction and oblivion.[18] The project of total mastery of the past was a goal of the Nazis, and one should not in general confuse either dubious monumentalization or the project of total *Bewältigung* with legitimate forms of memory, overcoming, and working-through.

Throughout this text, I have been insisting that a crucial issue raised by the *Historikerstreit* is how precisely the emphasis on uniqueness or comparability functions in the historian's own context. I have also suggested that this issue can be illuminated through a judicious, nonreductive use of certain psychoanalytic concepts—a use attuned to the relationship between psychoanalysis and sociopolitical issues. I would like to conclude with a few brief and inadequate statements about the general requirements of an attempt to work through problems rather than to deny or act them out.

Working-through requires the recognition that we are involved in transferential relations to the past in ways that vary according to the subject positions we find ourselves in, rework, and invent. It also involves the attempt to counteract the projective reprocessing of the past through which we deny certain of its features and act out our own desires for self-confirming or identity-forming meaning. By contrast, working-through is bound up with the role of problematic but significant distinctions, including the distinction between accurate reconstruction of the past and committed exchange with it. These distinctions should neither be reified into binary oppositions and separate spheres nor collapsed into an indiscriminate will to rewrite the past. In addition, working-through relies on a certain use of memory and judgment—a use that involves the critique of ideology, prominently including the critique of the scapegoat mechanism that had a historically specific and not simply arbitrary or abstract role in the Nazi treatment of the Jews. What is not confronted critically does not disappear; it tends to return as the repressed.[19]

How language is used is a crucial consideration in working-through problems, and the historiographical use of language confronts specific difficulties and challenges in the face of limiting cases that may reduce one to silence. Auschwitz as reality and as metonym is the extreme limiting case that threatens classifications, categories, and comparisons. It may reduce one to silence. Silence that is not a sign of utter defeat, however, is itself a potentially ritual attitude; but in this sense it is a *silence survenu* intricately bound up with certain uses of language.

The attempt to come to terms with extremely traumatizing events involves the work of mourning.[20] This work encompasses a relation between language and silence that is in some sense ritualized. Certain rituals teach us that this work does not exclude forms of humor, and gallows humor has been an important response to extreme situations on the part of victims themselves. Needless to say, the employment of humor is one of the most delicate and complicated issues in the light (or darkness) of certain events.

Historical understanding is not furthered by routine oppositions between "scientific" history and its stereotypical if not scapegoated "other," which often appears in the form of myth, ritual, or memory. Such oppositions serve primarily as mechanisms of defense and denial that signal overreaction to the possibility of acting-out—overreaction prompting a confinement of historiography to self-defeating positivistic protocols that may stimulate a return of the repressed in relatively uncontrolled and uncritical forms. In cases of extreme trauma, certain kinds of acting-out may not be entirely overcome, and working-through may itself require the recognition of loss that cannot be made good: scars that will not disappear and even wounds that will not heal. The problem facing historians—a problem that is itself inflected by the other subject positions occupied by given historians—is how to articulate the relation between the requirements of scientific expertise and the less easily definable demands placed on the use of language by the difficult attempt to work through transferential relations in a dialogue with the past having implications for the present and future. This dialogue is not purely personal or psychological. One of its vital aspects is the exploration of how different approaches relate to the generation of viable institutions of both discourse and social life that effectively resist the recurrence of anything comparable to the Nazi regime. More generally, in the dialogic dimension of historical study one seeks not abstracted meaning but meaningful guides to thought and practice, and one seeks them not in a hypostatized past or in some teleological master code but in and through one's very exchange with the past. But to be critical and self-critical, this undertaking must be sensitive to the problem of the possibilities and limits of meaning, including the threat of finding oneself at the point of irrecoverable loss and empty silence. The quest for a "positive" identity or for normalization through denial provides only illusory meaning and does not further the emergence of an acceptable future. A reckoning with the past in keeping with democratic values requires the ability—or at least the attempt—to read scars and to affirm only what deserves affirmation as one turns the lamp of critical reflection on oneself and one's own.

< 8 >

Historical Understanding and Counterrationality: The *Judenrat* as Epistemological Vantage

Dan Diner

The difficulty inherent in describing National Socialism—or, more precisely, in describing and presenting the mass extermination in historiographic terms—is an expression of the inconceivability, the basic unimaginability of the event itself. Such an observation might sound trivial if the problem of describability and representation did not entail an epistemologically guided question—one that is directly bound up with the entire complex of the comprehensibility of the National Socialist phenomenon. Moreover, the recent debate between the late Martin Broszat and Saul Friedlander on the historization of that incriminated era has demonstrated just how narrow the boundaries indeed are of a mode of describability aimed at achieving historiographical understanding, *Verstehen*.[1] In that debate it became clear that there must be a considerable theoretical effort prior to any attempt at historization of National Socialism—an analytical endeavor that would have to lead to prehistoriographical clarifications.

A decade ago George Kren and Leon Rappaport termed National Socialism and its core event, the mass extermination, a "historical crisis" and pointed out that "in more formal terms, the historical crisis involves events that shatter the credibility of pre-existing epistemologies."[2] Using concrete metaphor, they symbolized the annulment of customary approaches of knowing and description evoked by the event, noting that "one cannot measure pain with a ruler, or the temperature of a blast furnace with a fever thermometer."[3] Such a critique of traditional historiographic approaches in respect to the mass extermination thus broaches a basic question, one that is anterior to all description and pertains to the comprehensibility, the amenability to *Verstehen*, of social and political processes or events. According to Kren and Rappaport, one should assume that the phenomenon of the "Final

< 128 >

Solution" transcends traditional patterns of historical understanding. In order to specify more precisely the epistemological mutation of the subject, it is necessary to recall conceptions of historical understanding regarded as valid and accepted in previous historiography.

Beginning with Droysen, if not sooner, research in the historical sciences has proceeded on the assumption that a *Verstehen*-oriented reconstruction of a historical—and thus social—context is possible only under one condition: namely, when that reconstruction can be subjectively meaningful for the observer.[4] Seen from this perspective, a historical event is understandable in the sense of an empathetic reexperiencing and consequent concrete comprehension (*Nachvollziehen*) only if the observer or the reconstructing historian can rely on what is familiar to him from his own previous experience for support in his attempt to comprehend the respective situation. Moreover, in his project of experientially based understanding, he must also obey the dictates of reason.[5]

This notion of understanding as a process in which conclusions are drawn about an internal motive from external manifestations is based on the assumption that the person investigating history proceeds in the same way as one who makes history.[6] Or to formulate it in terms that seem less tautological: that both historical reconstruction and the action of the historical subject are guided in a similar fashion by reason.[7] In short, it is assumed that the anticipated logical connection between *explanans* and *explanandum* is present and operative in the process of understanding.[8] From this perspective, the subjective meaningfulness of the intertemporal dialogue between present and past is based on an intersubjectively generalizable, and thus objective, medium of communication—namely, that of *rational discourse*.[9] Consequently, what we are attempting to discover in the historical object by means of an approach aimed at *Verstehen*, guided by rationality, is always and only its interpretable core, that is, what is accessible to reason and amenable to experiential comprehension. That is also the case when historians find themselves confronted with a subject that appears to them to be irrational.[10]

Despite all protestations to the contrary—namely, that they are faced with an incomprehensible set of events—historians approach National Socialism and the mass extermination on the basis of a key assumption: that these phenomena are nonetheless amenable to a process of comprehension guided by criteria of rationality. That supposi-

tion is present, for example, when they note an extreme disparity between ends and means—a relation generally assumed to be socially
operative—such as the interlinkage between conduct of the war and
the mass extermination. That covert hypothesis regarding the ultimate
rationality of conduct also guides the approach to the ideologically motivated aims of the Nazis themselves. By dint of the fact that they sur-
pass the power of imagination of the rational personality, those aims
are consequently classified as "irrational." Such a label indicates that
the historian disqualifies this behavior as basically incomprehensible—when judged, of course, in terms of customary and accepted criteria of rationality.

Yet this commonly advanced characterization of Nazi behavior as irrational is far from being nonproblematical, since it raises two epistemically relevant consequences for historiography worth further examination. Thus, the popularly held view that Nazi behavior and action can
be grasped only in terms of irrationality serves as an impediment to
analysis: it blocks any further intention that is oriented toward criteria
of rationality in understanding phenomena and at least aspires to comprehend the nature of what remains past understanding. A priori, *Verstehen* would necessarily lapse and be impossible given such a previously decided and agreed-upon supposition: if one argues that the
actions of the Nazis, aimed purely at destruction, constitute a complex
of events that can only be evaluated as irrational by definition, then
such a structure of events is, fundamentally and by its nature, not amenable to rational understanding and insight.

   Moreover, classifying National Socialist behavior bent upon destruction as irrational contains a second salient and epistemically relevant
dimension: a view centered on the irrationality of Nazi conduct implies
the presence of a highly particularistic perspective, one guided by a
specific collective experience. Such a perspective leads to a vantage
that is hobbled by its subjectivity and has a fundamentally detrimental
impact on any attempts at understanding. Because if one explores the
accepted denotative meaning of the presumed irrationality of National
Socialist action, culminating in annihilation, it is evident that "irrational" in everyday linguistic usage means to signify just this: that the
Nazis did not act in an adequate manner—which is to say, that their
conduct was not in keeping with a rational pursuit of their *own* interests. This implies, quite intuitively and pretheoretically, that their

behavior caused intolerable injury and harm to the collective whose leadership they commandeered and whose fate they had been presumptuous enough to try to control—namely, the German people. Thus, the notion of the irrationality of National Socialist action—with its apogee in the mass extermination—would, from this vantage, be viewed as an expression of some particularistic German perception.[11]

The particularistic character of the notion of the irrationality of National Socialist action becomes clearer via a shift in perspective. If we cross over to view events from the angle of the victims, the notion of the irrational dimension of the mass extermination emerges as a kind of mocking euphemism within the total context of Nazi policy toward the Jews—as if, for example, one could classify such anti-Jewish measures as mass expulsion, graded below the critical threshold of the "Final Solution" and evaluated in terms of it, as being "rational" events by contrast. Those actions may appear positive or "reasonable" when judged from the standpoint of traditional antisemites, but that certainly does not render them rational.

Nonetheless, owing to the sheer weight and mass of the extermination, all National Socialist measures anterior to this event would, in the eyes of the victims of those measures, seem to claim, almost by default, the attribute of rationality. Indeed, it is arguable that such a classificatory label could be regarded as part of a quite specific experiential perspective, namely that of the victims. This vantage, in turn, might derive from a dimension of Jewish historical consciousness: in the life-world of the victims, the measures antecedent to the mass extermination may well have appeared to Jews as being reminiscent of a familiar complex of antisemitic traditions—that is, seemingly they conformed with the practices of a traditional, virulent form of anti-Jewish enmity. And in point of fact, to the extent that they could be presupposed as being already familiar phenomena, appearing as a kind of historical repetition, those measures could even possess a certain element of calculability and predictability in their presumed familiarity.

Thus, such measures, contrasted with the enormity of the mass extermination, may well have appeared rational to anyone who was a potential victim of that collective death verdict—because beyond the boundaries of the unimaginable, everything somehow seems "rational" by desperate comparison. Significantly, both Hannah Arendt and the sociologist Norbert Elias, motivated by a biographical-existential concern, commented on the "Final Solution" along these lines. Elias even ascribed a "strong element of realism and rationality" to those Jewish policies of the Nazis that stopped short of extermination.[12] Hannah Arendt, in focusing on deeds that tax all conceivable limits of common reason—acts neither "committed due to passion nor for one's own advantage"[13]—claimed that the antisemitic suppression and expulsion of the Jews was an "atrocious and criminal act, yet one that was completely rational and purposeful [*zweckrational*]."[14]

The existential experience of the victims does not readily allow for the transposition of their specific, historically subjective classification of the events onto a more general plane. It would constitute an embarrassing anomaly if, in fact, persons belonging to the collective implicated in the crimes were to classify those anti-Jewish measures that were anterior to, and thus seemingly in contrast with, the mass extermination as being rational. Rather, the proper task of the historians here is to attempt to arrive at a departicularized, universally acceptable classification of the mass extermination, and to develop an adequate definition of what *rational* can mean in this context. That definition is a necessary prerequisite to evolve meaningful categories of understanding for a universally valid historiographic reconstruction of events.

If one proceeds in terms of concepts based on decision theory—that is, on the basis of an assessment of the character of social relations in intersubjective communication—George Shackle's observation that "rationality means something only for the outside observer" is useful as a point of departure in trying to characterize the content of rationality of any act.[15] What Shackle means to state is that it is impossible to determine the rational content of actions from the internal perspective of the actor. Rather, it can only be assessed by those who evaluate the action from the outside, according to the yardstick of their own action. In regard to the historical subject at hand, such a proviso on the proper vantage for probing the meaning of the term *rational* is interpretable as follows: the content of rationality in National Socialist action, including the mass extermination, cannot be meaningfully judged and evaluated by the Nazis themselves. On the contrary: that rational content can only be assessed by those who stand outside, or, even better, by those who have been directly exposed to the events and were at their mercy.

After all, an internal National Socialist perspective on the Nazis' own actions could easily arrive at the conclusion that they acted quite rationally, that is, in accordance with their own criteria, objectives, and so on. In a seeming paradox, the particularistic perspective of action and reaction of the victims of systematic annihilation becomes a cognitively universal coign from which to view the event as such and to assess its rational content. This is a vantage point also taken up—indeed, specifically so—by reconstructing historians guided by their intention, in terms of historiographical *Verstehen,* to understand.

Thus, both the rational content and the historical comprehensibility of the mass extermination can be determined and judged utilizing a particularistic tool: the perception and form of behavior of the victims. To that extent, the existentially sharpened perspective of the victims assumes something like the importance of a practical epistemological vantage, a kind of observation point for reconstructing historians in their efforts to arrive at an understanding of events. It is hypothesized that such a vantage can enable us adequately to characterize the National Socialist system confronting its victims as being neither rational nor irrational, but rather *counterrational.*

In order to explicate National Socialist behavior aimed at annihilation as counterrational, it is necessary to illustrate that behavior in terms of a concrete, historically existent object. The experiential context that lends itself to a presentation of the problem of rationality is a situation of diagnostic radicality: namely, that in which the organs of what the Nazis termed Jewish "self-administration" in the ghettos, the so-called Jewish Councils (or *Judenräte*), found themselves entangled. Isaiah Trunk, the distinguished historian of the *Judenräte* in occupied Poland and the western Soviet Union,[16] refers in a somewhat lesser-known article to the exceptional epistemic value of the situation in which the Jewish Councils found themselves—a situation, I would contend, from which one can effectively perceive the counterrational effect of National Socialist behavior. In his analysis, Trunk points out that the situation of the Jews in the ghettos differed from all other situations in which Nazi victims were trapped. The ghettos, he states, "were the only places where the tragic endeavors for survival and adjustment could manifest themselves."[17] Thus, the significance of the ghetto lay in the fact that the Jews, confined there in a condition characterized by seeming, albeit specious, self-determination, were able to contemplate options for action and thus to reflect upon their own situation vis-à-vis the Nazis. They were allowed just enough social normality and the semblance of political will so as to nurture the illusion that they could act in furtherance of their own survival. Such a dilemma-ridden boundary experience could crystallize and evolve only in this sort of opaque state of affairs, strung between total subjugation and a modicum of self-activity and self-organization.

That boundary experience is what marks the situation of the *Judenräte* in a historical sense. Only in such a condition of apparent or genuine indecision regarding their ultimate fate were the victims still given sufficient socially maneuverable time to act. This leeway permitted them to perceive their predicament and their relation toward their hangmen during the respite between the verdict of collective death and its postponed execution. In this respect, their situation differed fundamentally from that of victims confined in the concentration camps, especially the extermination camps. In those camps, the individual, due to the absolute loss of all will, had no options for action whatsoever, and thus no dilemmatic alternatives.

As a result of the genuine or presumed alternatives for action upon which the Jewish Councils were repeatedly called to deal with anew, they found it constantly necessary, in the interest of the Jews who had entrusted themselves to their care, and in the interest of their own survival, to *anticipate* Nazi behavior, in order to try to exert a moderating influence on Nazi actions by means of anticipatory action; this could be termed a preemptive attempt to "think the Nazis."

Such real historical positioning brings the situation of the Jewish Council to a characteristic perception that takes on a key epistemic importance. Based on this importance, it is possible, according to George Shackle, to determine what can be evaluated as rational and how far Nazi behavior followed criteria of rationality as viewed from the vantage of action theory. To that extent, the experience of the *Judenräte*, which found themselves in the absolute and extreme situation of a historical boundary experience, can also function something like a universal cognitive prism, especially for the reconstructing historian. As such a cognitive prism, it can likewise serve as a historiographical tool, helping to lead to an analytical approach that annuls or suspends, as it were, those rational criteria of understanding on which the later historical reconstruction of a social reality customarily tries to base itself, founded on the logical connection between *explanans* and *explanandum*.

The behavior of the Nazis, seemingly counterrational for the consciousness of the victims, can be usefully explicated utilizing a key notion: the concept of labor within the ghettos.[18] In this connection, there are, historically speaking, three different meanings of *labor* involved here. First of all, there is labor in its immediate role as a practical activity aimed at survival and based on material reproduction. As a result of ghettoization, the Jews had been torn from the social context that had previously functioned to guarantee their livelihood and material existence. They had been pauperized by expropriation measures and the loss of their jobs to such an extent that they were left with no other choice: the only potential employers who could offer them work under the exceptional conditions of domination and servitude that had evolved were the Nazis themselves.

In addition to the role of work as the only value that Jews could exchange for food, it had another meaning and function bound up with the role of the *Judenräte:* that is, to provide the Germans in an organized manner with Jewish labor via the councils. In Lodz or Warsaw,[19] for example, the councils wished to "rationalize" the Nazis, which meant attempting to render amenable to calculation the arbitrary and unpredictable behavior of the Nazis toward the Jewish population. One principal aim was to try to exercise a mitigating influence on the extremely cruel practice of snatching up Jews on the street and then deporting them to toil at low-skill jobs as forced laborers. The organized labor services offered by the councils were intended to help make such practices more transparent and to regulate and curtail them. This had suggested itself as a viable option, since activities in the sphere of production were involved. In turn, such jobs presupposed certain skills and a more complex social context. Work was thus utilized as a means of rationalization and a medium of social communication, as it were, in the hope to "civilize" the Nazis by means of the obligations and ties this relation engendered. Such a strategy of survival was based on an assumption relevant for societal communication and preshaped by social forms of exchange, a notion of behavioral reciprocity that one's opponent would find cause, merely as a result of the behavior demonstrated toward him, to assume an equivalent attitude. To that extent, the *Judenräte* acted in accordance with the following socially self-evident stipulation: an organization of human cooperative endeavor and a self-rationalizing structure of interreferential behavioral modes was possible only if they made use of an *external* fact.[20] And work was such an external, self-objectifying fact.

The social trust placed by the Jewish Councils in the act of exchange, toward which they were constrained for lack of any alternative, would later develop into a trap. Initially they had offered their labor at their own initiative, but soon thereafter it was demanded by the Nazis themselves. An additional third meaning of labor is involved here, a function labor assumed as a result of knowledge, or at least premonition, of the possible ultimate aims of deportation. In view of the suspicions or certainty about Nazi designs to liquidate the ghettos, the Jewish Councils no longer tried only to "rationalize" the Nazis in a communication-relevant sense by means of work; rather, they also made a particular attempt to postpone the death verdict via the use of the value-creating function of human labor power, using work as a means of forestalling. The rational anticipatory supposition operative here can be summed up as follows: it was to the obvious benefit of the Nazis—indeed, in their own best interest, at least in the light of the ongoing war effort—to give priority to the exploitation of Jewish labor power over the ideologically motivated death verdict. Such priority would be based, it was reasoned, on considerations of advantage for the Nazis and their own self-preservation.

Proceeding from forms of everyday social behavior guided by rationality, the strategy of "rescue through labor" pursued by the Jewish Councils appeared to be well-founded to some degree. Thus, the economization that took place suggested to the Jews that an economic relationship was now the predominant one. At least, the everywhere valid form of economy, visible for all to see, had awakened the impression that a logic was operative here that was similar to or a close analogue of, social normality. It was in keeping with traditional social reality to behave toward that logic in an equivalent fashion.

The very *form* of work demanded from the Jews—productivity, effectiveness, and efficiency—indicated this logic.[21] It was thus unavoidable that the form of labor necessarily generated a blinding effect, masking from its intended victims the design to push ahead with annihilation—an intention that, on top of everything else, had been kept relatively concealed from its targeted victims. Faced with such forms, individuals who have been socialized on the basis of criteria of rationality will assume intuitively, in an almost Pavlovian sense, that their opponent's behavior is in fact rational and purposive, guided by material interests. And they will make this assumption even under conditions of being subjected by force and compulsion to the will of that opponent; indeed, they will especially adhere to this assumption under such specific conditions of constraint. Compulsion does not deny the traditional meaning and purpose of labor as such but only negates the voluntary quality with which it otherwise is exchanged. The economic content of forced labor indicated by the form of work thus becomes a confirmation of pursuit of interests and ultimately of societal rationality. Indeed, it is possible to contend that in its evident external effect, the form of labor symbolizes a kind of materialized rationality.

In the light of the labor demanded of them by the Nazis, the Jewish Councils, despite all signals to the contrary, were only able, when it came to the relevance for action, to conclude that the Nazis were presumably guided by utilitarian motives and thus by a more broadly operative civilizing logic of *homo oeconomicus*. Moreover, there was a rationality deriving from this logic,[22] especially since the system of action of *homo oeconomicus* was not simply oriented toward maximizing utility and minimizing costs, but rather proceeded on the supposition quite generally that acting subjects were indeed reasonable. *Homo oeconomicus* transposes the maxims of reason of economic life to the sphere of social action in general.[23] To that extent, such behavior could be regarded as being founded on utilitarian ethics, especially since economically based decisions are also viewed as correct in an ethical sense.[24]

No matter how narrow and constricted the arena left by the Nazis for free decision and in which the Jewish Councils believed they were acting, the form of economic utility calculation predominant therein suggested a high degree of socially grounded suppositions about rationality, especially since the criteria of economizing occur immediately to the mind of a person faced with a decision.[25] Inherently, the mere form of calculation of economic utility contains a high degree of assumed rationality. Consequently, every theory of decision making that regards itself as rational is based on calculations of utility—especially since no human activity is accorded greater rationality than the effort to engage in gainful pursuits. If contrafactual informational input is received by a person faced with the constant necessity to make decisions, the information accorded a greater degree of probability is that which appears to be in keeping with the utilitarian character of the form of economy.

Only that information is permitted to enter consciousness that points to an alternative relevant for action. When, for example, Jewish skilled workers in Czestochowa received word about the deportation

of similarly qualified workers in Warsaw, they failed to draw any conclusions from this about their own possible fate. The effect of a lived
and immediate, utilitarian, action-relevant manner of thinking indebted to economic rationality was far more important than the mediated negation of such rationality that had been reported to them.[26]
Due to its power of total refutation, news about the annihilation of
others was blocked out: it could not, must not be heeded in any way
that might have an impact on consciousness and reality. The principle
of rationality, materialized in the form of labor, and the associated options for perceiving reality remained dominant. In an insightful remark, Uriel Tal has formulated a terse imperative to express the justification for being and existence by means of work bound up with the
principle of survival and the strategy of the Jewish Councils: "I act
economically, ergo I exist."[27]

It appears that the *Judenräte* had no option except to anticipate the
Nazis economically and to utilize the associated rationality, given the
pervasive presence of universally traditional, longstanding forms of
utilitarian thought and action. These are forms that have been internalized to a considerable degree as a result of socialization and are
patterned in terms of economic categories. Based on the situation and
its internal perception, this choice constituted an impressive and quite
plausible attempt to draw conclusions from the *means*—namely, labor—about the *ends*—namely, the production of value. In this way,
the councils fell victim to a fundamental and yet necessary mispercep-
tion, because the form of labor was not supposed to take on any *systemic* meaning for the Nazis. In the final analysis, it remained external
to their real intention: annihilation.

Yet here too, on the basis of a generally valid relation between
means and ends, the behavior of the *Judenräte* possessed a high degree of supposed rationality, since it is not only the ends that follow a
value determination, but the means as well. In respect to value scales,
means cannot be indifferent or neutral.[28] The *form* of the means alone
makes that impossible as an option. From the perspective of ethical
action, the determination of value thus refers to the entire sequence of
an event, the comprehensive whole of the ends-means complex, and
not just to its anticipated final result. Consequently, the *Judenräte* had
virtually no other choice than constantly to cherish and rekindle the
hope that labor would somehow lose its exceptional character and be
transformed, after all, into a life-sustaining regularity, a normal rou-

tine. Or, viewed differently, that the form (labor) would finally shift from its meaning as a mere means to encompass the ends as well, thus ultimately negating annihilation in its own nature as negation of any rational pursuit of interests.

In retrospect, however, it would appear that the *Judenräte*, faced with the National Socialist intention to destroy the Jews, tried to defend themselves against the Nazis by using forms of thought and action that were unsuitable—inappropriate, because they were indebted to criteria of rationality. But this is really only the retrospective impression. Labor as the materialized form of communicative social rationality was not isolated in this context, but rather interlinked with a key strategic aspect that concerned the *Judenräte:* protraction, forestalling, the struggle for "time."

Labor thus stands for the materialization of concretized rationality, in the specific historical case for the form of thought and action of the *Judenräte*, oriented toward presumably utilitarian motives on the part of the Germans, and later functioning as a psychological denial filter to block out the ever more obvious and constrictive hopelessness of the victims. In contrast, the category of time here represents a strategic element to which everything else is subordinate. The *Judenräte* tried to gain more time, or to protract the period of "borrowed time" allotted them by the Nazis, by expending their sole asset: the physical labor power at their disposal. In the early phase the councils hoped that by the ploy of gaining time, some miracle might occur; later they harbored illusory hopes that the front would soon be approaching or that, for whatever reason, there would be some saving shift in German policy. Yet the struggle to gain time by expenditure of labor was bound up with a further element: the actual dimension of terror as a reversal of the formal-ethical proportionality of ends and means. The strategy aimed at gaining precious time made it necessary for the *Judenräte* to make decisions in keeping with the logic of utilitarian considerations. However, the original rational aspect of that forestalling logic—namely, the intention to ward off the worst by means of the lesser evil—successively shifted and was ultimately reversed.

One sees here the ultimate consequence of the process of forced self-selection, designed to be implemented by the *Judenräte* themselves: a program of participatory self-destruction by means of self-preservation. Because the Nazis continued to remain the masters of time—due, for example, to the fact that the front was not approaching with expected rapidity—the process of weighing options, a process that earlier had appeared justified in terms of an ethics of ends and means, now shifted to its diametrical opposite. The small numbers of those fated to die as a result of the self-selection repeatedly forced on the *Judenräte* by the Nazis had, in the course of events, long since become multitudes. The upshot of this was that the councils, bereft of any other alternative, directed the reversal of values engendered by the Nazis—the value-ethics of ends and means, and the associated, generally effective assumptions of rationality—against themselves, and against the Jewish communities in the ghettos entrusted to their care.

The *Judenräte* were subservient to a reality in which the rationality of action aimed at self-preservation was transformed to self-destruction as a result of that reversal. Such a reversal, because it became a reality, is not only a part of Jewish experience but can be regarded as the practical negation of the basic assumptions of the civilizing power of rational judgment as such. Seen in this analytical light, the mass extermination is not "irrational"; rather, because of the negation of rational judgment, it is imbued with a decidedly *counterrational* meaning perceived via the corresponding perspective of the victims. That perspective was experienced existentially by the *Judenräte*, and can be cognitively comprehended in reconstruction by others; it therefore is in keeping with universally valid forms of thought and action.

The behavior of the Nazis, perceived as counterrational from the perspective of the *Judenräte*, permits an assessment of the extent to which the rupture of forms of thought, action, and communication on which civilizing discourse is founded can also infect historiography, the domain of activity generally dependent on historical reconstruction. The behavior that appears counterrational when refracted through the prism of the perspective of the *Judenräte* necessarily extends into the sphere of historiography via the logical connection between *explanans* and *explanandum*. Historians, guided by an intention to understand that is beholden to rational forms of thought, will find themselves largely thwarted in that goal and approach in their search for the supposedly rational structure of Nazi behavior—rational at least in the sense of the Nazis' own self-preservation. Such a negatively thwarted intention to comprehend leads to a retreat: in reaction, historians may flee into a realm of explanation where they divest themselves of all criteria for comprehensibility and thus for rational understanding.

They also find it necessary to rationalize Nazi behavior tautologically as irrational: that is, by viewing it more generally as a direct product of Nazi irrational ideology and by adopting finalistic patterns of interpretation.

By contrast, a historiographical perspective that appropriates the experiential view of the *Judenräte* will proceed along a quite different path. Such a vantage can open up diverse and varied insights highly relevant for strategies of research. For the simple reason alone that the *Judenräte* found it necessary—for purposes of forestallment and survival—to anticipate Nazi behavior, they had good cause to explore the Nazi bureaucracy in thought and deed. The objective was to fathom its internal decision-making structures, deeply fissured by competition and rivalries over power and authority. Indeed, it was perceived as necessary by each *Judenrat* to penetrate as "participant players," so to speak, into the bureaucratic-administrative apparatus they were confronted with. That process can be comprehended in several concrete cases by examining the strategic deliberations and actions of the *Judenräte* in Lodz, Vilna, and Bialystok.[29]

The strategy of trying to influence the Nazi bureaucratic apparatus by offering genuine or presumed support to various factional interests seemingly more concerned with exploiting Jewish ghetto labor than with immediate annihilation makes the *Judenrat* in a double sense an epistemologically relevant indicator for assessing the adequacy of a given theoretical-methodological approach. Thus, perceptions taking the *Judenrat* as point of departure reveal just how closely the structuralist historiographical paradigm of National Socialism models reality. On the other hand, the practical failure of *Judenrat* strategy in the light of the ultimate implementation of annihilation reflects a salient fact: despite the chaos of conflicting authorities and powers—or perhaps precisely because of this confusing administrative welter—the designs of the Nazis to destroy the Jews were ultimately carried through.

Be that as it may: via the perspective of the *Judenrat*—an institution set up by the Nazis and active under its supervision and at its bidding, though simultaneously a Jewish institution centered on objectives of survival running counter to Nazi will—it is possible to arrive at the conclusion that if rationality was involved here at all, it could be termed "fractured." The associated historiographical approach followed in reconstruction of events is analogous to that of rational administrative behavior. This is the case because historians, in reconstructing an event or process like that of the mass extermination—an action carried out by a bureaucratic state apparatus—make use in their analysis almost intuitively, so to speak, of precisely the corresponding logic of bureaucratic-administrative action. But they must recognize that such an assumed rationality is negated, fractured by the reality the Nazis created.[30]

The consequences of the mediating, methodologically fertile significance of the *Judenrat* for historiographical *Verstehen*—the abiding intention of the historian to fathom the National Socialist period and its core event, the mass extermination—should now be evident. The demolition of action-guiding assumptions of rationality that are generally considered universally valid, transforming them into their destructive opposites, also has a direct impact on the approach of the historian, necessarily so. That approach is guided by the desire to comprehend and is therefore traditionally indebted to criteria of rationality. Thus, the very subject matter acts to cancel, to deactivate the connections among an assumption of rationality, the ability to understand, and meaningful reconstruction.

To that extent, the endeavor to describe National Socialism and the mass extermination requires what can be termed a "negative cognition of history"—since historians must first become aware of the cancellation of assumptions of rationality in historical reconstruction before they can venture to engage in the enterprise of historization. Or, to phrase it differently: due to the loss of its imaginability, it is necessary first to *think* Auschwitz before it can be written about historically.

Translated by Bill Templer

< 9 >

History beyond the Pleasure Principle: Some Thoughts on the Representation of Trauma

Eric L. Santner

I find it increasingly difficult to reflect on the theoretical and ethical limits to historical and artistic representations of Nazism and the "Final Solution" without also thinking about recent events in Central Europe and, above all, about the unification of the two Germanys. If the stories one tells about the past (and, more specifically, about how one came to be who one is or thinks one is) are at some level determined by the present social, psychological, and political needs of the teller and his or her audience, then the radical developments that have taken place in Europe over the last several years cannot help but powerfully influence the repertoire of available representations of the events and phenomena that are our concern here. You will recall Elie Wiesel's concerns regarding the place of a particular date, 9 November, in the historical imagination of contemporary German society.[1] The date of the Kristallnacht as well as of the first breach in the Berlin Wall, fifty-one years later, had apparently become a site of struggle between competing narratives.[2] The story of the destruction of European Jewry, which entered a new stage with the Kristallnacht pogroms, was being displaced—or at least this was Wiesel's worry—by a rather different narrative, the story of the German struggle against, and ultimate triumph over, Marxism-Leninism. In a sense, Wiesel's question was this: Would the shattered glass of 1938 be buried and, as it were, metamorphosed under the sheer weight of all that crumbling concrete of November 1989?

Those familiar with the West German political and cultural scene of the 1970s and 1980s will recognize in the struggle over the narrative inscription of this particular date the contours of a process that has increasingly come to occupy the German historical imagination and political unconscious over the last decade or so.[3] This process might be

< 143 >

described as a series of mnemonic readjustments and rearrangements, enacted in the framework of public rituals, narratives, and various other modes of cultural production, whereby dates, events, names, concepts, locations, institutions, and historical agents are made newly available for libidinal investments.[4]

The most notorious public ritual in this regard was, perhaps, the ceremony of reconciliation staged at Bitburg in May 1985, the subtext of which seemed to involve not only the sentimental equalization of all victims of the war but, more insidiously, a repositioning of the SS within a narrative of the long "Western" struggle against Bolshevism.

In the course of the following two years, this general tendency and direction of mnemonic readjustment became the central issue in the *Historikerstreit*, a discursive event which has not ceased to have repercussions for the way one thinks about recent German history and, perhaps more important, the way one thinks about the ambiguous and often dubious role of the historian in the process of national identity formation. The details of this debate are well known and I will not rehearse them again here. I would simply like to note how a certain "narrative fetishism" has figured in this controversy.

By narrative fetishism I mean the construction and deployment of a narrative consciously or unconsciously designed to expunge the traces of the trauma or loss that called that narrative into being in the first place. The use of narrative as fetish may be contrasted with that rather different mode of symbolic behavior that Freud called *Trauerarbeit* or the "work of mourning." Both narrative fetishism and mourning are responses to loss, to a past that refuses to go away due to its traumatic impact. The work of mourning is a process of elaborating and integrating the reality of loss or traumatic shock by remembering and repeating it in symbolically and dialogically mediated doses; it is a process of translating, troping, and figuring loss and, as Dominick LaCapra has noted in his chapter, may encompass "a relation between language and silence that is in some sense ritualized."[5] Narrative fetishism, by contrast, is the way an inability or refusal to mourn emplots traumatic events; it is a strategy of undoing, in fantasy, the need for mourning by simulating a condition of intactness, typically by situating the site and origin of loss elsewhere. Narrative fetishism releases one from the burden of having to reconstitute one's self-identity under "posttraumatic" conditions; in narrative fetishism, the "post" is indefinitely postponed.

Here, of course, it might be said that it is unrealistic and may perhaps even represent a sort of category mistake to expect that historiography could or should perform *Trauerarbeit*. Historians, after all, strive for intellectual and not psychic mastery of events. In this context I would recall LaCapra's deconstruction of this opposition between intellectual and psychic mastery, cognitive and affective dimensions of representation, "scientific" and "mythic" or "ritualized" approaches to the past.[6] As LaCapra's reading of the historians' debate suggests, one might argue that because of the kinds and intensities of transferential dynamics it calls forth, a traumatic event is by definition one that implicates the historian in labors of psychic mastery. Any historical account of such an event will, in other words, include, explicitly or implicitly, an elaboration of what might be called the historian's own context of survivorship. Such an elaboration will typically involve efforts to differentiate and distance one's own moral, political, and psychological dispositions from those associated with the traumatic event. The affect, style, and velocity with which this work of differentiation is undertaken is often an indication of the intensity of the transferential relations that continue to bind one to the trauma. The transferential dynamic will, moreover, vary radically according to the features of the particular context of survivorship or, to cite LaCapra once more, according to the particular subject position of the historian. The transferential relations of a non-Jewish German historian to Nazism and the Final Solution will differ enormously from those of an Israeli historian to the same events. And certainly not only the national and cultural background but also the age of the historian, his or her temporal distance to the events in question, will play a significant role in the definition of the subject position.[7] But central to any elaboration of survivorship is, I would argue, the work of mourning. As should be clear by now, my primary concern in the present context is with the tasks and burdens of mourning that continue to afflict and, as it were, interrupt processes of identity formation in postwar Germany. In other words, I am concerned here with the project and *dilemma* of elaborating a post-Holocaust German national and cultural identity. Germans are faced with the paradoxical task of having to constitute their "Germanness" in the awareness of the horrors generated by a previous production of national and cultural identity.[8]

Perhaps Freud's most compelling characterization of the work of mourning is his discussion, in *Beyond the Pleasure Principle*, of the *fort/da* game that he had observed in the behavior of his one-and-a-half-year-old grandson. In this game the child is seen to master his grief over separation from the mother by staging his own performance of disappearance and return with props that D. W. Winnicott would call transitional objects. Bereft by the mother's absence, and more generally by the dawning awareness that the interval between himself and his mother opens up a whole range of unpredictable and potentially treacherous possibilities, he reenacts the opening of that abysmal interval within the controlled space of a primitive ritual. The child is translating, as it were, his fragmented narcissism (which might otherwise pose a psychotic risk—the risk of psychological disintegration) into the formalized rhythms of symbolic behavior; thanks to this procedure, he is able to administer in controlled doses the absence he is mourning. The capacity to dose out and to represent absence by means of substitutive figures at a remove from what one might call their "transcendental signifier," is what allows the child to avoid psychotic breakdown and transform his lost sense of omnipotence into a chastened form of empowerment. The work of mourning performed in the *fort/ da* game has attracted so much attention in recent literary and critical theory because it displays so clearly the way in which a human self constitutes itself out of the ruins of its narcissism.[9]

The dosing out of a certain negative—a thanatotic—element as a strategy of mastering a real and traumatic loss is a fundamentally homeopathic procedure. In a homeopathic procedure the controlled introduction of a negative element—a symbolic or, in medical contexts, real poison—helps to heal a system infected by a similar poisonous substance. The poison becomes a cure by empowering the individual to master the potentially traumatic effects of large doses of the morphologically related poison.[10] In the *fort/da* game it is the rhythmic manipulation of signifiers and figures, objects and syllables instituting an absence, that serves as the poison that cures. These signifiers are controlled symbolic doses of absence and renunciation that help the child to survive and (ideally) be empowered by the negativity of the mother's absence.

To put these matters in a somewhat different light, one might say that the work of mourning is the way human beings restore the regime of the pleasure principle in the wake of trauma or loss. I call your attention to Freud's remarks in *Beyond the Pleasure Principle*, shortly following his discussion of the *fort/da* game, regarding the behavior of *Unfallsneurotiker*, individuals who have experienced and then repressed some trauma but return to it over and over again in their dreams. Concerning this oneiric repetition compulsion, Freud says the following:

> We may assume . . . that dreams are here helping to carry out an-
> other task, which must be accomplished before the dominance of the
> pleasure principle can even begin. These dreams are endeavouring
> to master the stimulus retrospectively, by developing the anxiety
> whose omission was the cause of the traumatic neurosis. They thus
> afford us a view of a function of the mental apparatus which, though
> it does not contradict the pleasure principle, is nevertheless inde-
> pendent of it and seems to be more primitive than the purpose of
> gaining pleasure and avoiding unpleasure.[11]

Given the homologies Freud underlined between the symptoms of the trauma victim and the symbolic behavior of the child at play, one may conclude that these other, more primitive psychic tasks are the tasks of mourning that serve to constitute the self and that must, at some level, be reiterated with all later experiences of loss or traumatic shock (Freud was thinking here of the great number of traumatized soldiers returning from World War I).[12] Both the child trying to master his separateness from the mother and the trauma victim returning, in dream, to the site of shock are locked in a repetition compulsion: an effort to recuperate, in the controlled context of symbolic behavior, the *Angstbereitschaft* or readiness to feel anxiety, absent during the initial shock or loss. It was Freud's thought that the absence of appropriate affect—anxiety—rather than loss per se is what leads to traumatiza-tion. Until such anxiety has been recuperated and worked through, the loss will continue to represent a past that refuses to go away. At the end of this process of psychic mastery, the ego becomes, as Freud says elsewhere, "free and uninhibited" and open to new libidinal invest-ments, that is, open to object relations under the regime of the plea-sure principle. Fetishism, as I am using the term here, is, by contrast, a strategy whereby one seeks voluntaristically to reinstate the pleasure principle without addressing and working through those other tasks which, as Freud insists, "must be accomplished before the dominance of the pleasure principle can even begin." Far from providing a sym-bolic space for the recuperation of anxiety, narrative fetishism directly or indirectly offers reassurances that there was no need for anxiety in the first place.

When Ernst Nolte asks—to return now to the context of the historians' debate—whether it is "not likely that the Nazis and Hitler committed this 'Asiatic' deed [the "Final Solution"] because they saw themselves and others like them as potential or real victims of an 'Asiatic' deed [the gulag],"[13] he is, so to speak, inviting his readers to locate themselves in a place—call it simply somewhere to the west of Asia—where they can feel morally and psychologically unthreatened by the traumas and losses—what I am calling the psychotic risk—signified by Nazism and the "Final Solution." According to Nolte, in this magical zone to the west of Asia, the regime of the pleasure principle was never in any danger.

A similar fetishistic use of narrative may be found, I think, in other contributions to the historians' debate. In his *Zweierlei Untergang*, for example, Andreas Hillgruber more or less programmatically sets out to restore his German audience's capacity libidinally to cathect and unproblematically to identify with the defenders of Germany's eastern territories during the period of their collapse, even though these "valiant" efforts to hold back the anticipated reprisals of the Red Army— efforts evoked with considerable narrative pleasure—allowed for the machinery of the death camps to continue unabated.[14] As Saul Friedlander has noted of Hillgruber's fetishistic reinscription of the Wehrmacht and the events of 1944–45:

> In the new representation, the Wehrmacht becomes the heroic defender of the victims threatened by the Soviet onslaught. The crimes of the Wehrmacht are not denied by Hillgruber, although he prefers to speak of the "revenge orgy" of the Red Army. Whereas this revenge orgy is described with considerable pathos . . . its origin, the tens of millions of dead left by the Wehrmacht in the wake of its onslaughts on Germany's neighbors—particularly on the Soviet Union—does not seem to reenter the picture with any forcefulness.[15]

But even in morally and historiographically far more responsible efforts to historicize Nazism and the "Final Solution," one may discover an inclination to reinvoke prematurely a condition of normalcy, that is, a condition in which the normal functioning of the pleasure principle has not been significantly disrupted and exposed to psychotic risk.

Arguing his case several years ago for more vigorous, plastic, and richly colored narrative strategies of historicizing National Socialism, Martin Broszat bemoaned the fact that when historians turn to this period of history their capacity for empathic interpretation and what he called the "pleasure in historical narration" [*die Lust am geschicht-lichen Erzählen*] appears to be blocked.[16] Broszat's plea for historiciza-tion was thus, among other things, a plea for a certain primacy of the pleasure principle in historical narration even, paradoxically, when it comes to narrating events the traumatic impact of which would seem to call the normal functioning of that principle into question. Friedlan-der's critique of Broszat's appeal to narrative pleasure will be familiar to those who have followed the theoretical debates on the problem of representation with regard to Nazism and the "Final Solution." The gist of this critique, as I understand it, is the claim that the events in question—Nazism and the "Final Solution"—mark a shattering of the regime of normal social and psychological functioning and therewith a crossing over into a realm of psychotic experience that may be inaccessible to empathic interpretation, that may not be redeemable within an economy of narrative pleasure.[17]

Finally, I would like to discuss very briefly the dynamics of narrative fetishism as it functions in a realm of cultural production where narrative and visual pleasure freely intermingle, namely film.[18] I take my example from Edgar Reitz's hugely successful film *Heimat*, which was first broadcast on German television in the fall of 1984. (Reitz is cur-rently involved in the postproduction of a sequel to *Heimat*.) This film is important for all kinds of reasons I cannot go into here.[19] In the pres-ent context, however, it is especially interesting to note that one of the effects of the film—whether this was intentional one can only sur-mise—has been to make the word "Heimat" newly available for libidi-nal investment in Germany, if only as the elegiac token of something lost. Not unlike the case of a particular date discussed earlier, the word "Heimat" becomes, in and through Reitz's film, a site of competing narratives. A word—one might say a "mytheme"—that has figured prominently in the story of the social marginalization and eventual de-struction of European Jewry, is, as it were, reoccupied within a new ideological and narrative ensemble in which Germans can see and cathect themselves as bereft victim, as the dispossessed.

This reoccupation of "Heimat" takes on further resonance when one recalls that Reitz made his as a kind of counterfilm to the American television production *Holocaust*. His own film was intended, in large part, as a strategy of reclaiming memories—and, perhaps more impor-tant, the pleasure in their narration—that Germans have been forced to renounce under the sway of the American culture industry in general and media events like *Holocaust* in particular. (Reitz polemically refers to the aesthetics embodied by *Holocaust* as the "real terror" of the twentieth century.)[20] Germans have, Reitz claims, abandoned their unique, regionally inflected experiences and memories, because they have been morally terrorized by spectacles like *Holocaust*.[21] Reitz's own work of resistance to this "terror" therefore lies in the salvaging of local experience, local history, local memories:

> There are thousands of stories among our people that are worth being filmed, that are based on irritatingly detailed experiences which apparently do not contribute to judging or explaining history, but whose sum total would actually fill this gap. We mustn't let ourselves be prevented from taking our personal lives seriously . . . Authors all over the world are trying to take possession of their own history and therewith of the history of the group to which they belong. But they often find that their own history is torn out of their hands. The most serious act of expropriation occurs when a person is deprived of his or her own history. With *Holocaust*, the Americans have taken away our history.[22]

With *Heimat*, the pleasure in the historical narration of twentieth-century German history is taken back and reinstated with a vengeance. But as numerous critics have noted, Reitz's restoration of narrative and visual pleasure would seem to proceed along the route of the fetish, that is, at the price of disavowing the trauma signified by the "Final Solution." Here it is important to keep in mind that one can acknowledge the *fact* of an event, that is, that it happened, and yet continue to disavow the traumatizing impact of the same event.

The scene that perhaps best illustrates the fetishistic aspect of Reitz's particular deployment of narrative and visual pleasure comes in the first episode of the film. This scene prefigures, quite remarkably, the scenario evoked by Elie Wiesel regarding November 9. It is 1923; Eduard and Pauline make an afternoon excursion to Simmern, the largest town near Schabbach. Pauline wanders off alone and finds herself looking at the window display of the town watchmaker and jeweler. Suddenly a group of young men run up behind her—including Eduard, armed as usual with camera and tripod—and begin throwing rocks at the window of the apartment above the watchmaker's shop where, as we learn, a Jew—in this case also branded as a separatist—resides. They are chased off by police, but the shards of fallen glass have cut Pauline's hand. Robert Kröber, the watchmaker, signals her to come into the shop where he cleans her wound, thereby initiating the love story of Pauline and Robert. Later on in the film—it is 1933—we hear that the now married Pauline and Robert are buying the Jew's apartment. As Robert remarks, "The house belongs to him and now he wants to sell it . . . The Jews don't have it so easy anymore."

This small Kristallnacht sequence shows how the shards of the Jew's shattered existence—we never see him in the flesh—are immediately absorbed into a sentimental story of love and courtship in the provinces. Though it is the filmmaker who alerts us to the ways in which experience (and narrative) construct themselves around such blind spots, Reitz refuses to allow such potentially traumatic moments to disrupt the economy of narrative and visual pleasure maintained throughout his fifteen and a half hours of film. This consistency is surely one of the reasons for the incredible success of the film. *Heimat* offers its viewers the opportunity to witness a chronicle of twentieth-century German history in which *die Lust am geschichtlichen Erzählen* is never in any serious danger.

I have argued in these pages that Nazism and the "Final Solution" need to be theorized under the sign of massive trauma, meaning that these events must be confronted and analyzed in their capacity to endanger and overwhelm the composition and coherence of individual and collective identities that enter into their deadly field of force. To use, once more, metaphors suggested by Freud's discussion of traumatic neurosis, the events in question may represent for those whose lives have been touched by them, even across the distance of one or more generations, a degree of overstimulation to psychic structures and economies such that normal psychic functioning (under the auspices of the pleasure principle) may be interrupted and other, more "primitive" tasks may take precedence. These are the tasks of repairing what Freud referred to as the *Reizschutz,* the protective shield or psychic skin that normally regulates the flow of stimuli and information across the boundaries of the self. To quote, once more, from *Beyond the Pleasure Principle,* Freud's most ambitious effort to formulate a theory of trauma:

> We describe as "traumatic" any excitations from outside which are powerful enough to break through the protective shield [*Reizschutz*]. It seems to me that the concept of trauma necessarily implies a connection of this kind with a breach in an otherwise efficacious barrier against stimuli. Such an event as an external trauma is

bound to provoke a disturbance on a large scale in the functioning of the organism's energy and to set in motion every possible defense measure. At the same time, the pleasure principle is for the moment put out of action. There is no longer any possibility of preventing the mental apparatus from being flooded with large amounts of stimulus, and another problem arises instead—the problem of mastering the amounts of stimulus which have broken in and of binding them, in the psychical sense, so that they can then be disposed of.[23]

Here it is most important to keep in mind the *textual* quality of this *Reizschutz,* to remember that it is made from symbolic materials, that it is a culturally constructed and maintained organization of individual and group identities. As Robert Lifton has put it, "In the case of severe trauma we can say that there has been an important break in the life-line that can leave one permanently engaged in either repair or the acquisition of new twine. And here we come to the survivor's overall task, that of formulation, evolving new inner forms that include the traumatic event."[24]

Both mourning and narrative fetishism as I have defined these terms are strategies whereby groups and individuals reconstruct their vitality and identity in the wake of trauma. The crucial difference between the two modes of repair has to do with the willingness or capacity to include the traumatic event in one's efforts to reformulate and reconstitute identity.

There are a number of paths along which such an integration might proceed. Important aspects of this work have, I would argue, figured prominently in theoretical discourses of recent years—call them "postmodern"—that have concerned themselves with the cultural construction and deployment of "difference" in particular historical contexts. These discourses have invited the citizens of Western industrial and postindustrial societies to acknowledge and work through fundamental complicities between certain modes of identity formation and the violence and destruction perpetrated in emblematic fashion by German fascism against Jews and other groups deemed to be threatening to the composition and coherence of the German subject.[25] Feminist critiques, in particular, of the patriarchal subject and its various historical institutions suggest that the tasks facing post-Holocaust societies in general, that is, societies willing to work through the traumatic impact of Nazism and the "Final Solution," include that of a radical rethinking and reformulation of the very notions of boundaries and borderlines, of that "protective shield" regulating exchange between the inside and the outside of individuals and groups. The goal of such reformulations is, as I see it, the development of a capacity to constitute boundaries that can create a dynamic space of mutual recognition (between self and other, indigenous and foreign); in the absence of such a capacity it would seem that one is condemned to produce only rigid fortifications that can secure little more than the inert space of a thoroughly homogeneous and ultimately paranoid "Heimat."[26]

To summarize: To take seriously Nazism and the "Final Solution" as massive trauma means to shift one's theoretical, ethical, and political attention to the psychic and social sites where individual and group identities are constituted, destroyed, and reconstructed. This mode of attention is one which, to paraphrase Freud, though it may not always contradict the pleasure principle, is nevertheless independent of it and is addressed to issues that are more primitive than the purpose, narrative or otherwise, of gaining pleasure and avoiding unpleasure. It is furthermore a mode of attention that requires a capacity and willingness to work through anxiety.

Let me conclude by returning very briefly to the possible influence of contemporary political events on the ways that Nazism and the "Final Solution" may come to be represented both in popular and more properly scientific historiographical discourses. There are signs that the narratives being constructed around the collapse of Central and Eastern European communism and the unification of the two Germanys will have a tendency to reduce the available moral, conceptual, and psychic space within which Nazism and its crimes can still be worked through as a trauma that shook *the West* at its very foundations. All around one hears stories of triumph: of a vital and dynamic Western economic and political culture over a moribund socialism somehow considered to be "Eastern," not to say "Asiatic." At some level, it is as if events in Europe had opened the gates to ever more unconflicted "enactments" of the revisionist narratives constructed by Nolte and Hillgruber in the mid-eighties. It is difficult not to get the sense that the crisis of socialism is being appropriated at the level of what might be called the "political imaginary" to exorcize from the body of the West— from its patterns and projects of modernization—the violence, destruction, and human suffering that have belonged to and continue to belong to its history. In Germany, the velocity, affect, and style with which unification has been undertaken suggest a manic element, not unlike that which typified the work of reconstruction in the early post-war years. This manic element has attached itself, as earlier, to images and ideals of economic, technological, and bureaucratic *mastery*.

In a political and cultural climate in which the operative metaphor has been that of a powerful machine moving relentlessly forward—the image of a train which has left the station and cannot be halted or slowed down has strangely, uncannily, come to dominate the public discourse on unification—there is, perhaps, little reason to be hopeful that this crucial period of national reconstitution might become a real opportunity for reflection: not only on the issues associated with the breakdown of state socialism, which are indeed formidable, but also on a wide range of moral, political, and psychological questions that have not ceased to emanate from the traumas of Nazism and the "Final Solution."

< 10 >

Habermas, Enlightenment, and Antisemitism

VINCENT P. PECORA

The German *Historikerstreit* is an argument which, in its most basic
political terms, Nietzsche could have subtitled. It is about the "Nutzen
und Nachteil," the advantage and the disadvantage, of history for
present-day life. Of course, immediately this approach may seem to
miss the mark. For surely, everyone on both sides, from Andreas Hillgruber to Jürgen Habermas, has implicitly agreed that there are only
disadvantages in continuing to forget, to repress, or to renounce history altogether. Within Germany, Habermas has been an indispensable example of conscience and reflection, protesting eloquently
against the very possibility of a return to a pre-Nazi German identity.
From his critical perspective, "the Nazi period will be much less of an
obstacle to us, the more calmly we are able to consider it as a filter
through which the substance of our culture must be passed, insofar as
this substance is adopted voluntarily and consciously."[1] The "normalizing" urge of a nationalist historiography, on the other hand, must be
rejected.

In a deeper sense, however, even Habermas' eminently useful
words here show a strain that good intentions cannot fully outweigh,
for they are implicitly aimed at sublimating an "obstacle" which "history" has thrown in the way. Even for Habermas, that is, the *Nachteil*
of history is obvious, however much it must be confronted calmly if a
rational social order is to be achieved. In what follows, I would like to
examine a few of the implications of this situation for the Western intellectual—and here I include those inside and outside the German
debate—who struggles to confront the massive obstacles of modern
Western history from within the West and its self-proclaimed tradition
of enlightened thought. By reopening in the latter portion of this discussion certain issues addressed already by Theodor Adorno and Max
Horkheimer in *Dialectic of Enlightenment,* I hope to raise fundamental questions about the nature of the contemporary debate over the

< 155 >

"singularity" of the "Final Solution," about the singular difficulty of the Western intellectual in such debate, and about what is in danger of being repressed concerning the West even as the necessary work of historical retrieval goes on.

In the perhaps inescapable contradictions lurking in Habermas' words, the duplicity of Nietzsche's phrase returns. History is always, *pace* Santayana, in some sense a disadvantage for the living, and especially so in the context of any society which tries to build its monuments on the bones and ashes of an implicit destiny which it believes it fulfills. What Nazism means for the contemporary period is, to some extent, a deracination of that question about history's "value" which Nietzsche still thought he could address. To return to a tradition or an identity *before* Nazism is out of the question (though this *Sehnsucht* is obviously still alive and well on the German right), if only because such a gesture actually repeats the nostalgic, selective, and dangerous historiography of the National Socialism which is the very impetus behind contemporary debate. But to stand up and be counted, on the other hand, as one who acknowledges a destructive heritage, who returns in calm yet critical consideration to the painful roots of a social identity lost in repression and amnesia—can such an archaeology really be said to yield only a "filter" through which the otherwise intact "substance" of a culture can be passed, as if to purge that culture through tragic understanding?

In the final lines of Walter Abish's novel *How German Is It?/Wie Deutsche Ist Es?* the hero (born in 1945, and perhaps a bastard) willingly undergoes hypnosis in order to "reexperience his childhood"— in order, that is, both to exorcise his ghosts and to find a name to which he can answer. In what can be read simultaneously as a test of the effectivity of the hypnosis and as a paradigmatic gesture of self-identification, allegiance, acknowledgment, oath-taking—all that Louis Althusser would have defined as forms of interpellation of the subject—the hero raises his right hand at the doctor's request. In this case, however, the hypnosis which lifts repression is doomed to fail, for the sign of its success would be precisely the sign—a salute—of the false self-identification that is to be lifted. "Is it possible for anyone in Germany, nowadays, to raise his right hand, for whatever the reason, and not be flooded by the memory of a dream to end all dreams?"[2] Abish's final question, I would submit, lies at the heart of the current struggle over memory in Germany today, and it profoundly complicates Habermas' more sanguine metaphors of "filter" and "substance"—unless, that is, one can imagine a filter that contaminates even as it cleans.

To say this, of course, is to say that Habermas' call for a cultural tradition and a history that are critically adopted "voluntarily and consciously" is simultaneously the only responsible political position to adopt, and a liberal's dream fraught with contradiction. Under present conditions, the New Germany now emerging could not exist if the "filter" Habermas imagines were actually to be used: it would soon become impassable. Identities formed by continuous cultures which have achieved a measure of real power and authority in world history, let alone the totalitarian status of the Third Reich, cannot be cleansed in this fashion. American culture and American identity, despite numerous attempts at self-criticism, will never be able to filter intact the substance of its culture through a historical "memory" which is in fact completely dependent, first, on the conscious and voluntary eradication of a native Indian population, and second, on the conscious and voluntary eradication of that eradication. Cultural identity formed in the crucible of political power is contaminated at its core, in its very "substance."

I am of course aware that such sweeping statements merely reiterate—like the mantra of the appropriately concerned historian—Walter Benjamin's famous aphorism: "There is no document of civilization which is not at the same time a document of barbarism."[3] Habermas himself invokes the line in a recent essay on "posttraditional identity," with the claim that Benjamin was thinking of the "public use made of history by national movements and nation states in the nineteenth century"—an interpretation usefully directed at contemporary German revisionism.[4] But I would like to think that the aphorism could also be read so as to resonate beyond Habermas' narrowly drawn limits of *national* self-reassurance. Habermas vigorously attacks any reclamation of the myth of a specifically "German" identity—well and good. But he then substitutes for it something which many in the world today would find only marginally better—the myth of Western Man, of a "Western civilization" from which "we Germans dissociated ourselves."[5]

What do *modernity, enlightenment,* and *the West* mean in the context of Habermas' response to the new German conservatism? Habermas himself elaborates two large sets of oppositions that bear on these terms and that define his own position toward them. First, he points to a distinction between "cultural modernity" and "social modernity," between a secularized, rational ethico-political culture and the "economic and administrative" rationalization of capitalist society.[6] In broad terms, the "new conservatism" in Germany (and the United States) favors the latter, and is radically opposed to the former. Habermas, on the other hand, understands "cultural modernity" as being the basis for a life-world in which individual self-fulfillment and universal ethics first become possible. As such, it is the crucial complement to social modernity.[7] Second, and in parallel with the first opposition, Habermas draws a distinction between what might be called the idea of Western enlightenment and the pragmatic benefits of enlightened Western capitalism.[8] Again, the new conservatism favors the latter without the former, whereas Habermas renounces the latter, or at least subordinates it to the higher interests of the former.

One could hardly quarrel with Habermas' critique on its own terms. His main point—that conservatives read contradictions in the economic and administrative base of social modernity as if these were the result of the destruction of a traditional *ethos* by a secularizing cultural modernity, and thus "confuse cause and effect"[9]—has indeed been, ever since Marx, a founding tenet of left-liberal social criticism. But something always remains masked by such neat formulations. As long as "cultural modernity" can be made identical to the idea of Western enlightenment, and both made to signify *only* obvious benefits like "self-fulfillment" and "universal ethics," with no remnant, then the term simply becomes a predetermined code. But to what extent is "cultural modernity" or "Western enlightenment" exhausted by this code? Habermas' work has been uniformly silent on the obvious historical fact that "enlightenment" and "modernity" almost always came to the *West* at the expense of those colonized and exploited peoples whose labor, land, resources, and markets stoked its "social modernity," and whose presence has been more or less uniformly ignored or denied by the grand institutions of "cultural modernity" Habermas champions. Indeed, by always managing to stress the *idea* of modern, Western enlightenment—self-fulfillment and universal ethics—regardless of its historical *actuality*, Habermas situates himself within a long tradition of "enlightened" imperialist thought: it is, after all, precisely the idea of the West which Charlie Marlow thought he could save at the end of *Heart of Darkness*.

And yet wherever one looks in the *Historikerstreit*, on the right and on the left, one is made queasy by the intimation that, for its participants, what is finally at stake is once again nothing less than the fate of Western civilization. Has not the "rest" of the world already learned to fear for its very existence whenever it gets wind of "Western" intellectuals beginning to argue once again about how best to define the West? The Third Reich itself made use of a lively *Ostforschung* industry in academia—akin to other "orientalist" traditions—which arose during the Weimar period in response to borders set at Versailles; which helped authorize a quest for Lebensraum in the East; and which survived the war remarkably intact by adapting its rhetoric to serve anti-Soviet Cold War policies in the West.[10]

At the end of a most persuasive essay, forged as a sharp polemic against the mindlessness of Ernst Nolte's claim that National Socialism came to commit "Asiatic" deeds because of its justified fear of being a victim of "Asiatic" deeds, Habermas writes, "The unreserved opening of the Federal Republic to the political culture of the West is the great intellectual achievement of the postwar period, of which my generation in particular could be proud."[11] Where, one might ask, does Habermas really think German "political culture," at least from the eighteenth century on, has actually been?[12] Indeed, even as he cogently attacks the right-wing image of a proud German republic "firmly anchored in the Atlantic community of values," he cannot resist projecting the same image himself: "The only patriotism which does not alienate us from the West is a constitutional patriotism."[13] Throughout Habermas' much-needed replies to the new conservative revisionism, such disturbing strains can be heard, like Wagnerian motifs which stir recollection but not recognition. What appears in the end to be at stake for Habermas is "our link with the West"—that is, Germany's link with "civilization" itself. Inevitably, such a connection is threatened by the obstruction called Auschwitz. To demonstrate that it deserves its hard-won status as a "Western," civilized nation, Germany must, in Habermas' view, atone for its sins. Thus emerges Habermas' call for a "posttraditional" identity located "in the untroubled consciousness of a break with our disastrous traditions" and for an "unreserved openness to the political culture of the West."[14] But can this convenient notion of a "Western" identity, supplanting a German one, really bear the weight Habermas loads onto it? Does not this seemingly "critical" transformation of traditional German identity in fact require nothing short of a massive repression of everything "the West" has actually represented in the face of struggles for self-fulfillment and universal justice around the globe, as opposed simply to what Habermas wants "the West"—the Western idea—to mean?

It is not simply that, in reaffirming the primacy of the "political culture of the West" and Germany's moral salvation within it, Habermas inadvertently manages to re-demonize all that is non-Western. It is also that such rhetoric subtly serves precisely to absolve the West from its own obvious complicity, not only in Germany's war crimes, but also in the long narrative of Western imperial power. Which "political cultures" were responsible for turning away boatloads of Jewish refugees? Which "political cultures" found no great burden in knowingly collaborating with genocidal policies? Which "political cultures" actively supported a climate of antisemitism so strong that Hitler and his followers felt certain "the West" would thank Germany for its troubles?

Of course, why should the complicity of the enlightened West in Nazi crimes surprise any but the naive, when Western culture has routinely sustained itself by destroying its others for so long? Which "political cultures" were responsible for those noble works of man accomplished in the modern period in the African Congo, in Algeria, in South Africa, in Egypt, in India, in China, in Southeast Asia, in Central and South America? At such moments, Frantz Fanon's strong words are a necessary rein on the self-satisfied claims to "rationality" by Western intellectuals.

> Every time Western values are mentioned they produce in the native a sort of stiffening or muscular lockjaw. During the period of decolonization, the native's reason is appealed to. He is offered definite values, he is told . . . that he must put his trust in qualities which are well-tried, solid and highly esteemed. But it so happens that when the native hears a speech about Western culture he pulls out his knife—or at least makes sure it is within reach. The violence with which the supremacy of white values is affirmed and the aggressiveness which has permeated the victory of these values over the ways of life and of thought of the native mean that in revenge, the native laughs in mockery when Western values are mentioned in front of him. [15]

Through the idealization of "the West" that occurs with such disturbing frequency in the Western media *and* in its "critical" discourse, Fanon's experience is systematically repressed.

I do not wish to be understood as lending the merest sliver of support to the revisionism which seeks to "normalize" and "balance accounts" by recalling the barbarity of so much "non-German" culture. What National Socialism called the "Final Solution" of the "Jewish Question" indeed possesses a horrific singularity; but it does so only in the context of more or less continuous, increasingly systematic, "Western"—and terrifyingly *Christian*—traditions of religious, political, economic, and cultural persecution of the Jews. In this sense, the attempt to eradicate the Jews is not some strange, irrational swerve away from that benevolent practice Habermas calls "the political culture of the West"—it has been lurking near its heart from the beginning. Likewise, I do not wish to be understood as offering some wholesale or sophomoric (or worse, neo-Heideggerian) denunciation of Enlightenment notions of human reason, universalizing moral judgment, representative government, technological progress, and so forth. But as long as such positive gains are understood to have suddenly "happened" without recognizing their cost in the West's massive, centuries-old, and increasingly effective persecution of its others—and the Jew has been perhaps the oldest and most persistent "other" of the Christian West *inside* the West—even "enlightened" attempts to discuss the "Final Solution" will prove to be hopelessly tainted with a Eurocentric megalomania. And finally, I do not wish to be understood as implying that those who have suffered unspeakable persecution are therefore automatically immune from taking up the role of persecutor. The state of Israel, for all its "Western" traditions, has proven no more capable of cleansing itself of the deepseated racism at its heart than has Europe or America before it. Indeed, given its almost total oppression of an indigenous Arab Palestinian population, Israel has demonstrated anew just how elusive the idea of enlightenment can be.

Western political culture is in the forefront of Arno Mayer's analysis in *Why Did the Heavens Not Darken?* Although he retains his focus on the "Jewish catastrophe" and on its specificity, Mayer nevertheless demands that the event be rigorously "historicized"—whatever its nature, the "Final Solution" needs to be understood "in history," and not as a providentially ordained "Holocaust" which can be turned to sectarian purposes, commemorated, reified, confined to a "prescriptive 'memory' unconducive to critical and contextual thinking" and "beyond historical reimagining."[16] Mayer thus emphasizes, correctly I think, the need for a "profane," secular historiography built on Enlightenment notions of "causality and accuracy." He counters the "central premise" of prescriptive commemoration—that the Nazi "victimization of the Jews . . . is absolutely unprecedented, completely *sui generis*"—with a notion of a political and ideological "general crisis" running from 1914 to 1945.[17]

Mayer's notion of a modern general crisis depends on political instability and ideological fanaticism. In fact, an irrationalist "causal nexus" links the National Socialist "absolute war" against its Bolshevik ideological rivals with institutionalized antisemitism: the Judeocide occurred when the first began to fail in 1941, and ideological fury turned to the second. (Mayer even goes so far as to suggest that the mass killings would not have occurred had Hitler succeeded in Russia.) Underlying such claims is the notion that the "mainspring" of all general crises is unreason itself—neither technical or bureaucratic skill, nor the latest instruments of violence, nor the power and competitiveness of big business were the driving forces beyond the "general crisis" of 1914–1945. A strange contradiction thus haunts Mayer's thesis of ideological irrationality, and it is prompted by the specificity of the "Final Solution" itself. For although Mayer emphasizes the values of enlightened, profane historiography and of historical precedent, he also recognizes the need to describe the Judeocide in terms that will differentiate it in meaningful ways—history does not simply repeat itself, after all. But what emerges at the heart of this irrational thirty-year epoch, what most distinguishes the Judeocide from all previous and related atrocities, is nothing so much as a more efficient means–ends rationality applied to the business of mass murder.[18] In fact, wherever Mayer pauses in his "second epoch of general crisis" to distinguish the Judeocide from the furious brutalities of previous crises, he ends up invoking the organized, planned, systematized, rationally controlled nature of its destructive power. That is, at the center of this thirty-year whirlwind of ideology and unreason are the more or less calm, dispassionate, and efficient workings of railway timetables and the measurement of a crematorium's capacity.

What I want to suggest is that, for Mayer too, something about the West, and about the "political culture" of its modernity, is at stake. This likelihood is nowhere more evident than when he notes that, in the very circles of hell, such as the Lódz Ghetto, chroniclers "unlike those of earlier times" were recording their observations "in the spirit of Enlightenment history."[19] What is finally at stake for Mayer as a historian is a Western tradition and a modernity the fates of which are curiously intertwined for him with that of the Jews. What remains is a vertiginous *mise en abîme*—a more or less "normal" history, interrupted by periods of irrational crisis, at the heart of which one finds unspeakable yet quite systematized cruelty, in the midst of which chroniclers devote themselves to the spirit of the Enlightenment. My point is simply that, like Habermas, Mayer seems unable or unwilling to acknowledge systematic and rationally planned barbarity as an intrinsic, ubiquitous complement to "enlightened" Western traditions and, even more so, to their modernity. In the same decades when the United States was putting into practice a constitution which many consider the first true political product of the Enlightenment, it was also systematically eradicating a supposedly inferior native population in its search for Lebensraum and calmly pursuing planned race slavery.

This point is absolutely crucial. If the specific and terrifying suffering endured by the victims of Nazi persecution is not mobilized to remind the West of the barbarity folded into even its most admirable traditions, but instead serves to obscure it, and perhaps to foster surreptitiously a smug sense of political complacency and assuredness, then that suffering will end up serving barbaric purposes all over again. What Mayer calls the Judeocide should in no case be "normalized"—but neither should anyone take false comfort in the possible inference that all else in the enlightened West already is.

A rereading of Adorno and Horkheimer's *Dialektik der Aufklärung* (Dialectic of enlightenment), emphasizing their last chapter, "Elements of Antisemitism," might serve to counterbalance the apotheosis of Western modernity that is evident throughout Habermas' later work and implicit in much of the contemporary discussion of the "Final Solution." Today it is of course quite fashionable to dismiss *Dialektik der Aufklärung* as the site of the wrong turn in Frankfurt School critical theory, an irrational swerve toward sweeping anthropological generalization, a sort of reverse Hegelianism, now linking reason and freedom only by means of a duplicitous, rather than a progressive, dialectic. It is a turn that has evoked hostility on many fronts, from the orthodox Marxian left to positivist sociology.[20] In many ways Habermas has led the attack.[21] For him, *Dialektik der Aufklärung* could be reduced to the Nietzschean irony that implies a totalizing, self-destructive corruption of all normative standards for critique, an abandonment of Enlightenment ideals of science and morality, which leaves in its wake only the theoretical abyss of unresolved antinomies, "performative contradiction," and "determinate negation."[22] Given Habermas' devotion to such norms and ideals, this critique is to be expected. More important, perhaps, one could not help but agree with much of his response. After all, Adorno and Horkheimer themselves start from Habermas' basic claim: "We have no doubt—and therein lies our *petitio principii*—that social freedom is inseparable from enlightened thought."[23] This statement hardly implies an abandonment of the ideals of Western reason.

Nevertheless, Adorno and Horkheimer articulate a challenge to the perennial myopia of the Western intellectual that must not be forgotten amid all the clamor of the *Historikerstreit*.

> Just as the Enlightenment expresses the actual movement of civil society as a whole under the aspect of its idea embodied in persons and institutions, so truth names not merely rational consciousness but equally its actual form in reality . . . Even the sincere reformer who recommends innovation in hackneyed language, through his adoption of polished modes of categorization and the bad philosophy concealed therein, strengthens the power of what exists, which he wishes to break . . . What is at stake is not culture as value, as the critics of civilization, Huxley, Jaspers, Ortega y Gasset and others, have in mind, but rather that the Enlightenment must reflect on itself [that is, must recollect itself: *muss sich auf sich selbst besinnen*], if men are not to be betrayed altogether. The task is not the conservation of the past, but rather the redemption of past hope.[24]

And what constitutes such self-consideration for Adorno and Horkheimer? It is precisely the active recollection that "what men wish to learn from nature is how to use it in order to dominate it and other men completely. Nothing else matters. Ruthlessly, in spite of itself, the Enlightenment has burned out the last remnants of its own self-consciousness. Only thought that does violence to itself is hard enough to shatter myths."[25] These are not, of course, easily "proven" observations. Nor, for that matter, are they particularly congenial to a Eurocentric perspective whose power in world affairs is completely dependent on its ability to calculate and control the force of nature, and of human beings, better than any other. The point is that it is not only Germany which represses its past. The "enlightened West" has also learned to forget those who have paid the price for its escape from the bonds of mystified nature.

To be sure, Habermas' point about the "performative contradictions" around which such observations inevitably turn—around which Adorno's later work as a whole turns, many would say—is well taken. For it is with *Dialektik der Aufklärung* that the later philosophical antinomies of Adorno's *Negative Dialectics* first emerge in fully developed form. In the earlier text, the "leveling domination" of abstract equivalence in capitalist modernity, and the need for strict calculability and repetition in industrial production—issues already much elaborated by Weber and Lukács, among others—are understood to be inextricably tied to the larger process of enlightenment. For Adorno especially, such a perspective demands a sustained interrogation of equivalence and the identitarian concept as such. "The concept, which one would like to define as the sign-manifestation [*Merkmalseinheit*] of whatever is seized under it, rather was from the beginning the product of dialectical thinking, in which everything remains only what it is while it also becomes what it is not.²⁶ Against Aristotelian logic—though in many ways in perfect harmony with Marxian epistemology—Adorno will press a dialectical insistence on the inescapability of contradiction, even at the most basic conceptual levels. Thus, positivist science and rationality discover their efficacy only at those points where conceptual identity can be maintained. But such conceptual identity is all too readily fetishized at the level of the social reproduction of thought, and can thus be immediately turned to the service of social domination.

In *Negative Dialectics* Adorno focuses on the "ontological need" revealed by all conceptual fetishization. His goal is nothing other than the disenchantment of that philosophical insistence on the rational concept as objectively given. "A changed philosophy would have . . . to cease persuading others and itself that it has the infinite at its disposal."²⁷ One can perhaps see how, in spite of the fact that Heidegger is the immediate and unmistakable target of Adorno's later philosophy,²⁸ Habermas would come to link Adorno's attack on identitarian thinking with Derrida's "deconstruction" of phenomenology, and through Derrida to a longer tradition of "irrationalism" culminating in Heidegger. But is Habermas not throwing out the baby with the bathwater here? That is, Habermas maintains too little distinction between one perspective (Adorno's) that insists on recalling the "remnant" inevitably left out, or behind, in all achieved (and instrumentally necessary) conceptual identity, and another (Derrida's, for example) which insists, in good Heideggerian fashion, on the value of playing the perpetual beginner and which assumes as its raison d'être the endlessly repeatable gesture of dismantling the very possibility—the concept itself, one might say—of all pretension to conceptual coherence. That Habermas finds little difference between these two approaches is what allows him, I think, to make statements such as the following: "Of course it is not possible to characterize the history of the mentality of the Federal Republic in a few sentences. What I want to emphasize is this: If one disregards marginal groups, both of these ongoing controversies [about external alliances and internal 'political culture'] were conducted on the basis of a choice in favor of the West that was not seriously questioned."[29] Habermas may of course have in mind only those "marginal groups" which renounce any claim to social justice whatsoever. But is not modern political life precisely the complex imbrication of "marginal groups" struggling to find a space, and a voice, even within the "enlightened" culture of the West? When America defends its borders against the flow of Mexicans searching for better conditions, it justifies itself on the grounds that only in this way can the "good life" of its existing citizenry—their "cultural modernity," one might say—be preserved. But how much would be left out of such conclusions, even if they could be shown to be true? It is above all at such points that Habermas' fetishization of the West must be subjected to dialectical questioning: something, or someone, is almost always being excluded in the process.

I referred above to the special value of rereading Adorno and Horkheimer's chapter on antisemitism for precisely such reasons. For the Jews would surely rank high among all those groups systematically marginalized throughout the long history of "the West." In unmistakable ways, "Elements of Antisemitism" is the essay toward which *Dialektik der Aufklärung* as a whole has been directed, for antisemitism forms a precise instance—perhaps the primary exhibit—of "the actual return of enlightened civilization to barbarism."[30] And yet, throughout Habermas' summary and critique of *Dialektik der Aufklärung* and of the theoretical swerve instantiated by it, there is almost no mention of antisemitism or of the Adorno/Horkheimer discussion of it. In a chapter of a book which purports to address the "philosophical discourse" of modernity, there is only one mention of "Elements of Antisemitism," buried in a larger discussion of Bataille. The issue of "mimesis" is raised, but neither Jews nor antisemitism nor racism of any kind is ever mentioned.[31] Surely the omission is a curious one in a project dedicated to the efficacy of intersubjective rationality in the modern period. It is as if the specific nature of the problem that the resurgence and victory of barbaric racialist dogma raises for Habermas' benignly progressive history of rationalizing modernity has been conveniently airbrushed from memory.

By reintegrating the final chapter of *Dialektik der Aufklärung* into the trajectory of the work as a whole, I want to suggest the continuing relevance of Adorno and Horkheimer's interrogation of the relation between a Western "political culture" self-conceived as enlightened modernity and a long, brutal history of the West's domination of its others. That is, even though the term *imperialism* is more or less absent from the text itself, my claim is that Adorno and Horkheimer's thesis of a neurotic will within "enlightenment" toward the wholesale domination of nature can best be understood as the elucidation of a knowledge/power nexus central to imperialist relations. What Mayer calls the Judeocide, then, would gain its specificity not only from its extraordinary viciousness and systematicity but from the fact that it represents an uncanny episode in the enlightened West's need to define itself against its others. It is precisely because the Jews, perhaps more than any other people defined a priori as alien to the West and its traditions, are understood to have infiltrated the culture of reference at its core, that they represent the most destabilizing threat to their host culture. The image of the Jew as a "parasite," which runs throughout National Socialist dogma, would be impossible without the Jews' characterization as internalized aliens, as the enemy within. Their eradication must be seen, then, as a project spawned not only by their relation to an external threat to Western hegemony—as Bolshevism functions in Mayer's account—but as their embodiment of the non-West within the West, the internal difference that the West simultaneously most wishes to disavow and can never manage to disavow fully. As long as Germany could regard itself as the guardian of the West, the Jew would have a privileged place as the ineluctable discrepancy at the heart of a *Western*—not just German—fantasy of cultural unity, continuity, singularity, and identity. The Aryan racist had convinced himself that, beyond the uniqueness of his own blood line, the fate of civilization itself in the West rested on his shoulders. In a sense, the "singularity" of the "Final Solution" becomes a revealing problem only to the extent that it is understood to be inseparable from the West's own conception of itself as a singular and privileged culture of reference.

There are perhaps three ways in which "Elements of Antisemitism" might still contribute to an important reexamination of how Western civilization—including, without apology, its supposedly "modern" and "enlightened" phases—produces and reproduces a phantasm of superiority over its others. First, antisemitism, especially in its modern versions, reveals the inevitable link between a dominating culture and its imaginary construction of those it comes to dominate. "In the image of the Jews that the nationalists [*Völkischen*] erect for the world, they express their own essence. Their craving is for exclusive possession, appropriation, unlimited power, at any price. As masters, they deride and crucify the Jews, who are burdened with their guilt for this, endlessly repeating a sacrifice the efficacy of which they cannot believe in."[32] The destruction of the Jews thus becomes the figure par excellence of "enlightened" culture's attempt to destroy the memory and the guilt of the power to control which enlightened thought itself has enabled. Like Kurtz, who cries, "Destroy the brutes!" in Conrad's story, the Nazi hopes to eradicate the trace of his own barbarity projected onto those he dominates.

Second, through their confinement to commerce and trade and their banishment from productive forces and state authority, the Jews become identified with the growth of capitalism in the West, and specifically with the sphere of circulation. Indeed, Adorno and Horkheimer seem to be imagining a series of equations based on their sense of the Jews as the mediating element between production and consumption. Not only does the Jewish "middleman" become the object of the resentment of those who suffer under capitalism and whose real oppressors are safely out of reach; moreover, the Jew, tied to bourgeois merchandising and economic circulation, also becomes the image of intellectual mediation, that is, of the reflective mechanisms of conscience. Like Hamlet, those who doubt and weigh reasons—who perceive the contradiction where others see only identity, one might say—become identified with hesitation and impotence, but also with the dangerous, subversive power of the parasitical and "nonproductive" modern thinker.[33] In this way, the "Final Solution" of the "Jewish problem" is also (and quite ironically, given Habermas' anti-Nietzscheanism) the desire to resolve, finally and forever, reason's age-old tendency to turn on itself, to undo its own prerogatives and assuredness—to halt, one might say, the often debilitating self-doubt that reflection and conscience foster. The Jew becomes the very symbol of the modern, self-conscious, angst-ridden intellectual—Freud is the model here—and for that very reason becomes an intolerable threat to the untroubled link between power and knowledge which "enlightenment" hopes to attain.

Finally, and perhaps most important, antisemitism throughout Western history is the contradictory yet growing expression of enlightened culture's fear of being seduced by, and adapting to, uncontrolled nature—in sharp juxtaposition, that is, to the Nazi cult of a romantically heroized and contained nature. "[The Jews] had not extirpated assimilation to nature, but sublimated [*aufgehoben*] it in clear duties of ritual . . . So they are reputed to be left behind by civilization and much too far ahead of it, similar and dissimilar, clever and stupid. They are said to be guilty of that which they, as the first burghers, were the first to break themselves of: the allure of nature, the pull toward animal and earth, the service of images. Because they invented the concept of kosher, they are persecuted as swine. The antisemites make themselves the executors of the Old Testament: they see to it that the Jews, when they have eaten of the tree of knowledge, turn into dust."[34] The partial accommodation with nature achieved by Jewish ritual, especially given the more rationalized forms of modern Christianity, becomes the object of a profound ambivalence. It is simultaneously coveted as an organic tie with the earliest forms of human relations, now forbidden by self-repressive ideals of morality and civilization, and transformed into a monstrous pact with prehuman existence.

Indeed, I want to claim that the mechanism that Adorno and Horkheimer call "repressed mimesis"—the repression of the reproduction of undominated nature—can help to illuminate not only the paradigmatic contradictions of antisemitism, but also those of racialist dogma in general within Western imperialism. Racism's hysteric relation to its object simultaneously masks and reveals a repression of mimetic desire, a repression which racism's victims always appear uncannily to have avoided. Frantz Fanon quotes a friend who had been living in the United States: "The presence of Negroes beside whites is in a way an insurance policy on humanness. When whites feel that they have become too mechanized, they turn to men of color and ask them for a little human sustenance."[35] Edward Said, concentrating on the professional production of the discourse of orientalism, points out that the Orient was simultaneously "overvalued for its pantheism, its spirituality, its stability, its longevity, its primitivity, and so forth"; and then suddenly devalued as "lamentably under-humanized, antidemocratic, backward, barbaric, and so forth."[36] One could also point to James Clifford's discussion of a "modernist primitivism," especially in Europe's regard for "l'art nègre": "The discovery of things 'nègre' by the European avant-garde was mediated by an imaginary America, a land of noble savages simultaneously standing for the past and future of humanity—a perfect affinity of primitive and modern. For example, jazz was associated with primal sources (wild, erotic passions) and with technology (the mechanical rhythm of brushed drums, the gleaming saxophone)."[37] And one could turn to Klaus Theweleit's analysis of the roots of fascism in the ambivalences of male self-image and misogyny in the Freikorps.[38] In the texts of Europe's construction of its others— in Hegel's *Philosophy of History,* in Balzac's *Peau de chagrin,* in Flaubert's *Salammbô*—and in the work of psychoanalysts of colonialism like Fanon, one finds further testimony to those paradoxes of repressed mimesis expressed with such extraordinary viciousness in the modern and systematic antisemitism of the Third Reich.

Unless the internal relations between antisemitism and the long history of the West's exclusionary policies toward those it defines as alien are kept in mind, a truly reflective and critical attitude toward those events defined by the notion of a "Final Solution" will be impossible. It is not at all a question of forsaking the imperatives of reason, of evidence, of normative values, or of an ideal of enlightened thought and behavior—such a formulation would be a reductive deflection of that critical spirit which is not satisfied to denounce certain mistakes or "crises" while implicitly salvaging the good intentions and beneficence of the modern West's "political culture." Habermas is never more correct than when he upholds the imperatives of reasoned reflection in the face of counterfactual, racist, or irrational impulses within his own country. But aborting critical reflection where he does is the real "performative contradiction" in Western thought.

< 11 >

Between Image and Phrase:
Progressive History and the
"Final Solution" as Dispossession

SANDE COHEN

I am concerned with the event of extermination known as the "Final Solution," especially with the cultural formation of this name and its status as image and concept in the context of contemporary critical thinking.

I believe it is worthwhile to pursue the sense of contemporary enlightenment which Habermas has attached to the "Final Solution" and relate this conception to Lyotard's skepticism regarding the credibility of enlightenment today. Elaborating on the different portions of the arguments, and how they engender cultural and intellectual positions concerning the "Final Solution," will make it immediately apparent that the view of language-as-representation is at stake. Lyotard's arguments propose the writing of the "Final Solution" as a challenge to language, cultural criticism, and historiography, whereas Habermas' recent work on the "Final Solution" stands for a Hegelian-Freudian synthesis.

Habermas' Model

Historicism has been variously defined, but I suggest we consider it as an attempt to achieve a cultural "timeless time," an image which holds together categories such as origin and result. Historicism enables one to "take account of the number of moves around the dial the hand has made by the end of the period of observation," and renders an image of an unavoidable presentation handed down by "history" which braids past, present, and future in the here and now.[1] One is at once anchored to both a date and an image; one starts one's narration by setting the clock at a metaphoric midnight—time "counts" because the historian imputes this clock to the events recounted. (There are restorative countings, apocalyptic ones, and so on.) As a cultural arrangement,

< 171 >

historicism is severely pressured when the idea of capital is exception-
ally dynamic, or when the economic genre itself becomes sublime,
that is, "a finality of antifinality and a pleasure of pain" (consumerism),
which produces for many an unreal sense of "history."[2]

In taking up the historians' debate, Habermas does not pursue Saul
Friedlander's call "[for] a new style . . . to be introduced for the purpose of historical description . . . The duty of the historian may well
be to forgo the attempt to visualize, precisely so that he can fulfill his
task in terms of documentary precision and rendition of the events."[3]
On the contrary, Habermas does not waver in connecting historicization and visuality, a mode of classical German historiography in its concern with national, monumental narrations. For Habermas, the visual
anchor between narrativity, the "Final Solution," and the present is
secured in the following way:

> Today the grandchildren of those who at the close of World War II
> . . . are already growing up. Memory . . . has not become corre-
> spondingly distantiated. Contemporary history remains fixated on
> the period between 1933 and 1945. It does not move beyond the
> horizon of its own life-history; it remains tied up in sensitivities and
> reactions that . . . still always have the same point of departure: *the
> images of that unloading ramp at Auschwitz. This traumatic refusal
> to pass away of a moral imperfect past tense that has been burned
> into our national history entered the consciousness of the general
> population only in the 1980s.*[4] (my italics)

Time here "does not move"; it is sutured to a present urgency, an
intense identity between past and present. What happened then is
embedded in a continuity of not-forgetting: the sense of "has been
burned," the "traumatic refusal." These luxurious synecdoches (*pace*
Hayden White) of pain have not blended with an "objective past." Privileged is the psychological dimension, designated as the "traumatic refusal," the inability to engage with unacceptable images.[5] The "landing-ramp" at Auschwitz which "burns" is the result of the assertive
force of a statement which does not want to be challenged in the creation of a philosophy of history; it is the *universality of inclusive traditions,* established by the imposition of psychologically negative continuities on all levels of contemporary German relations.

Past and memory are thus secondary to psychological projections
which count in the present or hold accountable the writings of culturally engaged German historians. The time-continuum accessed by psy-

chological trauma is treated as a universal and national fact, as the substance of psychological judgments. In Habermas' terminology, "national histories" are treated as unproblematical extensions of individual feelings, and such psychology legitimizes enlightened politics. Entailed in Habermas' *New Conservatism* is that there can be no really enlightened society or nation until the melancholy of the survivors is recognized as determining that "the survival of all of us stand[s] under the *curse,* in attenuated form, of having merely escaped . . . an intersubjective liability . . . for distorted life circumstances."[6] This curse renders identity negative at least and thereby offsets a society which day by day becomes more fractured in terms of capitalist dynamics. Habermas seems unaware here that the philosophy of history is itself an "exceptional" relation of capitalist society.[7]

This psychological *result* ("curse") makes up the substance of a new historical consciousness of the "Final Solution." But it unfortunately involves regression to the level of an invoked organic form, here in the shape of an unreflective use of the term *milieu:* "Our own life is linked to the life context in which Auschwitz was possible not by contingent circumstances but intrinsically. Our form of life is connected with that of our parents and grandparents . . . through a historical milieu that made us what and who we are today. None of us can escape this milieu, because our identities, both as individuals and as Germans, are indissolubly interwoven with it . . . We have to stand by our traditions, then, if we do not want to disavow ourselves."[8] The "curse" which has fallen on the "people" becomes the "milieu" of an identity which occurred in the past but which must not be "disavowed"; the entity named "German" must retain its particularity, no matter what. This metapsychological curse may never be "reparable" but it can be "treated," as it were, by "historical reflection."

The aim, the rehistoricization of public life, supposes an engagement in collective "therapy" for a curse asserted as the form of German collectivity. The treatment of this curse is one of the proper activities for intellectuals and artists and for future intellectual-political involvement, hence a (progressive) bureaucratization of a cultural problematic (finding the proper therapies).

There is thus an *irreversible* demand made by Habermas, directed against what Peter Sloterdijk has called the "radical ironization of ethics and social convention . . . as if the general laws were only meant for the stupid."[9] That is, Habermas proposes the reinvention of a national life controlled by a "gaze educated by the moral catastrophe" and precluding the fragmentation that Sloterdijk says is irresistible.[10] In place of ordinary "history" it entails an extraordinary liability and a psychologically based moral economy, a mixture of law and ethics by which to dissolve a past which blocks "our path like a locked door." Habermas has created a cultural machine: it combines psychology with a progressive political agenda anchored in Marx and Freud and restricts the role of intellectuals to preparations for enlightenment, wherein "our cognitive meanings, moral expectations, subjective expressions and evaluations must relate to one another."[11] In the face of the shatterings performed by the "Final Solution" on value, on meaning, on law, the category of intellectual is severed from any possible antimodernity. One could read *The New Conservatism* as the state-building exclusion of those who would disavow enlightenment.

Habermas imposes unquestioned notions of German identity like "our national life" on every German, a contemporary version of the burdened will:[12] the past experienced as perpetual sadness. Present Germans, of every generation it seems, have yet to "synthesize the initially competing images of the good and the bad parents into complex images of the *same* person . . . The weak ego acquires its strength only through nonselective interaction with an ambivalent environment."[13] Or again: "In adults the need to defuse the corresponding cognitive dissonances is still alive." The projection of these needs, of a speculative faculty of psychic synthesis, necessitates a language which can detect the satisfaction and frustration of needs. The reference of course is to the "ideal speech situation," which would ensure the survival of what Habermas calls "the supply of motivation and meaning" to limit illicit power plays and "merge elements of public education, social welfare, liberalized punishment, and therapy for mental illness."[14] Thus the German dilemma of a "corrupted effective history" requires the merging of critical therapy and its grafting to redemptive reflection so as "to reclaim encumbered traditions."[15] The "Final Solution" can now release a doubly critical usefulness for Germans and for everyone. It serves as the litmus test of one's current "reflexive, scrutinizing attitude toward one's own identity-forming traditions" and it thus *de-problematizes* contemporary relations, which cannot properly be taken up until the "Final Solution" is resolved by a historico-therapeutic model.

To summarize: Historicism writes the meaning of the date and name

"Final Solution," 1942–1945. The result of the "Final Solution" is the "curse" which does not end. The "Final Solution" is at once the origin of a contemporary burden of reconciliation—the "blocked door" between present and past—and the substance of a collective critical self-examination mirrored in a universal uniqueness of Germany now: "No one can take our place in the liability required of us."[16] Thus, the Germans receive the archaic Hegelian category of an *unacceptable identity*, where the cultural force of religion, philosophy, and sociology has now given way to psychology.

Just as *The New Conservatism* asserts that there are no grounds for normalization of the "Final Solution," it emphasizes that there are no convincing grounds for the formation of a postenlightenment social critique. As neoconservatism practices moral neutralization of the "Final Solution," so too contemporary dissident critics are represented as revealing an attitude of fundamentalism in not accepting the model of "a society based on communication . . . limited to the formal aspects of an undamaged subjectivity."[17]

Habermas ties together the neoconservatives of historical normalization and the postmodernist critique of the West. The repressive integration of the former (with its stress on normalization of tradition) and the deconstructive pragmatism of the latter (its dystopian force) are linked by their rejection of modernity, by their having fallen into "one-sided" perspectives. To Habermas, the neoconservative's reliance on tradition and the postmodernist rejection of diagnostic thinking constantly press in on enlightenment. This judgment repeats Freud's gesture of calling psychoanalysis a discipline under attack. Habermas cannot lose in a politics based on psychological needs which no "mere" critique of politics is allowed to affect.

It is crucial to note that where the exception of the "Final Solution" offered opportunities for cultural learning, contemporary capitalism is presented as virtually normal in terms of its determination of social contradictions. Just as the memory of the "Final Solution" allows for *no break* concerning "our more sinister traditions,"[18] or negative continuity, there is *no break* from capitalism, which receives an affirmative continuity: "reformed conditions of employment retain a position of central importance."[19] Capitalism is acknowledged to be a source of crisis, but in a telling phrase, Habermas says that the goal of capitalism—as of the welfare state—"is the establishment of forms of life that are structured in an egalitarian way and that at the same time open up arenas for individual self-realization and spontaneity," a goal that saves the possibility of a finality in which "hope" is directive and willed, and damns only the means of the "legal and administrative . . . practice of normalization and surveillance."[20]

The exceptionality of the "Final Solution" is anchored to the nonexceptionality of capitalism. That capitalism should be given the capacity to provide for "a higher level of reflection," as Habermas puts it in "The New Obscurity," is disturbing. Why is capitalism—which makes mincemeat of real argumentation by its homogenization of signifiers, not accomplished, for example, by the media's excessive displacement of analysis or the marginalization of unfamiliar cultural and social voices—rendered more critically?[21] There are disjunctions between capitalism and democracy that are not raised by Habermas. Why is the economic mode so accepted in the first place? Why is criticism so often an opposition by exclusion? Why is there so much repetition by the same political players? What is not forgiven in the "historical" sphere is barely criticized in terms of the sphere of living social entanglements. Habermas' interest in the cognitive *control of dissidence* is ominous, since those who argue for any "normalization" of the "Final Solution" are lumped with those who make up the new "antiproductivist alliance." We are told that "the old and the young, women and the unemployed, gays and the handicapped, believers and nonbelievers" might reject a "productivist vision of progress that the legitimists [of capital and the welfare state] share with the neoconservatives."[22] This semiotic "machine" aims at cultural transcendence: the rationalization of the irreversibility of the power of capitalism to clear away what limits it. The intellectual's role can only be that of smoothing the effects of being reactive in the first place.

Finally, the parallel between the "exceptionality" of the "Final Solution" and the crisis of contemporary capitalism is that both have a similar referent: learning, enlightenment, reflection. Habermas' language targets the category of the dissident—those who argue for the normality of the "Final Solution" (neoconservatives) and those who argue for the impossibility of reflection as adequate to contest capital (the young conservatives, whom Habermas equates with postmodernism). The former do not accept a "detached understanding [which] liberates the power of reflective remembrance and thus extends the possibilities for dealing autonomously with an ambivalent tradition,"[23] whereas those who reject liberation *within* capitalism are said to deny a "reflection and steering" which means rejecting the new utopia of communication—"the formal aspects of an undamaged subjectivity," the "democratic generalization of interest positions and a universalist justification of norms."[24] The realized nihilism of capitalism is thus displaced, just as speculative psychology presents every German for whom the "Final Solution" was not an experience with a "need" to reflect on it. Of course one wants to see a "sensitized" youth, but also many dissident ones!

In sum, *The New Conservatism* contributes to the debate on the "Final Solution" by setting aside the repeated crises of modernity insofar as they are not allowed to call enlightenment and critique into question.[25] The image of the landing-ramp at Auschwitz carries an enormous cultural-political agenda, but it does so through the language of psychological historicism, which gives present-day progressive audiences a stable cultural anchor.

Lyotard's Notion of Dispossession

The intellectual context for Lyotard's consideration of names and images attending to the "Final Solution" is writings where Western historicism (*Postmodern Condition*) and philosophy (*The Differend*) based upon a Hegel-Marx-Freud conjunction such as the acceptance of speculative dialectics have been challenged by what G. Bennington calls a Kantian move: language thought of and employed as "the origin" of history and not a result of it.[26] Here it seems impossible fully to reduce some modernist processes to the language games of critical practice. Interpretation is challenged by Lyotard's version of pragmatism, which tries to *listen* to events, objects, and texts instead of interpreting them according to a preexisting script. Criticism and art-making are linked by activating differences instead of by synthesizing consequences.

Dispossession has a number of senses, but it commonly refers to events which prevent consciousness from being the subject of traditions, disciplines, and interpretations. The disseizure through insight, a person's refusal to agree with an oedipalizing evaluation, a painting's ability to frustrate one's subjective expectations, the momentary appearance of the sublime, are examples of dispossession. An "it happens" is momentarily unconnected to acts of thought, to what has "already been thought, written, painted in order to determine what hasn't been." Dispossession is antithetical to phenomenologies of meaning, including the ascription of "formal commonalities that are constitutive for reaching any understanding at all." [27]

Criticism is often the epitome of such possessive seizure, insofar as it promises the form of answer for problematical phenomena. Unlike sociological and historicizing criticism, "dispossession" opens onto what "remains to be determined, something that hasn't been determined before." [28] One is not dealing with absence and nothingness in which a relation is thought to lack meanings to be restored—as in psychoanalysis[29]—but with "disarming all grasping intelligence": a "protection of the occurrence 'before' defending it, by illustration of commentary" shifts cognition from its fanatical dependency on representations to experiences which may be without reason. [30] Modernity may itself be theorized as "dispossessive" insofar as more and more segments of it are "ruled" by aleatory factors.

"No consistent symbols" is the way Lyotard puts it in considering the systematic suspension of identification, including its negative variety (for instance, Adorno's aesthetic theory with its notion of art as a "martyred witness" to suffering). [31] In arguments from "Freud According to Cézanne," "dispossession" is aimed against the privileged representation of tragedy, against the machinery for the elaboration of Oedipus. Oedipalized paintings, for example, lodged in the space of a "hallucinatory representation and deception" and subject to the truth value of psychoanalytic statements, allow for an audience's desire to achieve identification and the release of an "incitement premium." Such works are believed to raise "the barriers of repression." Dispossession, on the other hand, would construe painting, in this case, "to be itself an object, to be no longer a message, threat, beseechment, defense, exorcism, lesson or allusion in a symbolic relation, but rather an absolute object, delivered of transferential relation, indifferent to the order of relations, active only in the order of energies, in the silence of the body . . . Both desire and the fascinated gaze are spurned." [32] Dispossession refers to practices wherein objects do not symbolize: they do not connect desire and history or desire and sociality, but instead allow for an *exteriorization* of force which sidesteps the collective sociological ego. [33] Seurat's *Grande Jatte* as described by Tim Clark is an instance where extremes of pleasure and pain suspend any one interpretation to be everyone's narrative. When dispossession is active, according to Lyotard, it modernizes: any "Final Solution" which presents itself as the way to achieve an artistic goal or social end or verbal consensus is suspended.

In the matter of language, dispossession is enacted as the "differend," part of which is familiar in everyday life as the expression "perhaps" which interrupts (and departs from) a conversation, and part of which is revealed in epistemic uncertainty concerning what J. Tagg has called "grounds of dispute" where consensus worsens our pragmatic ability to think of interesting ideas. As the differend, dispossession will be like the "unstable state and instant of language wherein something which must be able to be put into phrases cannot yet be."[34] Silence, vague feelings, pausing, postponements, refusals to judge even the most "obvious" of errors and faults, and constant delay in affixing names situate "phrasing" within a virtual bind of (1) the "impossibility of indifference" and (2) the "absence of a universal genre of discourse to regulate [events]."[35] One is always making phrases which are incomplete; there is always surplus of content and form, constrained by "the social," but it is capitalism which is not bound by phrases. For Lyotard, nothing could be more "dispossessive" than capitalism's reduction of other modes of becoming, the binding of language to economy and not to an expansion of things to say.

The concept of dispossession as differend implies that the "Final Solution" cannot be entirely cognized by phrases, a point that is exploited by "revisionists" such as Faurisson, who deny its having taken place. But the issue is less one of truth than one of the nature of the wrong and its silence. The most forceful problematic is whether the "Final Solution" can be "phrased" in the register of a *result* of German or Western history. Habermas' nonspeculative use of a speculative model—"our sinister traditions"—encodes speculation through psychology, which for Lyotard misses the point about the "Final Solution" as a differend.[36] The coupling "speculation/result" would anchor consciousness in a social determination from which there would be no more phrases: the criminal state, the terror of racism, satisfactions of the psychological formation of modernity. In short, the notion of dispossession makes it more difficult for any of us to stabilize the proper names of the causality of the "Final Solution."

The Differend evades the overcoded Hegelian straitjacket of speculative determinations. The incessant integration of negative universals is set aside. Auschwitz "would be the proper name of a para-

experience or even of a destruction of experience" rather than Habermas' "pluperfect past that will not pass away." The latter is based upon a model of "continuities of German history," the "sinister traditions" mentioned above.[37] For Lyotard, the "continuities" of the "sinister" are too remote from events, since the phrase structure of the death camps annihilated the phrase *we* amidst the "solitude and silence" of the victims. The question is not whether a "sinister tradition" was "revived" from the past (which was then never "past"), but how to express "shame and anger over the explanations and interpretations—as sophisticated as they may be—by thinkers who claim to have found sense to this shit."[38] The conflict is between a historicization of the "Final Solution" *for the present* and what can be said now to resist such historicization. What is called into question is the ability of any representational system to erect what Karl Bohrer has called a "falsely objectified tradition" that blocks the articulation of a heterogenous past *and* present.[39]

Lyotard asks us to imagine that a cultural formula for "Auschwitz" as thought by Nazi phrasing is like this: "It is a norm decreed by y that it is obligatory for x to die," and that this death has no sociality left to it, since it is not a question of there having been alternatives such as options, discussions, reasons, or even rationalizations; the formula manifests an unmodalized "you must die," which entails "your right to life is not recognized" and because of this structure there is no *after* reason to the event. The Nazis practiced a countersemiotic: their speaking, phrasing, is not something we can restore in a form which answers our "why" questions, regardless of survivors' and critics' "recountings of all kinds."[40] *There having been no norm fulfilled or satisfied by the individual deaths of the "Final Solution,"* their death destroyed even the proper name of death; in this sense, "Auschwitz is the forbiddance of the beautiful death . . . The canonical formula of 'Auschwitz' . . . would be, if we focus on the SS as 'legislator': That s/he die, I decree it; or, if we focus on the deportee as the one 'obligated': That I die, s/he decrees it. The authority of the SS comes out of a we from which the deportee is excepted once and for all: the race, which grants not only the right to command, but also the right to live, that is, to place oneself at the various instances of a phrase universe."[41]

No action by a Jew was even differentiating: they were caught by the other's narration in a place within that narration which annulled existence a priori. They were dead within the SS narrative; and the murder committed by Nazi stories "dispossesses" our attempts at analyzing Nazi psyche and culture.[42]

What happened to make Auschwitz occur was thus dispossessed in its very doing. Nazism shares this dangerous feature with other, even progressive events of modernity—a generalized "dismantling of the bastion of signification."[43] There is no room here for a Habermasian "history of the German People"; the event in question was itself a conjunction between a racist phrase regimen and an institutionalization of the type SS. There are no continuous links to the present. Instead of retaining general terms like *history,* Lyotard's countermodel "dispossesses" positive and negative histories based on either the psychologization of "becoming-normal again" (Nolte and others) or on Habermas' "exceptionalism," which relies on the psychology of debt and curse.

So the encoding of the "Final Solution" was itself a masterwork of death to language. Jews and others were not ordered to die according to the "logic" of SS "discourse" or because of something "in" German history. They did not have the "right to life" in the first place, since the racialist narrative was precisely that which decreed, "Death is legitimate because one's life is illegitimate." In such thinking, serial numbers "naturally" replaced individual names, a "desire" which takes the SS into a metaphysics: "This death must therefore be killed, and that is what is worse than death. For, if death can be exterminated, it is because there is nothing to kill. Not even the name Jew."[44] There is no pseudolegitimation from the SS by which we can access their "unconscious," for there is no point at which Nazi and Jew intersect in a manner that would establish figures of identity or even disidentity. As Lyotard puts it: "Dispersion is at its height. My law kills them who have no relevance to it. My death is due to their law, to which I owe nothing. Delegitimation is complete."[45] Is the absolute reactivity of the victims at Auschwitz not modern?

Frighteningly dispersive, negative, and analytic—just as racist thinking is intellectually anti-intellectual—the machine set in motion by the Nazis engenders no room for critical thinking to come along and make sense. The insistence upon memory and the cultural obligation to transmit knowledge to "youth" are only reactive formations *for ourselves.* It becomes precisely impossible to derive a generalization of the effect which Freud called *Nachträglichkeit,* where a past has not "passed" but continues to work within a future-present toward the presentation of a decisive "that's it." Given the "dispossession" which obtains between the phrase universe of the Nazi and the objectless non-subjectivity of the Jew, the only connection between them would be that of myth (including psychoanalytic myth, which establishes negative "mirroring" or "disidentification" or psychosis between Nazi and victim). The Nazi as the "failed child" and the victim as the "trapped infant" could only refer to our fantasy of symbolizing and appropriating some cultural use-value for ourselves, whose narcissism lies in continuing to pretend that there is sense.

What sense of history is applicable then? The landing-ramp at Auschwitz gives an image of the fright experienced by victims. The power and horror of the image is such that it is directed at those in the present who would "forget." But from the perspective of "dispossession," Nazism does not signify or represent events reducible to a factual consensus for cultural politics. This precludes any "general history of Germany and Nazism," as Nazi murder was a superstition revealing no "universal" whatsoever (not even one concerning mass psychology), and its victims experienced nothing by which we, now, can narrate what their deaths were "sacrifices for." Stripped of the positivity which results from such extreme negativity, bereft of Hegelianism, Nazism reaches us in a manner that makes it impossible to be sure which concepts *really apply* to those events. In such a feelingscape, instead of postulating curses and landing-ramps and liabilities, it would be better to maintain skepticism.

So where is the concrete linkage between present-day Germans and the Aryan savage narrative? How is it possible that present-day Germans born after the collapse of Nazism and who are not racist have to come to terms with the supposed "past that will not go away," as Habermas insists? Is it to be supposed that *all* Germans now, in practicing "historical remembrance," are potential racists? And if that is so, if the potentiality of racism is the referred yet exorcised part which actually informs Habermas' model of cultural criticism, then why doesn't *The New Conservatism* address that topic instead of putative "universals" of German history and culture?

In sum, Lyotard's workup of "dispossession" makes it possible to think of the "Final Solution" as an event that "devours names" instead of providing materials for historicizing.

Conclusion: Myth and Criticism

The savage narratives of Nazism are criticized by Habermas through the evocation of their criminality. It is doubtful whether Nazism is reducible to criminality, a category of law. It is wishful thinking to postulate law and its breaking as a foundation for understanding. Similarly, law and concepts of criminality will not help us address the question, why did the Americans drop *two* atomic bombs? Notions of criminality are not the issue and in fact signify an agenda of nostalgia—the criminal, after all, has been judged and society has, in that judgment, been vindicated.[46] Nazism made law irrelevant; the Nazis showed law to be an ambiguous formation within modernity. This implies that enlightenment after the fact can be inappropriate to what happened, as in the delusion that names enunciated "after the fact" have value. They may not. Habermas' landing-ramp at Auschwitz would culturally empower an Everyone to possess the "Final Solution" in a manner which renders it no longer argumentative, since the image and name of the landing-ramp operate a priori as object and limit on other images and, in fact, govern the power to image.

What does the phrase *German history* mean? Or *German people?* Or *German nation?* It is highly implausible that these terms stand for actualities other than formal ones. Modern capitalism is far too active in the register of splitting apart and recombining such "wholes." The reiteration of *German* smacks of a deictic mytheme, an overcoded cultural wish-projection. Habermas would set aside the false "normalization" of the "Final Solution," but at the same this negation of the false supposes the "true" belongs to a psychological "recognition"—which supposes "consensus" in the here and now by every "German." The landing-ramp at Auschwitz would be an encapsulating image. But there is no sense to the "Final Solution" which "reflection" can take hold of, apart from these overcharged psychologemes; if anything needs to be explained, it is not the epideictics or display of the Aryan "beautiful death" in which the Nazis projected making their name something immortal (one dies in order to have one's name live), but the contemporary language game(s) of psychological historicism.

Put another way, in the word conflicts over the "Final Solution," Habermas practices a dangerous game: he does not see that modern capitalism may be "dispossessive" of the very "reason" he wants to establish. On the one hand, a term such as *German* or *reflection* or *life-*

context is intended to convey certain socially and linguistically negative continuities when connected to the "exceptional" aspects of the
"Final Solution" ("our sinister traditions"). These overcharged terms
are also connected to an affirmative predicate—mourning, remembrance, and "detached philosophical thinking"—an amalgam intended
to signify an enlightened perspective. There is thus a negative and
positive of "continuity." But this enlightenment turns out to be an affirmation of myth, where the West is defined in empty terms and where
every cultural or political move which is not enlightened is negated.
The affirmative myth-judgment concerning the West as a model of positivity obscures the counterjudgment that capitalism is not aligned,
safely, with "fundamental liberalization."

Because Habermas does not consider capitalism to share the
semantic-real space of irrationality, he rejects the so-called young conservatives (postmodernists) as antirational and antimodern, and hence
approximate Nazis. It seems to me that if Habermas were to consider
capitalism within the semantic orb of criminality he would wish to dis-
mantle the construction of the "Final Solution" as an event of both
"exceptionality" *and* "learning"—because to acknowledge the "civilized nihilism" or the "acceptable criminality" of capitalism would
mean a nonmediated encounter with *facts of the present.*

As opposed to Habermas' endeavors to salvage modernity—no matter how evil and criminal—Lyotard's treatment of Nazi phrasing suggests that the "Final Solution" is not intrinsically attached to any "historical" mode of comprehension. It is our Western narcissism which
conflates modernity and present, present and "history." Dispossession
and the concept of the differend remind us that modernity is not itself
a necessarily "historical" phenomenon. An analysis of the ambivalences and dangers built into modernity (for example, the "normal"
asociality of capitalism) might show that the "Final Solution" pushed
its own dispossession beyond limit, beyond "speculative dialectics," by
its connection to a mythic narrative which, paradoxically, resulted in
"Silences, instead of a *Resultat.*" The real fright concerning modernity
is that it still expands in the political and social-economic spheres while
in the cultural and critical spheres it is trapped by premodern belief
formations.

< 12 >

Science, Modernity, and the "Final Solution"

Mario Biagioli

A number of publications in German and English have begun to fill a conspicuous gap in the historiography of German medicine and life sciences in the Nazi period, and recent debates on the use of scientific data from Nazi experiments on camp prisoners have spread the discussion among nonspecialists.[1]

Some narratives on Nazi medicine and life sciences offer well-documented analyses not only of Nazi medical crimes—events that began to emerge at the Nuremberg and Frankfurt trials—but also of the role played by doctors as a professional body in the scientific justification, development, and implementation of Nazi racial policies from the beginning of the Nazi regime until the so-called Final Solution. However, most of these works tend (in various ways and to different extents) to present Nazi scientific practices as a major anomaly within the history of science.

Although the modalities of this bracketing vary in relation to the historian's professional, national, ethnic, and political background, they seem to share a common denominator in that they generally reflect an essentially positive view of science, one which stands in the way of recognizing what some Nazi doctors did as "science." Such a representation of science seems to reflect not only appreciation of the cognitive effectiveness of scientific method but also a belief in the symbiosis between science and the values of modernity as expressed in the culture of Western democracy.

The belief in this symbiosis goes back to the Enlightenment and reemerged very conspicuously during World War II when both science and democracy were perceived by non-German analysts as being seriously threatened. Writing in 1942, the American sociologist of science Robert Merton presented a normative view of the social system of science as a mirror image of a Western capitalistic democracy organized around the principle of a competitive free market.[2] In those years, the

< 185 >

nexus between "good" society and "good" science was stressed also by two British Marxist scientists and historians of science, John Bernal in 1939 and Joseph Needham in 1941.[3] Although Bernal and Needham probably would have disagreed with Merton on what a "good" society should look like, they all shared the belief that the same rationality that produced "good" science was that which produced politically just social structures.[4] With the partial exception of Bernal, these authors also suggested that bad science (and the Nazi example must have been in their minds) was the result of external influences rather than of dynamics inherent in science itself.[5]

As shown by most interpretations of Nazi medicine written in the 1980s and by some histories of Nazi physicists, authors who believe in the symbiosis between the values of modernity and those of science are caught in a bind. Admitting that Nazi science (including experimentation on humans) was a form of science rather than its aberration would automatically proliferate into a questioning of their beliefs not only in science but also in modernity and its values.[6]

Because it is both about the Holocaust and about science, the history of the role of German life sciences in the Final Solution shares in the thorny historiographical problems both of the Holocaust and of science. As shown by the recent "historians' debate," Holocaust scholars are struggling with the interpretive problems posed by an event like the Final Solution, which took place within the framework of modernity and yet seemed to subvert all the values commonly associated with that culture. On the other hand, recent studies of science have developed increasingly complex views of scientific change that are exposing the tensions in what was previously perceived as the unproblematic and mutually reinforcing link between the culture and historical development of science and modernity. What follows is an attempt to locate some of the problems of writing the history of Nazi science in the concentration camps within the problematic space framed by the intersection of the post-Kuhnian debate in science studies and the so-called historians' debate.

Bracketing Nazi Science

Perhaps the most common bracketing device displayed by recent histories of Nazi medicine is the shift from talking about science to talking about scientists. As one can guess from the title, Michael Kater's very recent *Doctors under Hitler* (like Beyerchen's older *Scientists under*

Hitler or Lifton's *Nazi Doctors*) is an exemplar of this type of historiography. Kater does not claim to be a professional historian of science or medicine and, in fact, his other well-known book is a prosopographical analysis of Nazi party leadership. Consequently, *Doctors under Hitler* does not focus primarily on medical theories and practices of German medicine during National Socialism but rather produces a very detailed, biography-oriented, sociopolitical history of the medical profession under Nazi rule. Because of his ethical stance and his relative lack of interest in the technical dimensions of the history of medicine, Kater believes that any assessment of the scientific content of Nazi medicine would be completely pointless: "It is my contention that these ethical violations by themselves were sufficient to discount any nominal progress that might have been accomplished by the profession . . . for ethics supersedes all considerations."[7]

Both in the book and in articles, Kater states his view that Nazi medicine was not real medicine but an incomprehensible perversion of it.[8] In his most recent work, he suggests that Nazi medicine deviated from proper medical practice because of its uncritical adoption of the method of the physical sciences. According to Kater, this methodological borrowing led to an extreme objectification of the patient and to the alienation of the doctors from their commitment to healing. Eventually, these attitudes reacted in lethal ways with what he considers to have been irrational notions about race that had been injected into the medical students' curricula.[9]

Although Kater is well aware that a demonization of a few Nazi doctors would actually prevent a fuller historical understanding of the broader role of German physicians and medicine in the Final Solution, his suggestions about how to achieve such an understanding are still based on a perception that what some Nazi doctors did was incommensurable with normal medical practice.[10] By not questioning the very complex relationship between healing practices and medical research, or the processes through which notions that we now consider irrational were once regarded as scientifically legitimate and to be incorporated in medical curricula, Kater ends up in the paradoxical position of criticizing the demonization of Nazi doctors while, in practice, ruling out the analyses that may have avoided it.

Benno Müller-Hill is an accomplished German geneticist trained after World War II. Troubled by the silence his profession has systematically maintained on physicians' involvement in the Nazi regime and in the

Final Solution, Müller-Hill has produced a short but powerful book which presents a range of previously unpublished archival material and concludes with a long series of probing interviews with a few former Nazi doctors or people close to them.

Müller-Hill's clear though somewhat unreflexive views on the history of the natural sciences are stated at the very beginning of the book: "The history of the natural sciences has two themes, one, the formation of their foundations, and the other, an account of their effects on society. Everyone who follows the calling of a natural scientist experiences pleasure, when his work is done, in studying the unfolding of knowledge in his science; it is a story both beautiful and true."[11]

Committed, as Müller-Hill is, to preserving the belief in the truth-finding character of the discipline he has successfully practiced for years, he claims that science may influence society but excludes the possibility that society may have any influence on science. Because of this purity-preserving, one-way influence between science and society he cannot, I think, blame the horrors of Nazi science on the social circumstances that may have corrupted it. Moreover, his belief in the truth-producing character of genetics seems to prevent him from considering that genetics may have been directly involved in the development of Nazi racial hygiene.

Consequently, he tries to argue that the culprit behind Nazi racial hygiene is not the "natural" science of genetics but the "soft" sciences of anthropology (or human genetics), psychiatry, and psychology which, because of their scientific "immaturity," misused real genetics in lethal ways: "In these sciences it is easy to think that only what is new is true. But when I think today of the story of how genetics was once put to use in anthropology and psychiatry, I see a wasteland of desolation and destruction . . . The recent history of these genetically oriented human sciences in action is full of chaos and crime as a nightmare."[12]

This strategy of disciplinary blame is played out throughout the book: the "soft" sciences are blamed for the disaster while the "natural" science of genetics is barely mentioned and never in any accusatory fashion.[13] Very similar views emerge also in one of his later articles: "It seems to me most revealing that so many German professors of psychiatry, anthropology or human genetics used their knowledge to have their clients mutilated or killed by others in the name of science. This and the fact that they did not express remorse or guilt should have automatically made these sciences internationally suspect after the war. Sciences or arts whose members find it that easy to maim and to kill should be analysed very, very carefully for their content."[14]

Müller-Hill seems to think that the reason these "soft" sciences contributed to the Final Solution was because their practitioners were anxiously trying to get the recognition and power they could not gain through the low scientific status of their discipline: "What kind of position did anthropologists and psychiatrists hold in National Socialist society? They had no power. Yet as scientists, they helped by justifying robbery and murder. They gave a scientific gloss and tidiness to the Nazi programme."[15] In other words, they sold their scientific soul to the Nazis to fulfill their frustrated scientific ambitions by other means.[16] As Müller-Hill puts it, "Finally they were respected as the experts they were to straighten out the problems of workers, soldiers, and murderers alike."[17]

However, Müller-Hill's intricate attempt to save "good" science through the selective scapegoating of "bad" scientific disciplines runs aground soon. In fact, the modern taxonomy of scientific disciplines in which he roots his strategy does not match the disciplinary scenario of the Nazi period.[18] Moreover, the involvement of geneticists in racial hygiene was institutional as well as scientific. Most of the members of the *Beirat für Rassenhygiene*—the first official German institution for eugenics and racial hygiene—established by the Prussian Ministry of Public Welfare as early as May 1920 were geneticists. And geneticists were those who lobbied for an increasingly stronger relationship between eugenics and social policies in the interwar period—contributing to setting the stage for the events that led to the Final Solution.[19]

The bracketing of Nazi medicine one finds in Robert Jay Lifton's *Nazi Doctors* is less intricate than Müller-Hill's, but its methodological and ethical consequences are more complex.[20] Lifton sees Nazi doctors as having subverted medicine from a practice of healing (to which he thinks doctors should be bound by the Hippocratic oath) to a science of killing. Lifton's bracketing of Nazi medicine is global. Nazi medicine was not just corrupted: it was inverted.[21]

Different from Kater and others who see Nazi medicine as plagued by perversions beyond comprehension, Lifton's perception of it as the inversion of normal medicine allows him to keep an ethical distance between himself (a Jew and a healer) and the Nazi medical killers. At the same time, this view gives him a framework within which to study the phenomenon of Nazi medicine. In fact, a phenomenon that is the opposite of the norm can be better grasped than a random aberration. At the same time, seeing Nazi medicine as the opposite of what he takes medicine (and his own practice as a doctor) to be allows him to have some sort of "inverted empathy" that proves important to his study.

It is not that Lifton becomes empathetic with the Nazi doctors he studies.[22] Rather, his "method of inversion" allows him not to feel "polluted" by trying to figure out the thoughts and motives of a Mengele. In fact, by representing them as being precisely the opposite of his own, he rules out any possibility for complicity. Yet, by "inverting" his own thoughts, he also seems to gain some access to Mengele's mentality. Basically, Lifton perceives Auschwitz as a hospital upside down.

Let me give an example of the workings of this method. At one point Lifton writes that "Mengele was relentless in tracking down Gypsies, especially children, who tried to escape their fate. Though the assumption [for Mengele's research on Gypsies] was factually wrong, its psychic truth lay in Mengele's inexorable commitment to the Nazi principle of murder-selection."[23]

Lifton begins by stating that Mengele's research was unscientific— and this would be where Kater and others who see Nazi medicine as an incomprehensible aberration would probably end their analyses. However, he then takes a next step and talks about the "psychic truth" of Mengele's behavior, one that he does not relate to principles of ethically and scientifically acceptable medicine but rather to a "negative axiom," that is, to the Nazi inversion of the Hippocratic oath into a commitment to killing.

Not every sentence of the book reflects this "method of inversion." Nevertheless, this overarching belief allows Lifton to go further than most other historians of Nazi medicine. His reflections on the psychological dimensions of the process of socialization of the doctors in the "Auschwitz system" reflects a methodological stance that gives visibility to the institutional conditions that triggered the inversion from healers to killers.[24]

Although Lifton tends to be either critical or dismissive about the cognitive relevance of the science produced by the Nazi doctors in the camps, he does report the favorable comments on the soundness of Mengele's scientific method he has received during interviews with survivors like Doctor Teresa W.[25] For comparison, similar views on Mengele expressed by his Jewish captive assistant Miklos Nyiszli moved Bruno Bettelheim to warn the reader of their problematicity. In his preface to Nyiszli's autobiography he writes, "How Dr. Nyiszli fooled himself can be seen, for example, in his repeatedly referring to his work as a doctor, though he worked as the assistant of a vicious criminal. He speaks of the Institute for Race, Biological and Anthropological Investigation as 'one of the most qualified medical centers of the Third Reich' though it was devoted to proving falsehoods."[26]

I believe that Lifton's judgment on the scientific work conducted at the institute of von Verschuer (Mengele's mentor and the recipient of the human material resulting from his experiments at Auschwitz) would not be different from Bettelheim's. However, Lifton—like any psychiatrist who does not need to state continuously his/her distance from the patient's delusions or dreams—would not feel compelled to back away so explicitly from Nyiszli's beliefs. Lifton's "method of inversion" grants him some ethical leeway for interpretation.[27]

For all the interesting aspects of Lifton's bracketing of Nazi science, his approach rests, I think, on assumptions that are historically problematic. My perplexities are not so much about his almost exclusive emphasis on the institutional-psychological processes through which normal physicians were inverted into killers within and by the Auschwitz system (an approach that pays minimal attention to the role that received theories of racial hygiene may have played in this inversion). What I find more problematic is the introduction of a historically unwarranted inversion between healers and killers as a way of demarcating normal medicine from the practices of the Nazi doctors.

A number of social histories of ancient medicine have indicated that the Hippocratic oath was not really a universal norm but an idealized, self-legitimizing representation of an emerging profession.[28] Although Lifton's endorsement of it as an inviolable norm speaks to his credit as a physician, the history of medicine indicates that the distinction between healers and killers is far from being so clear-cut. I am not talking about individual doctors that have killed patients because of incompetence, but about the problematic yet intimate relationship between healing and the dangers inherent to research[29] or to the social role of medical institutions—a relationship that, as shown by recent historiography of medicine, incorporates both healing and social control.

Consequently, Lifton's idealization of "normal" doctors and his representation of Nazi doctors as their negative image works a bit as an exorcism of the problematic aspects of "normal" medicine as displayed by its history. At the Nuremberg trial, the defense lawyers for the Nazi doctors were able to produce a list of fifty-three non-Nazi publications reporting human experiments on convicts, immigrants, invalids, children, soldiers, nurses, and sanitation employees.[30] Seventy percent of these articles did not mention the subjects' consent, and some of them referred to experiments conducted in the United States at the beginning of the century.[31]

Although the discourse of the Nuremberg defendants is very problematic in that it tries to present as unproblematic scientific practices that do not need to be accepted as such, it nevertheless exposes the myth of origins at the base of Lifton's views of medicine—a myth that prevents "normal" medical science from being seen as implicated in the Final Solution.

Experimentation on humans in the concentration camps and the Nazi doctors' role in the Final Solution are not the specific focus of Robert Proctor's *Racial Hygiene*, which instead is concerned with tracing the pre-Nazi development of theories of racial hygiene and the successive symbiosis between Nazi political culture and medicine.

A distinctive feature of Proctor's work (and one that I fully endorse) is that it represents the disastrous results of Nazi racial hygiene as historically exceptional but does not analyze the processes that led to those results as if they were unique. In his work, Nazi medicine is not bracketed off from the history of science but is analyzed as an example of how—in a certain sociohistorical context—the interaction between science and power led (and therefore could still lead) to unprecedented crimes.

Although there are important overlaps between his book and both Müller-Hill's and Kater's in terms of information, the picture presented here is not that of the "nazification" of German medicine, genetics, psychiatry, and anthropology but that of a full interaction and mutual reinforcement between Nazi politics and German life sciences. Proctor's narrative is neither about politics invading or perverting science (as is the case with Kater and Beyerchen) nor about a minority of power-hungry and genetics-ignorant physicians, anthropologists, and psychiatrists who fed the Nazis with racial myths in exchange for political recognition and power (as Müller-Hill has it).[32] Instead, Proctor suggests that the doctors were not nazified more than the Nazis were medicalized, and that this symbiosis was co-orchestrated by the top professionals in the medical sciences.[33]

By tracing the development and increasing popularity of theories of racial hygiene among German life scientists since the end of the nineteenth century, Proctor indicates that science set the stage for the Final Solution well before the arrival of National Socialism.[34] When the Nazis took over, the preexisting scientific discourse allowed the doctors to become the priests of the cult of the German blood as well as its medical keepers and the exterminators of its potential polluters. The symbiosis between Nazi politics and medicine seems to be rooted in the fact that they shared the same race-based "ontology." Race was the "natural" subject matter of medical science as well as the "natural" foundation for the German nation.[35]

However, Proctor does not present the collapse of the spheres of politics and science in Nazi Germany as implying that science and politics are always the same thing. His analysis suggests that the lethal symbiosis between science and politics that happened once in Germany under specific cultural and historical circumstances may or may not happen again depending on the structures of democratic management of science that are developed. In short, there are no safeguards in the scientific method or in scientific ethics to prevent such interplay from happening again.

Proctor does not present specific methodological parameters for sorting good from bad science. However, his analysis suggests that the least problematic option would be to make sure that each social constituency is democratically represented among scientific practitioners.[36] If one cannot define generally valid methodological rules to keep racist ideas out of science, at least one should make sure that people from social groups that may be affected by such views can be in positions to argue against them in the scientific arena.[37]

With the April 1933 Law for the Restoration of Civil Service, which excluded Jewish physicians from civil service in universities and health insurance companies, the Nazis (with the support of German doctors much eager to take over the jobs of the many Jewish practitioners) excluded from German medicine and science those who could have exposed its racist theories with scientific arguments. In a sense, Jews and other minorities became disempowered victims by being excluded from the scientific criticism of theories about them.

To Proctor, I think, camp science was bad science not because it represented an inverted image of normal science and healing medicine, but because it was a crime against humanity. As a result, Proctor does not focus—as Lifton does—on the Auschwitz microcosm to study the specific institutional and psychological processes that allowed for the inversion of physicians from healers to killers. To him, the key to understanding the role of the life sciences in the Final Solution (and to prevent it from happening again) is not so much in the reconstruction of what happened in the minds of the Nazi doctors operating in the camps or in the psychiatric hospitals, but in the fine mechanisms through which an accepted and respected scientific discourse allowed for the representation of certain ethnic and social groups as inferior and through which it legitimized (and was legitimized by) the culture of national socialism.

The Problems of "Normality" and "Exceptionality"

This brief survey seems to indicate the presence of certain homologies between the positions that have emerged from the debate over the history of Nazi science and those that have characterized the historians' debate. More specifically, the works of Kater, Müller-Hill, and Lifton could be seen as representing Nazi science as something exceptional or, at least, nonnormal. Proctor's approach, instead, may be perceived as arguing for the "normality" of the processes by which the discourse of racial hygiene became involved in the Final Solution. Because the debate over "normality" and "exceptionality" is central to the current discussions on the historical interpretation of the Final Solution, let me discuss and compare the meaning of these categories in recent science studies and in the historians' debate.

Since Thomas Kuhn's work, the field of history and philosophy of science has seen a steady increase in works that question representations of science as either a perfectly transparent and normal process structured by unproblematic rules or as a heroic quest for knowledge sometimes achieved through exceptional leaps of scientific genius. For instance, representations of science as a progressive, cumulative, and continuous enterprise and of scientific discoveries as "facts" routinely arrived at by scientists have been shown to be based on a fetishization of "facts" which renders invisible the complex processes through which facts are perceived and certified. Similarly, the notion of scientific genius is no longer viewed as an adequate interpretive category but as an opaque concept invoked in place of a careful empirical study of the nonexceptional processes that make scientific change possible.

Together with the questioning of both the reified normality of scientific progress and mythical exceptionality of scientific genius, recent analyses have also begun to perceive power as no longer external to science. Although there is considerable disagreement on the extent to which power is involved in the process of scientific production, historians, sociologists, and philosophers of science are paying increasing attention to the mechanisms through which science and power interact, modify, and legitimize each other.

The picture of science produced by post-Kuhnian science studies is that not of a methodologically or conceptually unified enterprise but of one that develops through a variety of context-specific negotiations. In a sense, this approach does not find exceptionality in science because no rigid norms are assumed about what science should concern or about how scientists should behave. This outlook does not mean that this historiographical approach denies the rationality of the scientific enterprise. It simply denies that the philosophers' reason should be used as an a priori, "master" category by which to assess (and normalize) the behavior and choices of the scientists under study. Paraphrasing Pierre Bourdieu, this approach may be called "fieldwork philosophy."[38]

Similarly, the distinction between common-sense knowledge and science is not placed within the distinction between opinion and truth but concerns ways common sense has been transformed into scientific thinking through specific educational, experimental, and institutional practices. In a sense, the post-Kuhnian project could be seen as the continuation of what Jack Goody outlined in his *Domesticization of the Savage Mind*—an analysis of the way literacy mediated the transition from so-called primitive mentalities to more recent forms of thinking.[39] As a result, the symbiosis between science and modernity is no longer perceived as a "natural" fact, but as a historically produced and mutually legitimizing representation of the development of both science and modernity.

But the understanding of the "normality" of science sought by recent science studies is not the "normality" that some participants in the historians' debate have predicated of the Final Solution. In fact, although science is being increasingly studied in its local expressions and "normal" everyday practices, the result is not a normalizing study. Here, contextualization does not mean "reduction to the context," because context is not treated as an absolute frame of reference for the evaluation of historical events "contained" by it. In a sense, the context itself is reinterpreted while interpreting the event that took place in it. Contrary to the type of historicism expounded by Nolte, the aim of this approach to the study of scientific change is to show how a specific context and specific scientific norms and ethos were constructed.[40]

From this point of view, the conflation of "analogy" and "explanation," or the use of context as a reservoir of analogies through which to normalize a given event, is a category mistake. To say, as Nolte does, that the horrors of the Final Solution are comparable to those of other massacres is a tendentious misuse of the explanatory features of analogy.[41] What is particularly problematic in Nolte's position is not the use of analogy per se, but the fact that he "naturalizes" his terms of comparison. His "explanation" rests on the tacit assumption that we should take for granted the massacres of modern history and that we should treat them as "facts" and employ them in explaining "similar" events. Consequently, he does not use analogy as a tool for a dialogical interpretation of an event and its context, but as a device by which two explananda (Stalin's and Hitler's massacres) are magically transformed into "normal facts."[42] In Nolte's hands, analogy becomes a cover-up device rather than a tool for "working-through."

However, the critique of normalization outlined here does not imply an endorsement of unqualified uses of the category of "exceptionality" in historical interpretations. Although I endorse Habermas' exposé of the neoconservative agenda of recent German historiographical revisionism, I cannot agree with his representation of the exceptionality of Auschwitz as a necessary component of the response to the recent re-emergence of conservative and nationalistic tendencies in Germany.[43] By stressing the exceptionality of the Final Solution, Habermas may be in fact doing more than just responding to the neoconservative agenda of Nolte and his cohorts. To Habermas, Auschwitz is not only an exceptional crime but also a devastating anomaly to his modernistic philosophical agenda based on the discourse of Enlightenment rationality. If we keep this perspective in mind, Habermas' emphatic claims of the exceptionality of the Holocaust can be also perceived as a sort of politico-philosophical exorcism.[44] In a sense, the strong negative reaction provoked by the extremity of Nolte's claims may have helped the perception of Habermas' emphasis on the exceptionality of the Final Solution as a politically correct move while hiding its exorcistic dimensions.

Following very different political agendas, Nolte and Habermas assess the normality or exceptionality of the Holocaust within the framework offered by the discourse of modernity. To Nolte, the Holocaust is not exceptional because it shares in the genealogy of other massacres of modern history. Habermas, instead, stresses the exceptionality of Auschwitz because he cannot fit it into his view of modernity rooted in a mythical representation of the discourse of the Enlightenment. In short, notions of "normality" and "exceptionality" as introduced in the historians' debate belong to a historiographical discourse that (in very different ways and with very different goals) tries to legitimize views of the present and of modernity. Some of these considerations can be transferred to the analysis of recent representations of Nazi science.

The bracketing of Nazi science found in the works of Kater, Lifton, and (to a lesser extent) Müller-Hill share in Habermas' attempt to prevent Enlightenment rationality and modernity from being perceived as involved in the Final Solution.[45] But there are also views of Nazi science that share in the methodology (though not in the political agenda) of Nolte's interpretation of the Final Solution. These positions are not present in the literature on Nazi science discussed above but have emerged in debates on the ethics of using data coming from the Nazi hypothermia experiments.[46]

According to these views, science is a value-free enterprise. As a result, the data one obtains during a research planned and executed according to the standard scientific method are "facts" whose epistemological status cannot be questioned on ethical grounds. The analogy with Nolte is that this position presents the fact-producing features of scientific method as a given in the same way that Nolte takes modernity and capitalism as facts (in the sense of something "natural") that, consequently, cannot be questioned. The homology is not accidental but reflects a specific strategy that tries to defend the symbiosis between science and modernity by making it unfalsifiable.

In this case, the relationship between science and modernity is not the idyllic type produced by Lifton and Kater (who reify the Hippocratic oath into some sort of social contract) or by Habermas' utopian vision of a society operating around the principles of "communicative action." Science and its method are here presented as something that is neutral, value-free, and cognitively effective rather than as the carrier of "good" values. In this case, the symbiosis between science and the culture of modernity develops from the representation of science as being value-free, rational, and objective. This is done by presenting science as "natural" and therefore "good" by virtue of being natural. In turn, the "naturalness" of science is supposed to warrant the inherent "naturalness" of modernity—a culture represented as having developed from that type of "natural" reasoning. Consequently, science and modernity are represented as sharing in the good value of being value-free. The oxymoron is, I think, telling.

From the representation of science as a value-free enterprise, it follows that if science falls into the wrong hands, then it may produce disasters. But such disastrous results are nevertheless scientific and, as such, do not refute the epistemological status of science. Similarly, Nolte presents capitalism and modernity as a given, an axiom of civilized life, something that is historically produced and yet "natural." Like science, the logic of capitalism and modernity have proven very effective—in this case by bringing about major social, cultural, and economic changes. But, precisely because of their being "value-free," the dynamics of modernity can lead to tragedy once they fall into the hands of people like Hitler or Stalin. Consequently, Nolte does not present these tragedies as something leading to the questioning of the status of modernity, but rather as very sad "facts." To him, the "epoch of fascism" is an unfortunate and yet unsurprising consequence of the industrial revolution.[47]

Paradoxically, the crimes of Nazi science end up "proving" the "objectivity" of science because they indicate that, unfortunately, scientific method—precisely because it is "neutral"—works also in the hands of criminals. Similarly, in Nolte's narrative, the Final Solution and Stalin's massacres "prove" that the dynamics of modernity are value-free (and therefore "natural"); they also prove that the tragedies of modernity are "normal," in the sense both that they could (and did) happen and that—by happening—they confirm that the dynamics of modernity are value-free. In the case both of Nolte and of those who argue for the cognitive "normality" of Nazi science, what could have been read as a devastating critique of received representations of modernity and science (and of their symbiosis) is turned into a confirmation of those representations—one that is particularly powerful precisely because it acknowledges (while normalizing) the possibility of "things taking a sad turn."

Through this brief comparison of the use of the terms *exceptionality* and *normality* in the historians' debate and in narratives about Nazi science, I have indicated the ways modernistic agendas have framed their meaning. Despite apparently radical differences, the view of science as inherently good (and thus of Nazi science as nonscience) and that of science as neutral (and thus of Nazi science as the historical proof of science's being value-free) belong to the same discourse and share in the same attempt to defend (in very different ways) the symbiosis between science and modernity. The belief in this symbiosis entails a very high risk because it can be maintained only by trivializing or denying visibility to the processes through which science became (and could again become) involved in events like the Final Solution.

Instead of arguing about the inherent neutrality or goodness of science and about the normality or exceptionality of Nazi science, I will try to break away from this modernistic framework and, by using some of the approaches developed by late twentieth-century science studies, look at science as a process. In fact, views of science as either neutral or good reflect a similar essential assumption: science is a "thing" that has the essential quality of being either good or neutral. Instead, I want to propose a few examples that present science as an activity, as something that is produced and that has been (and still is) produced in very different ways in different contexts.

Buchenwald's Division for Typhus and Virus Research

Ludwik Fleck's 1935 *Genesis and Development of a Scientific Fact* is probably the most important historiographical ancestor of the new science studies methodologies sketched earlier in this chapter and one that informed Kuhn's influential *Structure of Scientific Revolutions*.[48]

In 1946, Fleck published "Problems of the Science of Science," a short piece that presented an analysis of the scientific practices of the "Division for Typhus and Virus Research" at Buchenwald—a laboratory with which Fleck was associated as a captive collaborator from December 1943 to spring 1945.[49] The medical crimes committed on Buchenwald's Block 46 by Ding-Schuler—the director of the research laboratory at Block 50 with which Fleck was associated—were judged at the Nuremberg Trials.[50] In his study of Ding-Schuler's research program, Fleck does not focus on the experiments on humans but rather on the internal dynamics of the research laboratory.

Fleck's interest in these processes is connected to his theory about the ways scientific consensus is developed in interacting groups of scientific practitioners. To him, science is not a truth-producing enterprise, but one in which—because of a very specific sociological and institutional context—scientists "tune" their beliefs to those of their colleagues who share a similar "thought style." What distinguishes such a system of scientific beliefs from other forms of coherent beliefs is the quantity of "links" established among the objects studied by that group—what Fleck calls a "thought collective." Very schematically, what distinguishes a scientific from a nonscientific world view is not its coherence (for both can be equally coherent) but rather its "tightness"—the density of the relations (what Fleck calls active and passive links) it weaves around and between the objects it tries to know.

Fleck presents the "Division for Typhus and Virus Research" as an example of what happens when the sociological mechanisms responsible for the production of what he calls "the harmony of illusions" operate among people who do not share the same thought style, that is, among people who have not been socialized in the same scientific specialization and have not, for instance, learned to see the things they are supposed to see in preparations under the microscope. Although several of the captive participants in the Buchenwald research group had a medical background, they were not specialists in serology. In fact, none of the Buchenwald researchers had ever seen the germ of typhus (*Rickettsia prowazecki*) but relied on current scientific textbooks to learn how to see and manipulate it to produce vaccines.

The result was that, also under the pressure of the boss Ding-Schuler, the members of the group managed to "see" (in good faith) *Rickettsias* in preparations that contained other germs but not these. The researchers then developed a sophisticated system of beliefs which managed to explain the various anomalies that kept emerging.[51] Following this much-welcome "discovery," a scientific routine of vaccine production was coherently developed around these "findings," which were also quickly sent outside the camp to internationally known German specialists who praised the results. When preparations with real *Rickettsias* finally arrived at the Division for Typhus and Virus Research from an outside microbiological laboratory and the researchers saw the real thing, they did not explicitly acknowledge the fictional character of the construction they had so coherently developed, but found a way to integrate the new evidence with the old beliefs.[52]

To Fleck, this was not an instance of "bad" science but an example that showed the process through which a scientific theory (one that no longer fits the current "thought style" of the discipline) was constructed.[53] In a sense, the science produced within Ding-Schuler's program was an example of anachronistic science—one that may have been produced in another time, when the "thought style" of typhus research was different. In fact, although the scientific activity of the Division for Typhus and Virus Research did not become a success story, Fleck presents it as a picture of standard dynamics in a scientific community, dynamics that, if operating in a "current" scientific setting, would have produced "current" science.

What is important in Fleck's example is that it does not assume any fixed norm by which the science of Ding-Schuler's group should be assessed. Although the context in which it developed had much to do with the anachronistic features of the science produced at the Division of Typhus Research, such an effect was not that of a corruption.

The Camps and the Discourse of Racial Hygiene

To understand something about the mechanisms through which a given scientific view of culture and race was legitimized and contributed to the development of concentration camps and, eventually, to the Final Solution (which in turn provided the setting for camp science) we may turn to the interaction between the discourse of racial hygiene and the institution of the concentration camp—an institution which objectified the prisoners and represented as scientific the norms that regulated life and death in the camps.[54]

This hypothesis is somewhat informed by an essay by Adi Ophir in which he approaches the Holocaust as an exceptional event but indicates its origin in an exceptional combination of normal processes.[55] Although the Foucaultian agenda of his essay is never made explicit, its foci (the relationship between discourse and the technologies of power, discipline, and surveillance) can easily be traced back to Foucault's analyses of some of the institutions of modernity: the penitentiary, the clinic, the asylum.

In fact, Ophir stresses the necessity to "understand the technology of power and the modes of 'excluding' discourse which made the Holocaust possible: the discourse which made it possible to exclude a group of people from within the borders of the human race, and the technology which made it possible to massively deport them to their deaths."[56] Although the aim of Ophir's piece is not that of providing a full-fledged plan for this analysis, it is safe to assume that racial hygiene was part of that discourse, that the concentration camp was the institution that embodied it, and that that institution and discourse tended to legitimize each other.

For instance, the exterminations of entire blocks in the camps were presented as medical actions ("selections") aimed at preventing the spread of diseases which Nazi theories of racial hygiene linked to the genetic makeup of non-Aryans. This process confirmed both the scientific soundness of the decision to exterminate (or "disinfect") a block or a group of people and the theories of racial hygiene that linked diseases to the genetic makeup of certain "inferior" races.

Similarly, while sending hundreds of thousands of Jews to the gas chambers as a routine extermination of individuals whose lives had been represented as not worth living by received theories of racial hygiene, Mengele was using Auschwitz as a scientific institution which offered exceptional possibilities to study usually rare individuals. These studies on twins and the handicapped were then used to confirm a discourse of racial hygiene which lent scientific legitimation to the institution of the concentration camp and to the genocide to which that institution had been dedicated.

These loops of mutual legitimation among discourse, institutions, and power remind one of the structurally similar patterns Foucault discusses in the case of the hospital and the penitentiary. These analogies suggest that the context in which experiments on humans were carried out was not simply an institution of social control and extermination that happened to employ many doctors. This suggestion is supported by the evidence uncovered by recent studies suggesting that the symbiosis between the discourse of racial hygiene, the medicalization of the Final Solution, the institution of the concentration camps, and the development of experimentation on humans was too tight and effective to be considered accidental. Although not all experimentations or medicalized selections in the camps were leading directly to a confirmation of beliefs in racial hygiene, we find a range of remarks indicating that the camps became quickly perceived as laboratories offering unique opportunities.

Programs of experimentation on prisoners were not usually pushed from above but developed from below by doctors who had perceived the exceptional experimental possibilities offered by the camps. For instance, on 15 May 1941, Dr. Rascher wrote Himmler that during a medical course on the effects of high-altitude flying, "considerable regret was expressed that no experiments on human beings have so far been possible for us because such experiments are very dangerous and nobody is volunteering. I therefore put the serious question: is there any possibility that two or three professional criminals can be made available for these experiments?"[57] Rascher was soon informed "that prisoners will, of course, be gladly made available for the high-flight researches."[58]

Rascher was not alone in perceiving the camps as sources of an unlimited number of "experimental subjects." At the Nuremberg Trials, the defense argued that prisoners had been experimented upon not only because of the dangerous nature of these tests, but mostly because prisoners provided a perfectly normalized experimental population: they all shared the same accommodation, diet, hours of sleep, and clothing.[59] The exceptional features of the camp system in terms of medical research were also noticed by some of the prisoner doctors. For instance, Dr. Nyiszli remarked that both because of the concentration of people and because of the extremely poor sanitary conditions, diseases like gas gangrene were easily found and "most promising" remedies had been developed.[60] Also, he remarked that the camp "offered vast possibilities for research, first in the field of forensic medicine, because of the high suicide rate, and also in the field of pathology, because of the relatively high percentage of dwarfs, giants and other abnormal types of human beings. The abundance—unequaled elsewhere in the world—of corpses, and the fact that one could dispose of them freely for purposes of research, opened even wider horizons.[61]

Lifton's work indicates the pervasive role of physicians in the camp system: they were in charge of the selection of incoming prisoners at the ramp, of the routine selections of "sickly" or "infectious" inmates, and of pouring Zyklon-B reagent in the chambers. He also shows that camp hospitals were death rows, that Red Cross vans were usually employed to take the prisoners to the "disinfection" chambers, and that the cans of Zyklon-B gas (stored in the camp's pharmacy together with the phenol used for lethal injections) were usually brought there in Red Cross ambulances.

By looking at Lifton's evidence through eyes informed by Proctor's analysis of the discourse of racial hygiene and by Ophir's proposal, one may disagree with Lifton's conclusion that "real" medicine was not implicated in the Final Solution and that Auschwitz was only a travesty of a medical institution. Instead, one may begin to see Auschwitz not only as a slave labor camp for I. G. Farben and an extermination center, but also as a medical research institution which both embedded and helped to confirm Nazi theories of racial hygiene. What is most striking is that these different functions went hand in hand.

It is in the context of these processes of mutual legitimation of the institution of the concentration camp and the discourse of Nazi racial hygiene that we may consider some of the representations of Mengele's work as a researcher. For instance, his captive assistant, Dr. Nyiszli, has exposed Mengele's cruelty but has not dismissed his scientific methodology. Nyiszli's diary is full of oscillations between a view of Mengele's research as pseudo-science and a respect for Mengele's careful scientific method, bordering on fanatical precision.[62] In a few isolated cases, it seems that Nyiszli even became involved with Mengele's research enough to share in some of his excitement about discoveries in the peculiarities of twins.[63]

Similarly, when interviewed by Lifton, Dr. Teresa W. expressed her inability to put together the picture of the Mengele who sent thousands of people to the gas chambers everyday (besides those he killed for his scientific experiments) and that of the Mengele whose scientific method she considered "more or less standard for the time, the norm for anthropological work"; she "recognized it as the same approach she had been trained in at her Polish university under a distinguished anthropologist with German pre-Nazi academic connections."[64] On a different occasion, Teresa W. confirmed her views on Mengele as somebody having a genuine scientific background and "absolutely capable of doing serious and appropriate scientific work" although she detected in him the same fanaticism for accuracy that Nyiszli had also noticed.[65]

I am not presenting the views of Nyiszli or Teresa W. on the scientific soundness of Mengele's method as final. The very few prisoners who managed to survive Mengele—some of whom had a medical background—expressed much different views of his science.[66] However, the limited evidence we have from Drs. Teresa W., Nyiszli, and Abraham (Mengele's captive radiologist) makes it possible, I think, to question the usual dismissal of Mengele's scientific credentials. Obviously, I am not doing so to reevaluate Mengele, but to point at the dangerous naiveté of the historiography that tries to prevent science from being implicated in the Final Solution by claiming that Nazi doctors were just ignorant, fraudulent, or methodologically incompetent scientists.[67]

I find Teresa W.'s remarks unusually significant. They indicate that certain anthropological methodologies that before World War II were considered scientifically legitimate also outside of Germany (including one that she said stressed "the biological foundation of the social environment"[68]) could lead to disaster. In particular, I think we should try to understand what prevented her from seeing that the anthropological theories and methods in which she was trained and continued to believe even while in Auschwitz were actually much implicated in the culture that had sent her to the camp.[69] I am not saying that Dr. Teresa W. was naive in not realizing the complicity of the science she was practicing in the culture that managed to represent her as somebody whose life was not worth living. Her perceptions cannot be dismissed as short-sighted but may be read, instead, as the "natural" result of social processes of legitimation of scientific discourse—processes that keep playing a crucial role in today's culture.

Although this sketch is very far from being a full-fledged approach to the science produced in the camps, it suggests that the processes (though not the results) of Nazi science were not exceptional. As I have argued in much of this chapter, they were neither normal (in Nolte's sense) nor exceptional (in Habermas'). They were certainly problematic, as problematic as are the norms (and the agenda behind them) by which many of the received views of Nazi science are trying to argue for the normality or exceptionality of Nazi science. Such a taxonomical exercise will not solve our problem, which is to understand how science became (and could again become) implicated in a tragedy such as the Final Solution.

< 13 >

Holocaust and the End of History:
Postmodern Historiography in Cinema

ANTON KAES

In 1984, in his essay "Of an Apocalyptic Tone Recently Adopted in Philosophy," Jacques Derrida parodied the proliferating discourse that takes it upon itself to proclaim the end, specifically "the end of history, the end of the class struggle, the end of philosophy, the death of God, the end of religions, the end of Christianity and morals, the end of the subject, the end of man, the end of the West, the end of Oedipus, the end of the earth, Apocalypse Now . . . also the end of literature, the end of painting, art as a thing of the past, the end of the past, the end of psychoanalysis, the end of the university, the end of phallocentrism and the phallogocentrism and I don't know what else."[1]

In this amusing inventory of odds and ends, Derrida alludes to a quiescent mood of *post-histoire* that has characterized Western European politics and culture since the 1970s. Following the exhaustion of the utopian impulses and revolutionary energies of the tumultuous sixties, a period of political inertia and *Endzeitstimmung* set in until it was ruptured by the events in Eastern Europe in the late eighties. At the same time, in the United States, Francis Fukuyama, deputy director of the state department's policy planning staff and former analyst at the RAND Corporation, published a much-discussed article entitled "The End of History?" in which he argued that with the demise of communism the ideological struggle between East and West had come to an end and no further evolution of human thought was to be expected.[2] Whatever the merits of such post-Hegelian and pseudo-Hegelian speculations, the very emergence of a new American discourse that predicts (and deplores) a universal posthistorical boredom for lack of ideological conflict should give us pause to think. In West Germany, similar debates about *post-histoire* have a different origin dating back to the apocalyptic finale of the Hitler regime. In 1945, history had indeed ended for more than fifty million victims of World

< 206 >

War II, among them six million killed in an industrial genocide. That *something* had come to an end was recognized by calling 1945 *Stunde Null*, as if history could ever begin at point zero. *Post-histoire* in Germany always means history after the apocalypse, in the face of Hitler and Auschwitz.

Theodor W. Adorno's often cited remark that no poem can be written in innocence after Auschwitz implies the same *post-histoire* sentiment: "After Auschwitz," he writes in his *Negative Dialectics*, "there is no word . . . not even a theological one, that has any rights unless it underwent a transformation."[3] Following Adorno, Jean-François Lyotard in his book *The Differend* also sees Auschwitz as an endpoint of the historical process as well as of rational reason. Seen from today, he argues, it is as if one sensed that some great disaster had struck, a disaster so massive and at the same time so distant and foreign that no one can adequately articulate it: "Suppose that an earthquake destroys not only lives, buildings, and objects but also the instruments used to measure earthquakes directly and indirectly. The impossibility of quantitatively measuring it does not prohibit, but rather inspires in the minds of the survivors the idea of a very great seismic force. The scholar claims to know nothing about it, but the common person has a complex feeling, the one aroused by the negative presentation of the indeterminate."[4]

The silence, Lyotard continues, that the crime of Auschwitz imposes upon the historian is a *sign* for the common person, indicating "that something . . . cannot be phrased in the accepted idioms."[5] Similarly, in his book *The Writing of the Disaster,* Maurice Blanchot constitutes Auschwitz as an unrepresentable event which has nevertheless left its impressions and traces on every sector of the political and cultural life, reminiscent of the devastations of an earthquake long ago.[6]

The insistence on the impossibility of adequately comprehending and describing the Final Solution has by now become a *topos* of Holocaust research.[7] As Saul Friedlander recently pointed out,[8] how can something that at least on the face of it lacks instrumental rationality find a rational explanation? How can this historical occurrence, which is less understood the more we know about it, be represented in the mass media of today's entertainment industry? We have become rightly skeptical about realistic reconstructions of concentration camp scenes as depicted in the American television mini-series *Holocaust*— one of the most popular and commercially successful Hollywood products, which was sold to fifty countries including West Germany, where its reception nearly caused a mass hysteria in 1978.[9] We also have become perturbed by the unabashed commercial exploitation and trivialization of human suffering as exemplified in such television specials as *Playing for Time* and *War and Remembrance*, or in such films as *Sophie's Choice* and *Enemies–A Love Story*—films in which the Holocaust serves more often than not as a mere backdrop to melodramatic private affairs.[10] And, finally, we have come to question films made in the strictly documentary style, such as Joachim C. Fest's highly successful documentary of 1977, *Hitler–A Career*, which, by drawing only on original footage, reproduces precisely those images that the Nazis employed in their skillful manipulation of film as an instrument of propaganda. What is sorely lacking (with few exceptions—Claude Lanzmann's semi-documentary *Shoah* is one of them) are films that deal with Nazism and the Holocaust in ways that challenge the narrowly circumscribed Hollywood conventions of storytelling and not only reflect self-critically on the limits and impasses of film but also utilize its specific potential in the representation of the past.

What Lyotard demands of the historian of Auschwitz, namely to lend an ear "to what is not presentable under the rules of knowledge,"[11] may well be the real domain of the filmmaker; it may, in fact, be expressible only in such a syncretistic medium as film, which makes use of theater, literature, painting, photography, and so on. It is the filmmaker (as visual artist) who can transcend the "rules of knowledge," that is, the documentary evidence, the facts and figures which the Nazis tried to conceal and to destroy. It is the filmmaker who can shed light on the social imagination, perverse as it may be, that underlies the unspeakable deeds. It is the filmmaker who can translate the fears and feelings, the hopes and delusions and suffering of the victims, all unrecorded and undocumented, into pre-verbal images and thereby trigger memories, associations, and emotions that precede the kind of rational reasoning and logical-linear discourse needed in historiographical writing. If it is agreed that the cataclysmic mass destruction that occurred a half-century ago defies not only historical description and quantitative determination but also rational explanation and linguistic articulation, then a new self-reflexive way of encoding history is called for.

I believe that Hans-Jürgen Syberberg's controversial seven-hour film of 1978, self-consciously entitled *Hitler–A Film from Germany*, represents one of the few attempts to come to terms with the Nazi phenomenon in a way that challenges Hollywood story-telling and, above all, utilizes the specific potential of film in the representation of the past. Internationally more acclaimed than other films of the New German Cinema, and more widely discussed abroad than literary works from West Germany, Syberberg's Hitler film has elicited strong reactions for and against its revolutionary postmodernist form as well as its neoconservative ideology. The main objections to the film (particularly among German intellectuals) were its emphasis on the irrational, mythical, and apocalyptic dimension of German history; its Wagnerian excess; its pastiche presentation; and its highly ambivalent exploration of the mesmerizing power of fascism. Syberberg's Hitler film was celebrated by critics in the United States and in France: Susan Sontag praised the symbolist and neosurrealist visual effects and placed Syberberg as avant-garde filmmaker in the tradition of Céline, Proust, and Joyce.[12] French critics hailed the film as an expression of the romantic, torn, irrational—in short, Faustian—German nature; it was even seen in its ambition and scope as a sequel to *Faust:* "Faust, Part III."[13] Scholars such as Philippe Lacoue-Labarthe and Jean-Luc Nancy acknowledge their indebtedness to Syberberg's film in their most recent essay on "The Nazi Myth," which deals with the role of aesthetics in fascist politics.[14]

In the following I will use Syberberg's Hitler film as a vantage point to bring into focus four concerns that seem central for a postmodern historiography on film (the kind of historiography that probes most radically the limits of representation): the rejection of narrativity, the specularization of history, the proliferation of perspectives, and the affirmation of nostalgia.

The Rejection of Narrativity

Highly self-aware of the conditions of the possibility of historical representation on film, Syberberg's Hitler film does not naively attempt to reconstruct the Nazi period or the life and times of Hitler. It has virtually no visual documentary footage, no authentic interviews, no location shots, no sustained linear narrative. The entire film is based on simulation and re-creation: it takes place in a studio on a sound stage, using the artificiality of the setting and the theatricality of the presentation as devices to counter any similarity to the conventionalized images that have come to signify Nazism in popular entertainment films. Syberberg's Hitler film openly acknowledges its own status as a construct, as a performance, as a history horror picture show that has its own aesthetic logic and is independent of any outside referent.

"No human story will be shown," says the master of ceremonies, standing in a circus ring, at the beginning of the Hitler film, "but the history of humanity. No disaster film, but disaster as a film. Apocalypse, flood, and cosmic death" (p. 41).[15] History in this film is "produced" and exhibited in the form of a circus show; it appears as a revue consisting of a large number of self-contained sketches and tableaux. Syberberg is interested less in constructing history as a story with cause and effect (thereby implying a logical development that can be "understood") than in presenting constellations and associations that surprise and shock the audience. His radically contrived and artificial mode of presentation also attacks all those allegedly authentic, in actual fact hopelessly platitudinous reconstructions of the past in which images shot by the Nazis themselves are recycled. Syberberg's film destroys direct referential illusion. What reality, after all, should the film mirror? Past reality is absent and not repeatable; it cannot be visited like a foreign country. A deep gulf separates history as experience from its re-presentation. What is presented can never be identical with the presentation itself.

Syberberg favors a self-reflexive play with images and linguistic signs that *refer to* history in associations that are not bound by time and place. Various temporal layers are interlocked through blatant anachronisms, radically undermining the illusion of continuity and linear development in narrated history. Historical time is stopped and recombined according to principles that derive not from chronology but from the power of association. Visual and aural leitmotifs recur throughout the film, often as only one layer of several on the soundtrack or in the image construction. Syberberg's complex sound-image collages neutralize the linear progress of time and bring history to a standstill. Instead of the "horizontal" development of a story, we have a *vertical* structure in which various levels of meaning and association coexist and resonate on many levels and in many voices.

Everything the camera registers takes place on a studio stage, which is hermetically sealed off from the outer world. Time becomes spatial, a dense web of quotations and references from literature, theater, music, and film. This radical intertextuality also has far-reaching consequences for Syberberg's treatment of historical material. Past events and characters, cut loose from their original contexts, become quotable set pieces in an aesthetic structure that follows its own laws. A closer look at one sequence in the first part of the film may illustrate how Syberberg transforms history into a gigantic sign system.

Against the backdrop of a soundstage cluttered with cardboard figures of the German Expressionist cinema, *Muspilli*, an apocalyptic poem from the ninth century, is read off-screen—"The mountains burn, the trees vanish from the earth, the rivers run dry, the moon falls, and finally the entire earth burns"—and, simultaneously, in original sound, a Hitler speech of 1932 is heard—"We have a goal and we will advocate it fanatically and relentlessly until the grave" (p. 40). The mythical prophecy of the end of the world in the ninth century is associatively related to Hitler's expression of a collective death wish. Such a double coding of old and new, of mythical and documentary, cannot be interpreted in a conventionally hermeneutic sense. These multilayered collages contain no transparent messages, but rather impressions and possibilities; no images of an independent reality, but articulations of autonomous artificial worlds; no straightforward stories, but intricate constellations and meandering paths of associations that do not converge in one point. In a review of the Hitler film the French film critic Christian Zimmer wrote: "No events are incapable of being retold, but there are cases where narration betrays reality and the memory of those who lived through what they themselves called 'unspeakable.' In such cases, the only legitimate and faithful truth is the scream . . . Narrative always involves a little of the hopes of the historian: Is not narrative an explanation and a rationalization of the unthinkable? Is it not a standardization of insanity? Does not narrative always excuse?"[16]

The Specularization of History

Syberberg's translation of historical reality into a self-sufficient cosmos of signs, intertexts, quotations, allusions, memories, and associations gives him the freedom to encode German history in a variety of specular forms: as circus spectacle and horror cabinet; as puppet theater, cabaret, and side show; as tribunal; and as allegorical, baroque *theatrum mundi*. The central project of the film is not the representation of Hitler himself but the representation of the various ways in which

Hitler has been represented. Syberberg's interest lies in the *possibilities* of presenting a figure which, he feels, "essentially cannot be represented realistically,"[17] not in the least because today the historical subject Hitler has dissolved into a plurality of images. Instead of reducing the phenomenon Hitler to *one* image, Syberberg proliferates images. Thus we are confronted, at the very beginning of the film, with the different roles Hitler plays in the popular imagination: Hitler as Charlie Chaplin in a scene from Chaplin's *The Great Dictator,* as house painter, as raving maniac, and so on, and finally as the compulsive sex killer from Fritz Lang's *M*, who recites his famous defense before invisible judges: "But who will believe me, who, who knows what compels me! I have to, I don't want to, I, I have to, I don't want, I have to, I can't help myself, I can't help myself. I have to, I have to do it, but nobody will believe me. I can't help it, I, I . . ." (p. 61). The monologue, spoken with self-lacerating theatricality by an Austrian actor wearing an SA uniform, is superimposed over a recording from Berlin of 1939, in which masses break out into "Sieg Heil, Sieg Heil" at Hitler's appearance. As the murderer is still whimpering "I can't help it, I, I . . . ," we hear the original soundtrack of an SA song.

It is left to the viewer what exactly to make of the connections between the paranoid child murderer from Lang's 1931 film and the Hitler of 1939, between the criminal's blubbering about innocence and the intoxicated masses whose collective madness expresses itself in their enthusiastic "Sieg Heil!" The hysteria of the people and the shocking wretchedness of the captured criminal are related to each other in a montage, but for what purpose? Is Hitler to be exculpated as a victim of his drives? Are we to place the blame on the masses who shouted for a "Führer"? Or is the hysteria of this scene supposed to evoke the atmosphere of the era? Syberberg offers no single interpretation but instead constructs spectacles that allow several readings simultaneously. In one interview he said, "For some Hitler was a god of light, for others a jack-in-the-box and carpet chewer. Both interpretations receive the same weight and are juxtaposed with each other in various forms."[18]

Hitler served the Germans as a screen onto which they could project all their wishes, anxieties, and hopes. He appears as the goal of the Germans' "most secret yearnings," as the object of their suppressed desire for subjugation and the executor of everything they longed for collectively. That is the point of the film's central monologue, spoken by an actor imitating Hitler's voice and gestures, who, in a hallucinatory image, emerges from Richard Wagner's open grave. Hitler, rising from the dead, sits in judgment over the living. To the utter consternation of the audience, Hitler says in his monologue, "After all, there was no one else who would, who could take over my desired role. And so they called upon me . . . I gave them what they put into me, what they wanted to hear, wanted to do, things they were afraid to do. I made and commanded for them, for it was all for them, not for me . . . I was and am the end of your most secret wishes, the legend and reality of your dreams, so we have to get through. Finally. The time of the end? Nightmares? Not by a long shot" (pp. 127–129).

Faced with such a spectacle, the viewer feels helplessly ambivalent, spellbound on the one hand by its visual power and excessive camp eccentricity but shocked on the other hand by the audacity that uses such consciously naive stage magic, in a manner verging on the burlesque and shamelessly mixing the sublime with the ridiculous. And Hitler's politically provocative speech of self-defense, which the spectator instinctively feels challenged to refute, is made unreal by its context, the overly obvious theatrical play. In the staging of such scenes Syberberg does not hesitate to use (in the tradition of Robert Wilson) images of striking simplicity and childlike naiveté, a technique that results, as a critic once put it, in the "paradox of highly reflective infantility."[19]

Transforming the Nazi phenomenon into a gigantic spectacle opens Syberberg up to the criticism of the aestheticization of politics, which for Walter Benjamin was the ultimate strategy of fascism.[20] For example, in a scene such as the one just described, the spectator is most likely too enchanted or bewildered to put up much resistance against the film's seductive pull. All the Brechtian distancing devices that are put in the film as safeguards break down in the face of the genuinely cinematic pleasure of looking. Still, fascism is unthinkable without aesthetics. Hitler and Goebbels, both failed artists, reformulated the political itself as a work of art and had the burning desire to be the creators of a new Germany as a *Gesamtkunstwerk*. Syberberg's film brings the aesthetic dimension of Nazism to the fore and alludes more than once to the underlying affinities between cinema and fascism: both rely on spectacle.

The Proliferation of Perspectives

In order to evoke the "Hitler in us" (one of the subtexts of the film),
Syberberg tries to level the distance between ourselves and the historical person; he achieves this by introducing the figure of Karl-Wilhelm
Krause, Hitler's conscientious and pedantic servant from 1934 on.
Krause's memories, recited drily into the camera for an entire grueling
half-hour, give an unusual view of Hitler as private person. The meticulous notation of the course of a day, which to Krause was the same,
day in, day out, shows Hitler from a pedestrian perspective that allows
the temporal distance between him and the viewer to disappear for
moments at a time. For instance, Krause describes the breakfast ritual:
"The breakfast always consisted of the same things. Two cups of mouth-
warm whole milk, as many as ten pieces of Leibniz zwieback cookies,
and then a third to a half of a bar of bittersweet chocolate broken into
small pieces . . . For his bath he used pine-needle tablets" (p. 143). In
the dull spectacle of our everyday lives, the film seems to suggest, we
are all identical. In the cycle of daily routines there is no change from
yesterday to today; once again history seems to evaporate in a timeless
present. Precisely through his commonplace daily life, his quaint little
idiosyncrasies, his ludicrous likes and dislikes—"Isn't it possible for
the Führer of the German people to get a pair of decent socks?" Krause
reports Hitler to have said one day—and through his dependence on
moods and emotions, Hitler becomes "one of us." With an obsessive
precision of language and a frighteningly flat voice, the servant also
describes Christmas Eve 1937, when he and Hitler wrapped presents
and drove incognito in a taxi through the streets of Munich. In the
film's pastiche style the private Christmas spirit of the petit bourgeois
from Braunau is juxtaposed with the political situation at Christmas
1942: the soundtrack that accompanies the servant's nostalgic description of 1937 features the famous radio broadcast on December 24,
1942, which brought together German soldiers from all fronts across
the globe. Sentimentality and expansionism, peaceful Christmas
whimsy and imperialist war, *Gemütlichkeit* and terror blend into one.

In the film, the radio broadcast is superimposed over Krause's monologue; he continues speaking, but the radio broadcast ultimately
drowns him out. Associative links are suggested between the unbro-
ken loyalty of the servant to his Führer and the fate of millions of German soldiers who died at the front out of loyalty to Germany; also be-

tween the administrative tone in which Krause talks about the human and banal side of Hitler and the rational bureaucratic ingenuity that was required to send three hundred thousand soldiers to Stalingrad and transport millions of Jews across Europe to the concentration camps in the east. (Lanzmann's film *Shoah* is similarly concerned with the sheer logistics and technicalities of efficiently murdering thousands of human beings a day.)

"The quality of Syberberg's film," said Michel Foucault in his review of the Hitler film, "consists in its statement that horror is banal, that banality in itself has dimensions of horror, that horror and banality are reversible."[21] Not only the madness and *Rausch* of antisemitic fervor but also the narrow bureaucratic diligence of an ordinary person like Krause was necessary to organize the assembly-line mass murders effectively and in an administratively "correct" way. The end of the scene, however, in Stalingrad, suggests a different, more ambivalent reading. Heavy snow starts falling down, gradually covering Krause, who is quite obviously standing in the middle of a studio. Krause's face finally freezes, an emblematic embodiment of the trapped and freezing German army outside of Stalingrad. The Germans appear as victims of their high conception of duty: like Krause, they obey the Führer to the end.

A further layer of associations is added to this scene through a musical collage that combines march music and motifs from Wagner's *Rienzi*, Hitler's favorite opera. The vertical structure of this scene is a product of the layering of various linguistic, musical, and visual codes. Its simultaneous effects can only be approximated in a nonspatial medium like writing or speaking. Private and political, fictional and authentic, trivial and worldhistorical matters are intertwined and evoked at the same time. And the ensuing scene, added through an abrupt cut, relativizes everything again: the closeup of the valet's head, covered with ice and snow, and the radio broadcast from Moscow in February 1943 announcing the defeat at Stalingrad are followed by a projection (a still) of William Blake's "Shrine of the Imagination," and André Heller instructing us (in a sudden cut to another scene) that "Astronomers at the University of California, Berkeley, have discovered the farthest known galaxy. This tremendous structure of over a trillion suns is more than eight billion light-years away. The light now reaching us from there was sent out at a time when our sun and its planetary system did not even exist" (p. 56). This unexpected shift of perspective from Hitler's private life and German history to the history of the cosmos seems extremely problematic, for it relativizes everything, suggesting that from the perspective of a billion light-years away *all* world events, including the Final Solution, seem completely inconsequential and trivial.

Even this (certainly most dubious) "cosmic" model only approximates what Syberberg calls "the whole." He is obsessed by the insight that Hitlerism cannot be explained by a single thesis, not by *one* story but by many. He circumnavigates his theme with a postmodern proliferation of different voices, actions, recorded memories, quotations from novels, poems, military reports, autobiographies, speeches, songs, pictures, melodies: all of them ways of approaching the secret center called Adolf Hitler, a subject that becomes concrete and comprehensible only in the distorting mirror of others, a hollow center that is filled to the degree that we project ourselves into it.

A similarly complex and problematic collage can be found in the representation of the Final Solution in the third part of the film. Heinrich Himmler, played by the same actor who also impersonates Hitler, is lying on a massage table and having his muscles loosened by his masseur; he speaks about his childhood dreams, his recently acquired Buddhist beliefs in nonviolence, and in the same tone of voice about his higher (and basically unpleasant) "duty" to murder millions of Jews. While he speaks, SS soldiers and concentration camp guards appear on the back projection screen to be marching toward the camera, one by one, like phantoms from another world, while an off-screen voice reads from eyewitness accounts of unspeakable crimes against women and children committed in the concentration camp as well as from official Nazi propaganda speeches justifying the genocide (pp. 163–189). There are also snippets intercut (in original sound) from the speech that a shaken Hitler delivered after the failure of the Staufenberg assassination plot in 1944. Himmler at the same time gushes forth about his plans to introduce a law for the protection of animals as soon as the war is over. "I was extraordinarily interested to hear recently," he muses, "that when the Buddhist monks walk through the town in the evening, they carry a little bell in order to make the forest creatures that they might crush underfoot move aside, so that they may suffer no harm" (p. 175f).

Himmler's infamous speech to the SS in Posen in 1943, which expresses his admiration for those who remained "decent" while facing a mounting heap of corpses, is repeated twice. Only a few still pictures of concentration camp victims are shown as backdrops to the repelling visages of SS soldiers who extol Germanic virtues which for them include the heroic determination to remain unmoved by the suffering caused by the industrial-style mass killing that the Führer has ordered. To have cold-blooded mass murder presented by SS soldiers as a challenging task and a selfless sacrifice surely creates in the spectator a critical distance that exposes in one flash the whole cruel and perverse absurdity of such reasoning.

Still, the construction of such a scene abounds with incongruities, tensions, contradictions, ambivalences, and sudden, troubling shifts of sympathy: Himmler's grotesque concern for the protection of helpless animals is juxtaposed against his ruthless extermination policies vis-à-vis helpless Jews, while he himself, lying half-naked and squirming under the hands of his masseur, is shown as vulnerable. Is the pathologized image of Himmler in this scene meant to humanize him or to demonstrate the utterly schizophrenic project of the Final Solution, in which family fathers were also mass murderers? Are we to associate (as consciously or unconsciously suggested on the soundtrack) the failed plot against Hitler with the stepped-up mass murder in the concentration camps? So many questions suggest an equal number of ways to read a scene like this, which refuses to reduce the contradictions to a single narrative. The film's postmodernist multiple coding and the constantly shifting position of the author/filmmaker as *bricoleur* require an audience ready and willing to enter the slippery realm of textuality (any recourse to statements by the filmmaker that would constrain the potential meaning of the film does injustice to the textual multivalence of the film's collage principle). Not surprisingly, the proliferation, disjunction, and layering of conflicting sounds and images in a *sujet* like Nazism and the Final Solution pose a danger. The sheer number of conflicting angles (including always the angle of the Nazi perpetrator) from which each event is simultaneously viewed leads inexorably to ambivalences that do not preclude readings of the film (such as the Germans in the role of victims, nostalgia for a *Heimat* and a sense of lost grandeur, and so on) that are clearly revisionist in their implication. The radical (Nietzschean, nihilist?) pluralism of postmodern aesthetics which characterizes this film also embraces conservative, sometimes provocatively reactionary and revisionist motifs and arguments, allusions and references, either expressed in the (often sarcastic) voice-over or evoked by the music of Richard Wagner who, in Syberberg's eyes, had cast a spell over Ludwig II, the romantic Bavarian King, as well as over Hitler. The burden is placed on the spectator to engage in a dialogue with the film and create his or her own version of the Nazi story, which the film lays out in all its daunting complexity.

The Affirmation of Nostalgia

Syberberg's stylistic strategies of proliferation, juxtaposition, pastiche, contradiction, and intertextuality demonstrate his affinity with a poetics of postmodernism,[22] while his apocalyptic world view, his cultural pessimism, and his static view of history place him in the philosophical tradition of what has become known as *post-histoire*. Postmodernist aesthetics and the tradition of *post-histoire* are related: the ease with which a postmodernist artist like Syberberg uses the past as "material" that can be quoted at will is based on the belief that history and progress have reached their limit and have come to a standstill; the present is itself no more than an assemblage of quotations from the past. In the epoch of the *post-histoire*, originality and innovation mean recycling and pastiche. In this sense postmodernism and *post-histoire* are indeed kindred concepts, with *post-histoire* being the larger term encompassing postmodernist strategies and styles. But while postmodernism has engendered a critical debate that is still growing by leaps and bounds, the term *post-histoire*, coined not accidentally in the restorative Adenauer period and revived in the 1970s, has gone almost unnoticed in this country.

As early as 1952 the German sociologist Arnold Gehlen adopted the expression *post-histoire* from the writings of Paul de Man's uncle, Hendrik de Man, a Belgian socialist thinker who later became a Nazi collaborator. He first used the term to designate an epoch characterized by a state of stability and rigidity, devoid of utopian ideas, change, or development.[23] In 1961, in an article appropriately entitled "Über kulturelle Kristallisation" (On cultural crystallization), Gehlen wrote, "I am predicting that the history of ideas has come to an end and that we have arrived at the epoch of *post-histoire*, so that now the advice Gottfried Benn gave the individual, 'Make do with what you have,' is valid for humanity as a whole. In the age in which the earth has become optically and informationally surveyable, when no event of importance can happen unnoticed, there are no more surprises."[24]

Syberberg takes up this motif of crystallization and glacial rigidity in his film about Hitler, and it is no accident that metaphors of coldness, ice, and ossification recur in much of contemporary German literature (most prominently in Enzensberger's long poem *Der Untergang der Titanic*). In the Hitler film the stage itself appears as an emblem of the frozen world. Since, in the philosophy of *post-histoire*, the future has no further prospects and history seems to have come to a halt, there is no longer any existing force that could function like a magnet to pull the fragments of the past into a meaningful (that is, narrative) order. The fragments remain fragments; they lie scattered around on Syberberg's stage, dead and without context. The "spatialization" of time to a confined area in which disconnected fragments from many historical eras are strewn about—the bits and pieces after the catastrophe, as it were—corresponds exactly to the idea of an eternal present expressed by adherents of *post-histoire*. Syberberg's *Hitler* has no forward movement; it evokes instead elegiac memories of past glories, nostalgia, and a sense of waiting for the apocalypse.[25]

This stasis becomes most obvious in the numerous monologues that André Heller carries on in a mock discussion with a puppet that has Hitler's features. At one point the Hitler puppet is addressed with, "You occupied everything and corrupted it with your actions,—everything, honor, loyalty, country life, hard work, movies, dignity, fatherland, pride, faith. You are the executor of Western civilization . . . the plague of our century. The words 'magic' and 'myth' and 'serving' and 'ruling,' 'Führer,' 'authority,' are ruined, are gone, exiled to eternal time. And we are finished. Nothing more will grow here. An entire nation stopped existing" (p. 242).

In this lament, Germany—its myths, its history, and its identity—is irretrievably lost. What remains, according to Syberberg, is a land without a national identity, full of neurotic uncertainties about its own dreams, desires, and myths that define and sustain identity. The act of mourning here turns toward Germany itself as Syberberg vainly attempts to deliver German culture from its fascist past. His film ends with the chorus "Ode to Joy," from Beethoven's Ninth Symphony playing behind a visionary tableau dominated by the black stone from Dürer's famous engraving, "Melancolia," controversially pointing the way from mourning to "salvation" and "healing."

Where no development or change is considered possible, the future vanishes. At the end of history, the artist works in an eternal process of recycling what is at hand. What John Barth argued as early as 1965 in one of the first manifestoes of postmodern literature, *The Literature of Exhaustion,* informs Syberberg's representation of German history: Everything has been said, originality is strictly confined to the recombination of fragments from the past. The entirety of Western culture is now available, a quarry to which one goes to pick out quotations. This is how Syberberg expressed it in 1981: "Now the world is divided up, relinquished to history and the traditions of culture, the source of our works. Huge mines of the old cultures for quotations, which build up by layers to new cultures. Everything we show or speak has been used before, been touched, and only a rearrangement of the systems and fragments produces, if it functions, something new . . . Today's mythologies of the wandering Odysseus are constructed of quotations from the discipline of our history, and the fear of today's Penelope threatens to create chaos on the horizon of our inner landscapes as a foreboding about the future—the end of all history." [26]

The end of Germany is evoked by the pervasive mythologizing of death throughout the film: the original recordings of the National Socialist funeral service for the victims of Hitler's putsch on November 9, 1923, are used regularly as a leitmotif on the soundtrack, and in a film clip from Christmas 1944, Goebbels says, "Forward over graves! The dead are more powerful armies than we on the land, than we on the sea. They stride ahead of us." Syberberg intensifies and totalizes the mysterious collective death wish, characteristic of the National Socialist ideology, into a global longing for the end of the world that can only be grasped through myth. All crimes against humanity, including the extermination of the Indians, which incidentally the film also mentions, and the annihilation of the Jews, are mere symptoms for the fatal disease of the moribund West. Even before the titles appear on the screen, the film announces its position in a voice-over: "Dances of death, dialogues of the dead, conversations in the kingdom of the dead, a hundred years later, a thousand years, millions. Passions, oratorios . . . leftovers of a lost civilization and of a lost life, our Europe before the collapse. Farewell to the West. *Sub specie aeternitatis* and everything on film, our new chance. The story of the death of the old light in which we lived, and of our culture, a remote singing" (p. 32).

The cultural pessimism of such passages allows the concrete guilt of the Germans to dissolve in the general malaise of *post-histoire.* Against the horizon of the apocalypse and of eternity ("sub specie aeternitatis"), "rational" distinctions between perpetrators and victims, between violence and suffering lose their meaning and even their justification. The specificity of the Final Solution is thus conveniently submerged in the problem of universal evil—an evil that for Syberberg is as much associated with the curse of modernity as it is with the Nazi genocide.

Seen from this perspective, Claude Lanzmann's 1985 documentary film *Shoah* offers the necessary corrective to Syberberg's film by drawing a sharp line between Nazi criminals and their victims.[27] Based on interviews with survivors and witnesses, former concentration camp guards and Nazi officials, and bystanders of varying degrees of complicity, the nine-and-one-half-hour documentary on the Final Solution evokes the past not through an illusionist "authentic" reconstruction but through the survivors' individual memories of the period. Lanzmann does not show any of the well-known and by now codified documentary concentration camp footage but focuses instead solely on the power (and failings) of personal memory and the (admittedly often staged) immediacy of oral history. He is engaged in *Spurensuche* (search for traces): in detective and reconstructive work undertaken in the hope of recovering and recording the traces of the distant disaster. It is as if the disaster itself resisted representation; it is grasped only afterwards by studying, as it were, the aftershocks.

As early as 1979 Lanzmann outlined his project for *Shoah*: "A film devoted to the Holocaust can only be a counter-myth, that is, an investigation into the presentness of the Holocaust, an investigation into a past whose wounds are so fresh and so keenly inscribed in consciousness that they are present in a haunting timelessness."[28] Thus Lanzmann's work throws Syberberg's project in relief: although both filmmakers believe in the presence of the past (which explains, on the formal level, their shared disregard for chronological narratives and their sense of *post-histoire*, of "timelessness"), ultimately their projects differ radically. Lanzmann sets out to prove irrefutably and with an enormous array of witnesses the existence of concentration camps; the film focuses almost exclusively on the annihilation process. Syberberg (not unlike Anselm Kiefer), on the other hand, stages the myths of the Nazi past—not to glorify them, but to find some redemptive way back to the spiritual *Heimat* of the Germans, which he believes has been lost to both fascism and postwar materialism. His undertaking is completely paradoxical: irrationalism, which the Hitler movement had ap-

propriated and exploited, is to be wrested away from its National Socialist associations by means of a film that celebrates irrationalism as
the essence of German identity. The attitude necessary for this task
simultaneously constructs and deconstructs, enchants and disillusions,
hypnotizes and alienates: hence the contradictory union of stylistic
models from Brecht and Wagner, and the vacillation between fascination and criticism in the presentation of Hitler and Nazism.

Syberberg places himself in the long tradition of German writers
and artists—Lessing, Goethe, Hölderlin, Nietzsche, Wagner, Tuchol-
sky—who designed an imaginary, excessively idealized Germany in
order to compare it with the unbearable real Germany which now—
after Hitler and Auschwitz—lives in a period of *post-histoire*, only a
shadow of its former self. It would be worth speculating whether the
obsessive preoccupation with the apocalypse and the imaginary anticipation of the end of the world in the 1970s and 1980s does not express
Germany's subconscious wish to eradicate its traumatic past once and
for all. The longing for the apocalypse and the end of history may be
provoked by the utopian hope to begin once more, to create a pure
moment of origin that is not contaminated by history.

< 14 >

Whose Story Is It, Anyway?
Ideology and Psychology in the Representation
of the Shoah in Israeli Literature

Yael S. Feldman

Reviewing a translated collection of Israeli fiction entitled *Facing the Holocaust*, Alan Berger concludes by referring to the "role of Holocaust fiction in a land where it may properly be thought of as a national literature."[1] This is a misconception, however. I would even say that *Facing the Forests*, A. B. Yehoshua's novella of the early 1960s, in which the protagonist, an alienated Israeli "anti-hero," discovers the ruins of an Arab village beneath the "national" forest he is supposed to guard, is much more representative of what is felt in Israel as national literature. Or perhaps I should say "what has been felt"; for as was pointed out in 1988 by Saul Friedlander, "For years one had the impression . . . that the events of the Shoah were disappearing from Israeli memory. Now, strangely enough, over the last two or three years, this past has come back into Israeli consciousness in the most vivid way, as it has almost everywhere else."[2]

What is in effect striking is the extent to which Israeli culture, particularly in its earlier phases, attempted to assimilate the experience of the Shoah to its overall Zionist perspective. Speaking here as an Israeli I can attest, not without mixed feelings, to the success of these efforts. For *my* generation grew up under the soothing images of heroic partisans, not under the sign of "the other planet." Katzetnik's mythicized chronicles of that planet (*Beit Haboobot* [*Dollhouse*], *Salamandra*, etc.) were there in the background, an isolated terrain within nascent Israeli literature, while centerstage was occupied (and quite literally so) by school plays about the Warsaw uprising or the heroic mission of Hanna Senesh. For us, *Yom hashoah vehagvurah* (Day of Holocaust and Heroism) was not "Martyrs day," as my *current* Israeli calendar translates it, but rather a celebration of resistance and national pride, a prolegomenon to the Israeli Day of Independence.

< 223 >

So this was the first story we were told—in public ceremonies, in school anthologies, in radio programs—and it was clearly exhilarating despite its tragic dimensions. It told of the victory of the spirit; it was easy to identify with; it was protective. Endowing loss and death with meaning, with a purpose, this story made our world a good place to grow up in.

And of course it was totally Hebraic. Everyone in this story spoke Hebrew: the ghetto mother singing a lullaby in the shadow of Ponar, the leaders of the Jewish resistance, and even the Polish underground. I must admit that even today I find it difficult to separate the emotional sediments of these early representations from the sonorous Hebrew in which they were encoded. Yes, the language was the message. It was *our* story; another link in the Hebrew-Israeli self-representation, emplotted in a tale of a goal-oriented, victorious struggle.

There are hardly any written samples of this story in the translated anthology that Berger was reviewing, nor in any other anthology. They are found primarily in popular and didactic literature. Curiously, and perhaps predictably, the canon of Israeli Shoah literature begins with the breakdown of that first story.[3] This breakdown takes place almost simultaneously in poetry and in drama, with fiction following suit nearly a decade later. Simultaneity does not mean similarity, however. Whereas Uri Zvi Greenberg's monumental poetic elegy, *Rehovot Hanahar* (*Streets of the River,* 1951), is a complex expression of protest, mourning, and painful acceptance,[4] Israeli drama in this period is conflict-ridden, illustrating the tension between the Sabra, or native Israeli, and the Holocaust survivor.

Composed mostly by Israelis who *did not experience* the Holocaust directly, these plays are all set in *post*-Holocaust Israel (or Europe, in one case), dramatizing the encounter between the "Israeli" and the "Jew" in all its alienation and lack of empathy. Although stereotypical Sabra perceptions are often the butt of the playwright's censure, one cannot escape the impression that once more, this is the *Sabra's* story rather than the survivor's; that what is at stake is the preservation of the *difference* Israelis have carved for themselves out of Jewish history and identity. Compared to what is considered "Holocaust drama" in the United States and in Europe, these plays can hardly be classified as such.[5] In fact, not until the eighties is there any attempt at documentary theater, a genre so popular in the West. In general, it is not the experience of the victim that is at the core of the drama, but rather the Israeli's difficulty in coming to terms with and validating the "otherness" of that experience.

This paradigm changed in the early eighties, in the dramatic productions of Hanoch Levin and Joshua Sobol. I have argued elsewhere that, their differences notwithstanding, both playwrights approach the source of violence itself, attempting to capture the relationship between victim and aggressor in all its gruesome implications.[6] By so doing, they suggest new perceptions of "the other" as being both external and internal to Israeli consciousness. While this process is rather obvious in Sobol's 1984 *Ghetto* (which I shall discuss), Levin conducts his inquiry in his 1981 play *Yisurei 'Iyov* (*The Passion of Job*) via a displacement to the Job–Jesus story. Only his rich system of contemporary allusions reveals that he too struggles with the impact of the Holocaust; in contrast to Sobol, he transposes his anxieties to a more abstract level of discourse, dramatizing the post-Holocaust polemics over the death of God, the banality of evil, and the possibility of the tragic. Despite this divergence, however, the two playwrights share a position unprecedented in Hebrew drama. Both dare to imagine the trauma itself; both present on stage victims experiencing the horror and the suffering, as well as the excruciating process of making moral choices; and, finally, both exemplify a psychological shift in the Israeli attitude to the Holocaust victim, from an external "other," one invoking shame and guilt and therefore to be defended against, to a subject in his or her own right, one whose experience can be internalized and even identified with.

My observation seems to concur, then, with the general revival of interest described by Friedlander in his statement quoted above: "The whole issue is coming back. But this time, I would say, it is coming back in a more mature society, one that has perhaps less self-assurance but more self-reflectiveness. There is no attempt to hide the Shoah; . . . there is no attempt, as far as I know, to identify it as part of a great historical interpretation. There is the facing of the catastrophe as such, not in search of something, nor even for coherence, but as a means of rediscovering the past" ("Roundtable," p. 289).

"Facing the catastrophe as such" may readily accommodate my own claim of treating the victim "as a subject in his own right." Yet my analysis of these plays, *Ghetto* in particular, does not allow for such an overall interpretation. On the contrary, it clearly demonstrates to what extent Sobol's selection of his "historical" materials is filtered through the powerful prism of the contemporary ideological crisis; how the ideological conflicts of his reconstructed Vilna ghetto closely (in fact, too closely) resemble those of Israel during the Lebanon war (1982–1984); and how this ostensibly documentary play draws its dramatic coherence from the all-too-familiar binary oppositions promoted by (Labor) Zionism: Yabne versus Jerusalem; diaspora versus Zion; Yiddish versus Hebrew; Talmud versus Bible; and—last but not least—(Jewish) spirituality, identified with vitality and survival, versus (German, but also Zionist and Israeli) recourse to force and aggression, identified as the death instinct.

That last dichotomy unravels Sobol's technique but also exposes the limits of his "new" representation: unable altogether to deconstruct the old oppositions, he simply inverts their markers, glorifying everything that has been traditionally marked as negative (all first terms in the above pairs) and debunking the previously valorized values. The result is an ostensible dramatization of a *psychological* mechanism ("identification with the aggressor") that is in fact dominated by the very *ideology* against which it rebels. As such, *Ghetto* highlights a literary trend that has recently taken hold of Israeli fiction as well—the appropriation of psychoanalysis for the critique of ideology ("Zionism on the literary couch," as I have elsewhere labeled it). It is my contention, however, that despite its apparent proliferation, Freudianism is used only as a metaphor; in the final analysis, it is ideology rather than individual psychology that is the primary force behind these literary representations.[7]

The same holds true for the use of the Holocaust in this literature. Again, *Ghetto* is typical of a certain literary fascination with the theme of the Shoah which is a far cry from a disinterested "rediscovery of the past." The ideological motivation of this literature, as in Sobol's case, is quite transparent—a response to a political constellation that has used and misused the Holocaust for its own purposes;[8] in the case of many less known, younger writers, however, the psychological motivation seems paramount, at least at first glance: their novels may be read as a literary "working-through" of the traumatic experience of the "second generation," the Israeli-born children of survivors, who only toward the end of the twentieth century have matured enough to identify with the hitherto untold past of their parents.[9] In fact, the therapeutic implications of this literature have been recognized by the Israeli psychologist Dina Wardi, who in her book *Nos'ei Hahotam* (*Memorial*

Candles) (Jerusalem: Keter, 1990) quotes fictional characters as lavishly as she does her patients, all children of survivors, born and raised in Israel. If the family dynamics described by Wardi are representative, then her findings seem to contradict earlier, more positive evaluations, propagated since the early seventies by the late Israeli psychoanalyst Hillel Klein and his colleagues. Viewed from this book's perspective, Klein's optimism about the effect of Israeli culture and identity, and particularly about the power of the collective (the kibbutz) on the process of adaptation and integration of Holocaust survivors, seems just as "slanted" by Zionist ideology as the fictional worlds created by the writers of his generation.

It is interesting to note, however, that none of the young writers who have tried to escape these very constraints (Oded Peleg, Navah Semel, Lily Perry-Amitai, Dorit Peleg, Yaakov Bochen, Itamar Levi, to name just a few) has been received so well by the literary mainstream as David Grossman, who has consciously tried to undermine them from within (more about him below). However, even in this literature one can detect the impact of a contemporary ideological crisis—the breakdown of the Zionist codes that emplotted earlier representations of the Holocaust. It was this breakdown, and the loss of the adolescentlike grandiose self accompanying it, that destabilized the old arch-opposition between "Jew" and "Israeli" and made possible a new position of empathy toward "the other," toward the Jew within the Israeli.[10]

What I would like to suggest, then, is that Israeli literature may serve as an important test case in the current debate on the limits of representation. For it sharpens and brings to focus—and perhaps to its own epistemological limits—the problematic dichotomy between historical and fictional truth. Indeed, we have learned enough about the uncanny power of narrativization (literary or other), emplotment, closure, and finally language itself, with all its figural "distortions," to know that the hope to face "the thing in itself" may be only wishful thinking.[11] We also know, however, that nowhere else is this issue so paradox-ridden as in the case of the Holocaust. In an intellectual climate that has practically erased the word *truth* from its dictionary, how are we even to express, let alone satisfy, our thirst to know what "really" happened and how it was possible? And in a philosophical discourse that insists on the necessarily figurative status of language, and hence of any human communication, how are we to come to terms with our natural abhorrence at what we perceive as an illegitimate, even immoral, metaphorization of this unique catastrophe?

These questions become painfully relevant in the division between survivors' and bystanders' (or second generation's) literatures, with all the ethical implications and hermeneutical risks that this division entails. As many discussions of the issue have made clear, the opposition between documentary realism and mediated recollection, raw testimony and literary construction, is not so final after all.[12] As Irving Howe says, "We are trapped. Our need for testimony that will forever place the Holocaust squarely within history requires that we respond to voice, nuance, personality. Our desire to see the Holocaust in weightier terms than the merely aesthetic lures us into a shy recognition of the moral reverberations of the aesthetic. This does not make us happy, but the only alternative is the silence we all remember, now and then, to praise."[13]

Implied in Howe's wry comment is not only the irony of so much talk about silence (pace Adorno and Steiner), but also the acceptance of the difference, of the moral imperative, of the paradoxical limits involved in writing and reading "aesthetically" about the Holocaust. And if this is true for works by survivors and eyewitnesses—who are, mainly, Howe's subject—it is much more so for long-distance observers and second- or third-generation writers. It is here that the ethical limits of representation are most acutely felt; and it is against literary works of this kind that most of the criticism has been raised. The heated debates that accompanied such diverse literary appropriations of the Holocaust as Sylvia Plath's *Ariel* poems, "Daddy" and "Lady Lazarus" ("I may be a bit of a Jew"); D. M. Thomas' *White Hotel;* William Styron's *Sophie's Choice;* and, in Israel, protest poetry written during the Lebanon war and its aftermath, are all expressions of a deepseated ambivalence: Somehow the rules of the hermeneutic game do not seem to apply here. There is a difference here that all (or most) of us sense, but are hardly able to make sense of.

This problematic difference is also behind the extreme position that decrees silence (*pace* Elie Wiesel) on whoever was not *there* (with the same success, one may add, as had Adorno's famous dictum). Yet it is precisely in this "forbidden" realm that Israeli writers are to be located. For most of Israeli Shoah literature, not only now—which is rather understandable—but from its very inception, is the work of writers who never experienced the terrors of the Holocaust firsthand.

This statement may come as a surprise. One may think immediately of Aharon Appelfeld, a survivor whose fiction has been generously translated into English. But Appelfeld is not representative of Israeli literature at large. In fact, he is the only survivor who actually "made the Hebrew canon" as a novelist. (The situation is quite different among Yiddish writers in Israel, for obvious reasons.)

The extent to which Israeli Shoah literature in Hebrew is *not* identified with first-hand testimony, with survivors' narratives, can be measured by the share they are allotted by literary critic Gershon Shaked in his afterword to the collection *Facing the Holocaust* mentioned above: out of fifteen printed pages only the last section, less than a page and a half in length, is devoted to "the writers who are survivors." Omitting Katzetnik (Yehiel Dinur) altogether, Shaked starts by stating the group's "difference" in that they write, "not surprisingly, shorter works—stories and novellas. They attempt to view the experience from a narrow angle of vision, to present testimony about what happened to them and to their protagonists, *not* to resolve historical issues and *not* to embody history in a symbol that comprehends the entire experience" (emphasis mine).[14] I believe the final two negative clauses speak for themselves. Although not openly judged, the otherness of the survivors' testimonial is measured against a tacit norm: the native-Israeli Shoah narrative to which most of the afterword is dedicated. This norm turns out to be, in its general lines, the one identified by many commentators (Ezrahi, Roskies, Mintz, Needler, Young) and theorized by Yosef Yerushalmi in *Zakhor*[15] as the typical Jewish/Hebraic response to catastrophe: mythization; collectivization; ritualization; in short, all processes that would embed the particular within the general and surrender the individual to the community—thereby endowing the narrative with a meaningful, life-affirming closure.

That this stock-in-trade reaction could be readily adapted to Zionist perspectives is quite clear. By the sixties, when Appelfeld began publishing, Hebrew fiction had caught up with the theater: in the wake of the Eichmann trial, it produced a variety of narratives that touched, in differing degrees of depth and engagement, upon the subject of the Holocaust. As in the case of the theater, very little attempt at documentary fiction is in evidence.[16] In the main, this is the literature of bystanders, whose imaginative energy is unavoidably directed elsewhere.

Some of these novels continue the thematic conflict elaborated earlier on the stage—the native Israeli's identity crisis when facing, for the first time, the typical diaspora "Jew" he was raised to reject.[17] Others fashion large epic structures, apparently trusting the explanatory powers of historical emplotment. The script here is a more sophisticated version of my childhood heroic dramas, with a closure that exposes the authors' Zionist world view despite the ostensibly epic narrative voice.[18] More personal, although no less embroiled in historical symbolization, are some fictional autobiographies that are structured around a journey to Europe, in search of a pre-Holocaust childhood. This time the conflict is internalized, and the symbolic or actual journey helps to heal the intrapsychic split between Jew and Israeli. The fact that these fictional introspections have a cathartic closure, back in Israel, is a sign of their adherence to the same narrative paradigm we are tracing here.[19]

It is not difficult to imagine how different Appelfeld's early short stories sounded against the background of this literature. In their short format, their sparse language, their lack of closure, and their refusal to be emplotted by the grand historical schemes of either the Jewish-Hebraic tradition or Zionist redemption,[20] they indeed introduced another script, "a new artistic code," as Israeli author A. B. Yehoshua has put it.

The point I want to make, however, is that it was not his originally "alienated" Shoah narrative that gained Appelfeld access to the canon; despite the stylistic and thematic continuities, Appelfeld of the seventies and eighties is quite different from the early Appelfeld. And I am not talking about linguistic growth and artistic maturity, which are of course factors as well; I am talking about a shift in the implied authorial stance of his narratives, beginning with *Ke'ishon Ha'ayin* (*Like the Apple of the Eye*, 1972), *Badenheim, 'Ir Nofesh* (*Badenheim*, 1972, 1974), and *Tor Hapela'ot* (*The Age of Wonders*, 1978). (The last two were, not accidentally, his first novellas to be translated into English in 1980 and 1981, respectively.)

My claim is that in these narratives Appelfeld gave up his initially bewildered, uncomprehending "take" on his experiences in the Shoah and its aftermath, and imperceptibly entered the old/new paradigm of the Jewish tradition. Alan Mintz may be right in placing the *early* Appelfeld outside of this tradition, but less so in his interpretation of the author's later move.[21] Appelfeld's journey to his pre-Holocaust *assimilated* childhood is not a nostalgic, approving return; it is a critical look back, full of apprehension and disapproval. This posture is possible (and makes sense) only from *within* the Jewish tradition. Moreover, his famous avoidance of direct representation of the Holocaust itself may be attributable not only to ethical inhibitions, as Howe would have it;[22] it may be his way to avoid the structural difficulty that such a representation of necessity entails. For it is not only the events of the war itself that are missing in Appelfeld's work. Even the postwar fate of survivors in Israel—a source of numerous narratives in his early tales—plays a smaller role in his recent work.

That theme culminated in his first novel, *Ha'or Vehakootonet* (*The Skin and the Gown*, 1971), which traces the failed attempts of two survivors who had been separated by the war to recreate their life together in Jerusalem. Their story ends in divorce, sickness and the intimation of death: "All night he was walking as if after a funeral. A journey in which first awareness slowly penetrated, like hard drops of poison . . . It dawned on him that this was death. First the body dies and then the soul evaporates until it is winged away by the morning breeze upon the earliest blush of dawn" (p. 166; my translation). Recently, however, only one of his works, *Hakootonet Vehapassim* (*The Gown and the Stripes*, 1983) reverberates with similar echoes.[23] It would seem that the later Appelfeld prefers the one portion of the story that lends itself to some "sense," that is amenable to a narrative closure, as gruesome as that may be. This is *not* the cathartic, life-affirming Zionist closure of his Israeli peers; and, paradoxically, it is not textually represented in his story. It is the unrepresentable extra-textual horror that represents—*in its absence*—the historically unavoidable closure of the assimilated culture of his childhood.

This is particularly true for several novels that could be defined as "group portraits" (*Badenheim*, 1972; *Hametzudah* [*The Retreat*], 1982; *Ritzpat Ha'esh* [*Tongue of Fire*], 1988), all set in Europe on the brink of the catastrophe. They dramatize different aspects of Jewish assimilation: its latent self-hatred; its refusal to face facts; the blow it received when confronted by open antisemitism. This theme is also central to the author's "family portraits" (*Like the Apple of the Eye*, 1971; *The Age of Wonders*, 1978), where it is played out against other options of Jewish existence. The struggle between these options is at the core of two of his latest novels, *Be'et Ube'onah 'Ahat* (*The Healer*, 1985) and *To the Land of the Cattails* (1986), each featuring a family split between the allure of gentile culture and the almost mystical attraction of the old tradition. Although in *The Healer* the conflict ends with a stale-mate, the journey to the "land of the cattails" has a chilling double closure: The spiritual awakening (first of the mother and, at the very end, also of her son, the scion of a gentile) is perforce entwined with a physical annihilation. Toni brings her son back to her Jewish home-town only to be swallowed by the maelstrom: "It was an old locomo-tive, drawing two old cars—the local, apparently. It went from station to station, scrupulously gathering up the remainder."[24]

Can we call the author of this unredeemed emplotment an outsider to the Hebraic tradition? Only if we read the letter, not the spirit. Appelfeld's Hebrew may indeed be "thin," devoid of traditional allu-sions and inherited literary formulas, but his goal is traditional enough: "From now on I am writing stories whose theme is—*Jewish destiny*," said Appelfeld in a press interview in 1975. "I am writing now about the historical Jew, the way he was in the diaspora. I want to show that what happened in the war was a process that had been fermenting for a long time, so I trace the footsteps that led to what is called Shoah. *I do not like the word 'shoah'; Shoah is a sudden event, whereas what happened had had its own preambles*" (my translation; emphasis added).[25] We have come full circle, then, not only to the Jewish tradi-tion, which Appelfeld has adopted in Israel, following the teaching of the late literary critic Dov Sadan[26] but to Zionist rhetoric as well.

And here we run into the most fascinating paradox in a writer who is known for his love of paradoxes:[27] "Let the assimilators admit their er-ror," screams one of the survivors in the 1980 novel *Michvat Ha'or* (*Searing Light*).[28] "If not for the assimilators, if not for the apostates . . . we would have looked different today." And when reminded that "they are gone, they are gone. What do you want from them, they were all burnt up," all he can do is whimper, "Let them admit their guilt, let them admit it in public."[29] Framed this way, in the hysterical diatribe of an enraged refugee (who turns out to be the past profes-sional rival of the young narrator's father, *and* a Zionist), Zionist ideol-ogy sounds little more than cliché and thin propaganda. This whole novel in fact reads as a ferocious parody of the Zionist enterprise of re-education, of the attempt to "baptize" the survivors as "new Jews."[30] It is a perfect mirror image of the earlier literary portrayals of the identity crisis of the native Israeli upon his first confrontation with the Jew from "over there"; except that here the perspective is reversed and we wit-ness the young survivor desperately clutching to a shattered identity, a trace of the self he might have been, even as he feigns (or, in some cases, refuses) to adopt a new one. That the carrier of this struggle is language itself is only natural. As Sidra Ezrahi has shown, it is the refugees' private "war of languages" that dramatizes the antagonism "between the privacy of biography and the tyranny of collective existence."[31]

Yet there is a darker underside to Appelfeld's "search for a language"[32] in this novel. For while parodying Zionist rhetoric, his narrator fashions his own perception of the events by using the well-defined and abused lexicon of the "Final Solution": "transports," "guards," "parasites," "insects." This does not make for easy reading, at least not for a reader of *my* background. It becomes extremely difficult when at certain moments the distinction between Zionist and Nazi rhetoric is blurred (as in the repetition of the phrase "Work is good. Work purifies"—pp. 43, 121, and 124, or in the constant talk about the survivors' deformities and blemishes (*moomim, pegamim*) that need "correction"). If this sounds too harsh and unbecoming of the Appelfeld you may know, consider, for example, the chilling closure of the novel, in my translation: "The truck arrived late at night. The driver came out of the cabin and angrily called out: 'Where are they. Where.' The irritated call forced us out of our sleep all at once. The driver pulled the stubborn catch and the door fell with a bang. And as it is in sleep, there was no need for words. Bodies rolled into the box one after another."

Could this nightmare be the protagonist's description of his conscription into the Israeli army shortly after arriving in Palestine? And if so, what is the ontological status of this representation: as a genuine subjective memory of the narrator who, being a refugee, had no other language in which to process his new experiences?—or as a deliberate choice of encoding by the extratextual implied author?

Whatever the answer, the implications are heavy. And if Appelfeld may not have been aware of them at the time (1980), he must have become so a few years later, when in the wake of the Lebanon war the identification of Zionism with Nazism became commonplace among writers on the political left. (This linkage is best exemplified by Sobol's use of "the identification with the aggressor" as a ploy in the dramatic argument of his play *Ghetto*, 1984, discussed above.) That *Searing Light* might be retrospectively absorbed by this new metaphor was probably not a welcome possibility for the author. And although this novel undoubtedly stands not only outside but in opposition to the Zionist script of history and the Holocaust, I doubt that this holds true for Appelfeld's oeuvre as a whole. For as much as he may rebel against the yoke of the collective, and as much as he may see himself as the spokesperson for the suppressed individual, he also admits that along the way of personal introspection the writer finds "not only himself but the scattered soul of his people as well."[33]

This insight is clearly borne out by his subsequent work, in which he seems to have left behind his experiential indictment of early Zionist practice, while adopting its overall historical perspective. So far, *Searing Light* stands alone in his oeuvre, an expression of unredeemed pain, perhaps an exercise in a personal working-through of long-buried conflicts. It has not been translated, and I doubt that it will be in the near future. (Rumor has it that the author forbade any translation of this work.) But it has no doubt cleared the way for Appelfeld's search for "Jewish destiny." That this destiny is conceptualized by him in terms of Zionism according to Dov Sadan should come as no surprise: after all, it was Sadan who offered a literary scheme in which the opposition of Jew versus Israeli would collapse. Reappropriating "the totality of Jewish experience," Appelfeld can now reclaim a Jewish identity that he had never had, in person, while turning against the assimilated culture of his youth along with its historical precedents and analogues.[34]

What this analysis suggests, then, is that in some sense even Appelfeld, *the* representative of Holocaust survivors among Hebrew novelists, has been coopted by the governing norm of the Israeli representation of the Shoah; and that despite his personal grudge, rooted in the psychological experiences of his youth, he is ideologically anchored within the Zionist camp and its collective, "closural" interpretation of history. Once again, psychology is subsumed by ideology, and the personal by the communal (albeit in a diametrically opposite direction from Sobol and his followers). One may even speculate that it was precisely this ideological-communal anchor that enabled Appelfeld to relinquish his initial post-Holocaust chaos and enter his current authorial (and authoritative) position.

We have to turn elsewhere, then, in our search for a break in the paradigm. Paradoxically, we find it among native novelists who, so far as I know, had no personal or even direct familial experience of the Shoah, but who are known for their clearly expressed ideological positions—somewhere to the left of the Israeli political consensus of the 1970s and 1980s. Since the correlation between the positions of these novelists and their literary representations of the Holocaust is less transparent than in the case of the theater (Sobol), a detailed demonstration of it will necessitate a separate analysis. Let me therefore just sketch out here the general lines of the new script in which they recast the Shoah, alluding to some of its ideological implications.

Yoram Kaniuk's *Adam Ben Kelev* (literally, "A human son of dog," but translated as *Adam Resurrected*) has come to figure as a major Shoah novel in every summary of the subject. Yet very little attention was given to it when it was published in 1969.[35] Kaniuk was the first writer who dared pit the survivor's pathology against the Israeli consensus of psychological normalcy. Mental pathology is almost legitimized here—a rather subversive gesture, even as a metaphor, for Israel of the late sixties. Kaniuk was also the first native Israeli to adopt the point of view of the survivor as an individual, without imposing on his story any collective or historical interpretive scheme. Redemptive closure is satirized in the plot several times over (the strong Christological allusions not excluded), and the role of the sane community is only marginal to that of the asylum—both the locus of the plot and the story's major symbol.

The Hebrew title, when understood in all its diverse punning, should hint at the "carnivalesque" quality of this novel, a sort of "Holocaust laughter" that the late Terrence Des Pres has recommended.[36] Realism is undermined here by a great measure of fantasy: the protagonist is endowed with supernatural skills of entertainment that saved his life in the concentration camp but were powerless to save his family—hence the guilt and self-punishment he "insanely" imposes on himself, and of which he will not let go.

All this should sound somewhat familiar to those who may not have read Kaniuk's novel but have read Grossman's 1986 novel *'Ayen 'Erech 'Ahavah* (*See Under: Love*). Nearly two decades separate the two novels, yet the latter would be inconceivable without the former.[37] Grossman gives up the asylum symbolism, but retains almost everything else—the carnivalesque humor, the fantasy, the validation of pathology as "artistic creation," the supernatural powers of the survivor, his powerlessness to save others, the less-than-diabolic Nazi officer, and, finally, the belief that faith in human love is the only possible redemption.

All this being said, we should give Grossman his due: He takes several giant steps beyond the "story" bequeathed to him by Kaniuk; and each of these steps have helped him "deconstruct," so to speak, the Hebraic-Zionist model with all its implications. What he ends up with is a sprawling postmodernist text, unique in Hebrew literature at large, in which several genres of Shoah literature commingle and interact: the stories of *l'univers concentrationnaire;* of resistance in the ghetto, though totally different from that with which we are familiar; of survivors in Israel; and finally, of the second generation's struggle to come to terms with the silences and denials of their parents.

It is within this last story that Grossman frames all the other narratives, and it is precisely this frame that aroused both admiration and criticism, not to mention a lot of confusion. Momik, his second-generation protagonist, whose traumatic childhood in the shadow of "the land of over there" has won the hearts of most readers, grows up to become a writer who tries to redeem the worst of all worlds by the power of his narrative art. This is an ironic reversal of the processes of public ritualization which have become the major channel through which young Israelis could learn about the Shoah. By emplotting this long journey into the heart of the death camps as an intensely personal odyssey, triggered by a writer's block and traced to the particular pathology of (single) children of survivors, Grossman has attempted to release the Shoah from the shackles of the collective and reclaim it as a subjective experience. Predictably, it is this very twist that many readers have found difficult to digest, both in Israel and in America. Accusing the author of self-centeredness, they read his interpretation as a trivialization, as a personalized emplotment which is too narrow for a cataclysm of such immense proportions. Yet individualism is only the obverse of universalism, and personal psychology only a foil in the encounter with collective ideology (a technique Grossman had elaborated *thematically* in his first novel, *Hiyooch Hagedi* [*The Smile of the Lamb*, 1983]).

Emphasizing the universal rather than the national, making redemption a relentless process rather than a historical or narrative closure (the novel does *not* end optimistically, despite its insistence on the presence of good even at the heart of evil), the author suggests a new set of attitudes that transform and transcend the old oppositions. His choice of Bruno Schultz, the epitome of assimilation, as his protagonist's literary ideal and source of inspiration is no accident. Through him Grossman offers a canonic analogue of the message developed in the noncanonic (and therefore subject to disregard) children's stories of Momik's "grandfather," Anshel Wasserman. Momik's infatuation with Schultz is presented as a mature version of his childhood fascination with his grandfather's naive, old-fashioned stories. In his long interior monologue (ostensibly addressed to the She-Ocean) he moves, in a kind of free association (presumably "changing the subject," p. 101), from his rendition of Bruno Schultz's life story to his discovery of Wasserman's place in the literary canon. In a critical article about "early-twentieth-century children's magazines in Poland," Momik finds that "'opinion is divided' on the quality and importance of his [Wasserman's] writing. The critic further remarks—not without a hint of reproach—that my grandfather was one of the few Hebrew authors 'writing at a time of national and linguistic revival . . . to deal chiefly with universal themes, scarcely touching on the issue of Jewish nationalism, indeed, ignoring it altogether. This may account for his favor with the children of the world and his attainment of a popular success beyond the reach of more masterful Hebrew writers imbued with a sense of Zionist mission.'"[38]

Is this straightforward reporting or parodic portrayal? Does one have to be intimately familiar with the internal feuds of modern Jewish culture to sense the grinning irony of the implied author? Possibly. Grossman, however, does not leave us in doubt about Momik's position: "I was furious at this pompous ass of a 'critic': you don't judge a man like Anshel Wasserman according to the commonplaces of literary analysis. Couldn't he see that?"[39] Momik's fury marks the national Hebrew critic's opinion as negative, thereby guiding the uninitiated reader towards a "correct" evaluation of its contents. But his fury is misguided, of course. For beneath "the commonplaces of literary analysis" lurk the commonplaces of ideological biases, this time in the garb of "nationalism" versus "universalism." It is this opposition that is the covert target of the implied author, and it is its subtle debunking that was a welcome change for some readers and a source of discontent for others.

That a major parameter of this change is a position of empathy toward any "other"—victim or aggressor, Jew or Gentile—even to the extent of identification and immersion in his mental world, should come as no surprise: after all, Grossman was also the first Israeli to imagine from within the psychological world of another victim—the eccentric Palestinian of *The Smile of the Lamb* (1983). And it is perhaps no accident that a similar move characterizes also Kaniuk and Sobol, both of whom tried to represent the other in his or her subject position, in the novel 'Aravi Tov (*A Good Arab,* 1984) and the play *Hapalestinayit* (*The Palestinian,* 1985; titled in English *Shooting Magda*), respectively.

We have come full circle then to the opening of my essay: "Facing the Holocaust" and "Facing the Forests" finally do meet. In 1988 Gershon Shaked lamented the fact that Hebrew literature still "lacks a plausible and necessary linking between the two core-experiences (Shoah and Restitution) that history has proven realizable despite their incomprehensibility."[40] He was talking about the literature of the older generation, those writers who either experienced or witnessed the Shoah in their lifetime. Paradoxically, it is only now, with the *second* generation, that such a link is being formed—though not in the way Shaked had anticipated.[41] And as if to add confusion to paradox, the novel that has actually put the "second generation" on the map was *not* written by a child of survivors. With an uncanny intuition, Grossman has tapped a new creative source while it was still in the making. *See Under: Love* crystallizes in a subtle and sophisticated fashion psychological and ideological shifts that are being expressed more crudely elsewhere in contemporary drama and documentary cinema ("Because of That War") and in the fiction of the second generation. Although the range of these shifts is rather broad, they share one common feature— a rejection of the collective model of representation that they inherited from their parents and cultural mentors.

Rather than finding the "necessary link" that this model aspires to, contemporary writers seek a close subjective encounter with the experiences that the ideology of that model of necessity suppressed. That they thereby undermine the historical closure assumed by that model is only too obvious. And it is precisely this disruption that brings us back to the source of the new developments: the extreme ideological polarization that governs the contemporary political scene in Israel. When the choice is limited to that between the victim or the victimizer, the oppressed or the oppressor, each of these tends to function as a "reaction formation," an automatic psychological mechanism that deprives the individual of his potentiality for freedom of choice and independent judgment. In response to this danger, Israeli writers now turn to the core experiences of their existence and reshape them in their own image. That by so doing they challenge and transform the limits of one model of representation is no doubt true. But that at the same time they unavoidably create a new set of limits is also true—a fact that in itself should have pragmatic, as well as philosophical, implications.

< 15 >

Translating Paul Celan's "Todesfuge": Rhythm and Repetition as Metaphor

John Felstiner

As to the rhythm, as to the effects and the after-effects of rhythm in Paul Celan's "Todesfuge,"[1] consider for a moment that since the 1950s, German high-schoolers have sometimes engaged with this poem by rendering it vocally, not only in unison but as part-song. Let them beforehand study fugues with their music instructor, one pedagogical journal suggests, then in German class students can each adopt a motif or voice to perform Celan's poem, so as (our journal says) "to make the polyphony audible."[2]

One can perhaps imagine how this might sound, but can hardly imagine, even with the most well-meaning teacher and sympathetic teenagers, what real effect such a performance might have—what mindfulness those nervously rehearsed and recited lines might generate. They aim "to make the polyphony audible," but what about that unresolvable dissonance the art of a fugue makes with Nazi genocide? A closer look at the teachers' journal doesn't elicit much hope. A dozen meticulous paragraphs analyze the contrapuntal elements in "Todesfuge," but not one sentence recognizes that the poem's very form, the rhythm and repetition so amenable to pedagogic technique, may itself—in miming German musical mastery—indict the nation that orchestrated mass murder.

What then did it take to evoke such an utterance as "Todesfuge," Celan's first published poem?* Some decades of Roumanian fascist antisemitism, let's say, behind the July 1941 irruption of an S.S. Einsatzkommando into Czernowitz, Bukovina, the plundering and burning and slaughter, the ghetto, the overnight deportation of Paul Celan's parents to Transnistria, the news of their brutal murder there when he was twenty-one, the year and a half he spent at forced labor, then in

---

*The complete text and translation of "Todesfuge" appear at the end of this chapter.

< 240 >

1944 the personal and newspaper accounts of Jews returning (or not returning) from Nazi camps.[3] It took all this, and at bottom it took a stroke of verbal nerve, to prompt the plural pronoun *wir* (we) in "Todesfuge"'s opening lines:

> *Schwarze Milch der Frühe wir trinken sie abends*
> *wir trinken sie mittags und morgens wir trinken sie nachts*
> *wir trinken und trinken*

> Black milk of daybreak we drink it at evening
> we drink it at midday and morning we drink it at night
> we drink and we drink

Above all, the immediacy of "Todesfuge," its compelling because compelled monologue driven as if by unremitting duress, has made two generations of readers assent to this poem's authenticity. So much so, in fact, that the catalogue for a recent exhibition of Anselm Kiefer's paintings, which embody lines from "Todesfuge," states that Celan's poem "was written in a concentration camp," and a *New York Times* article repeats that misinformation.[4] But in fact he composed the poem in Czernowitz in late 1944, not long after Soviet troops reoccupied Bukovina. If "Todesfuge" speaks as if immediately from a Nazi camp where the speaker is present, that owes to this lyric's decisive presentment of firsthand witness, its first-person, on-the-spot, unstopping present tense—*wir trinken und trinken.*

To speak of rhythm and repetition as metaphor in Celan's "Todesfuge," and in a translation of "Todesfuge," calls forth the question of music—the prosodic music of the verse itself as well as the music we are told of within the verse: that is, the cadence running or rising and falling and now and then ruptured, the alliteration and rare rhyme, the refrains or recurrent motifs, and the coda, as well as the whistling we hear about, the playing and dancing and singing, the fiddles and the fugue named in Celan's title. Strictly speaking, the poem's various motifs do not proceed fugally, but are more loosely permuted. Yet in coupling "fugue" to "death," this title drastically travesties everyone's paragon *Meister aus Deutschland*, Bach, with his *Kunst der Fuge* (Art of the Fugue). The title also sets this poem within, although desperately against the grain of, a profound tradition in German culture: the association of music with death, as in Wagner's *Liebestod*, Schubert's *Erlkönig*, and Bach's *Komm süsser Tod*. "*Spielt süsser den Tod*," says the "master" in Celan's "Todesfuge," "play death more sweetly."

Let us bring the question of music to bear on this lyric written not so much after as about (and reputedly even in) Auschwitz, and soon enough you will hear Theodor Adorno's much touted dictum, *Nach Auschwitz ein Gedicht zu schreiben ist barbarisch* (After Auschwitz, to write a poem is barbaric).[5] Adorno's stricture has to do with the pleasures of representation, questioning whether and how to represent aesthetically the Nazi genocide, how to make present again the human experience of it. If one way is through rhythm and repetition as metaphor, then we should first bring into question the matter of metaphor itself.

"What shall I take to witness for thee? what shall I liken to thee, O daughter of Jerusalem? what shall I equal to thee, that I may comfort thee?" This question, this outcry from Lamentations (2:13) seemingly casts in doubt the potency of metaphor—of figurative language, which is the stuff of poetry—to represent, much less to heal, utter duress. Yet that very personification of the solitary city, who is "become as a widow" and "weepeth sore in the night," sits at the source and origin of Judaic lamentation. "Todesfuge" enters into this tradition, taking Shulamith's "ashen hair" to witness for Jewish affliction.

"The prophets usèd much by metaphors / to set forth truth," says John Bunyan's apologia. "Truth" is not advanced much these days as a literary desideratum, but Paul Celan was never too fastidious to speak about truth in connection with poetry. Just after the war, for instance, a friend wondered how Celan could go on writing poems in the language that fashioned *Endlösung* ("Final Solution") and *judenrein* ("Jew-free"), slogans meant to obliterate such things as his poetry. After all, his Roumanian was near-native, his French perfectly fluent. Celan answered, "Only in the mother tongue can one speak his own truth; in a foreign tongue the poet lies."[6] And gradually, I believe, it came home to him that truths of the European Jewish catastrophe could be articulated only in German, precisely because—not although—the murderers spoke it.

This realization dawns in "Todesfuge," which absorbs into its verse the tokens of destruction—a rod, a bullet—and uncannily cites the perpetrator's words, "your golden hair Marguerite" from the commandant's letter home, embedding those words within the poem's own verse rhythm. But as the postwar West German public absorbed and assimilated Celan's Jewish elegy, his unintended gift to *Vergangenheitsbewältigung* (mastery of the past), he became acutely sensitive to the deceiving pleasures of representation, the deflecting effect of metaphor.

Celan's title itself creates the poem's elemental metaphor, and resists a single or simple rendering.[7] It can sound like a surrealist genitive, as for example "eyelids of night" might point to something beyond our reality. But "Fugue of Death," a correct translation, loses the German genitive *Todesfuge*'s compactness—the compact, as it were, between death and music, rupture and order, the word's two sides. Yet "Deathfugue" does not present the idea of belonging, of a train of events belonging to death. Possibly a difficult single word, "Deathsfugue," coins a strange enough equivalent?

Celan's opening, *Schwarze Milch der Frühe*, also becomes the refrain of "Todesfuge"—a refrain so catching that young Germans to whom I mention Paul Celan come up with "Schwarze Milch" before remembering the title. Beginning with the metaphor "black milk" implicitly announces that not description but only metaphor, the figure of speech that asserts something contrary to fact, can convey what must incredibly be known. And "black milk" forms an extreme, even the paradigm of oxymoron, a bittersweet that nullifies the maternal nourishment essential to humankind. Incidentally, Bruno Bettelheim has read *schwarze Milch* as "the image of a mother destroying her infant."[8] But this perhaps characteristically blames just the wrong party. I think Celan, whom the wrenching loss of his adored mother traumatized incurably, would have winced at this twist of his metaphor.

As it happens, Celan suffered acutely from a controversy over the inventiveness of *schwarze Milch*. Yvan Goll's widow accused him of having plagiarized her husband, and the German press helped publicize this groundless, drawn-out charge.[9] Celan, she said, had borrowed from this quatrain by Goll: *Nous buvons le lait noir,* "We drink the black milk / Of the cow Misery / When they butcher our brothers / In slaughterhouses." But these lines appeared in New York in 1942; it's highly unlikely that by 1944 Celan, in Roumanian labor camps and Soviet-occupied Czernowitz, could have known them. Besides, several other Jewish poets from Czernowitz used metaphors similar to "black milk," all of which might have some remoter origin.[10] *Schwarze Milch* could readily have been distilled from chapter four of Lamentations—"Her princes were . . . whiter than milk . . . Their visage is darker than black"—or could arise quite independently, for that matter.

The point here is that a plagiarism charge not only impugns originality, it also exacerbates the question of metaphorical truth, seeming to
vitiate the truth-claim of an image such as black milk. Doubtless Celan
felt attacked on both counts, originality and veracity, two not uncom-
panionable qualities. At bottom he saw the plagiarism campaign,
picked up in Germany, as a willingness to efface the past by blaming
its victim. "Hitlerism reborn," he said, accuses him of "duping the so
good people of Germany by . . . depicting in such a tragic way the
legend of my parents murdered by the Nazis."[11] In underlining "legend," a term Claire Goll had used about Celan's writings, he marks
how a poet's witness to the "Final Solution" can be dismissed as fiction.

Celan was always wary of questions about literary provenance, particularly those directed at him from Germany. In 1959 he responded
to the classical philologist Walter Jens about allusions to Democritus
and Dante; then in 1961, at the height of the plagiarism affair, Jens
must have queried him again about some other sources.[12] Celan replied with a kind of thin-ice politeness. About his poem "In Gestalt
eines Ebers" (In the form of a boar) he writes, "Well now I've asked
myself where I might have gotten my boar. Boars, dear Walter Jens, —
such things do exist [*das gibt es eben*]."

In this letter the poet also responds to a question about literary
precedents for his astonishing motif from "Todesfuge": *wir schaufeln
ein Grab in den Lüften da liegt man nicht eng* (we shovel a grave in the
air there you won't lie too cramped). Celan most revealingly says: "The
'grave in the air'—my dear Walter Jens, in *this* poem, God knows, it is
neither borrowing nor metaphor [*weiss Gott weder Entlehnung noch
Metapher*]." "God knows," indeed! We ourselves cannot know, and
might well adopt Celan's deploring, imploring phrase, "neither borrowing nor metaphor," as a touchstone in testing the limits of representation.

At least two Jewish survivors have known well enough what "a grave
in the air" had to do with. Jean Améry said in 1976 that German antisemitism is "playing with the fire that dug a grave in the air for so
many."[13] And when Primo Levi, who shared a block at Auschwitz with
Améry, invents the partisans' anthem for his 1982 novel *If Not Now,
When?*, they sing that their slaughtered brothers "have dug themselves a grave in the air."[14] I asked Levi how consciously he had used
the image from "Todesfuge." He said that Yes, he stole it, but that
"stealth" (his English word) was a form of homage—a particular hom-

age, I would add, because it credits Celan's words on Yiddish lips, indeed on the Yiddish lips of resistance fighters.

After all, *ein Grab in den Lüften* moves as metaphor beyond metaphor. In asserting what is not the case, it identifies a new datum. The East European *Luftmensch*, who cunningly lived on air, at last has "a grave in the air," has literally expired into the air over the chimneys. And the striking conjunction of "grave" and "air" also insists that countless Jews got no proper grave. So when even Rolf Hochhuth, wondering how to portray the horror of Auschwitz, remarks that "Todesfuge"'s "masterly" metaphors actually screen off reality, one might ask who is really being screened off.[15] And what if "black milk" is in fact no metaphor at all, but the very term camp inmates used to describe a liquid they were given? If so, *schwarze Milch* shows that in Nazi-ridden Europe, the real overtook the surreal, brute fact outfaced imagination. "Did you do this?" a Gestapo officer once asked Picasso in his Paris studio, gesturing at *Guernica*, and the painter replied, "No . . . you did."[16]

Fearing that "Todesfuge" could sound outlandish, its first publisher, in Bucharest in 1947, felt the need to precede it with a note assuring his readership that "the poem . . . is based on a real fact": in Maidanek and elsewhere, he says, "some of the condemned were forced to sing sad music while others dug graves."[17] This perhaps naive-sounding assurance does not necessarily relegate Celan's poem to the status of artifact. Maybe the magazine's readers needed some such orientation because in 1947, when "Todesfuge" appeared, Roumania was going Soviet; the same issue included a long and doubtless heartening poem called "The Tractor." What's more, in this first publication Celan's title was not "Todesfuge" but "Todestango" (Tango of death)—all the more reason for readers to suspect svelte rhythms giving the lie to graves and smoke.

Here too fact intervenes, documenting not so much "Todesfuge" as the destructive scheme this poem bodies forth. At the Janowska camp in Lemberg, an S.S. lieutenant made Jewish fiddlers play a new piece called "Death Tango" during camp functions.[18] And at Maidanek—this from a 1944 pamphlet that Moscow circulated in many languages—prisoners marched to the crematorium in columns five abreast: "Scores of loudspeakers began to emit the deafening strains of the foxtrot and the tango. And they blared all the morning, all day, all the evening, and all night."[19]

Suppose that Paul Celan in Soviet-occupied Czernowitz saw this 1944 account of the music blaring all morning, all day, all evening, all night. Then shortly afterwards he wrote: "Black milk of daybreak we drink it at evening / we drink it at midday and morning we drink it at night." Or even suppose that Celan wrote "Todesfuge" while actually in a camp. These assumptions only begin to touch the poem's authenticity. For a gap still exists between reported fact and cadenced verse. In sparking that gap, the poem reveals not fact but psychic actuality— an actuality about which Celan after 1945 stayed eloquently tacit. "What the life of a Jew was during the war years," he wrote once, "I need not mention." [20] Or else he simply called those years *das was geschah* (that which happened), or he resorted to necessary paradox, declaring himself (in Germany after the war) one who *mit seinem Dasein zur Sprache geht, wirklichkeitswund und Wirklichkeit suchend* (goes with his very being to language, stricken by and seeking reality) (*GW*, III, 186).

What kind of hold, then, has Celan's "Todesfuge" on the *Wirklichkeit*, the "reality" that both hurt and drew him? Or rather, what reality do his lines open up, open toward? Certainly the poem contains tokens enough of a murderous world: commandant, hounds, shovels, graves, smoke. This *univers concentrationnaire*, however, inheres essentially in the rhythm and repetitions of "Todesfuge" (which are, for better or worse, what induce German teachers to have it performed). Its rhythms, beneath everything else, make this lyric irrefutable. As the only poem Celan ever wrote with no punctuation whatsoever, it finds a beat by the first line—

> *wir trinken sie abends*
>
> we drink it at evening

—and keeps finding that rising-falling through to the end. Something enthralling about the rhythm makes it germane to this poem and no less so to any translation, if a listener is to sense the coercion locked within the allure of enthrallment. And Celan recited "Todesfuge" relentlessly, with no release of tempo or tension, iterating and reiterating a few turns of speech, voicing endless attrition. [21]

Endless attrition: here we perceive the poem's elemental signifying gesture, a timing of day-in, day-out fatality, eternal recurrence under what Nietzsche would call its "most dreadful" aspect: "wir trinken und trinken." [22] But if this poem managed no more than a compulsive repetition, that could only bring the trauma back, representing it helplessly. Instead, the plural voice stops saying "we drink it" and addresses the "black milk" directly: *wir trinken dich* (we drink you—or "we drink thee," I'm tempted to say, matching the intimate German *dich* with a form that English has lost except in biblical idiom). For these speakers to confront the poem's dominant figure of "black milk"—is it the gas itself?—seems an act of rhetorical resistance, almost outfacing the metaphor's objective authority.

Similarly, rather than succumb to the "master" narrative of the *Meister aus Deutschland,* whose epistolary utterance—"your golden hair Marguerite"—is heard in every stanza, some other voice interrupts with "your ashen hair Shulamith." This cannot be the commandant's but must be an alternative voice; that is, helpless repetition transforms momentarily into memorial litany.

What it feels like to hear *Faust*'s tragic heroine Margarete maudlinly invoked on S.S. lips is probably best attested by native Germans who grew up revering Goethe as the quintessential Enlightenment spirit. But does a rendering of *Margarete* as "Marguerite" deflect that irony? To my ear the French name, gathering gorgeous overtones from Gounod's and Berlioz's operas, emphasizes a deeper irony, that of the music counterpointing "Todesfuge"'s deathliness. And "Marguerite" even adds a bitter bilingual rhyme with the Hebrew "Shulamith."

As pertinent as the presence in "Todesfuge" of Goethe through his Margarete, I think, is the more favorably charged presence of Heinrich Heine, like Celan a German-speaking Jewish poet exiled in Paris with complexly ambivalent feelings toward Germany. When the commandant in Celan's poem writes home to his beloved *dein goldenes Haar Margarete,* he is tritely emulating Heine's most famous song to the Lorelei, the siren who "combs her golden hair." But whereas that type of allusion in Eliot's *Waste Land* would have mainly an ironic, undercutting effect, here such an emulation must strike us as profoundly sickening, given the fact that Nazi cultural commissars officially declared Heine's poems to be "anonymous" folksong. Celan was well aware of this literary purging, and came at times to identify himself with Heine. [23]

Sometimes in "Todesfuge" the cadence alone can subversively summon another text or historical moment, enlisting them within its own design. Listening to Celan's poem, we might well have in our ears another well-known lyric by Heine, "The Silesian Weavers" (1844), whose angry suffering stanzas directed against the vicious *Vaterland* now come to have a familiar refrain:

> We're busy weaving day and night—
> Old Germany, we weave your shroud,
> We weave the threefold curse in it,
>   We're weaving, we're weaving!

Wir weben, wir weben! From a century later, we hear the sound and cadence of *wir trinken und trinken,* in "Todesfuge." Heine's speakers were weaving the doom of their oppressors, though the actual Silesian weavers were brutally suppressed, not far from Oswiecim. Celan's speakers must passively drink their own doom.

For these reasons and others, it matters to keep the beat. *Wir trinken und trinken:* by line three, the poem's shortest verse, this rhythm has taken hold, and ought to hold in translation as well—"we're drinking and drinking." Although that sounds too vulgar for Celan's phrase, some such rollicking beat may call up a waltz-like sensation or, even more ironically, may bring out a sardonic hint in "Deathsfugue" of well-loved German drinking songs—of the Munich beer-hall, let's say, where Nazism arose: *wir trinken und trinken*—you can see the torsos swaying and hear the tankards clanking. Or else this hectic rhythm—*spielt weiter zum Tanz auf* (play on for the dancing)—can evoke the traditional medieval German emblem, the *Totentanz* or dance of death, *danse macabre*—and all right then, say grateful source-spotters, so that's all it is, the old *Totentanz!*

You may hear as well, in the opening verses of "Todesfuge," another, distantly familiar biblical rhythm, which I have come to recognize through translating. *Schwarze Milch der Frühe wir trinken sie abends:* I would like to say "Black milk of daybreak we drink it at dusk," so as to let alliteration imprint an inescapable dire recurrence. But instead of "dusk," "evening" for *abends* at the end of the line not only keeps Celan's metric, it also leads to "morning" in the next line, *morgens.* Now turn back behind this poem and recall Martin Luther's Genesis, *Da ward aus Abend und Morgen der erste Tag,* or the Buber-Rosenzweig version, *Abend ward und Morgen ward: Ein Tag* (There was evening and there was morning: one day). To call up this deeply recessed biblical rhythm, *Vay'hi erev vay'hi boker yom echad,* gives Celan's poem unlimited reach. And for a translator to say "evening," with the King

James version, rather than "dusk," sustains a radical parody, a countermand of Creation—though not so radical a parody, of course, as a Hebrew translation of the poem would present.

Celan's poem makes us think again about the limits of representation. The rhythmic reiteration in lines such as *wir trinken dich abends und morgens wir trinken und trinken,* where meter incessantly metes out a wretched daily ration; the overtones of beer hall and death dance whose mutual discrepancy only makes them more pertinent; the cadence of biblical Creation drawn into a kind of morning roll call that nullifies the founding myth—all this lyric activity drives deeper than any reportorial, documentary, or even testimonial task. In other words, where representation has its limits, presentation with such terrifying resonances does not.

Nothing like these resonances was audible, I suspect, when in 1952 Paul Celan first visited postwar Germany, for a Group 47 meeting. He read "Todesfuge," which was then virtually unknown, and witnesses differ somewhat as to how the reading went. He recited rapidly, with pathos, and had "an almost hypnotic effect," one person says,[24] but another recalls that some writers went around "sarcastically scanning: 'Schwarze Milch der Frühe . . .'" Reports speak of Celan's *"poésie pure,"* call him "ununderstandable," "not *engagé.*" Evidently his pathos and "visionary articulation" went over poorly, yet German radio wanted to broadcast him and a publisher signed him up. Later that year Celan's first book came out in Germany, and "Todesfuge" began its career as a *cause célèbre,* practically a national obsession.

One or two early responses met the poem head-on, but most, beguiled by its music, stuck to the label of *poésie pure.* A 1953 reviewer liked "Todesfuge" for its "enchantment," its "removal of everything concrete, absorptive rhythm, romanticizing metaphor, lyrical alchemy," and "Zen Buddhist satori-experience."[25] And Hans Egon Holthusen, in the influential monthly *Merkur,* praised Celan for "mastering" (yes, *bewältigen*) unimaginable horrors "with a few simple paradoxes"; for "singing one of the most ghastly and significant events in recent history . . . so that it escapes history's bloody chamber of horrors to rise into the ether of pure poetry."[26] Singing?—well, yes and no. But rising into the ether? That was the Jews this poem gives voice to, never the poem itself.

In Paris, where he eked out a living as a teacher and translator, Celan watched woundedly the German appropriation of his poems.

Sometime during the late 1950s he made the extraordinary recording of "Todesfuge" we now have, but he never recorded it again. And he would not permit the poem to be anthologized in collections that included authors sympathetic to Nazism during the war. In 1958, accepting the Bremen prize, he told his German audience that as a German-speaking Jew from eastern Europe, the only thing he had not lost was his mother tongue. "But it had to pass," he said, "through its own answerlessnesses, pass through frightful muting, pass through the thousand darknesses of deathbringing speech" (*GW*, III, 186). And in case that insistent phrasing was not *engagé* enough, he added: "A poem is not timeless . . . it seeks to reach through time—through it, not above and beyond it."

Just then, Celan was also composing "Engführung," a long poem, difficult to access, whose title, meaning a fugal *stretto*, suggests that in some sense it might supplant the "Todesfuge":

> *Asche.*
> *Asche, Asche.*
> *Nacht.*
> *Nacht-und-Nacht.*   (*GW*, I, 199)

Here the ashes and night from "Todesfuge" are rid of cadence and metaphor. Later in 1958 Celan spoke pointedly about German poetry's need to set aside "the 'melodiousness' that more or less untroubled still trips tunefully alongside what is most frightful" (*GW*, III, 167). And that year too, he wrote to a sympathetic German doctoral student: "What counts for me is truth, not euphony."[27] So much concern for the historical implication as against the lyric freedom of German poetry must bespeak an anxiety that "Todesfuge" was coming to serve as an instrument of alibi, of "reparation"—was even lapsing into invidious parallel with the orchestra at Auschwitz that doubtless gave S.S. officers a pleasurable diversion.

Then in 1960 came the plagiarism charge, followed by Celan's most Jewishly steeped poems. Meanwhile Adorno, in a 1962 radio talk that he also published in 1965, repeated his notorious sentence, "After Auschwitz, to write a poem is barbaric," and explained it: "Through the aesthetic principle of stylization . . . an unimaginable fate still seems as if it had some meaning; it becomes transfigured, with something of the horror removed."[28] Although Adorno probably did not have Celan in mind, others applied his stricture to "Todesfuge." Worst

of all, a 1965 article in *Merkur,* the journal that regularly housed Adorno's thoughts on music and literature, questioned "Todesfuge" and its
motifs, "all of them thoroughly composed in an elegant score—didn't
that show far too much pleasure in art, in art making 'beauty' from
despair?"[29]

Bitterly, in letters and conversation, Celan rejected the suggestion
(from Germany!) that a poet whose parents perished brutally at Nazi
hands and who himself barely survived forced labor might batten on
that history.[30] Indeed such a poet knows that when the common language has had to "pass through . . . that which happened," as Celan
said, then raw happening must pass through poems to actuate consciousness and conscience. Meanwhile his voicing of the German language was unquestionably changing, was estranging that language—
the "true- / stammered mouth" (*GW,* II, 42), as he put it in 1964, was
turning more oblique, staccato, enigmatic. He reportedly told someone: "I don't musicalize anymore, as at the time of the much-touted
'Todesfuge,' which by now has been threshed out in many a textbook."[31] Yet of course the poem had its own momentum. A friend has
shown me her high-school reader from the 1960s, with the word *Dak-
tylus* carefully penciled in above "Todesfuge." Maybe the fluent meter
was easier to teach than the abysmal irony. And since 1966, at least
seven German composers have set the poem for different vocal and
instrumental combinations.[32]

The question persists, then: Does "Todesfuge" read too well, accede
too easily, too musically? Certainly not, in my experience, especially
with listeners hearing Celan's voice for the first time. Even those who
do not understand German find his caustic enunciation and intensified
tempo stunning rather than pleasing. Likewise for those listeners, a
verse translation must seek some equivalent to the German, with its
movement of controlled violence. English, a cognate language, can
with some effort almost ritually approach this equivalence. For example, line four, *wir schaufeln ein Grab in den Lüften da liegt man
nicht eng,* translates as "we shovel a grave in the air there you won't lie
too cramped." That monosyllable *eng,* which Celan pronounced *engk,*
means "narrow" or "tight," but "cramped" voices the harshness and
avoids a rhyme with "night" in this poem where such rhyme would
prettify.

The poem's longest line, later in stanza one, can also be mimed
closely in translation: *er schreibt es und tritt vor das Haus und es*

blitzen die Sterne er pfeift seine Rüden herbei becomes "he writes it and steps out of doors and the stars are all sparkling he whistles his hounds to come close." Then in the next line, *er pfeift seine Juden hervor lässt schaufeln ein Grab in der Erde* (he whistles his Jews into rows has them shovel a grave in the ground), the slant-rhyme "close" with "rows" echoes Celan's abrasion of *Rüden* (hounds) against *Juden* (Jews)—a dissonance worth preserving for its reminder that the S.S. sometimes called their Jews "dogs" and their German shepherds "men."

Now why, after all, try to cleave faithfully to the syllabic and accentual measure of the original? Just *because*, I want to say—because here where Paul Celan's German language needed an incantatory impetus to speak out from the "thousand darknesses of deathbringing speech," anything less than ritual observance would deflect that impetus.

Toward the end of "Todesfuge," by the time it has evolved a time span of its own, rhythm and repetition have taken on thematic, systemic force. They permit no alternative, there is no escaping them, and that is precisely their metaphoric burden. After complex overlapping and counterpoint, the fugue's accumulations intensify in stanza four, most strikingly with a phrase that occurs here three times and has become the tagline for "Todesfuge":

> *der Tod ist ein Meister aus Deutschland sein Auge ist blau*
> *er trifft dich mit bleierner Kugel er trifft dich genau*

Clearly the poet had to stay in step; in this poem's only change from an early version, what had been *Aug* now reads *Auge*. And clearly a mock-balladic rhyme juts out ironically here:

> this Death is a master from Deutschland his eye it is blue
> he shoots you with shot made of lead shoots you level and true

The folkloric purity of that icy nordic eye seems to call for a folksy idiom and a hackneyed rhyme in translation. By the same token, I've kept *Deutschland* intact throughout my version. Its two syllables grip the rhythm better than "Germany," and anyway, the name's been made known everywhere—*Deutschland, Deutschland, über alles!* Celan used it only this once in his poetry and never again.

Something new is borne in on me here with the way *Deutschland* recurs, untranslated. Once having rendered this whole phrase, "Death is a master from Deutschland," the next time it occurs I've already got my translation, and then the next and the next. There's no need, no use in thinking anymore—and that very realization, that translator's sense of inexorable repetitiveness, itself enacts something inexorable: quotidian annihilation.

Then I wonder: given a *"fugue* of death"—this poem's musical logic—why not drive the catchphrase home as Celan does? Why not render it back to the German tongue? So the second time around I say "Death is a master *aus Deutschland"*; then, "Death is *ein Meister aus Deutschland"*; and finally, *"der Tod ist ein Meister aus Deutschland."* By thus veering around to its original, my version gets a "ring" of truth, so to speak, a tangential identity with verse written by Paul Celan— who said, after all, that "in a foreign tongue the poet lies." To sustain the exemplary force of this poem "after Auschwitz," maybe we must again hear it in the mother tongue become a mother's murderers' tongue. Meanwhile American ears may perhaps feel a strangeness of German, a salutary darkness, even an impinging or overcoming.

At last, through another veering or reversion, "Deathsfugue" comes to an end, as does "Todesfuge," when the twin motifs that have shadowed each other throughout this poem finally join—

> *dein goldenes Haar Margarete*
> *dein aschenes Haar Sulamith*

—in a chord that makes discord, a close with no closure, because the German and Jewish ideals will not coexist. In its own sense, this poem radically tests the limits of representation, for the termination of "Todesfuge" shows up the murderous euphemism of extermination. When any poem ends, of course, it has come to its limit of representation. "Todesfuge" comes to that limit with a vengeance, so to speak. The rhythmically synonymous evocations of Margarete and Shulamith— *dein goldenes Haar, dein aschenes Haar*—threaten to obliterate both figures mutually, unless some remnant letter or spirit may survive.

Whether, in ultimately reverting to Celan's mother tongue, my version acts somehow as restitution, restoring to the poet what was misappropriated, I cannot say. Evidently this poem keeps its representative status in Germany. On the fiftieth anniversary of Kristallnacht, an actress recited "Todesfuge" in the Bundestag.[33] Composers have set it, a German-Jewish dance troupe performs it in repertory, and West German television has broadcast a documentary on the "Final Solution" entitled "Der Tod ist ein Meister aus Deutschland."[34] The lines invoking Margarete and Shulamith figure starkly on several major canvases by Anselm Kiefer, which do not coopt them. And maybe this lyric says more to German high-schoolers since 1970, when Celan drowned himself in the Seine.

Later that year, as it happens, another pedagogical journal took up "Todesfuge," divining reconciliation in the closing couplet, a "loving meeting" between Margarete and Shulamith, and even "forgiveness."[35] But how shall *Faust's* Gretchen, the eternal feminine, join the Song of Song's "black but comely" maiden Shulamith, a figure of longing and return from exile, in German-Jewish symbiosis? At best that is wishful thinking; at worst, a willful imperviousness to the double blight or curse this poem's closing couplet may be pronouncing. And forgiveness is precluded by Paul Celan's recorded voice (if by nothing else) when just before the end of its vehement utterance, it breaks and catches on the "a" of *aschenes*, Shulamith's "ashen" hair, in almost a glottal stop: *dein—aschenes Haar Sulamith*.

With that break, Celan's fugue runs its course. And by running out on *Shulamith*, it enacts an ultimate metaphor. For this word resounds strangely in the German lexicon, as in the English. Being Hebrew, it forgoes, it preempts both languages. Being a name and a term that occurs once only in the Bible, it admits no translation. Within the shadow of *aschenes*, Paul Celan's "Todesfuge" still ends purely, by doing what Nazism attempted to forbid: naming the other. Archaic, inalienable, truly *Shulamith* has the last word, not to mention the silence resounding after.

Todesfuge

Schwarze Milch der Frühe wir trinken sie abends
wir trinken sie mittags und morgens wir trinken sie nachts
wir trinken und trinken
wir schaufeln ein Grab in den Lüften da liegt man nicht eng
Ein Mann wohnt im Haus der spielt mit den Schlangen der
    schreibt
der schreibt wenn es dunkelt nach Deutschland dein goldenes
    Haar Margarete
er schreibt es und tritt vor das Haus und es blitzen die Sterne er
    pfeift seine Rüden herbei
er pfeift seine Juden hervor lässt schaufeln ein Grab in der Erde
er befiehlt uns spielt auf nun zum Tanz

Schwarze Milch der Frühe wir trinken dich nachts
wir trinken dich morgens und mittags wir trinken dich abends
wir trinken und trinken
Ein Mann wohnt im Haus der spielt mit den Schlangen der
    schreibt
der schreibt wenn es dunkelt nach Deutschland dein goldenes
    Haar Margarete
Dein aschenes Haar Sulamith wir schaufeln ein Grab in den
    Lüften da liegt man nicht eng
Er ruft stecht tiefer ins Erdreich ihr einen ihr andern singet und
    spielt
er greift nach dem Eisen im Gurt er schwingts seine Augen sind
    blau
stecht tiefer die Spaten ihr einen ihr andern spielt weiter zum Tanz
    auf

Schwarze Milch der Frühe wir trinken dich nachts
wir trinken dich mittags und morgens wir trinken dich abends
wir trinken und trinken
ein Mann wohnt im Haus dein goldenes Haar Margarete
dein aschenes Haar Sulamith er spielt mit den Schlangen
Er ruft spielt süßer den Tod der Tod ist ein Meister aus
    Deutschland
er ruft streicht dunkler die Geigen dann steigt ihr als Rauch in die
    Luft
dann habt ihr ein Grab in den Wolken da liegt man nicht eng

Schwarze Milch der Frühe wir trinken dich nachts
wir trinken dich mittags der Tod ist ein Meister aus Deutschland
wir trinken dich abends und morgens wir trinken und trinken
der Tod ist ein Meister aus Deutschland sein Auge ist blau
er trifft dich mit bleierner Kugel er trifft dich genau
ein Mann wohnt im Haus dein goldenes Haar Margarete
er hetzt seine Rüden auf uns er schenkt uns ein Grab in der Luft
er spielt mit den Schlangen und träumet der Tod ist ein Meister
   aus Deutschland

dein goldenes Haar Margarete
dein aschenes Haar Sulamith

Deathsfugue

Black milk of daybreak we drink it at evening
we drink it at midday and morning we drink it at night
we drink and we drink
we shovel a grave in the air there you won't lie too cramped
A man lives in the house he plays with his vipers he writes
he writes when it grows dark to Deutschland your golden hair
    Marguerite
he writes it and steps out of doors and the stars are all sparkling he
    whistles his hounds to come close
he whistles his Jews into rows has them shovel a grave in the
    ground
he orders us strike up and play for the dance

Black milk of daybreak we drink you at night
we drink you at morning and midday we drink you at evening
we drink and we drink
A man lives in the house he plays with his vipers he writes
he writes when it grows dark to Deutschland your golden hair
    Marguerite
your ashen hair Shulamith we shovel a grave in the air there you
    won't lie too cramped
He shouts jab the earth deeper you there you others sing up and
    play
he grabs for the rod in his belt he swings it his eyes are blue
jab your spades deeper you there you others play on for the
    dancing

Black milk of daybreak we drink you at night
we drink you at midday and morning we drink you at evening
we drink and we drink
a man lives in the house your goldenes Haar Marguerite
your aschenes Haar Shulamith he plays with his vipers
He shouts play death more sweetly Death is a master from
    Deutschland
he shouts scrape your strings darker you'll rise then in smoke to
    the sky
you'll have a grave then in the clouds there you won't lie too
    cramped

Black milk of daybreak we drink you at night
we drink you at midday Death is a master aus Deutschland
we drink you at evening and morning we drink and we drink
this Death is ein Meister aus Deutschland his eye it is blue
he shoots you with shot made of lead shoots you level and true
a man lives in the house your goldenes Haar Margarete
he looses his hounds on us grants us a grave in the air
he plays with his vipers and daydreams der Tod ist ein Meister aus
    Deutschland

dein goldenes Haar Margarete
dein aschenes Haar Sulamith

Paul Celan, 1944–45
trans. John Felstiner

< 16 >

"The Grave in the Air": Unbound Metaphors in Post-Holocaust Poetry

Sidra DeKoven Ezrahi

In 1969, in what was to be one of his last major ventures before suicide, Paul Celan visited Israel and addressed the Hebrew Writers' Association. He spoke about the greening of the land and of the language: "Here," he said, "in your outer and inner landscape, I find much of the compulsion toward truth, much of the self-evidence, much of the world-open uniqueness of great poetry."[1] The world-embracing possibility that emanates from a reclaimed landscape, the self-evidence that allows public surfaces to speak, are remarkable concessions to the idea of repatriation on the part of this poet of private depths and unhinged languages. In that address, in that visit, and in the Hebrew words scattered throughout the poetry of his last years, he entered tentatively into a cultural space in which his own "Jewish loneliness"[2] might have found a different resolution.

But what becomes increasingly evident with time is the extent to which Celan and the Hebrew writers he was addressing remain embedded in two distinct universes of discourse. Within the global conversation among Jewish writers or between Jewish writers and their audiences, they represent radically different cultural options and forms of authorizing the past. The critical questions over aesthetic boundaries that were inaugurated by Theodor Adorno and have informed most readings of post-Holocaust poetry in America and Europe are rarely invoked in discussions of the Holocaust in Israel. As I will argue below, challenges to the adequacy or authenticity of poetic language, debates over its mimetic function and moral constraints, are negligible in the presence of a consensual historical narrative and a preexistent poetic vocabulary of catastrophe and martyrdom such as one finds in Hebrew culture. On the other hand, no consideration of the poetry of Paul Celan is possible, it seems, without reference to Adorno's dictum that "to write poetry after Auschwitz is barbaric."[3]

< 259 >

Said to have been originally occasioned by a reading of Celan's "To-desfuge," Adorno's statement has become explicitly linked with that poem so that the two are as intertwined as a talmudic commentary and its biblical source. Rarely, however, does one find any acknowledg-ment of the complexity of Adorno's position within the context of his philosophy of aesthetics or the dynamics of his own re-readings of Ce-lan. Rarely is it acknowledged that Adorno returned to "Auschwitz" again and again, refining and restating and qualifying his original state-ment in subsequent essays, probing but never quite resolving the con-tradictions that most of his readers tend to ignore altogether, that "the abundance of real suffering tolerates no forgetting . . . [that] this suf-fering . . . demands the continued existence of art [even as] . . . it prohibits it. It is now virtually in art alone that suffering can still find its own voice, consolation, without immediately being betrayed by it. The most important artists of the age have realized this."[4] As Adorno's dictum has been appropriated unreflectively since his death in 1969 by the very "culture industry" he so vigorously attacked in his lifetime, one is tempted to ask how, within the terms of his own critical theory, distinctions might be drawn between "barbarity," which is by defini-tion outside the civilized discourse, and liminality, which is not?

When examined more closely, the critical norms that have their ori-gins in (mis-)readings of Adorno relate not only to the so-called barbar-ity or betrayal but to a widespread if unarticulated sense of the *propri-ety* of the symbolic language that faces Auschwitz. Since the "scorched earth" which is the locus of this language cannot generate a natural audience for it, the issue of naturalization becomes crucial. Where, in our symbolic geography, do we locate Auschwitz or the Warsaw Ghetto: In Poland? In Nazi-occupied Europe? In the vast resonant spaces of Jewish memory? Or as the metonymic limit of Western civi-lization? The disruption between this place and its signs is greater than the common disjunctions between referents and their signifiers—and the controversy over nominative and metaphoric language settles in that great divide. Is Celan's "grave in the air" an open space with no boundaries? Or do certain images belong to specific symbolic worlds from which they are detached at considerable peril to both writer and reader? Are there Holocaust symbols or *topoi* so *over*determined that they cannot enter other existential universes without being either dis-ruptive or presumptuous—violating an unspoken principle of incom-mensurability (the Nazi as prototype of Sylvia Plath's "Daddy"; Ausch-

witz as William Styron's analogue of the American South; Babi Yar as
D. M. Thomas's configuration of Freudian—or Jungian—space; Rai-
ner Werner Fassbinder's "Hitler" as a blinding white emanation).[5] Or
is that which takes "Auschwitz" as its sign in fact so *under*determined,
in Lyotard's terms so "dissipated," by the premise of extermination that
it elides into a phraseless space?[6] It may be not only the limits of representation that are being probed here but the limits of *metaphor.*

There is no easy critical approach to the widely shared perception of
a decorum that renders specific poetic acts illegitimate or recalcitrant
in specific contexts and attempts to limit the polysemous potential of
certain symbolic vocabularies. That such a discussion often degener-
ates into competing claims for moral authority or for the guardianship
of memory may be a function not only of the ethical dimension, which
has become an acknowledged aspect of the enterprise of remembering, but also of a displaced poetic language that, like the survivors
themselves, may move randomly from one cultural realm to another
seeking a home. Images that are so decontextualized as to be considered illegitimate may in certain instances be acts of cultural disruption
in the most radical poetic sense: ungrounded and migrant, they may
be disruptive without being constitutive of alternative worlds. Even—
or especially—in the wake of catastrophe, a "redemptive aesthetic"
emerges along with public acts of commemoration to create soterio-
logical possibilities.

With reference to the idealizing function of art, Leo Bersani has
written, "A crucial assumption in the culture of redemption is that a
certain type of repetition of experience in art repairs inherently damaged or valueless experience . . . The catastrophes of history matter
much less if they are somehow compensated for in art, and art itself
gets reduced to a kind of superior patching function, is enslaved to
those very materials to which it presumably imparts value; the redemptive aesthetic asks us to consider art as a correction of life."[7] Yet
cultures that attempt to appropriate the dislocated languages of the
exiles may never succeed in domesticating the fragments of their broken worlds or in defending against the acidity of an irredeemable vision—a vision which not only resists corrective idealizing but positively exemplifies, through a series of defamiliarizing procedures, the
irretrievability and irreparability of the loss.

Perhaps the only version of utopianism that is compatible with the
most unregenerate responses to cataclysm is that reformulated by

Adorno in the postwar years. Resisting the totalizing philosophies that lead to fascism while affirming the potential of the most radical art forms to provide a "prefiguration of reconciled life" by which to measure flawed realities,[8] Adorno manages to rescue some of the utopian longings from the devastation of the war and of a failed Marxist orthodoxy: "The only philosophy which can be responsibly practised in face of despair is the attempt to contemplate all things as they would present themselves from the standpoint of redemption . . . Perspectives must be fashioned that displace and estrange the world, reveal it to be, with its rifts and crevices, as indigent and distorted as it will appear one day in the messianic light."[9]

Probably the most striking example of a displaced or estranged image in post-Holocaust poetry is the "black milk" which opens Celan's "Todesfuge" and provides its incantatory refrain. The "black milk" has become as much an icon of the Holocaust as the photograph of the little boy with his hands raised in the Warsaw Ghetto. But the oxymoron, no less palpable in our imagination for being an "impossible" image, is not only the rhetorical correlative of liminal reality; as the trope of ultimate contradiction that does not correct but defies the laws of both experience and logic, it relinquishes its compensatory function. That is, what may be so disruptive in such imagery is not its aesthetic properties per se but its defiance of a "redemptive aesthetic." Celan's poems, in Adorno's reading, "emulate a language that lies below the helpless prattle of human beings—even below the level of organized life as such . . . Celan translates into linguistic terms what happens to landscapes when they become more and more abstract."[10]

Yet the public status of "Todesfuge" would seem to belie its presumably subversive impact. The recitation of the poem in the Bundestag in 1988 to commemorate the fiftieth anniversary of Kristallnacht, its frequent quotation in film, in art, in dance, in music suggest that it has actually become a part of the official ritual of remembrance in Germany. It would appear, then, that the black milk and the ghetto child have become, in equal measure, constitutive texts in the regenerative semantic of their respective cultures.[11] But consider further. This poem, which has become a litmus test of the public attempt to come to terms with or to "master" the past—the *Vergangenheitsbewältigung*—yet remains somehow extraneous to the cultural conversations taking place in Germany. Why, one might ask, is the poem read so consistently as *poésie pure?* And why, if it has become a canonical text, has it lent itself to charges of plagiarism? The accusation, launched by Yvan Goll's widow, that Celan borrowed his black milk from her husband's poetry is in itself less significant—poets with Celan's visibility are not infrequently beset by claims that would impugn their originality— than the receptivity of sectors of the German public to such insinuations and the defensiveness of Celan's own response.[12] There is an implicit connection, I would submit, between the dislocation of the text and both its legitimating function and its provisional legitimacy within the society.

One point of departure for probing these questions could be a comparison of the textbook "misreadings" of "Todesfuge" in Germany with the simple intertextual acts practiced by such writers as Jean Améry and Primo Levi. Allusions to the "grave in the air" in an essay by Améry and in a novel and a poem by Levi—and Levi's disarming admission, when asked how conscious his borrowing had been, that his "stealth" [*sic*] was not really plagiary but "homage"[13]—illustrate not only the fine line between plagiary and allusion or quotation but the status of survivors such as Améry and Levi as a natural primary reading community for Celan's poem. The search for such a community is the compelling force that shapes the writing of every displaced writer.

Levi struggled to overcome his own "Jewish loneliness" by regrounding himself not only in his native tongue and native soil, but also in the positivistic principle of the transparent or correlative status of language vis-à-vis experience. The clarity of language relates here to the attempt to "objectify" experience as a property of culture, to rescue it from the irredeemably unique and therefore incommunicable. In Levi's view, the urge to communicate, the mandate of lucidity, and the subordination of language to the writer's "message" are betrayed in Celan's more obscure verses:

> If [Celan's writing] is a message, it gets lost in the 'background noise': it is not a communication, it is not a language, or at most it is a dark and truncated language precisely like that of a person who is about to die and is alone, as we all will be at the point of death. But since we the living are not alone, we must not write as if we were alone. As long as we live we have a responsibility. We must answer for what we write, word by word, and make sure that every word reaches its target . . . [Celan's] destiny [as a suicide] makes one think

about the obscurity of [his] poetry as a pre-suicide, a not-wanting-to-be, a flight from the world, of which the intentional death was the crown.[14]

The life urge is equated here with responsibility (that is, lucidity or communicability) and the death wish with inaccessibility. Yet what Levi is in fact demonstrating in his encounter with Celan's text, and in his special access to that text, is its existential, and not only or primarily its hermeneutic impact. ("I believe that Celan the poet should be meditated upon and pitied rather than imitated.")[15] Even when Levi takes issue with Celan's more opaque poetry, he identifies himself as the very reader whom Celan is seeking: Celan's writing, he admits, is "truly . . . a reflection of the obscurity of his fate and his generation, and it grows ever denser around the reader, gripping him as in an ice-cold iron vise."[16] So stricken, Levi reveals himself to be the worthy if reluctant recipient of the kind of literary assault defined by Kafka as piercing the "frozen sea within us."[17]

Levi's response to Celan dramatizes the perceived links between the survivor's personal, existential strategies and his authorial choices. Whether or not we regard Levi's own suicide in 1987 as a sign of his failure to find in the Italian language and soil adequate reflections of the precarious relations between the inner and outer landscapes of his imagination, we know from his very first book how desperate was his search for a language and an audience.[18] If we read his own death back into his life retrospectively, as he bids us do with Celan, his equation of life and "responsibility" renders his suicide, no matter what the circumstances that might have induced it, an admission of the failure to meet that responsibility.[19] Celan may be seen, then, as truly Levi's poetic foil, reflecting the attempt to integrate life with the inherent *irresponsibility* of a poetry surviving in a world whose symbolic geography has been convulsed, constituting a place "where all tropes and metaphors want to be led *ad absurdum.*"[20] Levi's insistence on the writer as witness and communicator, like the definition of the artist as builder of alternative worlds, retains some coherent vision or blueprint of the social order and a mandated relationship between history and art; it places the self in a specific, delineated position at a controlled distance from both that which has been survived and the tribunal to which the testimony is being addressed.

The image of a tribunal can be carried further. Read as *evidence,* this literature, its writers, and its readers seem to resemble nothing so much as presences in a judicial court. Even as Celan's allusions and citations penetrate into the deepest layers of several centuries of German literature and reach across several languages, he is also held to another accounting—one which relates to the representational or historical status of his poetry. In delineating audiences, conversations, and the very nature of the communicative act, the postmodernist discourse has significantly redefined, in ways we have already alluded to, the role of citation and quotation (plagiary's legitimate siblings).[21] Yet debates over those "Holocaust texts" indicted for having transgressed the limits tend to presume a unique decorum or protocol in regard to embedded citation or documentation. Consider, for example, the controversy that ensued over D. M. Thomas's alleged plagiarism of the Babi Yar sequence in *The White Hotel*. Far more memorable than the novel itself was Thomas's defense of his literary practice of borrowing passages from Anatoli Kuznetsov's novel, *Babi Yar,* in order to let history speak, unmediated by the imagination, as it were. The fact that he lifted those passages from the *English* translation of a *Russian* documentary *novel* with its own complicated publishing history[22]—not to mention the highly interventionist act of pinioning his heroine through the genitals in order to confer symbolic coherence at the moment of death—all this only underscores the tension between the urgency of the truth claim and the dislocation of the frames of language and experience without which it cannot be upheld.

Needless to say, the charges of plagiary directed at D. M. Thomas are of a different order from those suffered by Celan and only serve to underscore the differential weight of survivors as authenticating presences in the culture. Thomas's authority is, admittedly, located in historical documents or texts with a "documentary" valence; Celan's lies within his own person. And yet the weight of the written historical record, of recorded facts that would be admissible in some hypothetical court of law, often turns even the most abstract poetry into testimony. Rather than simply dismissing as irrelevant the accusations of plagiarism that were directed at "Todesfuge," John Felstiner presents in his discussions of the poem a series of counterarguments, among them one based on a kind of circumstantial evidence: he suggests that " 'black milk' may have been no metaphor at all but the very term camp inmates used to describe a liquid they were given"—and he cites Celan's declaration that "what counts for me is truth, not euphony."[23] Celan's own insistence on the veracity of the image or of the poem as a whole reflects more than the defensive posture of a poet vis-à-vis perceived misreadings of his work, just as the critical interest in his ongoing response reflects more than questions of intentionality. It is the survivor's unmediated access to experience, the survivor as ultimate reference, rather than the "correct" interpretation of the poem, that is being affirmed here as part of a struggle over the poem's cultural status. We should hardly be surprised, given the stakes, to discover that in 1988, forty-four years after its composition, "Todesfuge" was mistaken for an artifact, a "document" from the camps, in the catalogue of the Anselm Kiefer exhibit in Philadelphia and in a *New York Times* article. That sort of answer to the charge of plagiarism does not really challenge the terms of the discourse. Those texts, no matter how highly crafted, which appear to be "stolen" (or found) claim a valence that is essentially historical and documentary; in themselves they provide—or constitute—the citation or quotation that establishes authenticity. Their authorizing presence gives the ultimate lie to the charge of excessive aestheticization. Salient and indigestible, they remain appropriated but not fully naturalized into the conversation of the cultures in which they appear.

This may be even more perceptible in the realm of the visual arts. In discussing the two emblematic figures in "Todesfuge," Felstiner claims that the images of Shulamith and Margarete were not "coopted" in the Kiefer paintings that bear their names.[24] A close examination reveals the extent to which they do stand out as both text and image in these paintings, not fully quoted or absorbed into the canvas. Nazism, which in Lyotard's terms marks the end of the moral struggle, in that the subject—or the subject's right to "phrase"—has been effaced and reciprocity preempted,[25] allows Shulamith and Margarete to survive in the imagination as remainders of a mutual recognition that has become an annihilation of one by the other. In one of Kiefer's canvases entitled "Dein goldenes Haar, Margarethe" (1981), the hair could be the metonymic expression of that process of remaindering. Margarete's hair, straw embossed on an oil and emulsion painting of scorched fields, still retains its integral place in the rural landscape, whereas Shulamith's—a black curve that echoes the shape of Margarete's—is a sign of ruination and blight. As in many of Kiefer's other paintings, the text ("dein . . .") overlays and literalizes the nonliteral, nonfigurative painting and fixes the metaphoric field. The presence of figures in mourning or of memorial candles in other paintings in the Shulamith/ Margarete series—"Dein aschenes Haar, Sulamith" (1981), "Margarethe" (1981), and "Sulamith" (1983)—as well as the commemorative, ritualistic performances of "Todesfuge" throughout Germany suggest that there is nothing left to *do*.

Other Kiefer paintings which engage the Nazi past, such as the photographic series "Occupations" (1969) or the paintings "To the Unknown Painter" (1980–1983) are far more ambiguous, leaving more room for interpretation, for the unresolved moral struggle, evoking as well as ironizing the heroic, mythic images of the past. Unlike the "Occupations" series—in which the painter appearing in various "Sieg Heil" poses activates his audience to a wide range of possible, and very contradictory, responses to the invoked past, from celebration to revulsion[26]—the Shulamith/Margarete series implies a kind of self-limiting or self-chastizing in regard to the images and lines from "Todesfuge" that remain superimposed on the canvas—both as material and as text—suggesting the extent to which Celan's text remains superimposed upon German culture and resistant to being coopted into a more open, organic, intertextual dynamic. We confront once again the issue of the "propriety" as well as the overdetermined quality of certain tropes, their resistance to the ironizing or decontextualizing efforts of the artist and the complex cultural responses to them.

Actually, as has been amply documented in studies of the reception of the poem, while the substance remains recalcitrant, the metrical and musical *forms* of "Todesfuge" have been absorbed into an ongoing discourse on aesthetic forms in Germany. Celan himself is reported to have shared the perception that the focus on form may have preempted an assimilation of the poem's content; ironically, however, this admission also serves to support the argument attributed to Adorno that the more poetically crafted a text, the more inherently estranged from the reality it is meant to represent. While most readers continued to treat "Todesfuge" itself with deference, it became the prooftext for the danger that form would betray content, that any deviation from the strict historical account is a potential denial of its ontology. Rolf Hochhuth, in his stage directions for Act V of *The Deputy*, asserts that although in "Todesfuge" the "gassing of Jews is entirely translated into metaphors," it is a "masterly" poem; nevertheless, it cannot serve as a model for imaginative interpretation of that period, "for despite the tremendous force of suggestion emanating from sound and sense, metaphors still screen the infernal cynicism of what really took place—a reality so enormous and grotesque that even today [1963] . . . the impression of unreality it produces conspires with our natural strong tendency to treat the matter as a legend, as an incredible apocalyptic fable."[27]

It can be argued, perhaps, that at some subliminal level the Germans have come to *know* the poem the way a people knows its anthems and its liturgies, learning the words at such an early age and on such ceremonial occasions that it has become an incantational procedure rather than an attended text. The "performative" function of "Todesfuge"—what it does as distinguished from what it more strictly means—reflects the specific nature of the dialogue between this exiled writer and the culture he is addressing. What has been understood as a formidable denial of the contents of the poem may also be, for two generations of Germans at least, a particular form of knowing. We may be perceiving here a subtle reversal in the relations between aesthetic form and moral content. Rather than betraying the historical matter or obscuring its moral import, the aesthetic or ritualistic dimension may actually be the only possible conduit to what cannot be faced without mediation.

Beyond the impact of "Todesfuge," the fact that the insularity or incommunicability of Celan's mature verses has so absorbed the critical agenda could be a response not only to their inherent obscurity but also to their restless presence in the culture. The presumed impenetrability of neologisms and "hermetic" verses provides a defense against texts which are footloose, uncontained. It is in this sense perhaps that Celan's poetry becomes truly "barbaric," that the poet himself remains the original "barbarian" as foreigner or outlander—the one outside the community of selves, the one who in Germany most embodies an effaced otherness or nonidentity.

Although Celan himself insisted that he was "ganz und gar nicht hermetisch" (absolutely not hermetic),[28] we can find in this characterization more than a defensive strategy of reading; much of this poetry does appear uncontained in that it is *self*-contained, possibly even enclosing within itself the conversation usually transacted between text and reader. In the poem "In Eins," four languages—German, Hebrew, French, and Spanish—populate the first four lines: "Dreizehnter Feber. Im Herzmund / erwachtes Schibboleth. Mit dir, / Peuple / de Paris. No pasarán."[29] Jacques Derrida finds in this and related poems a "multiplicity and migration of languages . . . within the uniqueness of the poetic inscription."[30] The poem is bound by no single linguistic code or convention, place or situation.[31] Evan Watkin constructs a "counter-theory of lyric . . . at the point of missed connections between poet-self *and audience* . . . That would mean . . . [that one could] offer Celan's lyrics, his peculiarly social languages, as a not quite familiar but still responsive audience . . . an audience who *does* listen, the multiple languages which crowd his poems a moment of expectancy."[32]

For most of Celan's German readers, only one of these languages remains truly inscrutable: the Hebrew words scattered throughout. Like the small empty niches on the doorposts of formerly Jewish homes all over Eastern and Central Europe, Celan's Hebrew is a marker not only of the absent (and therefore indecipherable) Jewish culture but also of the absent reader. Recovering its status here as the language of origins, the primordial language, it remains uncorrupted, untried.[33] Translators and theoreticians have grappled with the untranslatability of Celan's foreign phrases; unique even within the polyphony of his verses, the Hebrew words from a scriptural or liturgical vocabulary remain as salient and unassimilated in his poetry as his poems are in German culture. The Hebrew words persist, then, unexamined, maintaining the status of a document, a relic, a ritual—or an incomplete memory.

It can be argued, further, that it is not only the languages which constitute multiple interlocutors within the poem but the addressed others ("mit dir, / peuple de Paris") who render Celan's poetry autonomous as an act that incorporates its own recipient. What is the status of the "you" (*du*) so often summoned in Celan's verses? Although a number of the later poems, especially, appear to be firmly located in the conventional lyrical address to a specific beloved, the less focused dialogical quest is thwarted in some of those texts in which it is most explicitly invoked. "The poem becomes conversation—often desperate conversation," Celan declared in his "Meridian" speech; "only the space of this conversation can establish what is addressed, can gather it into a 'you' around the naming and speaking I."[34] It is this *ars poetica* that informs the reading not only of his poetry but of his much-interpreted prose parable "Conversation in the Mountain" (*Gespräch im Gebirg*). The journey, which is both a parody and a recuperation of the romantic quest, begins, according to Stéphane Mosès, as a search for a true dialogic mode consistent with a Judeo-German vernacular and philosophy. But as the voice in the mountain echoes back upon itself, it becomes a kind of interior dialogue "of a single voice divided," and the search for otherness (*altérité*) issues in a nostalgic gesture—an "encounter with an other who has not come. Because in the absence of a You it is not given to the I to speak 'with the mouth and the tongue,' [this] . . . discourse can be compared, at its limit, to the language of the stone, 'who addresses no one.'"[35] This failed dialogic, this desperate search for the other that becomes a kind of self-proliferation, can be related to the yearning of the exile to return to some native ground, some original landscape in which he could be repatriated;[36] yet the passage transpires within a primordial mountainous landscape so generic, so nonspecific and elemental, that it becomes the ground of legend.[37]

The Bukovina region of Rumania was native ground to three German-speaking Jews who survived the war to become major writers elsewhere: Paul Celan, Dan Pagis, and Aharon Appelfeld. The first remained lost at sea, as it were, or stranded on a desert island, positing his poetry as a message sent out in a bottle[38]—potentially consequential but hardly hopeful of destination; the latter two washed ashore, in Palestine, on a language and a clearly-defined audience engaged in a collective act of repatriation.

In "Conversation in the Mountain," Celan recapitulates not only the legendary landscape but the conventional rhetoric of the wandering Jew: "One evening, when the sun had set and not only the sun, the Jew—Jew and son of a Jew—went off, left his house and went off . . . went under clouds, went in the shadow, his own and not his own—because the Jew, you know, what does he have that is really his own . . ."[39] The other two writers from Bukovina struggle with the allure—and the claustrophobia—of homecoming.[40] Pagis in particular invites the kind of comparison with Celan that would illuminate the provenance of each discourse, its poetic, existential, and cultural boundaries. There are striking similarities in their poetry that can be distinguished primarily, I believe, by the presumed presence or absence of a targeted reader and a specific gravitational force. Celan's neologisms are radical acts performed on the most primary lexemes of language; Pagis's assaults are performed within the larger unit of the social syntax. Whether we read Celan's last verses as "hermetic" in the sense of self-contained, autonomous, as the incorporation of text *and* audience—protected by a thick shield from the slings and arrows of outrageous readings—or as a gradual withdrawal into a private, impenetrable and indecipherable universe, to which suicide was a logical sequel, his self-inflicted death becomes the ultimate inscription of the fate of the survivor-writer with a phantom audience.

Since the language of discourse is Hebrew, there is no area in Pagis's linguistic universe comparable to the sacred space inhabited by the Hebrew words in Celan's—no unexamined, opaque or totemic images. Unlike Celan's, Pagis's personal exile is embedded within the noisy semantic of a collective homecoming.[41] The conversation is entirely a social one between reader and text, which presupposes a "storytelling circle." There are no lyrical subjects or objects, no significant addresses to an other within the poems themselves (the "you" who appears in an occasional poem tends to be an impersonal pronominal stand-in for both the integrity of the self and a significant other),[42] no real search for the dialogic moment—but there is, on the other hand, an implied reader as recipient of what becomes at times an urgent message. The appeal to an extratextual reader presupposes natural intralinguistic acts practiced by a living community. Pagis's "Written in Pencil in the Sealed Railway-Car" ("Katuv b'iparon bakaron hehatum") is one of the shortest poems in modern Hebrew; it is also, possibly, the most resonant, as canonic in its status in the Hebrew-speaking community as "Todesfuge" is in the German:

> here in this carload
> i am eve
> with abel my son
> if you see my other son
> cain son of man
> tell him that i[43]

The "you" addressed here is in second person plural ("'im tiru . . . tagidu . . ."), encompassing the grammatic potential of both male and female witnesses (which a second-person singular construct in the gender-tagged Hebrew would not have been able to accommodate). The reader summoned to perform a speech act ("tell him that i") is absolutely necessary to complete this most "nonhermetic" of poems.

Although it poses as a "found" text, naming its place of composition, suspended, in its lack of closure, as an interrupted inscription, this poem does not perform either an authenticating or a delegitimating role in the culture analogous to other "found" or "stolen" texts we have considered. It is, rather, the transmission of an unspoken but intuited message, *paideia* as a primary communal act, that is invoked here. I have suggested that within the realm of Hebrew literature some of the primary critical questions change. Whereas "i"-witness accounts have acquired over the years a narrow privilege in a community in which the historical terms of existence compete with and are subsumed into the mythical constructs of collective memory, there has been essentially no ongoing argument over symbolic language as a betrayal of the ground of historical memory comparable to the controversy that has focused on "Todesfuge." The collective narrative with its implicit moral consensus relieves the Hebrew writer of any historiographical responsibility, thereby conferring a kind of autonomy on the tropic discourse.

Pagis writes against this backdrop of an explicitly referential, sequential, and coherent *histoire*. One can argue that because the Holocaust narrative has itself become a convention, conforming more or less to contours drawn by writers like Primo Levi, both Pagis and Celan defamiliarize it in ways that retain the shock of unformulaic events. Both poets speak in codes, burying the referential layer deep within the poetic texture. But an essential difference lies in the status of the "master narrative" as primary reference for the Israeli writer. A critic like Berel Lang may be overlooking that difference when he claims that the poetry of Celan demonstrates the terms of a conflict that appears also in the poetry of (Israeli poets) Avraham Sutzkever, Abba Kovner, and Dan Pagis: "On the one hand, it seems evident that even if in the reading of his poems all knowledge of Celan's biography were put to one side, his imaginative power and the coercive horror of his subject would be recognized. On the other hand, it is far from certain that if the poems were read under a 'veil of ignorance' apart from his biography readers would associate the poems with the subject of the Nazi genocide, or (more strongly) that they would require this association in order to experience the force of the poems."[44] Lang then brings Celan's "Aspen Tree" as evidence that "poetic reference to specific historical settings becomes increasingly attenuated as the text is more fully realized poetically":

> Aspen tree your leaves glance white into the dark.
> My mother's hair was never white.

Dandelion, so green is the Ukraine.
My yellow-haired mother did not come home.

Rain cloud, above the well do you hover?
My quiet mother weeps for everyone.

Round star, you wind the golden loop.
My mother's heart was ripped by lead.

Oaken door, who lifted you off your hinges?
My gentle mother cannot return. [45]

Celan provides here, Lang argues, "only two indefinite clues concerning the circumstances of the death of the mother of the person in
whose voice the poem is expressed: the reader learns that she was shot
and that this occurred in the Ukraine." [46] Yet this poem is actually far
more confessional and less opaque than Pagis's "Written in Pencil . . ."
Like "Aspen Tree," Pagis's poem has only two circumstantial markers
that locate it historically: "sealed railway-car" and "carload" (*karon ha-
tum, mishloah*)—and even these are not exclusive or unambiguous
historical references.

Even if we accept the extreme terms of Lang's argument, namely,
that "documentary and historical writings about the genocide have
been more adequate and more compelling—in sum, more *valuable*—
than the imaginative writings about that subject," [47] we would have to
recognize that the contextual distance between the two poets from Bukovina actually alters the terms of the discourse. It is, simply, impossible for Pagis's primary audience to read his verse under a 'veil of
ignorance.' If we credit the "poetic tendency to dehistoricize even its
own quite explicit reference," [48] we might ask, in the name of what?
The issue in this context is certainly not the danger of a postmodernist
reading of reality as construct in the face of the moral urgency of representation.

The Yiddish poetry of Avraham Sutzkever, whom Lang cites along
with Celan, Pagis, and Kovner as embodying the paradox that the
more fully realized a poem is the greater the gap between it and an
authentic, historical referent, may actually be one of the best examples
of the inherently or potentially ludic function of the Holocaust writer
in Israel. In many of Sutzkever's ghetto poems the creative act is invoked as compensatory; the artist appears as empowered to provide
both representation of *and* symbolic reparation for history's horrors. [49]
By signing virtually all of these poems with the date and place of (presumed) composition ("Vilna Ghetto, January 17, 1942," "Vilna Ghetto,

July 28, 1943"), he endows these verses with a kind of documentary, evidentiary status that has the effect of *releasing* the imagination from the constraints of history.[50] Sutzkever's confident manipulation of the historical material both during and after the war and his personal poetic language, which is almost entirely devoid of archetypes from the public lexicon of responses to catastrophe, reflect not only his status as a survivor, but also his clear definition of his audience and of the changing exigencies of the regenerating Jewish community. Sutzkever's ability to address both the dead (within the confines of a poem) and the living (in an implicit space beyond)[51] presumes a continuum along which each has an assigned place, whereas the rudderless poetry of Celan is as unmoored and as inexorably present as the souls of the unburied dead: the dating of Sutzkever's ghetto poems renders them utterly *past*, while Celan's "Todesfuge" is set loose under the aspect of an eternal present ("we drink and we drink").

It is, therefore, not over the relative jurisdiction of referential and symbolic languages that the discussion of legitimacy takes place in Israel; rather, it is between innocent and subversive appropriations of the "master narrative." Whereas ironic appropriations of the philosophical and literary premises of Jewish survival are built into the dialectics of the lamentation tradition, a few contemporary writers have so assaulted the iconic configurations as to challenge the narrative in its most strategic places. In fiction, Yoram Kaniuk was one of the earliest and David Grossman one of the most recent writers to have co-opted the consensual symbols of the Holocaust and the Zionist story of collective regeneration into a radical parody of the paradigm of secular redemption.[52]

Through a series of temporal disjunctions, the poetry of Dan Pagis undermines the ideological, theological continuum that brings the past into a meaningful present. Through a series of spatial disruptions, the diffused self, whose most common element in a Pagis poem is air and whose most common thrust is centrifugal, enacts, in a way, the afterlife of one consigned to a "grave in the air"; yet unlike Celan's speaker, his response is not only (or even primarily) to the claustrophobia and confinement of the concentration camp but to the groundedness, the gravitational force of the collective homecoming.[53] Through juxtaposition or substitution that presupposes a semantic of destruction and regeneration, Pagis recasts the vocabulary of martyrdom. In the poem

"Written in Pencil . . ." as elsewhere, he replaces the archetypal victim, Isaac, with a composite figure, a fraternity of murder, Cain *and* Abel. The universal resonance of this poem only enhances its impact in the interpretive, "covenantal" community to which it is primarily addressed. Unlike the coupling of Margarete and Shulamith in Celan's "Todesfuge," in which, as we have seen, the presence of the one in effect annihilates the other, or in Kiefer's paintings, where they are fixed in memorial space—that is, cultural space devoid of significant moral tension—the brothers in the Cain and Abel poems remain moral alternatives; although invoking a history of Jewish martyrdom in which the identity of the Jew as victim is clear and absolute, they address a society in which the intimation of a possible interchange of identities (in one poem "Cain dreams that he is Abel"[54]) suggests an ongoing moral struggle. It should come as no surprise, then, that Pagis's poems are not read on memorial occasions, that they have not been granted a static, ceremonial presence within the culture.

Elsewhere, I have traced the attempt of Aharon Appelfeld and other survivor-writers to find a space for private memory vis-à-vis the collective remembering.[55] Here I would like to stress that, under the press of circumstances, most of the Hebrew writers, especially the native sons and daughters, are actually becoming more and more engaged with the "master narrative," which, in turn, is being transformed into a discourse on power and powerlessness, on victims and victimizers, which evolves in Israel as an ongoing response to the challenges of political sovereignty and collective power.

It may be that George Steiner, consistent with his lifelong argument for the Jewish text as homeland and the Jew as housed in many languages, overstates the purgative force in Celan's writing. In *After Babel*, he claims that Celan wrote German as if it were a foreign language: "All of Celan's own poetry is translated into German . . . It becomes a 'meta-language' cleansed of historical political dirt and thus, alone, usable by a profoundly Jewish voice after the Holocaust."[56] One can argue, of course, as Amy Colin has, that the "historical political dirt" is never fully eradicated, that the poet "intends to make readers aware" of just those absences within his language.[57] But just who *are* these readers? The survivors, I have suggested, form an inclusive and safe category of readers across all cultures and languages. But their mediating presence notwithstanding, the exiled German writer has no more "chosen" them than the Hebrew audience he addressed in 1969. The open borders of his reading community may correspond to the degree of insularity in his language. There is one anecdote that illustrates the profound distinction between readers carefully sought and those haphazardly found. Edmond Jabès is reported to have discovered Celan returning the manuscript of *The Book of Questions* to Jabès's mailbox, stating that the publication of such an unabashed treatment of Jewish themes would only bring new disasters upon them all. "The poet's fear that directness rendered his utterance ephemeral may have found its psychic counterpart in the troubled survivor's fear of renewed persecution and reprisal," writes Katharine Washburn in her introduction to a collection of Celan's last poems.[58] That is, at some level, the more social or accessible the language to a continually sought but ever elusive reading community, the more possibly consequential in ways the poet is powerless to determine or control. In conclusion, Washburn writes: "Anticipating a future in which . . . 'Auschwitz' . . . would . . . turn into threadbare metaphor, the coiner of words looked not only at the debasement of the currency which preceded him, but foresaw that which lay ahead. He has given us instead a host of invulnerable signs."[59] These signs signify a withdrawal into a private space that, far from being pre-suicidal, may be a form of inviolability or even immortality. Whereas the reader of Pagis's poetry tears off the public masks one by one, until the hollow contours of the skull appear where the self might have been, the reader of Celan's poetry constructs a profile out of the irreducible sounds that never quite enter public speech. The more personal or idiosyncratic the inscription, then, the more immune it is meant to be to both the debasement of metaphor and its reification in history. Ultimately, the grave in the air is the locus of a poetry which hovers over the earth, refusing re-creation.

< 17 >

The Dialectics of Unspeakability: Language, Silence, and the Narratives of Desubjectification

PETER HAIDU

For Paul Hajdu,
17 October 1907–16 March 1944

A historian addresses the work of other historians and their relation to the event. The major theoretical issues that attend the question of Holocaust historiography arise: the exceptionality of the event, its representability, its (un)speakability, indeed, its very (in)comprehensibility. That discussion is in the form of a preliminary draft, and bears across the cover sheet the words:

> Preliminary draft.
> Not to be reproduced or quoted in any form.

The formula is conventional enough. Given the importance of the topic, the solicitation of collegial reactions prior to the final draft for which one takes responsibility is admirable. Nevertheless, these normal professional considerations constitute an interdiction which produces the following situation: a scholar addresses an intellectual problem deployed by a colleague, without being able to cite that colleague's formulations. This inconclusive discourse perforce refers to an absent text which cannot be presentified. The historian's text, in turn, cites another text as potential document, and discusses its incomprehensibility, its unsayability.[1] In turn, that other text itself represents (in the sense of "makes the case for") the urgent need to curtail discourse, to impose silence, about its own topic, the extermination of the Jews.

Discourse on silence, a specific silence in an extraordinary historical situation, entails the issues of signification put forward by contemporary theory. Such a discourse, however, is a situated one, caught at a particular historical moment: the Bush supplement to the Reagan *im-*

< 277 >

perium. If it was important to Derrida, speaking in a different context about similar issues, to ward off any possible confusion between his discourse and dialectics,[2] it is essential to assert the necessity of dialectics in the present discourse, asserting both the discursive strategy of heuristic assertions, which later may be withdrawn or modified, and the complex interdependence of language and what it seeks to represent, always elusively: the domain of the real, postulated by language as its other. Only so can I hope to respond to "the obligation to think at the same time dialectically and undialectically."[3]

Silence is the antiworld of speech, and at least as polyvalent, constitutive, and fragile. The necessary refuge of the poet, the theologian, and the intellectual, it is equally the instrument of the bureaucrat, the demagogue, and the dictator. Silence can be the marker of courage and heroism or the cover of cowardice and self-interest; sometimes, it is the road sign of an impossible turning. Silence resembles words also in that each production of silence must be judged in its own contexts, in its own situations of enunciation. Silence can be a mere absence of speech; at other times, it is both the negation of speech and a production of meaning. At times, it has to be overcome, and for the same reasons the effort is made to index a "beyond" of language in full recognition of the fact that language is not to be transcended: silence is one of the ways in which we make sense of the world, and as such, it is one of the *différends* over which we struggle.

But silence is enfolded in its opposite, in language. As such, silence is simultaneously the contrary of language, its contradiction, and an integral part of language. Silence, in this sense, is the necessary discrepancy of language with itself, its constitutive alterity.

This discrepancy takes many forms. Theology—negative theology—long ago recognized language as inherently inadequate to the task of representing a divinity defined as alterity, as fundamentally other than the human-speaking subject. It has been the challenge of negative theology, starting with belief, to deploy modes of discourse that acknowledge divinity without presentifying it.

The traditional disciplines of language have amply recognized the interdependence of the said and the unsaid. Structures like elision, irony in its multiple forms, apostrophe, apophasis, and praeterition not only recognize the existence of the unsaid but define linguistic structures of representation which ground the said in the unsaid, making the unsaid the essential element of discourse. The semantic content of these rhetorical forms of structured silence was traditionally limitable; contemporary theory speculates about more fundamental linguistic instabilities which might preclude the limitative determination of both spoken and unspoken meanings.

The writer's thirst for "specificity"—which certainly includes the historian's desire to "get it right"—runs into the paradoxical functioning of his medium. The language employed to construct contemporary experiences is always already inscribed with past experiences, and cannot help but introduce elements of meaning that are of questionable relevance to the topic at hand. The debate about the name to be used to designate the event with which we are concerned is an extreme example. *Final Solution* implies the Jews as a social, political, ethical problem that, having festered in European culture and civilization for centuries, is finally to be resolved: we know the shape of resolution. *Holocaust* represents not only disaster and catastrophe, but functionalizes them as a burnt offering, a sacrifice willingly offered divinity, a divinity apparently hungry and thirsty for the blood of innocents, a sacrifice which, properly enacted, might allow the victims the possibility of an eventual redemption. Is *Shoah* an alternative? At least one Holocaust authority gives *Shoah* the purely secular meaning of disaster or catastrophe, but the Biblical references cited suggest otherwise: a number of those texts indicate that the disaster is sent by God.[4] My own solution is to speak of "the Event": the theoretical implications of this choice will become clear later.

The naming of an event bears with it implications of various kinds: narratological, theological, historical, political, rhetorical, and philosophical. Namings imply narratives and vice versa. The name, in the form of a noun, is the substantivation of an implicit narrative, and the verb is the narrativization of a noun. What is true of individual words is even more true of efforts at recounting events, whether the account is fictional or historical. "Point of view" theory was developed to account for the highly differentiated apprehensions of fictional narrative events as perceived by different characters. It is not only fiction that is concerned with point of view, however. Raul Hilberg, emphatic about the rules that would protect the nonfictional historiography of the Event, notes the difference of opinion as to whether the story should be told from the point of view of the victims or of the perpetrators.[5] A postmodern fragmentation may be posited which would present alternative "takes" on events, such as dedicating one part of a book to the point of view of the perpetrators and another to that of the victims.[6] This structure is fundamental in documentaries whose interviews provide alternative reports on the events narrated.

Before alluding to the *how* of historical writing, Raul Hilberg discusses the *what* of the telling. All narrative is "polemical," that is, representing the conflict of adversaries and their values systems. Hilberg is concerned with the incomplete and unbalanced character of his sources. German sources reveal the bureaucratic complexity of the process of extermination, but they deal with people only in the aggregate. The situation is reversed in the Jewish sources, which tell of particular experiences, but without grasping the larger process in which they were involved. Furthermore, the very number of survivors' testimonies is a historiographical problem. At last count, there were eighteen thousand such accounts, but that count was taken in the late 1950s.[7] The documentary mass is staggering. It presents the historian with a triple task: selecting the material, ordering it, and choosing the level of abstraction at which the story or stories are to be told. Can such choices avoid perspectivism?

This brief, empirical survey of the practice and the reflections of practicing historians rejoins the formulations of theory. The ordering of historical material itself is already a construction which implies shapings, perspectives, values, and textual morphologies.[8] These are, in one aspect, the technical problems of the historian's science and the rhetorical techniques of the historian's craft, but their implications transcend these instrumental considerations. That there is no value-free social science is an ancient discovery; but there is no value-free narrative or historiography either. These issues grow out of what may be called a "constructivist" historiography, one which conceives of history as a form of writing, hence as informed by the same structures as all forms of writing. But this constructivist historiography must be juxtaposed to a critique, not of the forms of textualization made available by language, but of language itself as well as its representational potentials.

Deconstruction has made a strong case of linguistic instability as an inherent characteristic of language, incorporating an endlessly regressive system of self-referentiality, whose representational claims and assumptions are contradicted or undermined by the actual and frequently contradictory functioning of the linguistic structures deployed. The issue is not accidental traps on the way to adequate representation, traps into which we may fall as the result of bad habits, faulty training, and inadequate methodologies. Nor is the issue whether language is to be used as an irresponsible game, in disregard of the serious matters of life, death, and history. It is rather the ineluctable structures and risks inherent in the representational process, including history as well as fiction, historical discourse as well as any other form of discourse. These structures and risks would appear to be the inherent cost of any and all representation, including all uses of language, including that form of representation we label "thought": they may be ubiquitous out of a necessity inherent to the processes they constitute.

These considerations identify a crucial aporia. History shares certain characteristics with fiction, not as an accidental weakness, but as the unavoidable price of being constituted as textualized thought and research. This conclusion runs directly counter to, and is absolutely unacceptable to, the sacred horror with which we cannot help but view the Event. There is a radical contradiction between what I will call a secular textual theory, along with its information of historiography, and an ethical and religious approach to the Event which addresses it with the requisite sense of responsibility toward the dead, their suffering, and the piety appropriate to the Event.

It is perhaps in the thought of Emmanuel Levinas that we find the most profoundly insistent example of the unity of ethics and religion: religion is the name given to the bond that is established between self and other, without constituting a totality.[9] Such a unity, adhering to the Jewish tradition itself, was elaborated after and perhaps partly in response to the Event. Levinas is to be taken literally when he places the Event in the center of "the scattered elements of his biography" as both presentiment and memory of the Nazi horror.[10] The resulting work is irreducible: it transforms the Jewish tradition into a radical challenge to Western ethical thought. Nevertheless, it is not a betrayal of that thought to see Levinas' work as a profound condemnation of the torment of the Jews in the camps—to whom Levinas refers as the Martyrs—and as a searching work of intelligence elaborated as a desired obstacle to recurrence.

In spite of accusations that Levinas' work slights history, his ethics is inextricably bound with history, and in exceedingly complex ways: it is simultaneously an escape from history, a response to history, and in the deepest sense an element of history itself.[11] World War II cedes us as primal narrative the face-to-face encounter of the guard, in a camp, with a victim. The fundamental ethical situation is that of the confrontation with the visage of the other, and the self's response to the other's "helpless eyes, absolutely deprived of protection," the "eyes without defense." That visage Levinas argues as being intelligible before the effects of culture and history; hence the response to it is universally obligatory. The presence of the other's visage requires a response to the other's immediacy as such, something possible only to an ego which has made itself vulnerable to the other, vulnerable to the point where it cannot escape the other's "naked neediness, the destitution inscribed upon his visage, his visage as a destitution which assigns responsibility to me."[12] The responsibility assigned by this encounter—the italics are Levinas' own—is an "*unlimited* responsibility."[13] It is a conception of the other's presence as an imperious call to self-abnegation in response to helplessness and need, a radical ethical imperative far less measured, far more imperious than the Kantian. Can a sharper contrast be envisaged to the behavior of persecutors of the Jews in the camps? Can a more ironclad guarantee of nonrecurrence be imagined, were this ethic universally adopted?

That last phrase poses the inevitable political question to ethics. The survival of groups in a multicultural world is a political question. However admirable in its challenge to moral somnolence, an ethic which can neither hope for general adoption nor meet the actual conditions of contemporary life hovers close to remaining the condemnatory luxury of survivor guilt. A world in which the face of experience is normally mediated—by linguistic structures and their ideological content; by social welfare organizations, whether governmental or private; by the representations of television as entertainment or news, or the representations of television cameras built into "smart" bombs, in which the face-to-face encounter with the victim is never even possible—such a world escapes the Levinasian narrative of encounter with the other's visage.

There is also a question both philosophical and ethical. No encounter between self and other is ahistorical. Immediacy per se does not walk up to us. Immediacy per se is an allegorical figure, reductively abstracted from real encounters. The narrative of "immediacy" avoids the recognition of the other in the concreteness of the other's social, cultural, and historical alterity. As Levinas himself has acknowledged, the ethics of *Totality and Infinity* fail in the effort at a heteronomy respectful of the other in the other's own terms.[14] The encounter that needs to be staged is the full one, in which the other comes garbed in yarmulke, Bedouin robes, Levis, or a business suit, in the black or the brown or the yellow of the other's skin, in the discrepancies between the other's language and our own. It is not phenomenological reductions that are constituted as subjects, victimized, or desubjectified: it is individuals and collectivities in the concrete habits of their cultures and social formations.

The call for recognition of and integral respect for the other cannot be gainsaid. It is precisely the urgency of that ethical claim which imposes the requirement for mediated forms of knowledge, the search for historical understanding, the effort to transcend cultural boundaries, as incorporated in the formalisms of the disciplines we inherit as historical creatures, as well as the social formalisms of governmental agencies. Hunger, as Levinas argues, is a phenomenon for ethical judgment and choice. So are torture and death. Hunger, torture, and death, if they implicate individuals in ethical judgments, are also social phenomena, with economic, political, and ideological aspects, parts of history folded into each other. The arguments as to the relative priorities of the different categories are perhaps of lesser importance to the victims than to academics who study them. Ethical judgment in particular is a luxury of the survivors, not of the victims, who perhaps would have asked far less than moral impeccability: survival does not require such high moral standards.

It is in any case my hope and my expectation that Levinas would disclaim any appropriation that employs his ethics to argue a moral condemnation addressed to the past and that at the same time disregards the present visage of the other. An ethic that works only for the satisfactions of moral superiority vis-à-vis the monsters of the past, without accepting concrete responsibility for the other who is present at our doorstep, seems to me a parody of Levinas' ethical thought.

The reference to negative theology, at the beginning of my remarks, was not accidental. The impossibility that attends the representations of the Event, as well as its designation as a unique event with a special status of "exceptionality," looks very much like the initial stage of an institutionalization of the divine. As such, it will be a divinity unlike that which we inherit as Jews, as Christians, or as atheists. The unspeakability of the Event, the horror which comes upon the historian as his gaze fixes on the documents of his research, enters into a tradition of the ineffability which attends appearances of the divine. The *topos* of ineffability is associated both with the experience of horror and with that of the sublime. What I wish to designate, however, precedes that distinction: the irruptions into human life of the divine as that which is awesome, that which strikes us with terror, inexplicable because of the unpredictability of its violence as well as the force of that violence. *Divinity*, here, might be the name given that violence Walter Benjamin considered constitutive.[15] It is a concept of divinity that precedes the moralization of divinity under the aegis of monotheism; it is a concept of divinity, I take it, that is pre-Judaic, intractable in moral terms, in which divinity bypasses human understanding, not necessarily as desirable perfection, but equally as an object of profound repugnance. It is a concept of divinity which culture and civilization, as we know them, hold at bay, rendering it also "unspeakable."

Let this incipient sacralization of the Event hang fire for a bit: I will return to it, turning now to a central historical text. It is a speech of Heinrich Himmler, delivered at Posen on 3 October 1943, to high-ranking officers who were his immediate subordinates in the SS.[16] In this speech, Himmler addresses the lieutenant generals who were his adjuvants. He speaks sometimes as a leader, sometimes as a teacher, sometimes as a bureaucrat: he is his interlocutors' destinator.[17] If there are references to the German nation, the welfare of its people, its future, and its needs, what is most immediately in the forefront of his concerns are the strength, the importance, and the welfare of his particular institution. He addresses his subordinates about their missions, past, present, and future; about the quality, morale, and morals of their troops; about the obstacles they face, both from external enemies of Germany and within the German polity. It is in a section with the subheading "Die Judenevakuierung" that the text enters a semantic domain characterized by a rhetoric of ambiguity, the use of euphemism, periphrasis, and all sorts of double-coding.[18] It is a text whose language is particularly unstable.

The text bears markers of an awareness of its own extraordinary nature. It takes note of its own situation of enunciation: it is entirely self-conscious as utterance. The leader of the SS addresses his immediate subordinates, those who in turn lead the elite forces that actually carry out the missions set for them. He will address topics that are usually left unspoken. He stresses his present openness on these topics by repetition, using that rhetorical stress to lead to paradox stated in the form of paranomasia (the play on meaning using different forms of the same word). He will be, for once (*einmal*), entirely open (*ganz offen*), and the matter will be discussed frankly: "und trotzdem werden wir in der Öffentlichkeit nie darüber reden" (in spite of the present "openness," never will we speak of this in "openness," that is, in more public circumstances). The norms, on this topic, are those of unspeakability: the present openness is an anomalous transgression of those norms. In the context of the elite membership present on the particular occasion, this extraordinary verbalization can—for once—be afforded.

The rhetoric presupposes a prior code of silence as a shared assumption between the speaker and his audience: a semiotic code, effective in real communication. During the purge of the SA in 1934, the SS murdered the rival organization's top officers and men. Himmler appeals to the same *Takt* (delicacy of feeling) which he and his subordinates have exercised regarding that event of 1934: never discussing it, never speaking of it. The event caused its participants to shudder (*es hat jeden geschaudert*)—the shudder of horror—but all were clear in their readiness to do it again, if so ordered. One distinction between the present elite and the outsiders excluded from that elite corps (the general, indeterminate, impersonal *man*, but also *die braven achtzig millionen Deutschen*) is that the members of the elite recognize the necessity of apophasis, of not speaking, of silencing certain matters, while the popular mass voices its concerns all too readily. Another distinction is that all Germans agree on the necessity of the extermination of the Jews in general, but not all are capable of acting according to the logic of the principle: each one comes forward with a favorite Jew, an exception to the general rule—*ein prima Jude*—who is to be spared. Without naming it, the text recognizes the human propensity to identify with another human being, and to protect the other. This behavioral potential is said to characterize the German polity in general: what is its status in the elite?

It is at this point that the leader appeals to the kind of experience that binds him and his subordinates in a collectivity driven by faith and a sense of mission. It is the appeal of a leader to military men, invoking the necessary sacrifice they all make to higher ideals. He and they have been hardened by the experience of seeing "a hundred corpses

lie side by side, or five hundred, or a thousand. To have endured this
. . . and in spite of that, to have remained decent" (*und dabei . . .
anständig geblieben zu sein*), that is what has made them hard. This
"hardness" is a quality to be desired, conjoined with "decency," both
being retained or achieved *in spite of* the sight of corpses of mass murder. No mention is made of the possible narrative role the individual
subject might have played, as an agent, in producing the scene before
his eyes. He is represented only in a passive and cognitive role: any
potential narrative is elided. The other rhetorical technique to be
noted is the assertion, as an assumption, of what would normally be
questioned as the result of the information given: the assertion of "decency." The "hardness" attained is the subjectivity of an elite, even
within the general German population, constructed in spite of, on top
of, the kind of reaction decried among *die braven achtzig millionen
Deutschen.* The reaction of identification with another suffering being
is a potential that is presupposed by the discourse as a danger, a possible obstacle to the development of that "hardness." It is a characteristic of the *vulgus,* which must be overcome by the elite, an elite
which, nevertheless and in spite of everything, remains *anständig.*

Addressing the issue of the event and its representation, the leader
turns to oxymoronic mysticism, to the paranomasiac paradoxicality
that language allows, to the linguistic transcendence of ordinary moral
and referential limits, as he posits an extraordinary theory of apophatic
historiography. The extermination of the Jews, the goal to be effec-
tuated, is to be *ein niemals geschriebenes und niemals zu schreibendes
Ruhmesblatt unserer Geschichte:* a never-written and never-to-be-
written page of glory in SS history. Never mind that *Ruhm* (glory,
honor, fame, renown) presupposes public knowledge, and that public
knowledge is exactly what is to be prevented by the fact that never is
this claim to glory to be written and thereby known: it is the rhetorical
coincidentia oppositorum that is postulated as the (non)representation
of the action of the SS, that will produce their glory and their fame.
The paradox of glory built on silence depends on the rule of apophasis,
the unspeakability of what the SS is being exhorted to do.

This goal is a demanding one. One of the traditional rewards of military action, the glory that implies admiration and more concrete rewards, is being denied the military. What will make men act with such
selflessness, such self-sacrifice? It is—as usual—"morality" that is invoked for the most immoral acts: it is a moral right (*das moralische*

Recht), a duty towards the people (*die Pflicht gegenüber unserem Volk*), to kill a people that had wanted to kill the enunciatory "us" (*das uns umbringen wollte*). The totalizing structure of the text shows that Himmler's speech here is geared to making a moral point: in spite of its striking linguistic rhetoric, killing the Jews is incidental, in the rhetorical structure of the speech, to a more encompassing issue, the morality of the SS. We have the right to kill the Jews, he says, "but we do not have the right to enrich ourselves with so much as a fur, a watch, a mark, or a cigarette or anything else" in performing that duty. The *Ausrottung des jüdischen Volkes* is a duty, an order (*ein Befehl*), one might say a responsibility. Pilfering the corpses, however, is forbidden: to give in to the temptation would be equivalent to being infected by the germ to be exterminated.[19]

The basic legitimizing principle (*Grundsatz*) had been enunciated earlier, in the context, not of Jews, but of "alien peoples" (*fremde Völker*) in general. Himmler warns against thinking that other peoples can share the spiritual qualities of the German people: "our inoffensive soul and feeling, our good nature, our idealism" (*unsere ganz harmlose Seele . . . unsere Gutmütigkeit, unseren Idealismus*).[20] The ethical imperatives to be enunciated have a restricted field of application, but within that field, they can be considered absolute. One basic principle had to be absolute for SS men: they had to be "honest, decent, loyal, and comradely to members of our blood . . . and to nobody else" (*ehrlich, anständig, treu, und kameradschaftlich zu Angehörigen unseres eigenen Blutes . . . und zu sonst niemandem*). Honor is entirely an ingroup concept, and its extension to the rest of the world is expressly denied. As a result, other peoples are literally worthless, without value: "Whether ten thousand Russian females drop from exhaustion while building an anti-tank ditch interests me only insofar as the anti-tank ditch gets finished for Germany's sake . . . It is a crime against our own blood to worry about them and give them ideas that will make it still harder for our sons and grandsons to cope with them . . . Our concern, our duty is to our people and our blood . . . Toward anything else we can be indifferent. I wish the SS to take this attitude in confronting the problem of all alien, non-Germanic peoples, especially the Russians. All else is just soap bubbles, is a fraud against our own nation" (*Seifenschaum, Betrug an unserem eigenen Volk*).

Sentimentality, morality, and ethical imperatives are not merely the personal qualities required by the millennial *socius*. These formulations are not merely general recommendations of a leader to his subordinates. They are orders, and orders are sacred (*heilig*): "Orders must be sacred. When generals obey, armies obey automatically. This sacredness of orders [*diese Heiligkeit des Befehls*] applies the more, the larger our territory grows." The duty to exterminate the Jews is one of these orders, falling into the category of the sacred.

The discourse of extermination, from the broad historical dimension of its beginning to its contorted invocation of apophasis and its unquestioning assertion of the right and duty to eradicate those it identifies as subhuman enemies, is cast in familiar tones: it is the familiar register of self-righteous moralism, deploying the language of responsibility for the welfare of an institution shared with the interlocutors and propounding the vision of a future polity to be served with self-sacrifice and devotion. It is a historical vision of the past, of present necessity and future service, legitimated in terms of recognizable values: honesty, decency, loyalty, solidarity, idealism, and so on.

Himmler, a patriotic idealist sincerely exhorting his subordinates? A hypocritical bureaucrat whose pretentious moralizing is obviously self-legitimating? Or is the silence a required part of a strategy which includes the refusal, by both Hitler and Himmler, to issue written orders for extermination, in spite of bureaucratic norms of justificatory paperwork—a strategy to elude judgment on the basis of documentary evidence? Was an eventual accounting foreseen, such as developed in the Nuremberg trials? Or was it a strategy to avoid a negative reaction from within their own polity?

These questions and hypotheses are all valid and are not mutually exclusive, but they are beside the point. The state of Himmler's soul, the workings of his mind, are equally accessible (nothing unusual in any of the possibilities mentioned), indeterminable (as questions of intentionality usually are), and profoundly indifferent. So, finally, is the expression of moral outrage at the appropriation of morality and idealism in the service of extermination. Neither individual empathy with the monsters of extermination, in some act of historical *Verstehen*, nor ritualistic condemnation provides the understanding that performs the necessary transgression of sacral apophasis. The force of outrage must be appropriated by the forging of tools of comprehension of the relation of the discourse of extermination to the enacted narrative history of extermination.

The concept of ideology allows for the presence of contradictions, such as that which displays thousands of genocidally murdered victims and claims "decency" as self-evident for the agents of their extermination. At a different level, the components of the Nazi belief system—antisemitism, social Darwinism, the geopolitics of eastern expansion, and anti-Marxism—formed a "syncretic ideology" of particularly weak linkages.[21] Ideology is not merely the self-interested representation of false consciousness, however. It is polymorphous, polyvalent, and ubiquitous. Furthermore, ideology plays an essential role in constituting subjectivity, endowing the individual with the possibility of social action within the institutions and normative parameters of a given society.[22] A generalized value system within a society, or a plurality of such value systems, ideology informs the discourses and actions of agents and representatives of various kinds, including administrators and soldiers. In the narrative of history, taking on the role of destinator, Himmler formulates the final goal, its instrumental means, and the ideology to knit those ends and means together to the concrete agents, assigned to specific tasks. Both means and ideology meet the obstacle already noted, the human propensity to identify with others, called "pity" by Rousseau.[23]

Himmler's is a practical, pragmatic concern and reveals a full consciousness of its enormity. The physical and mental tortures inflicted on the victims of the Nazi extermination processes were not without effects upon their perpetrators. Some may have found gratification in the *Rausch* of repeated extermination, indulging a "compelling lust for killing on an immense scale,"[24] particularly when combined with the "seething resentment fraught with avenging violence" of the Nazi regime:[25] for those so inclined, the camps gave ample opportunity for "acting out" the most inhumane components of humanity. But although occasions for sadism were frequent in the camps, one historian concludes that there were few sadists.[26] Rather, the major problem faced by Himmler and others was the effect of the extermination process on the morale of the "normal human beings," the "respectable fathers of families," the "ordinary law-abiding citizens" who carried out the cool, rational process of extermination as "cleanly" as possible: "The system and the rhythm of mass extermination were directed not by sadists . . . [but by] worthy family men brought up in the belief that anti-Semitism was a form of pest control, harnessed into an impersonal mechanical system working with the precision of militarized industry and relieving the individual of any sense of personal responsibility."[27]

The same individuals could have been both the ordinary, everyday fathers of families, bureaucratic automata to whom others' lives meant no more than the pieces of paper that sealed their torture, starvation, and gassing, *and* the bloodthirsty fanatics of the *Rausch*. This double conclusion is not at all impossible—there is ample evidence for each of the traits cited—but it requires a radically different view of human subjectivity than is usual in history or fiction: it would have to be a particularly postmodern and poststructuralist view of the subject to incorporate such aporetic narrative potentials.[28] It might operate a radical scission between the individual as characterized by a stable set of semantic traits ontologically categorized in clinical or sociological categories, and the actions attributable to that individual. The unity and self-identity of subjectivity would be put into question, as would the related issue of narrative and historical probability, what the French tradition calls the *vraisemblable:* that which has the appearance of truth.

Such scissions may be lived in a lighthearted manner, as when traditional forms of morality or politics are overthrown for new freedoms. But for some individual agents of the narrative of extermination, the process in which they participated proved a heavy burden. Highly educated and sophisticated, frequently drawn from intellectual professions such as academics, government officials, lawyers, even a priest and an opera singer,[29] the mid-level commanders were subject to increasing strains. As repugnant as their complaints are to read now, they experienced exhaustion, asked for transfers, avoided returning to duty after leaves, experienced nervous breakdowns, and even committed suicide.[30] Himmler himself was notoriously unable to stomach the sight of the actual extermination process.[31]

The administrative problem produced different, even contradictory solutions. On the one hand, a strategy was devised which attempted to elude guilt: the individual in an Einsatzgruppe was to have no contact with his victims, was to identify with a unit acting as such, and only on orders from a superior officer. On the other hand, another strategy posited collective blood guilt as the social cement that would bind the members of a unit together in comradeship and the "camaraderie of guilt."[32] Both solutions point to the same problem: the potential of a moral reaction of identification with the victims on the part of the perpetrators of extermination. It was these agents of extermination whose subjectivity had to be constructed in such a way as to enable them to carry out their "sacred" orders. It was their subjectivity that had to be shaped.

This is the delicate narrative, administrative, and political point at which much Nazi ideology and practice was aimed: the constitution of active subjects to carry out the prescribed programs of a particular ideology. The enactment of this program, however, also required the constitution of an appropriate victim. Terence Des Pres has described the "excremental assault" upon the inmates of the camps, the systematic assault upon their dignity and their self-identity as subjects. The negation of their subjectivity had to be internalized by the victims so as to be inscribed on their faces and in their bearing, marking them as subhuman and therefore fit for extermination. This systematic assault made their mass murder possible for those charged with their extermination. Asked why the incessant humiliation and cruelty, since all the victims were marked for extermination in any case, the Treblinka commander answered: "To condition those who actually had to carry out the policies . . . to make it possible for them to do what they did."[33] The desubjectification of the victim was a programmed precondition for his or her victimization, a precondition enabling the perpetrator's enactment of the narrative program of extermination.

Exclusive stress on the uniqueness of the Event, combined with its sacralization, results in its disconnectedness from history. The evolution of a cult of remembrance into a sectarian exclusionary ritual "[separates] the Jewish catastrophe from its secular historical setting."[34] The Event's uniqueness is reified; it is conceived as entirely *sui generis* and unprecedented: decontextualized, it therefore must escape historical comprehension. The stress on uniqueness leads, in ineluctable logic, to radical incomprehensibility. Worse, such a historical *hapax* also leads to dismissal of the event as irrelevant: if it is entirely unique and disconnected from human historicity, what can be its "relevance" for the perplexed, engaged in making historical or moral choices?[35]

My primary reason for avoiding this conclusion, or the profoundly religious silence to which it could lead, is a political one (conceiving of "politics" in this case in its broadest possible sense), in which it is equated with collective survival. Admitting "the mysterious quality . . . [of] every historical event," I would nevertheless insist on the necessity of pursuing the ideational *conatus*, the drive to understand, not for pure intellectuality of "research," but precisely because of the (partial) equation of power and knowledge. If the question of relevance is raised by one Holocaust historian, another (Bauer) complains of the "lack of realization of the here and now of the Holocaust, of its being a phenomenon, not of the past but of the present." It is our self-consciousness as extrusions of a specific history, living permanently on the edge of multiple destructions, that forces us to recognize our participation in the same genealogy as the Event: "The first thing to remember is that the Holocaust was an actual occurrence in our century. It was not the product of an inexplicable fate or of supernatural intervention, but one logical possible outcome of European history."[36] We are also "one logical possible outcome of European history": that duality is simultaneously the bane of our terror-laden awareness and the twisted skein our cognitive *conatus* follows as we desperately hang on to its burning knots.

In the discourse that is Himmler's, we can recognize modes of discourse that are all too uncomfortably familiar. What the historian sees in the discourse of the other, and what freezes him in terror, is not a cognition of alterity: it is the recognition of the already known. Even when the discourse deploys the linguistic structures from the most exalted reaches of human poetry and spirituality, these structures are familiar ones. What is so unacceptable is not anything that is readily dismissible as pure alterity, a discourse emanating from an instance and in forms that are radically different from those we know. This otherness was the problem of negative theology: it is not ours. On the contrary, Himmler's discourse is *unheimlich* because it reproduces, with all nuances and paradoxes in place, the discourses we know as the discourses of poetry and policy, of idealism and religion, of administration and bureaucracy.[37] Taken "straight" or as parody, however, the discursive strategies that weave their *tessura* in the texts of extermination are the ordinary furnishings of our institutional, intellectual and aesthetic lives. What is horrifying, what is monstrous, in this discourse, is not strangeness or alterity: its unspeakability derives from the recognition of our own modes of discourse, and of the subjectivities which, if they are not actually our own, are entirely within the grasp of our imaginations.

With one difference: the effects we know this discourse to have had, effects that are not accountable as linguistic, discursive, or theoretical. We cannot think of the Event without discourse and its textualizations; it is constituted in our minds and in our discourses by other representations, both narrative and discursive, including the postwar documentaries whose images etched themselves into our adolescent memories, including the videotapes of survivors, including all the discourses and texts of the historians. But the Event is more than language, text, and discourse. We can very readily question the use of the common noun, capitalized as I have used it, to simultaneously acknowledge and avoid the more frequently used terms in a periphrasis that is yet another form of apophasis. Its very visibility, I hope, will acknowledge the problematic of which it is the locus: what is *an* event, what is *the* event, is it a *single* event; how can one *abstract* from the enormous multiplicity of actions the notion of a single event; how can the evenemential, in its nonlinguistic aspect, make its way into language and representation? Such are the inevitable and proper questions of theory and history both, and it is necessary they be asked, above all in connection with the Event. The very reason they must be asked and pursued as theoretical questions, however, is the nontheoretical and nonlinguistic mass that eludes intellectual grasp and verbal circumscription: something happened about which we can never know enough, about which we always already know far too much, that remains equally insistent and absent in the nightmare language of historical reality.

Himmler's text parodies the rationality, the morality, the earnestness of our own subjectivity and reduces its universalizing assumptions, inherited from the Enlightenment, to the absolutistic hypostasis of tribal blood identity. That reduction was the ideological sine qua non for the extermination of the Jews. As a result, something other than a very large number of Jews was destroyed during the long sequences that led from the ghettos to the trains and into the gas chambers. The Nazi policies, as enacted in the narratives of our historians, also succeeded in killing off a certain kind of subjectivity. Its destruction, instrumental in the process of the physical extermination remains as the end result of that process. Both the diaspora and Israel are forced to develop new subjectivities, efforts whose results do not always meet our hopes. What strikes the reader with horror at the reading of Himmler's speech is that the very qualities we admire and defend, with which we inculcate our children as qualities of a desired subjectivity, are qualities claimed by his discourse as leading to the Event and to the destruction of that subjectivity. The reconstruction and the variabilities of subjectivity are the inevitable aftermaths of the Event.

The process of extermination, to a degree that must remain imprecise, resulted from the language of silence on which Himmler insisted and which he and Hitler practiced. It is this narrative connection, this sequential linkage of the speech of silence and the Event, that renders impermissible the erasure, the cancellation, the bracketing of the narrative that history performs with the silences of its agents upon the bodies of its victims. We cannot know the narrative directly, nor can we know it totally: even the direct survivors can know only one part of what a historian will constitute as the Event, and as we have seen, any historian will be exceedingly conscious of the Event as a construct of the process of writing history. Our grasp of the Event must inevitably be mediated by representations, with their baggage of indeterminacy. But this is a context in which theory is forced to reckon with reference—as unsatisfactory as contemporary accounts of reference may be—as a necessary function of language and all forms of representation. There are other arguments for reference: this is the argument of an ethics and a politics of history.

An admittedly atavistic reason to hesitate at the notion of "unspeakability" is that it constitutes an acceptance, after the fact and after the deaths, of the unspeakability argued by Himmler. It produces ourselves as the continuing agents of Himmler's narrative program of silence. There is another way of conceiving the issue of unspeakability, however, which may be more promising for the future. If I am correct, and the *unheimlich* quality of Himmler's speech derives from conjoining our recognition of his discourse as similar to our own[38] with the terror that strikes us in the realization of what that discourse led to in the narrative of history, then its "unspeakability" is less an inherent quality of the text than a product of our cognitive relation to the Event and to its texts. It is an effect of our own location in the genealogy that constructs both our subjectivity and that which produced the Event. It is as inheritors of that genealogy, it is because of our stake and our identity rooted in that genealogy, that we freeze in horror at simultaneously recognizing in Himmler's discourse the foundations and the destruction of our own subjectivity.

As repugnant as the idea may be, the reaction of unspeakability betokens the fact that we are the product of the same genealogy as the perpetrators of the Event and their discourse. We share the same culture, within certain limitations; we share similar ideological systems, as well as the same modes of discourse as the perpetrators and, it must be added, as their victims. Apophasis is a reaction of *our* historians, of *our* readers, of *our* congeners in the skein of a specific culture and history. Would a reading of the historical record of the programmed extermination of the Jews by a historian whose specific subjectivity was not implicated in the Event produce the same sense of "unspeakability"? Indeed, would the event strike that historian with the same sense of "exceptionality"?

Or would that historian recognize its specificity, as an event which could not have occurred without the bureaucratic structures that are typical of its historical period, which could not have claimed its relative efficacy without the easily reproducible technologies available in the mid-twentieth century, but which otherwise bears marked resemblances to other events, in other cultures, events which mark the sudden escalation of ordinary human violence and cruelty to extraordinary levels? This potential of human culture was conjoined for the first time with the military, technological, and bureaucratic systems required by the numbers implicit in this program of extermination. That particular exceptionality may well be a momentary temporal accident; but as these military, technological, and bureaucratic systems—the everyday components of our social lives—are spread throughout the world, as part of the culture we export for our cultural and historical others to imitate and adapt, they will also be taking in a deadly potential. The universalization of Western culture, which proceeds by the extermination of subjected cultures, implants the possibility of repeating its own patterns of extermination. The universalization of Western culture is hardly an unmixed blessing. "Never again" is a slogan that translates our hopeful reaction to the Event rather than a political judgment. Cynthia Ozick has pointed out that the historical facticity of the Event cannot be assumed to imply the unlikeliness of its recurrence: on the contrary, the fact that it happened more likely implies repetition. [39]

The arguments regarding the uniqueness of the Event are well known and will not be rehearsed here. But is uniqueness a unique quality? Historiography argues that every event is different, and hence unique. A historical event, though we speak of it in the singular, consists of a configuration of traits which together make up the event's uniqueness. Its components, however, could not be recognized were they not available in the remaining repertoire of human existence. It is the particular configuration of the event that endows it with unarguable uniqueness. Whether the uniqueness of the Event is located in the number of victims, in the methodological ambition of totalization, in the bureaucratization of the process, the individual traits are, in strict logical terms, comparable to other human experiences. Such comparison does not have the effect of reducing all the events considered to the same level; on the contrary, the comparison leads to recognition of specificity. The Jewish case was unquestionably unique, and denying the fact is to mystify history, but "to declare [on the other hand] that there are no parallels, and that the whole phenomenon is inexplicable, is equally a mystification."[40]

Among the traits of the comparable catastrophes is the desubjectification of the victims, both the killed and the survivors. Death in battle or resistance can signify the sacrifice of the individual for the sake of the survival of a collective subjectivity: it is an affirmation of subjectivity, even in the death of the subject. Death as the victim of an attempted collective extermination signifies the contrary: the radical desubjectification of the individual as part of the collective from which individual subjectivity derives. This phenomenon is not unique to any collective and its members: it is potentially universal. The interdependence of individual and collective subjectivity is a condition of human social life.

Let me suggest another, final direction, which will not only elude closure but actively seek an opening. It is an opening that is grounded in the freedom of the subject and the necessity of its employment. It is an effort to conclude with an ethical and political opening to others which will seek, not to redeem the dead by asserting their death possessed an inherent redemptive significance—a goal I find frightful and repugnant—but to endow their death and their torture with the retrospective meaning it is in our power to give. It is an effort to make present action the interpretant (to use C. S. Pierce's term) of the Martyrs' torture. One finds in Midrash the following from Rabbi Yohanan:

> Every distress that Israel and the nations of the world share is a
> distress indeed.
> Every distress that is Israel's alone
> is no distress.[41]

The rule, applied as inexorable Law, would be too harsh: the distress particular to Israel and the diaspora is a distress indeed. But the direction, toward continuity and interdependence, is the right one.

In the wake of World War II, and largely as a result of it, Jews in the United States gained access to the professions in a sudden and brilliant social success. Having just won the equality promised its subjects by the state, a generation of young Jews, impelled by the ethical and political passion for justice that was their inheritance, embraced the struggles of others for emancipation. The moving celebrations of the Passover known as the Freedom Seders during the sixties were a point of suture between religion and history, when Jews placed themselves in the forefront of the struggles of others for the freedom and rights they themselves had just won as full subjects of the state. At those seders were Jewish students and faculty, of course, but also large numbers of blacks, Porto Riqueños, and all those ready to recognize the concrete historical symbolism of the ritual event—its general emancipatory significance as well as its immediate political insertion. The role of Jews in the struggles of the sixties was an extraordinary and generous extension of a concrete historical experience, as a minority rising from subservience and oppression, to others still suffering as victims. Those victims were the poor and the black in our own society; they were also the foreign victims of our own warfare in distant lands. It was in recognition, not of the same subjectivity, but of the same subjection to unjustly exercised power and its effects of desubjectification, that Jews made common cause with those in yet more immediately distressful situations than their own. This recognition was based on an understanding of the continuity which links one form of desubjectification to another, without negating or ignoring the specificities of those forms.

Comparable desubjectifications continue in today's world. Their victims include the legions of *desaparecidos,* targets of South American death squads; South African blacks; the subject population of Cambodia, victimized by its own government. But they do not occur only in foreign lands and distant continents. They include, in our own streets and cities, the homeless, the more hidden victims of AIDS, and—still today—the blacks and the hispanics, increasingly silenced and isolated in their ghettos. The category also includes, as painful as it is to hear it said, the Palestinians under Israeli occupation. These are all persons whose subjection to the state has not brought them the active subjectivity implied by that subjection, the ability to act according to the values of the inculcating ideology that creates subjectivity.

None of these suffers as the equivalent of European Jewry targeted for Nazi destruction. None is the victim of a totalizing genocidal pro-

gram of extermination. All, however, share the inscription of desubjectification. We react to their increasing numbers with increasing indifference. Our indifference, our ability to live in silent contiguity to
their deprivation, is not unlike that of a German population that wel-
comed the deniability made possible by the official policy of apophasis.
One of the parameters that determined Jewish survivability during the
war was the attitude of non-Jewish neighbors, which could be life-
saving. In the absence of such protection, the Jews were left to the
mercies of the SS and their collaborators. According to one historian,
the "central historical problem . . . boils down to a moral challenge:
were the Gentiles their Jewish brothers' keepers?"[42] Isolating the Jews
was one goal of antisemitic propaganda, and it was largely effective.
"The majority of the population evinced an attitude of indifference
which, in the circumstances, meant abandonment of the hunted Jews
and noncooperation in their rescue."[43] Rather than any active hostility
toward Jews by the general population, what permitted the SS to be so
effective was a general attitude of "apathy, indifference, discomfort at
the thought of what was happening to the Jews," as well as fear of the
authorities.[44] Deniability has been erected into an operational theory
by our own government, in a kind of political apophasis, and is not
unknown in the practice of our population. It is a willful silence that
refuses the universalism of our own ideology and the subjectivity it
founds. It is a willful silence that may constitute the pre-condition for
far worse eventualities and their attendant narratives. It has done so in
the past.

Without impairing the continued constitutive role of the Event for
those directly implicated in its horror, the extension of its implications
to the analogous experiences of other groups on the face of the earth
will be the form of universalism that Judaism can hope to regain. It is
only as the exploration of the specificity of one historical experience is
extended to the analogous experiences of cultural and historical others, in full recognition of the differences between the experiences in
question, that the universalism will be enacted that was the basis of
the historic liberation of the Jews after the political emancipation of the
subjects of nation-states in the eighteenth century. That genealogical
adherence legitimizes our righteous anger at those persons, traits, and
institutions which were the conditions of possibility of the Event, including the silences that have attended the Event before, during, and

since the process of extermination and including the continuing processes of desubjectification in our own society. That genealogy also alerts us to the continuing danger to specificity and difference posed by the very universalism that is also the necessary condition of emancipation.

< 18 >

The Representation of Limits

BEREL LANG

The reference to the "limits of representation" in the title of this volume might seem to imply that limits themselves are not representations. Since the question confronted in the title asks whether or where limits occur beyond which representations of the "Final Solution" cannot or should not go, the limits referred to would not at the same time be themselves *within* the area "represented." And indeed, the issue tendentiously raised in this way is one of substance as well as logic. By definition, there will be a difference between a representation and its object *un*represented, with the former adding to or altering the other. In this sense, the opposite of *representational* is not *abstract* (applied, for example, to nonrepresentational painting) but *literal*—the object as it is before or apart from being re-presented.

There is, furthermore, a tacit preposition attached to the concept of representation and its exemplifications. Representations are characteristically representations *as,* with the implication in that locution of other possible "representations as." So, for example, the French Revolution could be "represented as" or "represented as not" having been a true class struggle—with no option for either, however, of escaping the qualifying preposition. One might think here of a space that obtrudes between an object or event and its representation, allowing, indeed requiring choices among the alternatives for which the space provides a means. Any representation, then, in addition to its manifest content, represents the exclusion of others. The latter appear not as a uniform phantom class, moreover, but with differing degrees of individuation which underscore the common factor of choice represented. No single representation, in effect, without the possibility of another.

This native pluralism in the concept of representation suggests an antagonism between it and the concept of limits—since the common function of limits, one supposes, is not to multiply alternatives but to

< 300 >

restrict them, in effect, to say "No." Indeed, the tension between representation and limits comes to light in the status of the limiting term *No* itself—as, for example, in the grammatical question of what "part of speech" that term is. Typically, the so-called parts of speech are understood representationally—verbs as representing actions, nouns as representing objects, and so on. But prima facie there seems no corresponding group-likeness with which the term *No* can be associated. The dictionary, with customary assurance, identifies it as an adverb; that is, as a representation of "how" events occur. But even this authority does not quite dispel the sense that the limit asserted in a flat denial requires a category that is also flat or one-dimensional—so single-minded that it may not, strictly speaking, be a part of speech or representational at all.

Yet it is also evident that few limits do say "No" unequivocally. More often what they exclude is already present or implied in the saying itself. For most limits that are asserted, other possibilities can be readily imagined; for many of *these*, the alternate limits are not only imagined but actual. Limits are asserted, in other words, in the presence of transgression, after (if not exactly because) violation has occurred. In fact, the representation of limits, the form that limits take and the function they have, is usefully understood at its origins in relation to the phenomenon of transgression—and this relation is then pertinent, in certain respects crucial, for characterizing the limits that apply to historical and literary accounts of the "Final Solution," the representations to be considered here.

One formal consideration may be brought up about both the "limits of representation" and (in my reversal of that phrase) the "representation of limits." In each, limits are referred to as if given—as though, notwithstanding disagreements about what or where they occur, there could be no question that they exist. But this apparent implication might be understood more immediately as no more than a manner of speaking, in the way that religion or morality have at times been posited only to turn out in discussion to be large-scale fictions. Viewed from this perspective, the concept or phenomenon of limits would be recognizable as a representation of something else, perhaps of a psychological or biological impulse for boundaries and taboos, perhaps of an intrinsic incompleteness in all systematic structures. Those two "deep" versions of limits are neatly joined, as it happens, in Mary

Douglas' description of the recurrence in cultural structures of the phenomenon of pollution. "Where there is dirt, there is system," her epigram on this goes. "Primitives and moderns, we are all subject to the same rules."[1]

Even this general claim, however, would not explain the specific forms that limits take or the processes that lead to them in the space of the imagination. In that space, the possibility that limits are no more than artifacts, freely chosen, perhaps self-consuming—in effect that for the imagination there *are* no limits—is proposed as a condition (if not exactly a limiting one). Thus, for example, Leonardo, in a well-known passage from his *Treatise on Painting*, offers advice to the aspiring artist: "You should look at certain walls stained with damp, or at stones of uneven color . . . You will be able to see in these the likeness of divine landscapes, adorned with mountains, ruins, rocks, woods, great plains, hills and valleys in great variety; and then again you will see these battles and strange figures in violent action, expressions of faces and clothes . . . In such walls the same things happen as in the sound of bells in whose stroke you may find every named word which you can imagine."[2]

Leonardo then goes on to caution the artist about the practical labor that remains *after* he "sees" the landscapes or faces in the stained walls and colored rocks. But the representations identified by Leonardo themselves serve as an image of representational freedom. When walls and stones yield the variety he details, there can hardly be limits on whatever more might be discerned there: anything, we infer, can come to represent anything else, and conversely, any representation can have anything else as its object or source.

The extreme possibilities, then, are marked. On the one hand, limits exist because they must: human culture or consciousness cannot do without them. On the other hand, limits (at least the limits of representation) are at most conventional and thus open to continuing, even limitless variation because they cannot be more than that: any specific representation, if not the act itself, is in these terms unnatural. The general force claimed by these contradictory statements suggests that their own status is a priori and thus beyond argument altogether. What is clearly not beyond discussion, however, is the fact that most representations of limits stand between those extremes. The examination of limits in this middle ground may be informative about the extremes as well; even without this benefit, however, such scrutiny will disclose the role of limits in practice—the point at which the representation of limits begins to shape the limits of representation.

Transgression and Representation

I refer to this unlikely conjunction nonetheless in a strong sense: transgression as a *condition* for representation. Once again, the phenomenon of artistic representation illustrates the claim, in Wölfflin's assertion of the limits that circumscribe the development of artistic style: "Not everything is possible," he writes about that history, "at every time"[3]—in effect denying the artist at a particular time at least some of what either later or earlier are indeed artistic options. It should be noted that these limits posited by Wölfflin constrain not only what at a given moment can be painted but, because of what the act of painting entails, also what the artist can imagine. There could be no representation of the limit that acts here because to imagine its terms would be already to transgress them; for the artist to conceive what he cannot do—to imagine what it is he cannot imagine—would already be to do the artist's work. Even the characteristic estrangement or defamiliarization found in art by the Russian formalists would not violate this further, nonrepresentational limit; those terms are themselves, after all, literary counterparts of transgression or violation.[4] In such formulations, the relation between transgression and representation is posed negatively. There is no possibility of arriving at a representation of the limit without transgressing it; yet the limit is indeed posited—thus, however, without representation.

It might be objected that this example depends heavily on one, disputed view of art history; but the same negative argument for the relation between transgression and representation appears no less emphatically in the Aristotelian "law" of contradiction. In Aristotle's own terms at least, the claim that something cannot both be and not be itself in the same respect at the same time cannot be meaningfully denied (or violated) without presupposing that very assertion. The limit posed, in other words, *cannot* be transgressed; to do so, as Aristotle concludes, would occur not humanly but in the life of a vegetable.[5] In this example as in the first one, then, transgression is not only impossible in fact, but unimaginable—incapable of representation because of the implicit exclusion of alternatives. The assertion of the limit here is thus not representational but literal or iconic, pointing (at most) only to itself.

The form of the relation thus asserted in the definition of limits between transgression and representation is not the only one that the relation can take; three alternate forms reflect other permutations in the two variables involved. As the transgression of its limits is judged in the first example as both impossible in fact and unimaginable, transgression can otherwise be seen as

imaginable but impossible;
unimaginable but possible;
imaginable and possible.

Like the original conception, the first and second of these alternate conceptions are only indirectly pertinent here, although they too underscore the relation claimed between transgression and representation. The first combination referred to is exemplified in physical limits—in the law of the conservation of energy, for example, or in the limit defined by the speed of light. Such limits assert the physical impossibility of transgression—but the limits pose no barrier (even, I assume, for those who fully understand their grounds) to imagining such violation—the existence, for example, of a particle that moves at 187,000 miles rather than 186,000 per second (insofar as *that* can be imagined). But here as in the original version of the relation between transgression and representation, no special constraints are implied for historical representations: physical limits that apply generally would also hold, we assume, both for past events and their present representations. And although it is possible to write about (hence, to imagine) a historical event in terms that violate recognized physical limits, nothing more than that would need to be known to discredit the account: anachronisms (for example) not only do not but cannot represent the past.

The second alternative relation cited between transgression and representation may seem puzzling or even self-contradictory: how can the transgression of a limit be possible and yet unimaginable? The conjunction here appears to strain intelligibility—but it is exactly this combination of features that Kant finds to characterize the sublime. In that conception, the recognition of a transcendence which, because of its limitlessness, cannot be represented impels the experience, distinguishing it from the more conventional (limited) aesthetic judgment with which Kant contrasts it.[6] So, in his example, the limitlessness of the power and expanse of the ocean cannot itself be represented—but the viewer's recognition of that limitlessness attests to his capacity for going beyond his own limits. A relation is thus claimed between the possible and the unimaginable, with the transgression of limits once again at the basis of their definition.

To be sure, for Kant and the tradition following him the "fact" of the sublime exalts the human subject, with moral implications proportionately elevated and with little suggestion of anything analogous entailed in acts of moral enormity. Yet Kant's conception of "radical evil" (as in *Groundwork of the Metaphysic of Morals*) approximates an inversion of the sublime that, joined to the historical evidence, might indeed characterize the Nazi genocide—as moved by an impulse not only to transgress limits but to deny that such limits apply at all. Transgression "downward" would, in these terms, be a counterpart to the "upward" movement of the sublime.

This version of the relation between transgression and representation would itself be dependent, however, on the final alternative cited—since it is here, in the transgression of limits as both possible and imaginable that the conception of limits as moral are first defined. The reason for locating moral limits under this heading should be readily evident: historically as well as psychologically, the representation of those limits assumes not only the possibility but the actuality of transgression. The *possibility* of transgression is presupposed if the limits are to be at all relevant—since without that possibility (reflected in the role attached by moral deliberation to free will), adherence to a limit could have no moral weight. (Without that possibility, the conception of a limit would be a parody—like drawing a bull's-eye on a target after an arrow had hit it.) The *actuality* of transgression is presupposed in identifying the specific point at which a limit is set. That the determination of this point is often a matter of convention does not mean that it is arbitrarily chosen; on even a restrained view of the functional strategies of culture, limits would hardly be asserted unless the practice prohibited had occurred in fact. So, for example, Braudel, the historian of everyday life, traces the spread in the Arab world of the dangerous new substance, coffee, and deduces one particular turn of that history: "[We know that] it had reached Mecca by 1511 since in that year its consumption was forbidden there."[7] Transgression figures here as a condition for the representation of limits, a condition which for Braudel is doubled in its occurrence: once in Mecca, as the prohibition was formulated, and once in Paris, as the historian rehearsed it. First, then, for limits, and secondly for the history of limits.

A Moral Radical of Historical Representation

To ask about the limits that apply to representations of the "Final Solution" is minimally to refer to that event in historical terms. It is clear that those terms, too, have in some sense to be imagined; indeed, the challenge to conceptualization and to language in the Nazi genocide is undeniable, for its agents no less than for those who reflect on it (consider only the complex although brief history of the term *genocide*).[8] But it is unlikely that we would be inquiring now about the limits of representation in respect to the "Final Solution" if its representations were taken to be only fictions, however demotic. The schema that has been outlined, of limits as reflecting the relation between transgression and representation, thus impels the question as to which, among the four versions just discussed, would serve as a basis for the limits of historical representation.

I have already suggested that the first of them, where transgression affirms or presupposes the limit transgressed, would not apply to historical representation more than to any other: logic, in this appearance, is historically indifferent. Nor, for most historical claims, whether at the level of chronicle or at that of interpretation, would alternative versions or even their contradiction be precluded by limits of physical impossibility (except insofar as history in general is subjected to a *meta*physical decree of determinism). No physical necessity blocks the reflection that Caesar might not have crossed the Rubicon, and a historical narrative which took that possibility seriously might nonetheless illuminate the accepted account. For reasons already given, moreover, the category of the sublime, viewed either straight-on or inverted—transgression as possible but beyond representation—would be applicable to historical assertion only insofar as authentic limits had first been defined that the "historical sublime" might then challenge.

If limits apply to historical representation, they will appear first, then, in the final alternative cited, where transgression is both imaginable and possible. The example cited of this relation was the representation of moral, not of historical, limits; that the latter comes under the same category does not imply an intrinsic connection between them, though that connection may exist. In fact, it is on the basis of that connection that the applicability of limits to representations of the "Final Solution" comes most clearly into view.

There are two levels at which the connection of moral to historical representation can be made evident. The first of these is at the level of historical chronicle, which I take to be foundational for historiography. The assertion—or its denial—that on 20 January 1942 certain members of the Nazi hierarchy, meeting at Wannsee, discussed the terms— and the term itself—of the "Final Solution" is separable from the causal or other interpretive accounts that might elaborate it. To be sure, the criteria to which even this assertion answers presuppose a conception of evidence and to that extent also of interpretation; such presuppositions are pertinent also in explaining why certain events rather than others are selectively cited. But what is validated or rejected in the form of chronicle does not, it seems to me, require contextualization or a narrative account that goes beyond its own grounds. In this sense, the chronicle remains systematically a point zero in historiography, with disagreement about any of its assertions capable in principle of adjudication in terms of the chronicle itself.[9]

I recognize the danger of positing this (or any other) foundation for a form of discourse. It is evident, moreover, that the chronicle itself is a literary genre, that it assumes certain conventions which are themselves representations; like facts in scientific discourse, the chronicle in historiography reflects a process of abstraction. But to admit these qualifications, even to concede that the citing of particular items in a chronicle may have moral or other suasive origins does not mean that no substantive differences distinguish those items in *this* appearance from their nonhistorical counterparts. If historical representations are to be at all distinguishable from those of fiction, the difference will be located here at the level of chronicle—if only *faute de mieux*. (The specific fictional analogue—and differentia—to the temporal references of chronicle is an atemporal constant: "Once upon a time . . .") Even at the level of chronicle, to be sure, assertions made within the chronicle's limits can be challenged. But the issue in these cases is, it seems to me, of a different order from that raised at a second—for example, narrative—level of historical statement for which the citations of chronicle are only a starting point. Even consensus at the level of chronicle leaves the way open to divergence at the levels beyond it.

The foundational role thus ascribed to chronicle appears with unusual force in representations of the "Final Solution" because of the
specific way those representations build on the *absence* of certain details of chronicle—an absence which, incorporated, leads to significant
differences in the second-level or narrative accounts of that event. I
refer most immediately here to the absence of (or at least the failure so
far to locate) a specific "Führer order" that, then recorded as an item
of chronicle, would serve as a basis for representing historically, at a
second level, the causal development of the "Final Solution." To a considerable extent, the reaction against the standard intentional accounts
of the "Final Solution" originates here—contesting the intentionalist
willingness not only to posit an overall shape for intention (where intentions are concerned, this must always be posited), but also to assume, even before that shape, the particular act that such a large-scale
intention presupposes—namely, the written or oral order given by
Hitler. In a formal or systematic sense, then, the absence of the latter
has served as a condition for the functionalist accounts that still pose
the weightiest alternative to intentionalist representations. It might be
possible, even with the discovery of a "Hitler order," to adhere still to
the functionalist representation of the "Final Solution" as an incremen-
tal process contributed to by independent, sometimes competing
forces within the Nazi hierarchy—but obviously the representation
would then be more difficult to defend. [10]

Much can be said, of course, about various aspects of these two conflicting second-level accounts, but for the moment I focus only on one,
albeit a large issue in the dispute between them: the question, namely,
of how (or whether) responsibility is to be ascribed for the "Final Solution"—with the consequences that conflicting answers to this have not
only for the historiography of that event, but also for history in the
present (that is, the way history is now incorporated). It is clear that
differences on this issue have significant moral and social consequences. Are such differences in consequence—*present* history—pertinent to the way that the history of the past is or should be written?
There can be little doubt that they do affect the writing of history; and
in referring to what I call a "moral radical of historical representation,"
I mean to suggest that there is a basis for this connection in the elements of historical representation itself, in the general relation involved there between fact and value.

The claim made in the formula I propose for the radical of historical representation holds that the differences among variant historical accounts of the "same" event include a factor based on the moral consequences of the respective accounts. The formula thus asserts that the risk or burden of evidence incurred in choosing among alternative historical representations increases—first—in proportion to the distance between the alternative chosen and those rejected; and secondly, with that distance multiplied by a moral weight assigned to the common issue at stake between them. In its mathematical form this would be $R = (A_1 - A_2) \times W$. How the "weight" (of W) is determined is not itself part of the formula, although it emerges as a function of the moral community in which the judgment is made.

An application of the radical of historical representation is indicated in the "distance" that separates the intentionalist and functionalist accounts. The disagreement between those accounts does not occur at the level of chronicle: the functionalist position need not and in general does not entail a denial that genocide or at least mass murder was an outcome of Nazi acts, however uncoordinated or collectively unintended those acts allegedly were. The differences between the two versions occur then, even in explaining the apparent absence of the Führer order, at the second level of interpretation. It is likewise at the second level that the differences in consequence of the two conflicting accounts—the differences articulated in the radical of historical representation—become pertinent.

There can be no doubt that whatever else is involved, a strong moral tension has underlain the differences at issue in the intentionalist and functionalist accounts, even in aspects that do not bear directly on the issues of intention or responsibility. In terms of the radical of representation, this tension is not adventitious but substantive.

This distinction is not to say that the moral weight of issues on which the second-level accounts disagree—like the question of responsibility—by itself should determine what then emerges as the content of historical representation. But it does mean that the decisions incorporated in such representation also include decisions on the moral implications of the elements that comprise the representation. This factor, the historian's moral risk, is then, willingly or not, an ingredient in the representation and also in the limits by which the representation is subsequently to be measured.

The differences that appear under such analysis in the "nest" of representations of the "Final Solution" come most blatantly to view, of course, in the revisionist alternative that denies not only intentionality, but the phenomenon of genocide or mass murder in the Nazi period. In terms of the radical of historical representation, the distance among the alternative representations increases from a starting point in intentionalism to that point defined by the differences between intentionalism and functionalism, and then increases sharply when the question in historical representation is not whether mass murder occurred by design but whether it occurred at all. Here, even more strongly, it is evident that the representational differences involve more than simply a determination of "matters of fact." The consequences of being right or wrong *about* the matters of fact in the conflicting accounts have a moral weight that marks the representation "chosen" by the historian from the nest of possibilities. The difference here lies between there being a "Final Solution" or not; and what turns on that difference is an element in the historical representation itself.

To be sure, even a large increase in risk as determined by the radical of representation does not mean that a limit of representation has been transgressed. But it does suggest how (and that) such a limit would emerge, and it indicates also what the terms of transgression would be. Indeed, as the distance in consequence among the alternatives posed increases, a representation that does not incorporate recognition of this fact—not simply by describing the difference, but by basing the proportions of the representation on it—seems already to violate a two-fold limit: a formal limit of material difference (by treating all possibilities of chronicle as equal); and, in failing to recognize the specific character of the "Final Solution," a substantive limit based on individual moral weight.

Representation and the Moral Community

The question remains to be addressed of how the moral weight claimed for matters of fact in the radical of historical representation is to be determined, and I refer here to only one of a number of factors that would be involved (and even that, largely by example): namely, the role of moral community. By this reference, I mean that the moral weight ascribed to an issue analyzed in terms of the radical will reflect the context of social identity in which the historical representation is addressed—in the present, that is, rather than in the past represented. In one sense, this claim may seem too obvious to need saying:

we speak always in the here and now. Just so, for example, it is the "Final Solution" for which the limits of representation are probed in this volume, not another of the many instances of moral enormity to which the same question might have been directed. Few of the authors who write here, moreover, would be in doubt about our own reasons for acknowledging this distinction.

Yet there would also almost certainly be agreement—as against this acknowledgment—that the moral quality of an act ought to be judged apart from any particular historical or social context. The distance separating the present from the age of the Caesars hardly alters the evildoing of a Caligula or a Nero. Nor is there a plausible way morally of distinguishing among like instances of wrongdoing, even murder and even (or perhaps especially) in terms of numbers. Yet just as it is undeniable that the effect on us of what happens in the lives or deaths of relatives and friends differs from the effect of what happens to "strangers," so too, events embedded in social identity reflect that identity as a factor in the significance associated with them.

It might be objected that even if the latter claim is true psychologically and historically, the analogy is morally wanting: the weight attached to a wrong should not, it seems, depend on the time or location in which the wrong is committed or on the particular persons or groups affected by it. This tension between the universal and the particular in moral judgment cannot be considered here except insofar as it bears on the radical of historical representation; but there, it seems to me, the claim for the particularity of moral judgment is compelling. The instances of historical representation judged in that formula are individual events; no less necessarily, the weights attached to them reflect the same particularity.

That there is no algorithm which would enable us to determine the weight assigned to every possible event itself suggests that the determination here will be contextual. And the context most directly pertinent to its formation is, it seems to me, provided by the notion of a moral community—the interwoven dependencies and claims which, ill-defined as their boundaries are, are distinguishable from the conception (indeed from the possibility) of a universal moral language, on the one hand, or a private moral language, on the other. The vagaries and so the dangers in relying on this contextual ground are evident— but they are no larger, I think it can be shown, than what is entailed by their alternatives.

Let me cite two examples of what I mean here, the first of them with special relevance to this volume since Saul Friedlander has a part in it. In the question period after a lecture that he delivered at a conference (also bearing on the "Final Solution") at Northwestern University, the first question directed to Friedlander came from a member of the audience who was identified as Arthur Butz, a faculty member at Northwestern. Since the Friedlander lecture was not restricted to conference registrants, Butz clearly had the right to be present; in the order of the meeting, he arguably had a right to be recognized by the chair and to ask questions. What he did not have a right to—or obversely, what the speaker was not obligated to provide—was a response to his question, even to the relatively straightforward one that he asked. And in deciding not to respond to the author of *The Hoax of the Twentieth Century*—consciously overriding the academy's commitment to open discussion—Friedlander was, it seems to me, asserting a twofold limit: in one aspect, on the moral possibilities of historical representation, and in a second aspect, on the extent of the moral community that is itself a part of that representation and from which, on this matter at least, Friedlander judged Butz to have separated himself. (I should emphasize that this is my own gloss on the exchange, not Saul Friedlander's.)

Obviously, the assertion of either aspect of this limit involves the risk of a slippery slope—and a more immediate challenge of justifying even the one step down it. But a premise of Friedlander's refusal to respond to Butz was, I take it, that there is a still larger risk and challenge on the other side: in the assumptions that questions are detachable from those who raise them; that questioners are themselves separable from the contexts in which they speak; and most fundamentally, that historical representations have no intrinsic or necessary moral standing. It seems to me that all three of these claims are rightfully disputed, not uniquely in their bearing on accounts of the "Final Solution," but certainly and markedly there—a crux that then becomes itself a ground for the representation of limits.

A second example is provided by a statement published by a group of thirty-four French historians in *Le Monde* (21 February 1979), in the context of the then strengthening denial in France of the means—and so by implication, the occurrence—of the "Final Solution": "Everyone is free to interpret a phenomenon like the Hitlerian genocide according to his philosophy . . . Everyone is free to apply to it one or another means of explication; everyone is free, up to the limit, to imagine or dream that these monstrous facts did not take place. They unfortunately did take place, and no one can deny their existence without outrage to the truth . . . This is the obligatory starting point of any historical inquiry on the subject . . . It is impossible to have a debate on the existence of the gas chambers."

It is clear that the limit thus asserted is not drawn around anything like a "simple" matter of fact—for on that basis, to deny the existence of the gas chambers would be no more excluded from discussion or representation than any other denial. What is being asserted, I take it, is a moral *presence* for matters of fact—and thus a quite different account of what facts are, here or elsewhere.

Again, the menace of the slippery slope threatens here; even for this one step, there is the necessity of defending it, given the frequency with which piety finds itself turned into moralism. It is not unreasonable, at any rate, to ask at a theoretical level whether a claim of the sort made by the French historians could *ever* be legitimate. For analysis that takes as a premise what has come to be known as the naturalistic fallacy, with the sharp line drawn there between fact and value, the answer to this question would obviously be "No": facts immaculately conceived could only be immaculately judged. But if one rejects that premise—on the grounds, for one thing, that the moral weight of a fact may be as much an ingredient in it as any other of its features, then not only is it possible that limits such as the one asserted by the thirty-four historians should be sustained, but there would be something implausible, even contradictory, if at some point it were not. One could imagine here a Kafkaesque tale in which the existence of a limit was proclaimed but its exact prohibition was left unstated. The antihero of the tale is troubled, even obsessed by this absence; he grows old, then, beset by profligacy and angst in equal measures: try as he will, even his largest excesses fail to bring him into contact with the limit, to disclose what it is. He has not, he feels at the end, led a *full* life.

The claim that such representations of limits are warranted in general does not, to be sure, justify any particular assertion of them; the indistinctness of practical in contrast to theoretical judgment applies here as well, for worse as for better. But here also the radical of historical representation provides the basis for a useful distinction—although I recognize that as it bears on the issue of the "Final Solution," that formula may seem to hold a telescope to something that is all too plainly in sight.

Art within the Limits of History

Earlier, I referred to a statement by Leonardo concerned with artistic or pictorial rather than historical representation. For Leonardo, the "walls stained with damp, or stones of uneven color" were accidental, incentives to the power of invention which, once evoked, might then proceed on its own. Insofar as limits of representation applied here at all, they would be limits of the artist's imagination, not constraints imposed by the walls or stones themselves. The fact that what the artist "saw" could only equivocally be said to be representations of the walls or stones would be more than outweighed, one infers, by the limitlessness of their possibilities: anything imaginable could be represented here.

This ideal of artistic representation as boundless in principle recurs in post-Renaissance conceptions of art and aesthetics—at an extreme in romantic accounts of genius and originality, but persistent also in later, less dramatic formulations which in other respects oppose the romantic emphasis on individualism (including, of course, the corporate individual). So, for example, Salman Rushdie, confronted by unusually harsh claims for the limits of representation, reiterates even then his opposing view of literature as "the one place in any society where . . . we can hear the voices talk about everything in every possible way." [11]

It should be evident that the question of censorship can be separated from the question of whether there exist limits of artistic representation related to limits of historical representation like those I have proposed. For here again the issue is not one of an intrinsic or necessary boundary, since, as I have suggested, for the imagination to formulate a limit (to imagine what could not be imagined) would already be to exceed it. The question is then not what can or cannot be imagined, but whether limits apply to the forms that imagined representations do take.

In this connection, imaginative writing about the "Final Solution" shares certain constraints with imaginative accounts of any historical subject. Where history figures in artistic representation, the details of historical chronicle have a role that would be absent or much reduced in representations where specific historical events have no part. To be sure, the line between what is and what is not historical fiction (in this instance, what is often referred to as Holocaust writing) will almost certainly remain unclear. So, for example, in Saul Bellow's novel *Mr. Sammler's Planet,* Sammler—the reader learns piecemeal—had fought as a partisan in the European destruction; but this literary fact is quite off-center from the primary representation of the novel set in the turmoil and uncertainty of New York middle-class and intellectual life in the late 1960s. Or in a more distinctive (because less serious) example: several pages in a mystery novel by R. D. Rosen, *Strike Three You're Dead,* depict an encounter between the detective-hero of the mystery and a tailor who is a concentration camp survivor, where this fact about the latter's biography, although given in some detail, is unrelated to the book's mystery. The encounter amounts, in effect, to a citation rather than a representation of the "Final Solution."

At issue here is the more general problem for aesthetics of how an artistic or literary work's representation—what it is "about"—is determined. But because specific judgments of this issue can be disputed does not imply that the general problem is irresolvable. For many texts that involve the "Final Solution," the problem is not to determine *whether* that event is their subject but to assess its "representation as" their subject—especially as they reach or pass its representative limits. I would argue in respect to literary representation that the force of the historical limits that apply is compounded as the constraints (and so, risks) on historical representation are joined by constraints that hold specifically for artistic representation.

The effect of this compounding of limits is noticeable even at the first, "chronicled" levels of literary and historical fact. The writer may imagine, as George Steiner does in *The Portage to San Cristobal of A. H.,* that Hitler had survived the war, later to emerge from hiding in South America—or, as Philip Roth does in *The Ghost Writer,* that Anne Frank, having somehow escaped Bergen-Belsen, would then reappear as an aspiring young writer in wintry New England. But these imagined representations depend for their effects on straightforwardly historical premises which the texts assume are known to the reader—namely, that the imagined possibilities are at once fictional *and* false: they might have been the case, but they were not.

In this way (and obviously there are other, more extensive and important examples), the limits of historical representation—a fortiori for representation beyond the level of chronicle—apply also to historical fiction, with the added burden now of taking account of what is entailed in designedly figurative or tropic representation. About this question, only a few rudimentary words. Whatever else it does, figurative discourse and the elaboration of figurative space obtrudes the author's voice and a range of imaginative turns and decisions on the literary subject, irrespective of that subject's character and irrespective of—indeed defying—the "facts" of that subject which might otherwise have spoken for themselves and which, at the very least, do not depend on the author's voice for their existence. The claim is entailed in imaginative representation that the facts *do not* speak for themselves, that figurative condensation and displacement and the authorial presence these articulate will turn or supplement the historical subject (whatever it is) in a way that represents the subject more compellingly or effectively—in the end, more truly—than would be the case without them.

It seems to me important to recognize that there are possible subjects of artistic representation which challenge this premise; and that imagined representations of the "Final Solution" provide one such instance—not in the sense that the challenge there is insuperable, but that it is unavoidable, and that it has both unusual force and an unusual form. The denial of individuality and personhood in the act of genocide; the abstract bureaucracy that empowered the "Final Solution," moved by an almost indistinguishable combination of corporate and individual will and blindness to evil, constitute a subject that in its elements seems at odds with the insulation of figurative discourse and the individuation of character and motivation that literary "making" tends to impose on its subjects. With this, a risk is added to the already severe one chanced in the decisions of historical representation—a risk that would hold even for subjects less heavily weighted morally than the "Final Solution" but that, with that weight, becomes itself a substantive part of the representation.[12]

Adorno's assertion of the barbarism—not the impossibility, but the barbarism—of writing lyric poetry after Auschwitz (a fortiori, *about* Auschwitz)—is one formulation of this representational limit and ought, in its premises at least, to be taken seriously in the judgment of all imaginative writing about the "Final Solution." Admittedly, even if Adorno's claim were accepted at face value (he himself subsequently qualified it),[13] a justification might be argued for the barbarism he warns against as a defense against still greater barbarism—against denial, for example, or against forgetfulness. On this basis, in fact, it could be held that even certain common *mis*representations of the "Final Solution" in imaginative writing—representations that seek the effects of melodrama or sentimentality or prurience—may nonetheless be warranted as within the limits; such writing, too, it could be maintained, serves a purpose in calling attention to the historical occurrence itself. In this sense, an unusual plea might be entered, based on an unusual subject, also for admittedly barbaric—"bad" or "false"—writing.

Not even this justification, however, would override what seems to me the most general limit of representation—the limit against which all representation, and all other representational limits, will in the end be measured and which applies to writing about the "Final Solution" only more obviously than it does to other writing. This is the limit, and thus the alternative, of silence—and I do not mean here a silence intended to express the impossibility, the intrinsic inadequacy of all representation of the "Final Solution" (as suggested at various times by writers as diverse as George Steiner and Elie Wiesel). It seems to me that sufficient evidence, both theoretical and in fact, argues against any such claim—as much, at all events, as it argues against the unintelligibility of evil in any of its appearances. I mean rather a silence that emerges as a limit precisely because of the *possibility* of representation and the risks which that possibility entails. In these terms, silence is a limit for particular representations as it happens, not intrinsically for representation as such. It seems harsh enough, after all, to say of any particular representation that, in comparison to its voice, silence would have been more accurate or truthful.

< 19 >

The Book of the Destruction

Geoffrey H. Hartman

The point was not, of course, to produce the biggest and saddest coffee-table book ever. Would it, in any case, have been a book? It is said that a museum, filled with replicas of the vanished life, especially the burnt and plundered temples, also exhibited a Scroll of Fire. Our sages of blessed memory and fertile wit pondered whether that scroll was really a book, and if so what kind of fire had inscribed it. One of them said in the name of a man "from Czernowitz" that it was written in black fire on black milk. Another claimed that it was written with dying embers that could only be seen at night.

> Asche.
> Asche, Asche.
> Nacht.
> Nacht-und-Nacht.

Reb Jabes, son of Jabes, said that the Scroll of Fire was that pillar by which the Blessed and Merciful One redeems the impurity of the night every single dawn. It burned without smoke and turned mourning into morning. But Abel, Kajis, and Ish-Chanit said that in those days history returned and everything was seen again, illumined by a strange cold flame. The pagans Mozart, Napoleon, and Van Gogh, as well as a certain Nazarene, returned that way. Going from light to heavy, even the Haman of that time, may his name and image be erased, would have come back like a vampire whose coffin can never be secured, however many curses nail it shut. Reb Idel taught there was such a book in a form beyond letters; witness the *remez* in Samuel and Joshua to a missing *sefer hayashar.* There surely existed a Book of the Destruction but it was not meant to be found. And to what may this be compared? To a king who made himself sick reading and reading, and decreed that there be no more accounts of the destruction. He appointed seventy elders to draft a single volume, a *sefer hashoah* that

< 318 >

would be consecrated in a great convocation and recited to the people. After a year and a day the elders came and said to him: O King, whose mercy is like the rays of the setting sun, we cannot do what you have commanded. You yourself must gather it together, in your wisdom and strength. For we are inspired only by fear and awe, that bring discord rather than unity. The dead cannot praise, but in this matter the living cannot praise either. Such a book would need six hundred thousand margins, one for each soul at Sinai, if the Covenant is to hold in the face of the slaughter. The king answered, like the Holy One that sits and roars when he remembers his children in distress among the nations: You have endured only two watches of the night, come back when you have sat all three. He also said, Names and Testimonies, Testimonies and Names: not praise, not blame, not commentary. In a year and a day the elders appeared once more at the foot of the throne, fearful as a woman on the birthing-stool, and said, O King, whose mercy et cetera, we cannot do as you have decreed. For the names and testimonies stretch to the very end of the world, and whenever we choose one rather than another, or tell the thousands as a single tale, there is pain as well as satisfaction. Silence is better: O let not the Accuser snuff the smell of mortal change. Have you not taught us, through the hand of your servant, in the Pirkei Hayim Nizokaim: to wrest pleasure from pain is forbidden, or to throw fodder to Gath and Ashkelon.

My latter-day parable is meant to be more than an expression of reader's insomnia. It is hard to give up the idea that a *Yizkor* or memorial book will emerge with something of biblical strength, one that could be read and understood by all. The very idea of such a book, at the same time, might produce a deceptive sense of totality, throwing into the shadows, even into oblivion, stories, details and unexpected points of view that keep the intellect active and the memory digging. Every ambitious writer, nevertheless, projects a work of that kind, or a poetics leading to it—though the idea of the Great Book is receding, and with it that of a canonical work about the Shoah.

We have been asked to probe the limits of representation of an event that is different in kind or degree from other catastrophic turns of history. I want to insert this topic into the field of literary studies. The question of the limits of representation has been important to poetics. The *genera dicendi* determined the level of style and prescribed what was fitting for each literary kind. Voltaire objected to the phrase the "blanket" of the dark in Shakespeare's *Macbeth* as too low an expression for tragedy. In French neoclassicism, which promoted such limits rigorously, it was as if everything were potentially to be shown at court, in the king's presence. That decorum prevailed as an ideal. Before pursuing a line of inquiry that might seem archaic, let me say a few words about what has happened to the limits of literary representation in the modern era.

Contemporary literature and art have almost total freedom of expression. When rules or norms enter, they do so mainly as a foil, in order to be breached. My first thought, therefore, is that even in the case of the Shoah there are no limits of representation, only limits of conceptualization. Though our technical capacity for depicting the extremest event is in place, it has outstripped the possibility of thinking conceptually or in terms of decorum about those representations, despite the growth of a literary and cultural criticism that wishes to overcome the intelligibility gap. Critical thought is somewhat desperate these days because the representations have multiplied and increasingly assume the force of fact. We are made to run after images (or between them, like the hero of the film *Enemies: A Love Story*), images whose aim seems to be a humiliation of the mind in favor of megareality or megafantasy.

Technique and the increasing gap between representation and conceptualization are of special relevance to the Shoah. Claude Lanzmann repeats Primo Levi's story of an SS man's welcome to KZ prisoners: "Hier ist kein Warum" ("There is no Why here"). Lanzmann himself will not probe the Why in his film, only and relentlessly the How— the how of technique, how exactly it was done, how many were processed, how long it took. Or, what did you know, hear, see, do? His questions avoid the one question that haunts us: Why?[1]

Perhaps the SS man was merely parroting what he had heard directed at himself during his own training. But he had also been compensated for the dismissal of all undisciplined and idle thoughts. For him a new motivation was provided by the *Weltanschauung* or master narrative Hitler promulgated as fundamental; whereas for the victim this same world view totally negated his human status and the right to live. Even the right to die in a human way: Jews were exterminated like dangerous or diseased animals. One difficulty in interpreting what happened may be related to the expulsion of the Why, which we might be willing, perhaps were willing, to relinquish, but cannot do so after this action of the murderers.

In every realistic depiction of the Shoah, the more it tries to be a raw representation, the more the Why rises up like an unsweet savor. We describe but cannot explain what happened. Could "unrealistic" depictions, then, alleviate the disparity? Is it a certain type of mimesis that troubles us, so that a more abstract or mythical art might escape our discontent—those works, precisely, whose artifice we most admire, or which seem to embody a reflection on representational limits? I could mention Celan, Appelfeld, Fink, Pagis, Grossmann, Ozick, Louis Malle: their art makes us feel there is something that cannot be presented, or—to quote Jean-François Lyotard's definition of the modern project—their technique "presents the fact that the unrepresentable exists."[2] The works I have mentioned release us from the presumption that realism can be absolute.

Yet Lyotard goes further. He does not view the gap between representation and the unpresentable as a defect but as a value. To harmonize them is to transgress a limit. He turns Kant's analytic of the sublime in a new direction. Kant linked the emotion of the sublime to a dynamic conflict between the faculty that conceives and the faculty that "presents": whereas feelings of beauty arise when an object gives pleasure without our having a conceptual understanding of that pleasure, so that we fall back on "taste" to validate it, sublime feelings arise when we conceive, for example, of the absolutely simple or the infinitely great, without being able to find an object or sense-presentation to make them rationally communicable. In the sublime there is at most a "negative presentation," as in Malevich's "white" squares or what is hinted at by the Bible's commandment against graven images. An aesthetics of the sublime, therefore, "will enable us to see only by making it impossible to see; it will please only by causing pain." The postmodern differs from the modern not essentially but by projecting "the unpresentable in presentation itself . . . [it] searches for new presentations, not in order to enjoy them but in order to impart a stronger sense of the unpresentable." According to Lyotard, this brings art and philosophy closer, for it is the business of both "not to supply reality but to invent allusions to the conceivable which cannot be presented" (*The Postmodern Condition*, pp. 79ff).

I want to read Lyotard's emphasis on unrepresentable reality in the specifying context of the Holocaust. He has the courage to attempt a post-Holocaust aesthetics. Usually the aesthetic as a dimension of culture is first to be targeted in moments of crisis or catastrophe: Adorno's "to write poetry after Auschwitz is barbaric" has become notorious. Yet here the aesthetic is saved as an aesthetics of the sublime. The mental blockage characteristic of the Kantian sublime is now said to arise not from a sense of nature's greatness or the idea of an absolute magnitude but from what Saul Friedlander has called the "modes of domination and terror at [the Holocaust's] very core."[3] These modes baffle the mind, not so much as historical realities, for the Final Solution, horrendous as it is, is comparable *at that level* to other large-scale massacres. It is when domination and terror become absolutes, that is, when they are *ideologized* and *totalized,* that we cannot discover in ourselves a possible scenario to explain what happened. We want to say, "It is inconceivable," yet we know it was conceived and acted upon systematically. We continue to harbor, therefore, a sense of improbability, not because there is any doubt whatsoever about the Shoah as fact but because what was lived through, or what we have learned about, cannot be a part of us: the mind rejects it, casts it out—or it casts out the mind. We are forced to admit that something in human behavior is alien to us, yet that it could be species-related. As Habermas has written, "A deep stratum of solidarity between all that bears a human countenance was touched."[4] I will return later to that "human countenance."

The Kantian sublime has a second movement, in which the blocked reason rebounds, and even feels uplift. That would seem impossible here. *This* trauma, even when experienced indirectly, requires a lengthy process of silence, mourning and recuperation. Shoshana Felman describes that process as an "impossible witnessing," and Eric Santner as a disruption of the economy of narrative pleasure. Any elation, then, can only be a nervous reflex: the head still smiling, for the fraction of a moment, after it has been cut off. Yet I will argue, at some risk, that Lyotard's work in this area, as well as our own work as historians, witnesses, writers, is itself *eine Art Schadensabwicklung:* the undoing of a blockage, a necessary *intellectual* response, more like the upbeat movement in the dialectic of the sublime than a nervous tic.

Lyotard's subject, even when his focus is on art, is really political anthropology: the nature of man as political animal and specifically, in the light of the Shoah, the nature of consent. The issue of consent becomes crucial after the Hitler era because our bafflement centers not only on the criminal actions of the regime but also on the deceptive consent of the bystanders (a similar kind of consent was overturned almost fifty years later in eastern Europe), the loyal or statutory consent of the perpetrators (which the courts and research such as Christopher Browning's have probed),[5] and a disabling of the consenting faculty in the victims, the substitution of automatism for autonomy. Lyotard extends to political theory Kant's remarks on the possibility of aesthetic judgment by drawing from the analytic of the sublime a *différend* (between what is conceivable and what is presentable) that always challenges unanimity, or the harmony achieved by eliminating dissent. He adopts, at the same time, Kant's refusal to sideline the issue of taste and art, since a consensus about the aesthetic does not lie beyond or below rational judgment. If the discourse of reason can be maintained in matters of art, there is—precisely through heeding the example of art—a hope for such discourse in politics too.[6]

Yet faith in a consensus achieved by reasoning together is modified by Lyotard's awareness of the limits of reason, an awareness made acute by history itself, where that reason—bureaucratized, instrumentalized—has turned into amoral technology and raison d'état. No wonder he is attracted, like the Frankfurt school, to the Kantian mode of critique rather than to Hegel's totalizing schema. He understands that in the past, and catastrophically in the recent past of the Nazi era, the price exacted for political stability and apparent consensus has been too high. The price was coercion and terror, and the result uniformity.

There are many unusual things about Lyotard's post-Holocaust aesthetics. Not least among them is that the representational limits of postmodern art turn out to be the limits of reason in Kant's aesthetic judgment. We breathe a double sigh of relief: art is reasonable (not irrational, myth-mongering, obscurantist), and art contributes by its *peculiar sublimity* or *différend* to an appropriate political philosophy after the Holocaust. It haunts us, it does not leave our mind, that after the Shoah we need a representation of the "human countenance" that will remove the distortion that countenance has suffered and will strengthen its glance. This retrieved humanism is also the high argument of Emmanuel Levinas.

Though such words as *high* and *sublime* have become difficult to use ("No word intoned from on high," Adorno wrote, "not even a theological one, exists rightfully after Auschwitz without a transformation"), the terror of the Shoah required a response which we cannot but depict as heroic. Acts of resistance, whatever their motive, are destined to be part of a monumental narrative. We understand them philosophically as a withholding of consent, as a rejection of the legitimating master narrative of the persecutors. After the fact, then, it is appropriate to ask whether that refusal was based on a narrative of its own, that is, a self-presentation or collective vision that was not fully articulated, but could have been deeply engrained as an ethos. If there was such a narrative, it is an obligation to represent it and keep it from disappearing into a vague sublimity. We need it to shore up our own resolve.

Yet the very fact of its appearing to be heroic given these circumstances, rather than ordinary as it might be in the conduct of daily life, makes us consider the conditions of its possibility. If we recall the Nazi "Rausch and Rhetoric," we quickly come to the conclusion that a counter-elation would be compromised from the outset. The retrieved narrative cannot be ordinary yet also cannot be sublime in the nazified sense. It is here that an extracanonical representation emerges, suspended between history and memory, suspended also between literature and documentary, whose subject is consistently the daily response to terror, and which provides the lineaments of that sublime yet ordinary story that is a necessity and not an indulgence if we still believe in educating the imagination. I refer to the genre, or rather the collective archive, of survivor testimonies, and I want to say something about its value.

For the survivors of the Holocaust, simply to tell their story is a restitution, however inadequate. Ordering one's life retrospectively brings some mastery, and so relief, to the unmastered portion. Yet that factor is less crucial than something that goes back to the special nature of their agony. In the camps they were systematically deprived of foresight: though they saw all too forcefully what was before their eyes, their ability to discern a normal pattern that could eventually be expressed in the form of a story was disrupted or disabled. Few could hope to make sense of the events, could hope to hope, could link what they had learned in the past to what now befell them. The promise of extending experience from past to future via the coherence of the stories we tell each other, stories that gather as a tradition—that promise was shattered. To remember forward—to transmit a personal story to children and grandchildren and all who should hear it—affirms a desegregation and the survivors' reentry into the human family. The story that links us to their past also links them to our future.

Whether survivor testimonies, especially the less rehearsed, oral kind, create a new text—a narrative representation significantly different—cannot be considered here at length. Lawrence Langer explores that aspect in *Holocaust Testimony: The Ruins of Memory*,[7] and his book involves the legitimacy of oral documentation as a whole, what sort of value it has as an account of those events. But we do know of shifts in the form of representation over the course of time. One such shift, described by Hayden White, takes us from annals to chronicles; another, less centered on chronology and more on character, has given dreams a language and created a new representation of reality on the basis of Freud. Thus the coherence of many novels, films, and biographies depends today on the explanatory power of dream and flashback. With or without recorded dreams, individual life is often construed like a Freudian dream. Do survivor testimonies signal another shift in the history of representation? If so, have previous shifts been triggered by collective traumatic experiences? How should we classify survivor narratives: what kind of text are we faced with?[8]

Such questions may sound overly scholarly, but their aim is respect for these documents. The memoirs of survivors are sometimes so vivid in their focus on detail, so condensed and overdetermined in their idiom, and so apocalyptic in their imagery, that whether or not we accept them as history they cast a shadow on all previous fiction that claims to depict human existence *in extremis*. Video testimonies are, in addition, countercinematic: a talking head, another talking head, a few awkward questions by an interviewer, are all that appears on screen. No theatricality or stage-managed illusions. Humiliating pictures shot for propaganda purposes by the killers are replaced by oral "photographs" told from the survivors' point of view. They constitute a roll-call of voices and dispel the anonymity of victimage.

The difficulty of seeing these accounts as representations comes only from the fact that they do not, like historical discourse, make the real desirable (if only as an object of knowledge), or the desirable real, in the manner of fictions. What is real here is not desirable; indeed, it is so repugnant that it may affect the will to live on. And what is desirable was once, in the camps, so removed from actuality that even now, recalled in the space of memory, it reveals an attaint that phantomizes the survivors' life and speech.

My long excursus, I am not ashamed to admit, is to assure survivor testimony a place in the Book of the Destruction. But I have not forgotten the question of limits as it affects art after the Holocaust. Even if, like Lyotard, we save aesthetics, and even if we avoid, in art or the discursive genres, a false sublimity, what limits representation of the Shoah is already expressed in survivor testimony as a sense of unreality that affects their past and present life. This question of "reality" is central, and the multiplication of facts in historical discourse or the sheer rate of publication of Holocaust-related films and books will not of itself contribute to belief or to quality of assent. It is not the disbelief of the revisionists alone that should concern us but also a limit of sensibility which surfaces here, and which the archaic rules of poetics I mentioned at the start have tried to respect.

Lyotard's phrase about "the conceivable which cannot be presented" should lead to the question: "Cannot be presented to whom?" In the aftermath of the Shoah silence about the audience is not just a refusal to overspecify. Let us complete his phrase to read "which cannot be presented to a society that considers itself civilized." As Ignacy Schipper wrote from Maidanek: "Nobody will *want* to believe us, because our disaster is the disaster of the entire civilized world."

Schipper's statement goes beyond acknowledging that we don't like to hear bad news about ourselves. It suggests a disbelief that is strangely symmetrical with Jewish disbelief of the *good news* that converted Christ's death into a redemptive event. It is now the Christian and "civilized" world that seems to adopt and even mock the Jews' prior disbelief; this turnabout makes Faurisson's proclamation of the "good news" that the gas chambers never existed all the more obscene. But the Holocaust threatens a secular as well as a religious gospel, faith in reason and progress as well as Christianity. It points, in that sense and that sense only, to a religious upheaval. It challenges the credibility of redemptive thinking.

So threatening was the Shoah that disbelief, as I have mentioned, touched the survivors themselves and added to the silence of the world. When speech returns, two phrases stand out in their testimony: "I was there" and "I could not believe what my eyes had seen." The second phrase is not purely rhetorical. Appelfeld writes, "Everything that happened was so gigantic, so inconceivable, that the witness even seemed like a fabricator to himself."[9] The nature of what was experienced and could scarcely be believed needs our attention; it has a similarity to what transpires in Shakespeare's Troilus when he sees before his eyes Cressida's infidelity and is tempted to renounce his eyes rather than give her up. Such trauma leads to a splitting of the image which is like a splitting of identity: we too could say, of our tainted civilization, "This is, and is not, Cressid."

Through film, moreover, one of the high points of technological achievement, the eyes have found a dominant form of representation, and this only increases the conflict between what was seen and what is believable. The thought of a limit to representation comes here from the very fact that through technical progress it *is* possible to provide a mimesis of everything, however extreme. The momentum of film, in fact, goes toward that extreme, as if the eyes had compulsively to test their own reality. This complicates Holocaust representation in the following manner.

Previously in civilized society, the limits of representation were linked to social decorum and to the limitations of a particular art medium. So Lessing's *Laocoon* argued that the distortion inflicted by pain on the human form was presentable in the temporal medium of poetry without transgressing art's law of beauty but not in the spatially static medium of statuary and painting. The thought here is not a squeamish one but expresses rather a sense of the vulnerability of civilized life, as if that sense were tied to a canon of physical beauty or, more precisely, as if the slightest sign of creatureliness, visible pain, and mortality could puncture—unless framed in the right manner—a dearly achieved complacency. The highest kind of art may "invent allusions" to our damaged life, to our mortality and persistent creaturely condition, but it may not present them as such. Voltaire's comment on Shakespeare's breaches of style points to the danger of a breach in consciousness itself, to a sense of the cosmetic rather than constitutive presence of what passes for civilization. It is possible to say, smugly, that all this neoclassical fuss reflects the density of a defensive psychic structure, and that we no longer avert our eyes that way. But this would be to ignore our persistent avertedness, even before the Shoah occurred. The neoclassical rules are gone; but their "alienation effect" may have been more realistic than we knew in their estimate of what will move rather than overwhelm or incite disbelief. We rediscover here Aristotle's criterion of probability. That the truth can offend probability is the dilemma of the artist who must follow truth without renouncing art.

It is not frivolous, therefore, to ask for a rethinking of poetics after the Shoah. Although Aristotle's treatise is but a series of notes, one senses in the importance it assigns to tragedy a shift of representational modes obscure in origin yet involving a different balance of human and divine, of human agency and a Dionysian sensibility. It is this shift Nietzsche reconstructs in *The Birth of Tragedy*. Are we living through another shift of this kind, and is it related to the Shoah?

These questions could be considered premature, and they require in any case a new Aristotle. I can but offer sketchy notes of my own. Concerning the continuing relevance of tragedy as a genre, Isaac Deutscher expresses his conviction in "The Jewish Tragedy and the Historian" that the passing of time will not lessen our sense of having been confronted by "a huge and ominous mystery of the degeneration of the human character," one to "forever baffle and terrify mankind." Yet Deutscher allows that "a modern Aeschylus and Sophocles" might cope with it, "on a level different from that of historical interpretation and explanation."[10]

The odds against this rebirth of tragedy are formidable, however, unless an older, pre-Enlightenment attitude returns. Deutscher, resolutely atheistic, won't look in that direction; he covers himself against the imputation of a return to myth or religion by choosing two of the greatest of ancient artists, who somehow transcend the issue of religious belief. Yet a host of questions remain. Did Aeschylus and Sophocles owe their ability to produce tragedies—so powerful that we continue to read and perform them two and a half millennia later—to their art or to their myths? Can we even distinguish between their art and their religious beliefs? Further, if we manage to isolate what enabled them to represent catastrophe, is their method transferable to the Holocaust era? In brief, is it a new or an older type of tragic art we are seeking?

We cannot wait on mystery to resolve mystery. Even should genius arise, it is unlikely to yield the secret of its art. Moreover, the relation of art to audience, which made those ancient tragedies effective public testimony—a contract, as it were, with the collective memory—that relation has changed. The religious matrix, which embedded the

Greek tragedies and gave them exposure, no longer prevails. And for any emerging art I do not discern a contemporary audience strong or constant enough to maintain a similar relation. For by pluralizing the curriculum and opening the canon, we have intensified the problem of consensus. Should a great work arise it could not be transmitted without a religious or parareligious reception.

Though I respect Deutscher and the way he has put the question, he is more radical about the limits of historical discourse than he is about art. The issue of whether tragedy can be an adequate interpretation of the events of the Shoah, or whether, to go beyond Deutscher, "the worst returns to laughter" in some new, as yet unrealized, form closer to the grotesque[11]—these are by no means idle questions, yet they do not go to the heart of the matter. Beyond genre, I have suggested, the very rule of probability has suffered a shock, a rule that cannot be relinquished without giving up art's crucial link to verisimilitude: to a mimetic and narratable dimension.

What threatens the mimetic is, to put it bluntly, the infinity of evil glimpsed by our generation, perhaps beyond other generations. Though the Shoah proved finite, and the thousand-year Reich lasted but a dozen years, a limit was dissolved and an abyss reopened. How do we find a bridge over that abyss, a representation more firm than Apollonian form or neoclassical rules? Is there, for example, a "plausible narrative representation" of that evil, in art or historical emplotment?[12] Should we turn to the leprous itch, the epidemic of figures, the disorderly excess of signifier over signified in Shakespeare's carnivalesque drama of errors, or to the opposite strictness of Greek hemistichs in dialogue, verging on the disclosure of unspeakable truth? Or is the mad, postmodern perspectivism of Syberberg the best we can do?

The trouble with infinity of any kind is that it dwarfs response and disables human agency. We feel compelled to demonize it, to divest the monster of human aspect and motivation, to create the stereotype of an evil empire. We romance ourselves into a psychically secure and ideologically upright posture, simplifying the representation of evil and the entire issue of mimesis. What is required, however, is a world that still has enough plausibility to represent what was almost destroyed: the trustworthiness of appearances, a consistency between the "human form divine" and what goes on within it, shielded from the eye.

The hurt inflicted on appearances—on a (harmonious) correspondence between outer and inner—is so acute that it leads to a stutter in the representational faculties. That stutter in verbal form is akin to poetry like Celan's, and in visual form it distorts, or simply divorces, features that once were kind. When Wordsworth as a young man hears for the first time the "voice of Woman utter blasphemy" (that is, a prostitute cursing), his reaction describes an ominous breach in the idea of the human, one that opens the possibility of deceptive look-alikes and, since the human form is not radically affected, drives a wedge between outward appearance and inner reality. It is as if the baffled eyes, unable to read the soul from a physical surface, were forced to invent an anti-race or dark double:

> I shuddered, for a barrier seemed at once
> Thrown in, that from humanity divorced
> Humanity, splitting the race of man
> In twain, yet leaving the same outward Form.

> (1850 *Prelude*, 7.388–391)

This troubled, ambivalent moment could breed either a deep compassion or a demonization of the other race. If the sense of evil gets the upper hand, scapegoating becomes inevitable as a way of marking the evil, of making its hidden presence biological and photogenic. The correspondence between inside and outside is saved, but a group is ritually excluded from the human community to bear the stigma of what is evil and now markedly inhuman.

The demonization of the Jews by the Nazis was a representation of this kind. Nazi propaganda seized on Wagner's characterization of the Jew as a "plastic demon of decadence." The demon is a shape-shifter, cold, vicious, unchangeable inside, yet on the outside able to mimic (assimilate) any national character or cultured facade. An entire subindustry invaded German education to aid a differentiation that would not have been necessary if Jews had the gross features which began to caricature them. The notorious children's book *The Poisonous Mushroom* was based on this same need to identify the "plastic demon" or deceptive look-alike. In short, the designation *Jew* allowed a demonizing solution to the dilemma of distinguishing appearance from "reality" when an overpowering sense of the indistinguishable presence of evil rendered useless ordinary skills of telling good from evil, or what was trustworthy from what was treacherous. The SS became "blade runners," and turned into the very androids from which they thought they were saving mankind.

If I stress visual representations it is because they environ us, and because the critic's search must be to separate kitsch from an authentic imagination of evil in the wake of the Shoah. The proliferation in science fiction of a manichean war against uncanny robotic enemies that no longer wear uniforms but have the metamorphic power to infiltrate as look-alikes may express in new coloration a very ancient fear. The challenge to visual representation, as I have said, does not come in the first place from lack of technique—we are still in the cinematic age and rarely talk about the limits of film—but comes principally from a doubt about the ethics of a certain kind of mimesis, or supermimesis. Just as the historical imagination often substitutes the violence of detail for the violence of violence, so the visual and cinematic imagination tends to save mimesis from a purely "negative presentation" by grotesquing what it touches, or surfeiting our need for clear and distinct identities. Hesiod said that the fear of the gods was alleviated by giving them distinct shapes; so too our fear of the evil in human beings is alleviated by marking them like Cain, though not for their protection. Lyotard and also Wallace Stevens would like to believe that art makes things a little harder to see, yet the present, popular exploitation of Holocaust themes suggests instead a repetition of the imaginative and ethical error that defamed the victims.

I began with the statement that there are no limits to representation, only limits to conceptualization, to the intelligibility of the Shoah. Yet when we turned specifically to art a further limit did appear: as the experience of evil explodes into a sense of the infinite presence of evil, a precarious element enters the very act of representation. The material overwhelms art; the rule of probability suffers a shock. Let us say, simply, the human countenance is obscured. What is presented becomes an offense, an aggression, and may arouse such strong defenses that—in a profound way—we do not believe that what we are made to feel and see is part of reality. Even our insistence on the exceptionality of the Shoah may become an isolating maneuver rather than purely and strongly an acknowledgment. Moreover, popular representations emerge that are uncomfortably close to fantasies that may have played their part in the genocide. Thus the problem of limits changes. It is not so much the finiteness of intellect as the finiteness of human empathy that comes into view.

Those limits of empathy are always being extended by art yet watched over by the rules of art. In classical tragedy, what Aristotle called *to pathos*, a scene of killing, wounding, and utmost suffering, was usually recited rather than shown. Survivor narratives are recitations of this kind and are far more bearable—despite the extremity of their *pathos*—than a modern sensationalism often bloodier than Jacobean tragedies or the terrible scene in *Lear* where Gloucester's eyes are torn out. Even a nonviolent representation, such as Cordelia's death, could be so painful as to have Dr. Johnson approve changing the ending and having Cordelia revive.

In this testing of the limits of our sensibility Claude Lanzmann's film is a powerful exhibit. *Shoah* blanches all other Holocaust depictions. It is an epic intervention that creates a rupture on the plane of consciousness like that of Auschwitz on the plane of history. By the authority of his art—the film is a judgment on previous art, as well as a documentary—Lanzmann places one issue at the center and marginalizes everything else, even the individual survivors and perpetrators who are made to talk. This singleminded concentration unifies the film but violates the privacy of those interviewed and exhausts the spectators. Primo Levi has written about the "incurable nature of the offense, that spreads like a contagion," affecting all who come in contact, victims as well as victimizers—and in *Shoah* it affects the artist too. The offense in question is not Lanzmann's direction, the obsessive honesty and ruthless irony that override every ordinary notion of decorum. For if the choice is between a precision that is traumatic and an imprecision that is obfuscating, then the choice must be for precision. The offense lies rather in the fact that the film, by a violence of its own, *forces* an act of recall, of anamnesis, from victim and victimizer alike, and forces it, in turn, on the spectator.

The interview genre, of course, as well as the recitational character of survivor testimony and Lanzmann's refusal to use archival footage, spare us from having to watch *to pathos* itself. There is an inbuilt and essential indirectness, despite which a question of limits arises. Is it not too much to have the narrative of extermination placed before our eyes so confrontationally and exclusively? The filmmaker has no interest in other aspects of the witness's life story. What is the purpose, then, of this massive film? The virulent stupidity of those who deny that death camps existed does not justify a production they would reject as they do all other evidence. Nor can the primary purpose be to instruct and move those who have remained ignorant: that goal would not have demanded such an outlay of spirit.

What then is Lanzmann's purpose? Though his film is a significant historical representation, it does not supply reality so much as it supplies art. The subject is hell itself: a state of victimage that before the Shoah had only been fantasized but that (as both Hannah Arendt and George Steiner have remarked) then became totally real through the Shoah. And if that is the case, it is not crucial that this hell was "Made in Germany" and a product of Nazi ideology. Rather, it is important historically, but it is not what makes the film an authentic epic. The artistic purpose, which cannot for once be distinguished from the historical, is that reality has displaced fantasy; and this fact, at once terrible and incredible, means that myth and fiction may now have to be devalued to playthings, discarded in the light of their grim fulfillment. The rupture, then, involves story as well as history: the story of hell, of its representations. The unpresentable has been presented. Before Auschwitz we were children in our imagination of evil; after Auschwitz we are no longer children.

This representational shift is like a fall: "We cannot not know," Terrence Des Pres wrote. The genocide makes us irreversibly aware of worldwide political torment. "Now a wretchedness of global extent has come into view; the spectacle of man-created suffering is *known*, observed with such constancy that a new shape of knowing invades the mind." Des Pres claims not that the world has changed but that we have changed as knowers, because of this "shift in the means of representation."[13]

Yet in such a world the problem of being a child, or more precisely, of remembering that childhood exists, remains. Holocaust museums which try to educate visitors, leading them from relative ignorance to knowledge, must take that problem into account: they may not become, whatever the enormity of the destruction, a chamber of horrors. Lanzmann, as epic artist, has elided the entire issue of pedagogy and audience accommodation: he assaults the averted or childlike in us. Helen K. says in a Yale testimony, "I cannot believe what my eyes have seen," at the point when she describes children lining up to be gassed; "such little children."[14] Irving Greenberg asks whether we can still utter the traditional prayers and not be haunted by an image of the murder of more than a million children. Here is a limit that cannot be removed without psychic danger.

Which does not mean we cannot work effectively with or within this limit. Art has always known this. A picture, story, or poem that allows reflection and interpretation may be more crucial—if the aim is an active rather than a passive response—than images that produce only shock and the defenses aroused by *to pathos*. The well-known Nazi photo of a Jewish boy, perhaps eight years old, with his hands in the air before armed German soldiers, is sad and eloquent enough: it can disclose the fact that no difference was made between children and adults in the Final Solution. Or read Günter Grass's *From the Diary of a Snail* and his account of its complex genesis in "What Shall We Tell Our Children?" Or recall Czeslaw Milosz's "Song about Porcelain," in which the poet admits he is moved more by the shards of "Rose-colored cup and saucer / Flowery demi-tasses" in a war-ravaged countryside than by the blackened, devastated field and its fresh graves:

> Of all things broken and lost
> The porcelain troubles me most.[15]

In the Book of the Destruction this lyric too has its place. An equation has formed in the poet's mind between that porcelain, nostalgic detritus of the bourgeois sensibility, decorated with roses, mowers, and shepherds, and the Pastoral as a healing mode of representation. The "small sad cry / Of cups and saucers breaking" suggests both the passing of an entire mode of life and the inadequacy of those fragile symbols. The fear, which I share, and on which I must close, is that what has been broken and lost is the pastoral sensibility itself, that the war and the Shoah have swept it away also. With it may have gone an art of obliquity that Milosz continues uniquely to practice. Our *sefer hashoah* will have to accomplish the impossible: allow the limits of representation to be healing limits yet not allow them to conceal an event we are obligated to recall and interpret, both to ourselves and those growing up unconscious of its shadow.

NOTES

CONTRIBUTORS

INDEX

Notes

Introduction

Epigraph: Etty Hillesum, *Letters from Westerbork* (New York, 1986), p. 142.

1. See Saul Friedlander, *Reflections of Nazism: An Essay on Kitsch and Death* (New York, 1984).
2. Jürgen Habermas, *Eine Art Schadensabwicklung* (Frankfurt-am-Main, 1987), p. 163. In English in *The New Conservatism: Cultural Criticism and the Historians' Debate* (Cambridge, Mass., 1989).
3. Jean-François Lyotard, *The Differend: Phrases in Dispute* (Minneapolis, 1988), pp. 56–57.
4. David Caroll, Foreword to Jean-François Lyotard, *Heidegger and "the Jews"* (Minneapolis, 1990), p. 11.
5. On Hayden White's closeness to a postmodern view of history see in particular F. R. Ankersmit, "Historiography and Postmodernism," *History and Theory*, 28, no. 2 (1989), as well as the ensuing debate in *History and Theory*, 29, no. 3 (1990).
6. Hayden White, *The Content of the Form: Narrative Discourse and Historical Representation* (Baltimore, 1987), p. 74.
7. Andreas Hillgruber, *Zweierlei Untergang: Die Zerschlagung des Deutschen Reiches und das Ende des europäischen Judentums* (Berlin, 1986).
8. Anselm Kiefer's paintings have sometimes raised issues similar to those evoked concerning Syberberg's film. Although the approach is almost similar, the ultimate effect of Kiefer's paintings, it seems to me, is contrary to Syberberg's *Hitler.* It would be worthwhile to identify the minute shifts of emphasis which create this difference. On related aspects of Kiefer's paintings, see Andreas Huyssen, "Anselm Kiefer: The Terror of History, the Temptation of Myth," *October*, 48 (Spring 1989).
9. Hans Jürgen Syberberg, *Vom Unglück und Glück der Kunst in Deutschland nach dem letzten Kriege* (Munich, 1990).
10. For an analysis of the aesthetic displacement technique, see in particular Gertrud Koch, "The Aesthetic Transformation of the Image of the Unimaginable: Notes on Claude Lanzmann's *Shoah*," *October*, 48 (Spring 1989).
11. Claude Lanzmann, *Shoah* (New York, 1985), p. 6. I am using Shoshana Felman's excerpting of Srebnik's words. See Shoshana Felman, "In an Era of Testimony: Claude Lanzmann's *Shoah*," *Yale French Studies*, November 1991, p. 61.

< 337 >

12. Primo Levi, *Survival in Auschwitz* (New York, 1961), pp. 5–6. This excerpt is quoted by Carlo Ginzburg, in chapter 5 of this volume.
13. Felman, "In an Era of Testimony," p. 41.
14. Avraham Tory, *Surviving the Holocaust: The Kovno Ghetto Diary* (Cambridge, Mass., 1990), p. 67.

1. German Memory, Judicial Interrogation, and Historical Reconstruction

1. This account is drawn from my *Ordinary Men: Reserve Police Battalion 101 and the Final Solution in Poland* (New York: Aaron Asher Books, Harper-Collins, 1992).
2. The afternoon before, when Trapp had informed the officers of this assignment, one man had indicated that, as a reserve lieutenant and Hamburg businessman, he could not participate in such an action in which defenseless women and children were shot. He asked for a different task and was assigned to guard the work Jews to be taken to Lublin.
3. Most important is Michael Marrus, *The Holocaust in History* (Hanover, N.H., 1987).
4. Raul Hilberg, *The Destruction of the European Jews* (Chicago, 1961). Hilberg was still working basically from the same document base of captured German records.
5. Tim Mason, "Intention and Explanation: A Current Controversy about the Interpretation of National Socialism," *Der Führerstaat: Mythos und Realität*, ed. Gerhard Hirschfeld and Lothar Kettenacker (Stuttgart, 1981), pp. 21–40; Christopher R. Browning, *Fateful Months: Essays on the Emergence of the Final Solution* (New York, 1985), pp. 8–38; Saul Friedlander, "From Anti-Semitism to Extermination: A Historiographical Study of Nazi Policies toward the Jews and an Essay in Interpretation," *Yad Vashem Studies*, 16 (1984), 1–50.
6. Richard Evans, "Perspectives on the West German *Historikerstreit*," *Journal of Modern History*, 59 (December 1987), 785. Evans concludes: "The whole debate ultimately has little to offer anyone with a serious scholarly interest in the German past. It brings no new facts to light; it embodies no new research; it makes no new contribution to historical understanding; it poses no new questions which might stimulate future work."
7. Charles Maier, *The Unmasterable Past: History, Holocaust, and German Nationalism* (Cambridge, Mass., 1988).
8. In addition to Eichmann, there was most notoriously Franz Stangl, commandant of Treblinka in Gitta Sereny's *Into That Darkness: From Mercy*

Killing to Mass Murder (London, 1974). Other case studies have focused on various professional groups: for example, Robert Lifton, *The Nazi Doctors: Medical Killing and the Psychology of Genocide* (New York, 1986); and Christopher R. Browning, *The Final Solution and the German Foreign Office* (New York, 1978).

9. Peter Novick, *That Noble Dream: The "Objectivity Question" and the American Historical Profession* (New York, 1988).

10. Hayden White, "The Value of Narrativity in the Representation of Reality," *The Content of the Form* (Baltimore, 1987), pp. 14, 20–25.

11. The following is based on the arguments developed by Douglas Christie, counsel for the defendant Ernst Zundel, a neo-Nazi publisher, in two trials in Toronto, Canada, in 1985 and 1988. Raul Hilberg served as the Crown's expert witness at the first trial; I did the same at the second.

12. A related argument, dealing with documentary evidence rather than postwar testimony, was made by Robert Faurisson, a deactivated professor of literature at the University of Lyons. During each trial he was in constant attendance as an adviser to Christie and was certified as an expert witness in "text criticism." Invoking the authority of recent theories of literary criticism, he claimed that the meaning of such terms found in Nazi documents as *resettlement* and *special treatment* could not be established by historical context. Since their meaning was indeterminate, an interpretation taking such terms literally and not as official euphemisms or code words for murder was quite valid. For Faurisson, of course, such literal interpretation also corresponded to objective historical truth. Neither he nor Christie has shied from working both sides of the objectivist-relativist fence.

13. Hayden White, "The Politics of Historical Interpretation," *The Content of the Form*, pp. 76–82.

14. Arno Mayer, *Why Did the Heavens Not Darken? The "Final Solution" in History* (New York, 1988), p. 365.

15. In addition to the works by Browning and Friedlander cited in n. 3, see the excellent recent work by Philippe Burrin, *Hitler et les Juifs: Genèse d'un génocide* (Paris, 1989). Also Martin Broszat, "Hitler und die Genesis der 'Endlösung.' Aus Anlass der Thesen von David Irving," *Vierteljahrshefte für Zeitgeschichte*, 25, no. 4 (October 1977), 739–775; and Hans Mommsen, "Die Realisierung des Utopischen: Die 'Endlösung der Judenfrage' im 'Dritten Reich,'" *Geschichte und Gesellschaft*, 9, no. 3 (1983), 381–420.

16. Leonidas Hill, "The Trial of Ernst Zundel: Revisionism and the Law in Canada," *Simon Wiesenthal Center Annual*, 6 (1989), 165–219. For a review of German law and Holocaust denial, see Eric Stein, "History

against Free Speech: The New German Law against the 'Auschwitz'—and other—'Lies,'" *Michigan Law Review,* 85, no. 2 (November 1986), 277–323.

17. Bruno Bettelheim, "Their Specialty Was Murder," *New York Times Book Review,* 15 October 1986, p. 62.

18. I am reminded by a colleague that shortly before his death at the hands of the Nazis, Marc Bloch wrote: "When all is said and done, a single word, 'understanding,' is the beacon light of our studies." *The Historian's Craft* (New York, 1964), p. 143.

19. Saul Friedlander, "The 'Final Solution': On the Unease in Historical Interpretation," *Lessons and Legacies: The Meaning of the Holocaust in a Changing World,* ed. Peter Hayes (Evanston, Ill., 1991).

2. Historical Emplotment and the Problem of Truth

1. Historical discourses consist also, obviously, of explanations cast in the form of arguments more or less formalizable. I do not address the issue of the relation between explanations cast in the mode of formal arguments and what I would call the "explanation-effects" produced by the narrativization of events. It is the felicitous combination of arguments with narrative representations which accounts for the appeal of a specifically "historical" representation of reality. But the precise nature of the relation between arguments and narrativizations in histories is unclear.

2. I have in mind here the farcical version of the events of 1848–1851 in France composed by Marx in open competition with the tragic and comic versions of those same events set forth by Hugo and Proudhon respectively.

3. Unless, that is, we are prepared to entertain the idea that any given body of facts is infinitely variously interpretable and that one aim of historical discourse is to *multiply* the number of interpretations we have of any given set of events rather than to work toward the production of a "best" interpretation. Cf. work by Paul Veyne, C. Behan McCullagh, Peter Munz, and F. R. Ankersmit.

4. Saul Friedlander, *Reflets du Nazisme* (Paris: Seuil, 1982), pp. 76ff.

5. Art Spiegelman, *Maus: A Survivor's Tale* (New York: Pantheon Books, 1986).

6. Berlin: Siedler, 1986, p. 64.

7. Thus Hillgruber writes: "Das sind Dimensionen, die ins Anthropologische, ins Sozialpsychologische und ins Individualpsychologische gehen und die Frageeiner möglichen Wiederholung unter anderem ideologischen Vorzeichen in tatsächlich oder vermeintlich wiederum extremen Situationen und Konstellationen aufwerfen. Das geht über jenes Wach-

halten der Erinnerung an der Millionen der Opfer hinaus, das dem Historiker aufgegeben ist. Denn hier wird ein zentrales Problem der Gegenwart und der Zukunft berührt und die Aufgabe des Historikers transzendiert. Hier geht es um eine fundamentale Herausforderung an jedermann." Ibid., pp. 98–99.

8. Most of the relevant documents can be found in *"Historikerstreit": Die Dokumentation der Kontroverse um die Einzigartigkeit der nationalsozialistischen Judenvernichtung* (Munich: Piper, 1989). See also "Special Issue on the *Historikerstreit,*" *New German Critique,* 44 (Spring/Summer 1988).

9. The plot type is a crucial element in the constitution of what Bakhtin calls the "chronotope," a socially structured domain of the natural world that defines the horizon of possible events, actions, agents, agencies, social roles, and so forth of all imaginative fictions—and all real stories, too. A dominant plot type determines the classes of things perceivable, the modes of their relationships, the periodicities of their development, and the possible meanings they can reveal. Every generic plot type presupposes a chronotope, and every chronotope presumes a limited number of the kinds of stories that can be told about events happening within its horizon.

10. George Steiner, quoted in Berel Lang, *Act and Idea in the Nazi Genocide* (Chicago: University of Chicago Press, 1990), p. 151.

11. Alice Eckhardt and A. R. Eckhardt, "Studying the Holocaust's Impact Today: Some Dilemmas of Language and Method," in *Echoes from the Holocaust: Philosophical Reflections on a Dark Time,* ed. Alan Rosenberg and Gerald E. Myers (Philadelphia: Temple University Press, 1989), p. 439.

12. Lang, *Act and Idea,* p. 160.

13. Ibid., p. 43.

14. Ibid., pp. 144–145.

15. Ibid., p. 146.

16. Ibid., pp. 146–147.

17. Ibid., pp. 157–158.

18. Ibid., pp. 158–159.

19. Ibid., p. 156.

20. Cf. Edith Milton, "The Dangers of Memory," *New York Times Book Review,* 28 January 1990, p. 27, for some perspicuous comments on the efforts of younger writers who, lacking any direct experience of the Holocaust, nonetheless attempt to make it "personal." This is a review of *Testimony: Contemporary Writers Make the Holocaust Personal,* ed. David Rosenberg (New York: Times Books, 1990). Milton remarks on the "obvious paradox at the heart of any anthology that offers to recollect genocide in tranquility." She goes on to praise only those essays which, "far

from pretending to come to grips with the Holocaust, . . . emphasize their authors' necessary aloofness. Indeed," she says, "since subjectivity and obliqueness are the only approaches possible," the best essays in the collection are those which "make a virtue of being subjective and oblique."

21. Lang, *Act and Idea*, p. xii.

22. Ibid., p. xiii.

23. As in, for example, such "performative" actions as those of promising or swearing an oath. In actions such as these in which the agent seems to act upon itself, the use of the middle voice permits avoidance of the notion that the subject is split in two, that is, into an agent who administers the oath and a patient who "takes" it. Thus, Attic Greek expresses the action of composing an oath in the active voice (*logou poiein*) and that of swearing an oath, not in the passive, but in the middle voice (*logou poiesthai*). Barthes gives the example of *thuein,* to offer a sacrifice for another (active), versus *thuesthai,* to offer a sacrifice for oneself (middle). Roland Barthes, "To Write: An Intransitive Verb?" in *The Rustle of Language,* trans. Richard Howard (Berkeley: University of California Press, 1989), p. 18.

24. Ibid., p. 19.

25. J. Derrida, "Différance," in *Speech and Phenomena and Other Essays on Husserl's Theory of Signs,* trans. David B. Allison (Evanston, Ill.: Northwestern University Press, 1973), p. 130.

26. Cf. Saul Friedlander's introduction to Gerald Fleming, *Hitler and the Final Solution* (Berkeley: University of California Press, 1984), where he writes: "On the limited level of the *analysis* of Nazi policies, *an answer* to the debate between the various groups *appears to be possible.* On the level of global *interpretation,* however, the real *difficulties remain.* The historian who is not encumbered with ideological or conceptual blinkers easily recognizes that it is Nazi anti-Semitism and the anti-Jewish policy of the Third Reich that gives Nazism its *sui generis* character. By virtue of this fact, inquiries into *the nature of Nazism* take on a new dimension that renders it *unclassifiable* . . . If [however] one admits that the Jewish problem was at the center, was the very essence of the system, many [studies of the Final Solution] lose their coherence, and *historiography is confronted with an enigma that defies normal interpretative categories* . . . We know in detail what occurred, we know the sequence of the events and their probable interaction, but *the profound dynamics of the phenomena escapes us*" (my italics).

27. Erich Auerbach, *Mimesis: The Representation of Reality in Western Literature,* trans. Willard Trask (Princeton: Princeton University Press, 1953), p. 491.

28. Ibid., pp. 534–539.
29. This is the view held by Fredric Jameson and most explicitly argued in *Fables of Aggression: Wyndham Lewis, the Modernist as Fascist* (Berkeley: University of California Press, 1979). It is a commonplace of leftist interpretations of modernism.

3. On Emplotment

1. Andreas Hillgruber, *Zweierlei Untergang: Die Zerschlagung des Deutschen Reiches und das Ende des europäischen Judentums* (Berlin, 1986). The original version of the first essay was published in 1985; that of the second essay was written in 1984.
2. Quintilian, *Institutio Oratoria*, 5.11.23, 8.3.77.
3. Hayden White, *Metahistory: The Historical Imagination in Nineteenth-Century Europe* (Baltimore, 1973), p. 427: "A given historian will be inclined to choose one or another of the different modes of explanation, on the level of argument, emplotment, or ideological implication, in response to the imperatives of the trope which informs the linguistic protocol he has used to prefigure the field of historical occurrence singled out by him for investigation."
4. Hillgruber, *Zweierlei Untergang*, p. 64.
5. Hayden White, "Narrativity in the Representation of Reality," *The Content of the Form* (Baltimore, 1987), pp. 21–25.
6. Hillgruber, *Zweierlei Untergang*, p. 98 ("historische Einmaligkeit").
7. See his fundamental essay, "Die 'Endlösung' und das deutsche Ostimperium als Kernstück des rassenideologischen Programms des Nationalsozialismus," in *Deutsche Grossmacht und Weltpolitik* (Dusseldorf, 1977), pp. 258–261.
8. Hillgruber, *Zweierlei Untergang*, pp. 81–83; *Germany and the Two World Wars* (Cambridge, Mass., 1981), pp. 41–44.
9. Hillgruber, *Zweierlei Untergang*, p. 98.
10. Hillgruber, *Deutsche Grossmacht und Weltpolitik*, p. 270.
11. Hillgruber, *Zweierlei Untergang*, p. 9.
12. Ibid.
13. Ibid., p. 67.
14. Ibid., pp. 10, 73–74.
15. Ibid., pp. 23–25. Note the subject specification: "Dies is das gerafft zusammengefasste und mit einigen deutlichen Akzenten versehene Geschehen des Zusammenbruchs im Osten 1944/1945, *wie es sich aus deutscher Sicht darstellt*" (p. 42).
16. See the commentaries of each in Hans-Ulrich Wehler, *Entsorgung der*

deutschen Vergangenheit? (Munich, 1988), pp. 49–53; Charles Maier, *The Unmasterable Past* (Cambridge, Mass., 1989), pp. 21–23.

17. See in particular Wehler, *Entsorgung der deutschen Vergangenheit?*, pp. 51–58.

18. Richard Evans, *In Hitler's Shadow: West German Historians and the Attempt to Escape the Nazi Past* (London, 1989), pp. 99, 95.

19. The ethnic composition of Poland's eastern *kresy*, in which Ukrainians and Belorussians formed a large majority, may now be beyond detailed reconstruction. Of a total population in these regions of some thirteen million in 1939, the Russians deported east over a million Poles, of whom large numbers perished, and after the war some two million made their way west.

20. Evans is mistaken in asserting, "Hillgruber's account [of the political background to the expulsions] is contradicted by recent research both in its detail and in its overall thrust" (*In Hitler's Shadow*, p. 95). The most scholarly recent work on the origins of the Oder-Neisse Line, Sarah Terry's study of Sikorski's wartime aims and their prewar background, *Poland's Place in Europe* (Princeton, 1983), makes it clear that Polish annexation of East Prussia, Pomerania, and Silesia was an objective entertained by the exile government without reference to the *kresy;* and that Churchill, within a few months of signing the Atlantic Charter, was assuring the exile government that principles of self-determination would not stand in the way of measures to break the power of Prussia (pp. 3–10, 272–286). It should be said that Hillgruber's account is not directed only at foreign powers: it does not spare the rulers of Germany either, from the Second Reich through Weimar to the Third, whom he charges with an increasing disregard for the safety of the inhabitants of the German East (*Zweierlei Untergang*, p. 69).

21. There is a curious lexical echo in the closing lines of the two most famous poems inspired by the events described in *Zweierlei Untergang*, Celan's *Todesfuge* and Solzhenitsyn's *Prusskie Nochi*. The blue eyes of *Der Tod ist ein Meister aus Deutschland sein auge ist blau* are those of a camp guard, seen by their Jewish victims; of *s bledno-sinimi glazami/neprivychno blizko sblizyas'* those of a peasant girl, seen by the Russian soldier who has forced her.

22. *Zweierlei Untergang*, pp. 72–74.

23. Jürgen Habermas, "Eine Art Schadensabwicklung," in *"Historikerstreit,"* ed. E. R. Piper (Munich, 1987), p. 76; Wehler, *Entsorgung der deutschen Vergangenheit?* p. 210.

24. "Für die Forschung gibt es kein Frageverbot," *"Historikerstreit,"* pp. 240–241.

25. Maier, *The Unmasterable Past*, p. 23.

26. Ibid., pp. 151–156.
27. "What makes history possible is that a sub-set of events is found, for a given period, to have approximately the same significance for a contingent of individuals . . . The dates appropriate to each class are irrational in relation to all those of other classes . . . History is therefore never history, but history-for." *The Savage Mind* (London, 1966), pp. 257, 260.

4. History, Counterhistory, and Narrative

Acknowledgments: I wish to thank Keith Baker, Saul Friedlander, and Sabine MacCormack for their comments, criticisms, and valuable suggestions.

1. Jakob Burckhardt, *Briefe*, ed. Max Burckhardt, 5 vols. (Wiesbaden, 1960), IV, 130.
2. It was not as yet the argument of Hayden White's *Metahistory: The Historical Imagination in Nineteenth-Century Europe* (Baltimore: Johns Hopkins University Press, 1973); see below n. 7.
3. Karl Marx, "Economic and Philosophic Manuscripts of 1844," in *Writings of the Young Marx on Philosophy and Society*, ed. and trans. Lloyd D. Easton and Kurt H. Guddat (Garden City, N.Y.: Doubleday, 1967), p. 335.
4. Franz Rosenzweig, *Briefe*, ed. Edith Rosenzweig (Berlin: Schocken Verlag, 1935), p. 19.
5. Oliver Sacks, *The Man Who Mistook His Wife for a Hat and Other Clinical Tales* (New York: Summit Books, 1970), p. 110; and the literature quoted therein (Luria). On other epistemological lessons of neurology see my forthcoming article "Motion, Similitude and Schematism: Kant and the Neoplatonic Tradition."
6. Ernst Troeltsch, *Der Historismus und seine Probleme* (Tübingen, 1922), p. 36; Friedrich Meinecke, "Klassizismus, Romantizismus und historisches Denken im 18. Jahrhundert," in *Werke*, IV, ed. Eberhard Kessel (Stuttgart: K. F. Koehler Verlag, 1965), p. 264.
7. White, *Metahistory*, p. 2, n. 5. White later also found this position untenable. An even more fundamental quaternity than the "tropes" is the quaternity of logical connectives "and" ($\wedge$) "or" ($\vee$) "if . . . then" ($\supset$) "if and only if" ($\leftrightarrow$). Why not characterize the modes of historical category formation as such that give weight to synchrony ("and"), argument ("or"), causality ("if then"), contextuality ("iff")? I raise this possibility to show that of quaternities there is no end, though I do not doubt their heuristic value.
8. See my article "The Persecution of Absolutes: On the Kantian and Neo-Kantian Theories of Science," *The Kaleidoscope of Science: The Israel*

Colloquium for the History and Philosophy of Science, I (1986), 329–348. Many of the fundamental insights of Ludwik Fleck or Karl Popper owe their origins to the neo-Kantian heritage.

9. The term was used by David Biale, *Kabbala and Counterhistory* (Cambridge, Mass.: Harvard University Press, 1979); and in an article of mine, "Anti-Jewish Propaganda: Pagan, Medieval and Modern," *Jerusalem Quarterly*, 19 (Spring 1981), 56–72.

10. In Benjamin's felicitous phrase. Walter Benjamin, *Illuminations*, ed. Hannah Arendt, trans. Harry Zohn (New York: Schocken Books, 1969), p. 257 ("Theses on the Philosophy of History" VII).

11. Manetho, *Aegyptiaca*, Fragment 54 (from Josephus, *Contra Apioneus*, I, sec. 26–31, sec. 227–287) (Cambridge, Mass.: Loeb Classical Library, 1940), pp. 119–147, pp. 62–86 (Manetho), pp. 389–416 (Apion). Also in Menachem Stern, *Greek and Roman Authors on Jews and Judaism*, I (Jerusalem: Israel Academy of Sciences, 1976).

12. Ibid. Cf. Tacitus, *Historiae*, V, 4, ed. Kenneth Wellesley (Teubner Publishing House): "Moyses quo sibi in posterum gentem firmaret, nouos ritus contrariosque ceteris mortalibus indidit. Profana illic omnia quae apud nos sacra, rursum concessa apud illos quae nobis incesta." Cf. Jochanan Levy, *Studies in Jewish Hellenism* (Jerusalem: Mossad Bialik, 1960) (in Hebrew), pp. 60–196.

13. *Religio licita* was never a legal term; it was first used by Tertullian. But Jewish religious rights were tolerated, whether by virtue of their being a *natio* (*laos*) or a permitted collegium. Cf. Theodor Mommsen, *Historische Zeitschrift*, 64 (1890), 389–419; Tertullian, *Apologeticus*, ed. Jean-Pierre Waltzing (Louvain, 1910), p. 125 (and the editor's comment); Jean Juster, *Les Juifs dans l'empire Romain* (Paris: P. Geuthner, 1914), I, 413–424 (denies that synagogues were *collegia*).

14. John Spencer, *De legibus et moribus Iudaeorum* (Cambridge, 1685), for example, p. 223. Cf. Julius Guttmann, "John Spencer's Erklärung der biblischen Gesetze in ihrer Beziehung zu Maimonides," in *Festskrift i anleding af Professor David Simonsen 70-årige foedselsdag* (Copenhagen, 1923), pp. 258–276; Shmuel Ettinger, "Jews and Judaism as Seen by English Deists of the Eighteenth Century," *Zion*, 29 (1964), 182.

15. Peter L. Berger and Thomas Luckmann, *The Social Construction of Reality* (Garden City, N.Y.: Irvington Publishers, 1980), pp. 166–167.

16. Tacitus, *Agricola*, 30. See Harold Fuchs, *Der geistige Widerstand gegen Rom in der antiken Welt* (Berlin: Wide Gruyler, 1964, reprint).

17. Augustine, *De Civitate Dei*, II, 21; IV, 4. *Corpus Christianorum, Series Latina*, 47, 52.

18. See Amos Funkenstein, *Heilsplan und natürliche Entwicklung* (Munich: Nymphenburger Verlagshandlung, 1965), pp. 43–50; more briefly: idem,

Theology and the Scientific Imagination from the Middle Ages to the Seventeenth Century (Princeton: Princeton University Press, 1986), pp. 256–261; against, for example, Alois Wachtel, *Beiträge zur Geschichtstheologie des Aurelius Augustinus* (Bonn: L. Roehrscheid, 1960). On Augustine's sources see Heinrich Scholz, *Glaube und Unglaube in der Weltgeschichte: ein Kommentar zu Augustin's De civitate Dei* (Leipzig: J. C. Hinrichs, 1911).

19. It was edited by Samuel Kraus, *Das Leben Jesu nach jüdischen Quellen* (Berlin: S. Calvary, 1902). Cf. Joseph Dan, *Hasipur ha'ivri biyme habenayim* (Jerusalem, 1974), pp. 122–132. Morton Smith, *Jesus the Magician* (San Francisco: Harper and Row, 1978), elaborates one of the narrative's main themes. In a way he, too, has written a counterhistory (to all *Leben Jesu* versions of modern Protestant theology). It is worthwhile to note, in passing, the difference between this or similar references to Jesus in the orthodox Jewish literature and the treatment of Jesus in the postemancipatory climate of acculturation, say in the nineteenth-century *Wissenschaft des Judentums*. The orthodox, traditional account agrees with Christians in the question of fact, but differs from Christianity in the evaluation: true, we killed Jesus, but he deserved it as a heretic and a magician. Nineteenth-century Jewish historians or theologians—say Geiger or Baeck—disagree about the facts: Jesus was a good Jew (a Pharisee to boot!), and we could not have killed him. But they agree in his evaluation with liberal Protestant theologians: he was the embodiment of ethics.

20. Herodotus, *Histories*, II, 34–35.

21. Funkenstein, *Heilsplan* (n. 18 above), pp. 70–77.

22. Isidor Hispalensis Episcopi, *Etymologiae sive origenes libri XX*, ed. W. M. Lindsay (London: Oxford University Press, 1st ed. 1911, reprint 1957), I, sec. 41, 1. See Isidor Hispalensis Episcopi, *De ordine creaturarum*, Migne, *Patrologia latina*, 83, 939–940: "historialiter facta sunt, et intellectualiter Ecclesiae mysteria per hoc designantur."

23. "Erit enim continua mundi historia: libri prophetici, Herodotus, Thucydides, Xenophon, Diodorus de Philippo, Alexandro et successoribus . . .": Philipp Melanchton, *Opera Omnia*, ed. Carlos G. Bretschneider, Halle\S (1844), XII, 714.

24. That history is rewritten anew every period from its unique *Gesichtskreis* was first claimed by Gattener, Chladenius, and others in the eighteenth century: Reinhart Koselleck, *Vergangene Zukunft: Zur Semantik geschichtlicher Zeiten* (Frankfurt am Main: Suhrkamp, 1979), pp. 176–203; Peter Reill, *The German Enlightenment and the Rise of Historicism* (Berkeley: University of California Press, 1975), pp. 125–126. Leibniz, we remember, spoke of each monad as representing a unique "point of view" of the whole world in which it is embedded.

25. John Greville Agard Pocock, *The Ancient Constitution and the Feudal Law: A Study of English Historical Thought in the Seventeenth Century* (Cambridge: Cambridge University Press, 1957), chap. 1; Donald R. Kelley, *Foundations of Modern Historical Reasoning: Language, Law, and History in the French Renaissance* (New York: Columbia University Press, 1970), pp. 19–50; Jerry H. Bentley, *Humanists and the Holy Writ: Neo-Testament Scholarship in the Renaissance* (Princeton: Princeton University Press, 1983).

26. The best study is still that of Erich Seeberg, *Gottfried Arnold: Die Wissenschaft und die Mystik seiner Zeit* (1923; reprint Darmstadt: Wissenschaftliche Buchgesellschaft, 1964). See also Biale, *Gershom Scholem: Kabbala and Counterhistory* (Scholem and Arnold) (Cambridge, Mass.: Harvard University Press, 1979).

27. Herbert Grundmann, "Opertet ut haereses esse: Das Problem der Ketzerei im Spiegel der Mittelalterlichen Bibelexegese," in *Archiv für Kulturgeschichte*, 45 (1963), 129–164.

28. Gottfried Arnold, *Unparteyische Kirchen- und Kezer Historie* (Schaffhausen, 1740), I, sec. 9, 24; cf. Seeberg, *Gottfried Arnold*, pp. 24, 224, 219–221.

29. On the origin and various fortunes of Mandeville's phrase see Walter Euchner, *Egoismus und Gemeinwohl: Studien zur Geschichte der bürgerlichen Philosophie* (Frankfurt am Main, 1973); and my *Theology and the Scientific Imagination*, pp. 202–205.

30. Karl Marx, "Zur Judenfrage," in *Karl Marx, Friedrich Engels: Werke* (Berlin: Dietz, 1956), I, 247–377. See also my article "The Political Theory of Jewish Emancipation from Mendelssohn to Herzl," *Jahrbuch des Instituts für deutsche Geschichte*, 3 (1980), 13–28, esp. 23–25.

31. Karl Marx, *Das Kapital* (Hamburg: Meissner, 1890–1894), I, 1. It is a variant (Marx would say: a concretization or a turning-on-its-feet) of the idealistic formula for the identity *cum* difference of the I and the non-I, A = B, identity and difference in the *Wesens Logik*. "The metaphorical" character of the commodity, to which White, *Metahistory* (see n. 32), draws attention, has its origin here.

32. Georg Wilhelm Friedrich Hegel, *Wissenschaft der Logik* (Nuremberg: Johann Leonhard Schrag, 1812–16). The most lucid explication of its moves was given by Dieter Henrich, "Hegels Logik der Reflexion," in *Hegel im Kontext* (Frankfurt am Main: Suhrkamp, 1971), pp. 95–156. I hope to develop this interpretation of Marx further at a later date. See also White, *Metahistory*, pp. 285–330, which shows in fact this dialectic (but without reference to Hegel's *Wesens Logik* or *Reflexions Logik*). The only mistake of this chapter is the assumption that "socially necessary time of labor" measures value of usage. The latter has no measure: "Als Ge-

brauchswerte sind Waren vor allem verschiedener Qualität, als Tausch-
werte können sie nur verschiedener Quantität sein, enthalten also kein
Atom Gebrauchswert" (Marx, *Das Kapital*, I, 1).

33. Franz Kafka, "Die Verwandlung," in *Kafkas Erzählungen*, ed. Brigitte
Flach (Bonn: Bouvier, 1967).

34. For a minimal construction of the meaning of collective memory see Amos
Funkenstein, "Collective Memory and Historical Consciousness," *History and Memory*, 1 (1989), 5–26.

35. The following relies on Pierre Vidal-Naquet, "Theses on Revisionism," in
Unanswered Questions: Nazi Germany and the Genocide of the Jews, ed.
François Furet (New York: Schocken Books, 1989), pp. 304–320.

36. Amos Funkenstein, "Changes in the Patterns of Christian Anti-Jewish Polemics in the Twelfth Century," *Zion*, 23 (1968), 126–145. That such a
change occurred in the way I sketched it there was the starting point of
Jeremy Cohen, *The Friars and the Jews: The Evolution of Medieval Anti-
Judaism* (Ithaca: Cornell University Press, 1982). He disagrees with me,
however, about the date; sees no traces of this change, as I did, in Peter
the Venerable or his times, and places the transformation of attitudes in
the thirteenth century (Raymundus Martini). I do not find this part of the
argument convincing.

37. Petrus Venerabilis, *Tractatus adversus Judaeorum inveteratam duritiem*,
V, Migne, *Patrologia latina*, 189, cols. 602, quotation: cols. 648–649. See
n. 36. This type of argument—at times the rationale for burning Jewish
postbiblical literature—continues through the seventeenth and eighteenth centuries. Johann Wagenseil's *Tella ignea satanis* was its most influential early modern example.

38. Thomas of Monmouth, *De vita et passione Sancti Wilhelmi Martyris Nor-
wicensis*, II, 9, ed. Augustus Jessopp and Montague Rhodes James (Cambridge, 1896), p. 93: "Referebat quidem in antiquis patrum nostrum scrip-
tis hebrei ludaeos sine sanguinis humani effusione nec libertatem adipisci
nec ad patrios fines quandoque regredi." On the *Protocolls* see Norman
Cohn, *Histoire d'un mythe, la conspiration juive et les protocoles des
Sages de Sion* (Paris: Gallimard, 1967).

39. George Steiner, *The Portage to St. Cristobal of A. H.* (New York: Simon
& Schuster, 1982). Of him we may say, with the medieval Archipoeta,
"Quaero mihi similis / et adjungor pravis."

40. I have argued against the "incomprehensibility" in "Theological Interpretations of the Holocaust," in *Unanswered Questions* (see n. 35), pp. 273–
303, esp. 302–303.

41. Hegel, *Phänomenologie des Geistes*, ed. Johannes Hofmeister (Hamburg:
Felix Meiner, 1952), pp. 141–150. The significance of these famous pages
is, among other things, that they are the first *philosophical* treatment of

self-consciousness as a through-and-through social phenomenon. The "I," or the *sum res cogitans* of Descartes, was not only a substance, but also a lonely one; its self-evidence needed no other self; its ideas were innate. Kant's "transcendental unity of the apperception"—the "I" that "accompanies all of my representations"—though not a *substance* anymore (Kant's position was very similar to Ryle's), was still a lonely affair. Hegel was the first to argue that self-consciousness, by definition, needs for its own constitution another self-consciousness to "recognize" (*anerkennen*) it. It identifies itself through the other.

5. Just One Witness

Acknowledgment: Many thanks to Nadine Tanio for her stylistic revision.

1. See J. Shatzmiller, "Les Juifs de Provence pendant la Peste Noire," *Revue des études juives*, 133 (1974), 457–480, esp. 469–472.

2. See *Storia notturna. Una decifrazione del sabba* (Turin: Einaudi, 1989), pp. 5–35.

3. See Bouquet, *Recueil des historiens des Gaules et de la France* (Paris, 1840), XX, 629–630.

4. See Josephus, *The Jewish War*, trans. G. A. Williamson, rev. E. M. Smallwood (Harmondsworth: Penguin Books, 1985). A subtle analysis of the parallels between the two passages has been given by P. Vidal-Naquet, "Flavius Josèphe et Masada," in *Les Juifs, la mémoire, le présent* (Paris: Maspero, 1981), pp. 43 ff.

5. Cf. Vidal-Naquet, "Flavius Josèphe," pp. 53 ff.

6. See *The Latin Josephus*, ed. F. Blatt (Aarhus: Universitetsforlaget, 1958), I, 15–16. See also G. N. Deutsch, *Iconographie et illustration de Flavius Josèphe au temps de Jean Fouquet* (Leiden: Brill, 1986), p. xi (map).

7. See P. Schmitz, "Les lectures de table à l'abbaye de Saint-Denis à la fin du Moyen Age," *Revue bénédictine*, 42 (1930), 163–167; A. Wilmart, "Le couvent et la bibliothèque de Cluny vers le milieu du XIe siècle," *Revue Mabillon*, 11 (1921), 89–124, esp. 93, 113.

8. See D. Nebbiai-Dalla Guarda, *La bibliothèque de l'abbaye de Saint-Denis en France du IXe au XVIIIe siècle* (Paris: Editions du CNRS, 1985), on a request sent from Reichenau to Saint-Denis in order to get a copy of Josephus' *Antiquitates Judaicae* (p. 61; see also ibid., p. 294).

9. B. N. Lat. 12511; cf. *The Latin Josephus*, p. 50.

10. *Hegesippi qui dicuntur historiarum libri V*, ed. V. Ussani (*Corpus Scriptorum Ecclesiasticorum Latinorum*, 66), Vindobonae, 1932, 1960, pref. K. Mras (on Masada's siege see 5, nos. 52–53, 407–417). The Bibliothèque Nationale in Paris owns twelve manuscripts of "Hegesippus," written be-

tween the tenth and the fifteenth centuries; see Deutsch, *Iconographie*, p. 15.

11. A translation of the latter essay has been published as "A Paper Eichmann?" (note the addition of a question mark to the original French title), *Democracy*, April 1981, pp. 67–95.

12. Maria Daraki's suggestion, mentioned by P. Vidal-Naquet (*Les Juifs*, p. 59, n. 48), that in the former case the parallel should be referred to the woman who denounced Josephus and his fellows seems to me less convincing.

13. See H. Van Vliet, *No Single Testimony*, Studia Theologica Rheno-Traiectina, 4 (Utrecht, 1958). See also, from a general (that is, logical) point of view, Vidal-Naquet, *Les Juifs*, p. 51. "More than one witness is necessary, because, so long as one affirms and another denies, nothing is proved, and the right which everyone has of being held innocent prevails," Beccaria wrote in 1764 in *Dei delitti e delle pene* (trans. J. A. Farrer, London, 1880, pp. 139–140: ed. F. Venturi [Turin, 1970], pp. 31–32). Today, at the very moment I am writing (2 May 1990), a totally opposite attitude prevails in Italian courts.

14. Cf. Van Vliet, *No Single Testimony*, p. 11.

15. Cf. A. Libois, "A propos des modes de preuve et plus spécialement de la preuve par témoins dans la juridiction de Léau au XVe siècle," in *Hommage au Professeur Paul Bonenfant (1899–1965)* (Brussels, 1965), pp. 532–546, esp. 539–542.

16. On this topic see the rather cursory remarks of P. Peeters, "Les aphorismes du droit dans la critique historique," *Académie Royale de Belgique, Bulletin de la classe des lettres*, 32 (1946), 82 ff. (pp. 95–96 on *testis unus, testis nullus*).

17. F. Baudouin, *De institutione historiae universae et ejus cum jurisprudentia conjunctione, prolegomenon libri II*, quoted by D. R. Kelley, *Foundations of Modern Historical Scholarship* (New York: Columbia University Press, 1970), esp. p. 116.

18. I consulted the second edition (Liège, 1770). The importance of this treatise was perceptively stressed by A. Johnson. *The Historian and Historical Evidence* (New York, 1934; 1st ed. 1926), p. 114, who called it "the most significant book on method after Mabillon's *De re diplomatica*." See also A. Momigliano, *Ancient History and the Antiquarian* (Contributo alla storia degli studi classici. Rome: Edizioni di storia e letteratura, 1979), p. 81.

19. See R. Faurisson, *Mémoire en défense. Contre ceux qui m'accusent de falsifier l'histoire. La question des chambres à gaz*, preface by Noam Chomsky (Paris: La Vieille Taupe, 1980).

20. *Michel de Certeau*, under the direction of L. Giard (Paris: Centre Georges Pompidou, 1987), pp. 71–72. From Vidal-Naquet's letter we also learn that his debate with de Certeau was ignited again by their involvement in the public discussion of François Hartog's thesis, published later on as *Le miroir d'Hérodote* (Paris: Gallimard, 1980). On some implications of this work see my postscript to the Italian translation of Natalie Davis, *The Return of Martin Guerre* (*Prove e possibilita'*, in *Il ritorno di Martin Guerre*. Turin: Einaudi, 1984, pp. 143–145).

21. The following pages are based on White's previously published work. His chapter in this volume suggests a milder (although somewhat self-contradictory) form of skepticism.

22. See C. Antoni, *From Historicism to Sociology* (Detroit: Wayne State University Press, 1959), translator's preface ("On History and Historicism"), pp. xxv–xxvi; see also the review by B. Mazlish in *History and Theory*, 1 (1960), 219–227.

23. See B. Croce, *Contributo alla critica di me stesso* (Bari: Laterza, 1926), pp. 32–33; R. G. Collingwood, *The Idea of History* (Oxford: Oxford University Press, 1956), pp. 91ff.

24. See H. White, *Metahistory: The Historical Imagination in Nineteenth-Century Europe* (Baltimore: Johns Hopkins University Press, 1973), pp. 281–288; B. Croce, *Primi saggi* (Bari: Laterza, 1927; second edition), pp. 3–41.

25. See White, *Metahistory*, p. 385.

26. Ibid., pp. 378, 434.

27. Ibid., p. 407.

28. E. Colorni, *L'estetica di Benedetto Croce. Studio critico* (Milan, 1934).

29. See G. Gentile, *Lettere a Benedetto Croce*, ed. S. Giannantoni, I (Florence: Sansoni, 1972); B. Croce, *Lettere a Giovanni Gentile*, ed. A. Croce (Milan: Mondadori, 1981).

30. See B. Croce, *Logica come scienza del concetto puro* (Bari: Laterza, 1971), pp. 193–195. See also G. Gentile, *Frammenti di critica letteraria* (Lanciano: Carabba, 1921), pp. 379 ff (review of B. Croce, *Il concetto della storia nelle sue relazioni col concetto dell'arte*, 1897).

31. Here I am developing some perceptive remarks made by Piero Gobetti in "Cattaneo," in P. Gobetti, *Scritti storici, letterari e filosofici* (Turin: Einaudi, 1969), p. 199; originally published in "L'Ordine Nuovo," 1922.

32. See G. Gentile, "The Transcending of Time in History" in *Philosophy and History. Essays Presented to Ernst Cassirer*, ed. R. Klibansky and H. J. Paton (Oxford: Oxford University Press, 1936), pp. 91–105, esp. 95, 100. Thirty years earlier Antonio Labriola, in a letter to Croce, had described the relationship between Croce and Gentile in curiously similar terms (A. Labriola, *Lettere a Benedetto Croce, 1885–1904* [Naples: nella sede

dell'Istituto, 1975], p. 376 [2 January 1904]: "io non capisco perche' il Gentile, che inveisce per fino in istile ieratico contro il reo mondo, non si dia proprio all'opera benigna (avendo il diavolo dentro casa) di convertire innanzitutto te"). On Gentile's allusion to Croce, see note 33.

33. See G. Gentile, "Il superamento del tempo nella storia," in *Memorie italiane e problemi della filosofia e della vita* (Rome, 1936), p. 308: "la metafisica storica (o storicismo) . . ."; the essay had been previously published in "Rendiconti della R. Accademia nazionale dei Lincei," classe di scienze morali, ser. 6, 11 (1935), 752–769. The words in parentheses, "(that is, historicism)," which are missing in the aforementioned English translation (*Philosophy and History*; the editors' preface is dated February 1936) were presumably added after the appearance of Croce's essay "Antistoricismo," first delivered at Oxford in 1930, but published only in *Ultimi saggi* (Bari: Laterza, 1935), pp. 246–258. Gentile delivered his lecture at the Accademia dei Lincei on 17 November 1935; he sent back the corrected proofs on 2 April 1936 (see *Rendiconti* cit., pp. 752, 769). For Croce's reaction to the essays collected in *Philosophy and History* see *La storia come pensiero e come azione* (Bari: Laterza, 1943 [1938]), pp. 319–327 (the entire section is missing from the English translation, *History as the Story of Liberty* [London, 1941]); on page 322 there is a polemical allusion to Gentile ("una torbida tendenza misticheggiante . . ."). See also in the same volume the pages on "Historiography as Liberation from History" (*History*, pp. 43–45 = *La storia* cit., pp. 30–32): "We are products of the past and we live immersed in the past, which encompasses us etc." In his much more radical and consistent idealism Gentile had emphasized that past, and time as well, are purely abstract notions, which are overcome in concrete spiritual life (*The Transcending of Time*, pp. 95–97). The relevance of Gentile's *Il superamento del tempo nella storia* has been emphasized by C. Garboli, *Scritti servili* (Turin, 1989), p. 205.

34. See G. Gentile, *Teoria generale dello spirito come atto puro* (2nd rev. enl. ed., Pisa, 1918), pp. 50–52.

35. I am not suggesting here a simple, unilinear causal relationship. White has undoubtedly reacted to Italian neoidealism through a distinctly American filter. But even White's pragmatism, implicitly pointed out by Perry Anderson at the end of his chapter, was presumably reinforced by the well-known pragmatist strain (through Giovanni Vailati's mediation) detectable in Croce's work, particularly in his *Logic*.

36. See H. White, "Interpretation in History" (1972–1973), in *Tropics of Discourse* (Baltimore: Johns Hopkins University Press, 1978), p. 75.

37. Ibid., p. 2.

38. "Foucault Decoded" (1973), in ibid., p. 254.

39. The index has only one entry under his name; but see also p. 24, n. 2,

where Barthes is listed with other scholars working on rhetorics, such as Kenneth Burke, Genette, Eco, Todorov.

40. G. Gentile, "La filosofia della praxis," in *La filosofia di Marx. Studi critici* (Pisa, 1899), pp. 51–157 (the book was dedicated to Croce).

41. Ibid., pp. 62–63.

42. See G. Bergami, *Il giovane Gramsci e il marxismo, 1911–1918* (Milan: Feltrinelli, 1977); A. Del Noce, *Il suicidio della rivoluzione* (Milan: Rusconi, 1978).

43. See S. Natoli, *Giovanni Gentile filosofo europeo* (Turin: Bollati-Boringhieri, 1989), pp. 94ff. (rather superficial). For Gramsci's judgment on futurism see *Socialismo e fascismo. L'Ordine Nuovo 1919–1922* (Turin: Einaudi, 1966), p. 22.

44. See B. Croce, *Antistoricismo*, in *Ultimi saggi*, pp. 246–258.

45. See *Tropics*, pp. 27–80.

46. See H. White, *The Content of the Form* (Baltimore: Johns Hopkins University Press, 1987), p. 63.

47. Ibid., p. 227 n. 12.

48. G. Gentile, *The Transcending of Time*, p. 99.

49. Cf. G. Gentile, "Caratteri religiosi della presente lotta politica," in *Che cosa e' il fascismo. Discorsi e polemiche* (Florence: Vallecchi, 1924 [1925]), pp. 143–151.

50. Cf. the section entitled "La violenza fascista" in ibid., pp. 29–32.

51. "State and individual . . . are one and the same; and the art of governing is the art of reconciling and identifying these two terms so that the maximum of liberty agrees with the maximum of public order . . . For always the maximum of liberty agrees with the maximum of public force of the state. Which force? Distinctions in this field are dear to those who do not welcome this concept of force, which is nevertheless essential to the state, and hence to liberty. And they distinguish moral from material force: the force of law freely voted and accepted from the force of violence which is rigidly opposed to the will of the citizen. Ingenuous distinctions, if made in good faith! Every force is a moral force, for it is always an expression of will; and whatever be the argument used—preaching or black-jacking— its efficacy can be none other than its ability finally to receive the inner support of a man and to persuade him to agree." I quote from the translation provided by H. W. Schneider in *Making the Fascist State* (New York: Oxford University Press, 1928, p. 347). The speech, delivered in Palermo on 31 March 1924, was first published in journals such as *La nuova politica liberale*, II, 2 (April 1924). In republishing it one year later, after the Matteotti crisis and its violent solution, Gentile, who had been dubbed "the blackjack philosopher," added a visibly embarrassed footnote in

which he made a distinction between private force and state force (the latter having been taken over, in a situation of vacancy, by the *squadristi*); see G. Gentile, "Il fascismo e la Sicilia," in *Che cosa e' il fascismo*, pp. 50–51. Text and footnote are strangely confused in H. W. Schneider's translation. Gentile's argument was not particularly original: see for instance B. Mussolini, *Forza e consenso*, in "Gerarchia," 1923 (= *Opera omnia*, ed. E. and D. Susmel, XIX, Florence: La Fenice, 1956, pp. 195–196; the article was translated by Schneider, *Making the Fascist State*, pp. 341–342).

52. "The Politics of Historical Interpretation" (1982), in *The Content of the Form*, pp. 74–75.

53. Ibid., p. 77. Italics are missing in the French text.

54. Ibid., p. 80. My italics.

55. Ibid., p. 227 n. 12.

56. On this latter point I am indebted to Stefano Levi Della Torre for some enlightening remarks.

57. See H. White, *The Content of the Form*, p. 74.

58. See R. Serra, *Scritti letterari, morali e politici*, ed. M. Isnenghi (Turin: Einaudi, 1974), pp. 278–288. A reading of this essay similar to the one I am suggesting here has been proposed by C. Garboli, *Falbalas* (Milan: Garzanti, 1990).

59. Cf. (but not exclusively) the well-known trittico *Gli addii* (*Quelli che vanno*, etc.) (1911), now at the Metropolitan Museum in New York.

60. Cf. R. Serra, *Epistolario*, ed. L. Ambrosini, G. De Robertis, A. Grilli (Florence: Le Monnier, 1953), pp. 454ff.

61. Cf. B. Croce, *Teoria e storia della storiografia* (Bari: Laterza, 1927), pp. 44–45.

62. Cf. R. Serra, *Epistolario*, p. 459 (November 11, 1912). The divergence with Croce has been emphasized by E. Garin, "Serra e Croce," in *Scritti in onore di Renato Serra per il cinquantenario della morte* (Florence: Le Monnier, 1974), pp. 85–88.

63. Cf. R. Serra, *Scritti letterari*, p. 286.

64. Ibid., p. 287.

65. See Hayden White's passage quoted above as well as his chapter.

66. Cf. J.-F. Lyotard, *The Differend: Phrases in Dispute* (Minneapolis: University of Minnesota Press, 1988; Paris, 1983), pp. 55–57.

67. P. Levi, *Survival in Auschwitz*, trans. S. Woolf (New York: Collier Books, 1961), pp. 5–6 (= *Se questo e' un uomo* [Turin: Einaudi, 1958], pp. 9–10).

68. Cf. E. Benveniste, *Indo-European Language and Society* (London: Faber, 1973 [1969]), pp. 522ff. (the difference between *testis* and *superstes* is discussed on p. 526).

6. Of Plots, Witnesses, and Judgments

1. Siegfried Kracauer, *History: The Last Things before the Last* (New York: Oxford University Press, 1969).

2. Perhaps the issue concerns the contradiction between two types of experience, which in German is expressed in the distinction between the raw shocks of *Erlebnis* and the meaningful coherence of *Erfahrung*. Whereas the victims experienced their fate largely in the former sense, historians tend to interpret it in the latter. Another way to make this point is to say that while the disaster of the Exodus from Egypt could be turned by the Jews into Haggadic truth, that of the Holocaust cannot. For more on the implications of the split in experience and the Holocaust, see my "Songs of Experience: Reflections on the Debate over *Alltagsgeschichte*," *Salmagundi*, 81 (Winter 1989), 29–41.

7. Representing the Holocaust

1. Ernst Nolte, "Vergangenheit, die nicht vergehen will," *Frankfurter Allgemeine Zeitung*, 6 June 1986. References to this article as "Vergangenheit" will be included in the text. Contributions to the *Historikerstreit* have been collected in Ernst Reinhard Piper, ed., *"Historikerstreit": Die Dokumentation der Kontroverse um die Einzigartigkeit der nationalsozialistischen Judenvernichtung* (Munich: Piper Verlag, 1987). See also the special issue of the *New German Critique*, 44 (Spring/Summer 1988).

2. Jürgen Habermas, "Eine Art Schadensabwicklung: Die apologetischen Tendenzen in der deutschen Zeitgeschichtsschreibung," *Die Zeit*, 11 July 1986; trans. Jeremy Leaman in *New German Critique*, 44 (1988), 25–39, as "A Kind of Settlement of Damages (Apologetic Tendencies)." "Vom öffentlichen Gebrauch der Historie," *Die Zeit*, 7 November 1986; trans. Jeremy Leaman in *New German Critique*, 44 (1988), 40–50, as "Concerning the Public Use of History." References will be to the English translations, and page numbers will be included in the text.

3. Charles Maier, *The Unmasterable Past* (Cambridge, Mass.: Harvard University Press, 1988), p. 1. See also Richard J. Evans' well-informed and lucid account, *In Hitler's Shadow: West German Historians and the Attempt to Escape the Nazi Past* (New York: Pantheon Books, 1989), which appeared after this text was largely completed. Evans' book is perhaps best read as a complement to Maier's, for it fills in background that Maier's more pointed and conceptualized analysis often takes for granted, and it devotes relatively little attention to facets of the *Historikerstreit* (such as Habermas' role) that Maier elaborates. Evans, however, often

seems to proceed on the assumption that an argument may be effectively countered by adducing and evaluating the evidence germane to its discrete claims. This approach, while obviously necessary, is not sufficient to address less rational aspects of certain "arguments" that are focused on in my analysis.

4. The term *Holocaust* is of course problematic. But one is in an area where there are no easy, uninvolved, or purely objective choices. Perhaps it is best not to become fixated on any one term but to use various terms with a continual indication of their limitations. In addressing limiting phenomena, one inevitably risks repeating the tendency to veer in the directions of either sacrificial elevation or bureaucratic reduction. Nonetheless, there are, I think, at least three reasons for using the term *Holocaust* even if one is aware of its problematic nature and resists giving it a privileged status: (1) Given the unavailability of innocent terms, *Holocaust* may be one of the better choices in an impossible, tension-ridden linguistic field. There is even the possibility that resorting to terms like *annihilation* or *final solution* will inadvertently repeat Nazi terminology. *Holocaust* is both less bureaucratic and less banal than some of the alternatives. (2) The term for various reasons has had a role in the discourse of the victims themselves, and there are ritual and ethical grounds for honoring their choice. (3) The rather prevalent use of the term, including its use by nonvictims, has to some extent routinized it and helped to counteract its sacrificial connotations without entirely reducing it to cliché, although one must beware of its role in what Alvin H. Rosenfeld has termed "a pornography of the Holocaust," promoted especially by popularization and commercialization in the mass media. See "Another Revisionism: Popular Culture and the Changing Image of the Holocaust" in *Bitburg in Moral and Political Perspective,* ed. Geoffrey Hartman (Bloomington: Indiana University Press, 1986), pp. 90–102. See also Saul Friedlander, *Reflections of Nazism: An Essay on Kitsch and Death,* trans. Thomas Weyr (New York: Harper & Row, 1984).

5. A fruitful beginning in addressing this problem is made by Theodor W. Adorno in "What Does Coming to Terms with [*Aufarbeitung*] the Past Mean?" trans. Timothy Bahti and Geoffrey Hartman in *Bitburg in Moral and Political Perspective,* ed. Hartman, pp. 114–129. As Adorno notes, "Enlightenment about what happened in the past must work, above all, against a forgetfulness that too easily goes along with and justifies what is forgotten" (p. 125). It should be noted that the concept of transference employed in my argument is not based on a simple analogy with the analytic situation but on the much stronger claim that the latter is a condensed version of a general transferential process characterizing relation-

ships—a process of which the Oedipal situation is one variant. On these issues see my "Psychoanalysis and History" in *Soundings in Critical Theory* (Ithaca: Cornell University Press, 1989), pp. 30–66.

6. "Working through" is a translation of Freud's term *durcharbeiten*. "Denial" or disavowal (*Verleugnung*) is of course meant here not in its ordinary sense but in its psychoanalytic sense, which may involve intricate and subtle modes of evasion, often through relatively complex (if at times paranoid and circular) modes of argumentation. (The more sophisticated modes of revisionism do not simply deny the existence of gas chambers.) In "acting-out," the past is compulsively repeated as if it were fully present, resistances are not confronted, and memory as well as judgment is undercut. The therapeutic goal is to further the movement from denial and "acting-out" to "working-through"—a recurrently renewed and easily impaired movement that may never be totally or definitively accomplished.

7. Eberhard Jäckel, "Die elende Praxis der Untersteller" in *Die Zeit*, 12 September 1986.

8. Ernst Nolte, "Between Myth and Revisionism? The Third Reich in the Perspective of the 1980s" in *Aspects of the Third Reich*, ed. H. W. Koch (London: Macmillan, 1985), p. 27.

9. Andreas Hillgruber, *Zweierlei Untergang: Die Zerschlagung des Deutschen Reiches und das Ende des europäischen Judentums* (Berlin: Siedler, 1986), p. 67.

10. Bitburg forms part of the larger context in which the *Historikerstreit* must be seen. In the article he wrote on Bitburg, Habermas prefigured some of the points he would make in the salvo that opened the *Historikerstreit*. See "Die Entsorgung der Vergangenheit: Ein kulturpolitisches Pamphlet," *Die Zeit*, 24 (May 1985); trans. Thomas Levin as "Defusing the Past: A Politico-Cultural Tract" in *Bitburg in Moral and Political Perspective*, ed. Hartman, pp. 43–51.

11. Jürgen Habermas, "Geschichtsbewusstsein und posttraditionale Identität: Die Westorientierung der Bundesrepublik," in *Eine Art Schadensabwicklung. Kleine politische Schriften VI* (Frankfurt am Main: Suhrkamp, 1987). All of Habermas' writings on the *Historikerstreit* may also be found in *The New Conservatism: Cultural Criticism and the Historians' Debate*, ed. and trans. Shierry Weber Nicholsen, intro. Richard Wolin (Cambridge, Mass.: MIT Press, 1989).

12. Martin Broszat, "A Controversy about the Historicization of National Socialism" in *New German Critique*, 44 (1988), 85–126. My discussion of Broszat does not imply that one may assimilate his views to those of Nolte or even Hillgruber. Nor do I address the problem of Broszat's own historical writing and research in his other publications. My analysis is ad-

dressed to certain aspects of Broszat's exchange with Friedlander in which the revisionist possibilities of a certain approach to social history are at issue. I nonetheless think it is misleading to go beyond the point of necessary distinction and to dissociate or detach the "theoretical and methodological problems" of "historicization" (*Historisierung*), as expounded by Broszat, from the "polemics" of the *Historikerstreit*, as Ian Kershaw attempts to do (*The Nazi Dictatorship: Problems and Perspectives of Interpretation*, 2nd ed., London: Edward Arnold, 1989, p. 150). This gesture "rescues" all of social history and *Alltagsgeschichte* at the risk of obscuring or downplaying the crucial issues of precisely how they are undertaken and the contextual functions they may be argued to serve.

13. It is noteworthy that Adorno asserts that "for countless people it wasn't all that bad under fascism. Terror's sharp edge was directed only against a few relatively well-defined groups." But he insists that a focus on this side of everyday life aggravates the "diminished faculty of memory" and furthers resistance to working through the problems posed by other aspects of the Nazi regime. See "What Does Coming to Terms with the Past Mean?" pp. 120–121.

14. The contribution of Christopher Browning to this collection (Chapter 1) attempts to investigate this complex interaction.

15. Oxford: Oxford University Press, 1987.

16. Hanover, 1985.

17. Here it may be useful to quote the most notorious passage of Himmler's 1943 Posen speech to members of the SS: "'The Jewish people must be exterminated,' say all party comrades, 'obviously, our party programme contains exclusion of the Jews, extermination, and we'll do it.' And then they all come, those honest eighty million Germans, and each and every one has his one decent Jew. Obviously, the other Jews are all swine, but this one is first class. Of all who talk like this not a single one has looked on, has endured it. Most of you, in contrast, well know what it means when a hundred corpses lie there together, five hundred, a thousand. To have endured *this* and—apart from a few exceptions of human weakness—to have remained decent, this is what has made us hard. This is a glorious page in our history which has never been written and will never be written." Quoted in Emil L. Fackenheim, "Concerning Authentic and Unauthentic Responses to the Holocaust" [first pub. 1975] in *The Nazi Holocaust,* ed. Michael R. Marrus, 1 (London: Meckler, 1989), p. 77. One may observe that Himmler's incredible conception of "decency" is itself made possible by an abusive notion of the division of life into discrete spheres.

18. On these problems, see James E. Young, "Memory and Monument," in *Bitburg in Moral and Political Perspective*, ed. Hartman, pp. 103–113.

19. There is a tragic sense in which Hitler, while losing the war, won the Holocaust—at least with respect to western and central European Jews. There are only 30,000 to 60,000 Jews in West Germany and 4,000 to 6,000 in East Germany. Although one should not underestimate the actual threat to remaining Jews, one of the more bizarre aspects of recent events in certain regions of Europe is antisemitism in the relative absence of real referents. One may perhaps call this phenomenon imaginary or fetishized antisemitism. It reveals in a heightened and almost clinical manner the role of the imaginary in antisemitism more generally—a role that can of course be attended by very real effects.

20. The problem of the work of mourning receives excellent treatment in Eric Santner's *Stranded Objects: Mourning, Memory, and Film in Postwar Germany* (Ithaca: Cornell University Press, 1990). Unfortunately, the book appeared too late for me to make fuller use of it in this chapter.

8. Historical Understanding and Counterrationality

1. Martin Broszat, Saul Friedlander, "Dokumentation: 'Ein Briefwechsel um die Historisierung des Nationalsozialismus,'" *Vierteljahreshefte für Zeitgeschichte*, 36 (1988), 339–372; English translation: "A Controversy about the Historization of National Socialism," *Yad Vashem Studies*, 19 (1988), 1–48.

2. George M. Kren, Leon Rappaport, *The Holocaust and the Crisis of Human Behavior* (New York: Holmes & Meier, 1980), p. 128.

3. Ibid., p. 12.

4. Johann Gustav Droysen, *Grundriss der Historik* (Munich: Oldenbourg, 1960; 1st ed., 1868), p. 9.

5. Wilhelm Dilthey, *Der Aufbau der geschichtlichen Welt in den Geisteswissenschaften* (1910/1927), 7: "Gesammelte Schriften" (Stuttgart: B. G. Teubner, 1958), p. 148; Gérard Gäfgen, *Theorie der wirtschaftlichen Entscheidung: Untersuchung zur Logik und ökonomischen Bedeutung des rationalen Handelns* (Tübingen: Mohr, Siebeck, 1963), p. 54.

6. Ibid., p. 278; see also Karl-Otto Apel, *Die Erklären-Verstehen-Kontroverse in tranzendentalpragmatischer Sicht* (Frankfurt am Main: Suhrkamp, 1979), p. 15.

7. Apel, *Die Erklären-Verstehen-Kontroverse*, p. 26.

8. William H. Dray, "Überlegungen zur historischen Erklärung von Handlungen," in *Methodologische Probleme der Sozialwissenschaften*, ed. Karl Acham (Darmstadt: Wissenschaftliche Buchgesellschaft, 1978), pp. 151–185; here, p. 158.

9. Apel, *Die Erklärung-Verstehen-Kontroverse*, p. 26.

10. Gäfgen, *Theorie der wirtschaftlichen Entscheidung*, p. 24.

11. On the particularistic experiential context of methodological approaches to National Socialism, see my essay "Historical Experience and Cognition: Perspectives on National Socialism," *History and Memory*, 2, no. 1 (1990), 84–110.

12. Norbert Elias, "Der Zusammenbruch der Zivilisation," in *Studien über die Deutschen* (Frankfurt am Main: Suhrkamp, 1989), pp. 391–516; here, p. 397.

13. Hannah Arendt, "Die vollendete Sinnlosigkeit," in *Nach Auschwitz* (Berlin: Triamat, 1989), p. 29.

14. Ibid., p. 11. In the English version of the article, "Social Science Techniques and the Study of Concentration Camps" (*Jewish Social Studies*, 12 [1950], 49–64), the term is simply *rational* rather than the more exact equivalent of the German *zweckrational*.

15. George L. S. Shackle, "Time and Thought," *British Journal for the Philosophy of Science*, 9 (1959), 290.

16. Isaiah Trunk, *Judenrat: The Jewish Councils in Eastern Europe under Nazi Occupation* (New York: Basic Books, 1977 [1972]).

17. Isaiah Trunk, "The Judenrat and Jewish Responses (Discussion)," in *The Holocaust as Historical Experience*, ed. Yehuda Bauer and Nathan Rotenstreich (London: Holmes & Meier, 1981), pp. 223–271; here, p. 268.

18. Yisrael Gutman, "The Concept of Labor in Judenrat Policy," in *Patterns of Jewish Leadership in Nazi Europe 1933/45.* Proceedings of the Third Yad Vashem International Historical Conference, Jerusalem, April 4–7, 1977, ed. Yisrael Gutman and Cynthia J. Haft (Jerusalem: Yad Vashem, 1979), pp. 151–180.

19. Ibid., p. 156.

20. See Arnold Gehlen, "Probleme einer soziologischen Handlungslehre," in *Soziologie und Leben: Die soziologische Dimension der Fachwissenschaften*, ed. Frank Altheim et al. (Tübingen, 1952), pp. 28–62; here, p. 33.

21. F. H. Knight, *The Ethics of Competition and Other Essays* (1935; reprinted Salem, N.H.: Ayer, 1955), p. 74: "Efficiency is a value category."

22. Otto v. Zwiedineck-Südenhorst, "Der Begriff homo oeconomicus und sein Lehrwert," *Jahrbücher für Nationalökonomie und Statistik*, 140 (1934), 513–532; here, p. 521.

23. Karl Acham, "Über einige Rationalitätskonzeptionen in den Sozialwissenschaften," in *Rationalität: Philosophische Beiträge*, ed. Herbert Schnädelbach (Frankfurt am Main: Suhrkamp, 1984), pp. 32–69; here, p. 34. See also G. Hartfiel, *Wirtschaftliche und soziale Rationalität: Untersuchungen zum Menschenbild in Ökonomie und Soziologie* (Stuttgart: Enke, 1968).

24. "Economic rationality is at the same time a concrete and universal descriptive principle and a normative principle." See Paul Diesing, "The

Nature and Limitations of Economic Rationality," *Ethics*, 61 (1950/51), 12–26; here, p. 13. The author to go furthest is probably John Rawls in his *Theory of Justice* (Cambridge, Mass.: Harvard University Press, 1971), in which utility calculations serve as a basis for morality (p. 25). Gäfgen, *Theorie der wirtschaftlichen Entscheidung*, notes that modern decision theory has led to a resurrection of utilitarianism: "Economics then becomes a formal ethics, as in Bentham . . ." (p. 7).

25. Gäfgen, ibid., p. 89.

26. Raul Hilberg, "The Ghetto as a Form of Government: An Analysis of Isaiah Trunk's Judenrat," in *The Holocaust as Historical Experience*, ed. Bauer and Rotenstreich, pp. 155–171; here, p. 165.

27. Uriel Tal, "Discussion," ibid., p. 237.

28. Gunnar Myrdal, "Das Zweck-Mittel-Denken in der Nationalökonomie," *Zeitschrift für Nationalökonomie*, 4 (1933), 305–329; here, p. 310.

29. Trunk, *Judenrat*, p. 410.

30. On the opposite effect of rational bureaucratic behavior in the Nazi system, see Dieter Rebentisch, *Führerstaat und Verwaltung im Zweiten Weltkrieg* (Stuttgart: Steiner, 1989), pp. 543 ff.

9. History beyond the Pleasure Principle

1. Elie Wiesel, "I Fear What Lies beyond the Wall," *New York Times*, 17 November 1989, Op-Ed. For a series of German responses to Wiesel's remarks, see *Die Zeit*, 22 December 1989, p. 12.

2. Even before 1938, 9 November was, of course, already overdetermined by historical events in Germany: 9 November 1918 was the date of the official beginning of the Weimar Republic; 9 November 1923 was the date of Hitler's failed *Putsch* (the *Kristallnacht* pogroms were linked to Nazi commemorations of the latter event).

3. The place of traumatic dates in the historical imagination and the textual and poetical procedures by which their inscription is facilitated or blocked are among the central themes of Paul Celan's Büchner Prize address, "Der Meridian." There Celan wonders, thinking no doubt of the date of the Wannsee Conference, "Perhaps one might venture to say that every poem is inscribed with its 'January 20'? Perhaps what is new about poems written today is precisely this: that here more than ever the effort is made to remain mindful of such dates?" *Ausgewählte Gedichte: Zwei Reden* (Frankfurt am Main: Suhrkamp, 1968), p. 142.

4. In this context I am reminded of André Heller's final monologue in Hans-Jürgen Syberberg's *Our Hitler*, in which Heller, speaking to a puppet of Hitler, lists some of the things no longer available to libidinal investment in postwar Germany: "You took away our sunsets, sunsets by Caspar David Friedrich. You are to blame that we can no longer look at a field of

grain without thinking of you. You made old Germany kitschy with your simplifying works and peasant pictures. And you are to blame that we have lost the pride of restaurants [*Stolz der Gasthäuser*], that people are driven into fast-food places for fear they might still love their work and something other than money, the harmlessly harmful, the only thing you left them with, since you occupied everything else and corrupted it with your actions, everything, honor, loyalty, country life, hard work, movies, dignity, Fatherland, pride, faith . . . The words 'magic' and 'myth' and 'serving' and 'ruling,' 'Führer,' 'authority,' are ruined, are gone, exiled to eternal time." Hans-Jürgen Syberberg, *Hitler, A Film from Germany,* trans. Joachim Neugroschel (New York: Farrar, Straus and Giroux, 1982), p. 242.

5. Dominick LaCapra, "Representing the Holocaust: Reflections on the Historians' Debate," Chapter 7 in this volume.

6. Ibid.

7. Thus, for example, Saul Friedlander has stressed the fact that a majority of the participants in the *Historikerstreit* are members of the "HJ-Generation," that is, the generation that would have passed through the formative experience of the Hitler Youth. See the published correspondence between Friedlander and Martin Broszat, "Um die 'Historisierung des Nationalsozialismus,' " *Vierteljahrshefte für Zeitgeschichte* (April 1988), pp. 339–372; an English translation of the correspondence may be found in *New German Critique* 44 (Spring/Summer 1988), 85–126, esp. pp. 366–67. In this context Helmut Kohl's now infamous declaration of the "grace of late birth" may be seen as an attempt not simply to deny guilt for the crimes of Nazism, which is understandable, but also to disavow any transferential relations to these events and the responsibilities that such relations bring.

8. For a more thorough discussion of issues of mourning in postwar Germany, see Alexander and Margarete Mitscherlich, *The Inability to Mourn: Principles of Collective Behavior,* trans. Beverley R. Placzek (New York: Grove Press, 1975), and Eric L. Santner, *Stranded Objects: Mourning, Memory, and Film in Postwar Germany* (Ithaca: Cornell University Press, 1990).

9. This characterization of the *fort/da* game is, admittedly, something of a negative caricature of a primal scene of coming to terms with difference. Separation and the entrance into the order of language and culture can be and, perhaps, more often than not is a process accompanied by great joy and exuberance, meaning that in a "good enough" holding environment, to use Winnicott's phrase, the psychic risks and conflicts associated with early encounters with difference and non-attunement can be contained and transformed into positive achievements.

10. Samuel Hahnemann's *Organon der rationellen Heilkunde,* first published

in 1810, is still the cornerstone of homeopathic medical practice. We read there, for example: "It follows . . . that substances become remedies and are able to destroy disease only by arousing certain manifestations and symptoms, i.e. particular artificial disease conditions, which are capable of eliminating and destroying the symptoms that already exist, i.e. the natural disease being treated" (*Organon of Medicine,* trans. Jost Künzli, Alain Naude, Peter Pendleton, Los Angeles: J. P. Tarcher, 1982, p. 24). And further: The homeopathic therapy "uses in appropriate dosage against *the totality of symptoms* of a natural disease a medicine capable of producing, in the healthy, symptoms as similar as possible" (p. 70).

11. Sigmund Freud, *Beyond the Pleasure Principle,* in *The Standard Edition of the Complete Psychological Works,* ed. James Strachey (London: Hogarth Press, 1953–1974), XVIII, 32.

12. Sigmund Freud, "Mourning and Melancholia," in *Standard Edition,* XIV, 245. The most comprehensive study of the effects of massive trauma on individuals and communities is Robert Jay Lifton, *The Broken Connection: On Death and the Continuity of Life* (New York: Simon and Schuster, 1979). Regarding the relation of early childhood experiences of loss to later experiences of loss or trauma, Lifton notes: "The survivor is one who has come into contact with death in some bodily or psychic fashion and has remained alive . . . The death imprint consists of the radical intrusion of an image-feeling of threat or end to life. That intrusion may be sudden, as in war experience and various forms of accidents, or it may take shape more gradually over time. Of great importance is the degree of unacceptability of death contained in the image—of prematurity, grotesqueness, and absurdity. *To be experienced, the death imprint must call forth prior imagery either of actual death or of death equivalents. In that sense every death encounter is itself a reactivation of earlier 'survivals' "* (p. 169; my emphasis).

13. Ernst Nolte, "Vergangenheit die nicht vergehen will," *Frankfurter Allgemeine Zeitung,* 6 June 1986.

14. Andreas Hillgruber, *Zweierlei Untergang: Die Zerschlagung des Deutschen Reiches und das Ende des europäischen Judentums* (Berlin: Siedler, 1986).

15. Saul Friedlander, "Historical Writing and the Memory of the Holocaust," in *Writing and the Holocaust,* ed. Berel Lang (New York: Holmes and Meier, 1988), pp. 74–75.

16. Martin Broszat, "Plädoyer für eine Historisierung des Nationalsozialismus," *Merkur,* 39 (May 1985), 375.

17. See once more the published correspondence between Friedlander and Broszat, "Um die 'Historisierung des Nationalsozialismus.'" In his second letter, Friedlander refers to a remark of Jürgen Habermas that seems to

identify what I have been characterizing as the psychotic layer of these events: "Something took place [in Auschwitz] which up until that time no one had even thought might be possible. A deep stratum of solidarity between all that bears a human countenance was touched here . . . Auschwitz has altered the conditions for the continuity of historical life connections—not only in Germany" (Jürgen Habermas, *Eine Art Schadensabwicklung*, Frankfurt am Main: Suhrkamp, 1987, p. 163). As Christopher Browning's excellent essay (Chapter 1 in this volume) on the writing of perpetrator history indicates, empathy and even a certain degree of narrative pleasure can be useful for the task of retrieving important details of the experiential history of participants in the mass murder. But as the conclusion of Browning's paper suggests, even for the members of Reserve Police Battalion 101, the immediate subject of his study, there reached a point at which horror and revulsion ceased and the killing became acceptable. There, however, Browning's story ends. And there, perhaps, the sort of narrative representation Browning is interested in finds its limits, despite appeals to the "all too human." Empathy, in other words, was able to guide Browning's narrative project as long as a certain degree of moral and psychic resistance to the killing on the part of the perpetrators was still accessible to the historian. Where the residues of such resistance have been sufficiently repressed or eliminated, empathy would seem to find its limits.

18. The following remarks have been informed in part by a reading of feminist analyses of voyeurism and fetishism in narrative cinema. See, for example, Laura Mulvey's by now canonical essay, "Visual Pleasure and Narrative Cinema," in *Film Theory and Criticism: Introductory Readings*, ed. Gerald Mast and Marshall Cohen (New York: Oxford University Press, 1985), pp. 803–816.

19. For more comprehensive discussions of the film, see my *Stranded Objects* and Anton Kaes, *From Hitler to "Heimat": The Return of History as Film* (Cambridge, Mass.: Harvard University Press, 1989).

20. Edgar Reitz, *Liebe zum Kino: Utopien und Gedanken zum Autorenfilm, 1962–1983* (Cologne: Verlag Köln 78, 1984), p. 141.

21. For a critique of the use of narrative and visual pleasure in *Holocaust*, see Elie Wiesel's remarks on the film in the *New York Times*, 16 April 1978. For a discussion of the aesthetics and politics of empathy—issues central to the old *Expressionismus-Debatte*—in the context of the West German reception of *Holocaust*, see *New German Critique*, 19 (Winter 1980), as well as Kaes's *From Hitler to "Heimat."*

22. Reitz, *Liebe zum Kino*, p. 102.

23. Freud, *Beyond the Pleasure Principle*, pp. 29–30.

24. Lifton, *The Broken Connection*, p. 176.

25. The work of Michel Foucault has been particularly helpful in illuminating such complicities. As Adi Ophir has argued, very much in the spirit of Foucault, our ability to truly enact the mourning work for and integration of the "Final Solution" depends on our capacity to acknowledge and explain "those modes of discourse which expelled the Jews from the domain of humanity, the technologies of power activated to implement the ideological statements, and the erotica of power used to guarantee complete execution of the mission, until the last moment, until the final breath." Ophir's remarks on the mode of identity formation that played so crucial a role in the "successes" of German fascism are especially relevant in the present context: "First of all . . . reference to another which serves as the borderline, as the archetype of negation; a package of 'excluding' oppositions wrapped in the same fundamental distinction and drawn after it: superior-inferior, authentic-inauthentic, holy-profane, pure-impure, healthy-sick, living-dead; a systematic application of the conceptual borderline (Aryan–non-Aryan) over geographic space (and also historical time: before and after the Jewish pollution, before and after the German revolution); the revealed and concealed mechanisms for encouraging, distributing and imposing the 'excluding' modes of discourse, its internal organization and principles of the hierarch contained within it, the sterilizing of channels of debate and blocking of the possibilities of disagreement and deviance" (Adi Ophir, "On Sanctifying the Holocaust: An Anti-Theological Treatise," in *Tikkun*, 2 [1987], 63; 64–65).

26. In this regard see especially Klaus Theweleit, *Männerphantasien* (1977; Reinbek: Rowohlt, 1989), and Jessica Benjamin, *The Bonds of Love: Psychoanalysis, Feminism, and the Problem of Domination* (New York: Pantheon, 1988).

10. Habermas, Enlightenment, and Antisemitism

1. Jürgen Habermas, "Concerning the Public Use of History," *New German Critique*, 44 (1988), 45; first published in *Die Zeit*, 7 November 1986.
2. Walter Abish, *How German Is It?/Wie Deutsche Ist Es?* (New York: New Directions, 1980), p. 252.
3. Walter Benjamin, *Illuminations*, trans. Harry Zohn (New York: Schocken Books, 1978), p. 256.
4. Jürgen Habermas, *The New Conservatism*, ed. and trans. Shierry Weber Nicholsen (Cambridge, Mass.: MIT Press, 1989), pp. 252–253.
5. Ibid., p. 250.
6. Ibid., pp. 26–27.
7. Ibid., pp. 29–31.
8. Ibid., pp. 37–45.

9. Ibid., p. 44.

10. See Michael Burleigh, *Germany Turns Eastwards: A Study of "Ostforschung" in the Third Reich* (Cambridge: Cambridge University Press, 1988).

11. Jürgen Habermas, "A Kind of Settlement of Damages (Apologetic Tendencies)," *New German Critique* 44 (1988), 39; first published in *Die Zeit*, 11 July 1986.

12. Useful alternatives to Habermas' more straightforward belief in the German *Sonderweg* and in Germany's detachment from the West until 1945 can be found in *Bürgertum im 19.Jahrhundert: Deutschland im europäischen Vergleich*, ed. Jürgen Kocka, 3 vols. (Munich: DTV, 1988). That liberal, parliamentary government was weak in Germany by comparison to England, that the German bourgeoisie was far more authoritarian in its development than the French—none of this can be denied. But can Germany's pre-Nazi development—socially and culturally—really be as neatly detached from that of "the West" as Habermas wants his contemporary readers to believe? And how should one evaluate the motives behind such an argument?

13. Habermas, "A Kind of Settlement of Damages," pp. 27, 39.

14. Habermas, *The New Conservatism*, p. 251.

15. Frantz Fanon, *The Wretched of the Earth*, trans. Constance Farrington (New York: Grove Press, 1963), p. 43.

16. Arno Mayer, *Why Did the Heavens Not Darken?* (New York: Pantheon Books, 1988), pp. 16–17.

17. Ibid., p. 18.

18. See ibid., pp. 14, 15, 31.

19. Ibid., p. 17.

20. For a positivist critique, see Axel van den Berg, "Critical Theory: Is There Still Hope?" *American Journal of Sociology*, 86, no. 3 (1980), 449–478.

21. See Jürgen Habermas, "The Entwinement of Myth and Enlightenment: Re-Reading *Dialectic of Enlightenment*," *New German Critique*, 26 (1982), 13–30; *The Theory of Communicative Action*, trans. Thomas McCarthy (Boston: Beacon Press, 1984), I, 339–399; and *The Philosophical Discourse of Modernity*, trans. Frederick Lawrence (Cambridge, Mass.: MIT Press, 1987).

22. See, for example, Habermas, "The Entwinement of Myth and Enlightenment," pp. 28–29.

23. Theodor Adorno and Max Horkheimer, *Dialektik der Aufklärung, Gesammelte Schriften*, 3 (Frankfurt am Main: Suhrkamp, 1981), p. 13; see also *Dialectic of Enlightenment*, trans. John Cumming (New York: Continuum, 1972), p. xiii. Subsequent quotations from this work are my translations from the Suhrkamp edition.

24. Ibid., pp. 14–15.
25. Ibid., p. 20.
26. Ibid., p. 32.
27. Theodor Adorno, *Negative Dialectics*, trans. E. B. Ashton (New York: Continuum, 1983), p. 13.
28. See especially Adorno, *Negative Dialectics*, pp. 61–131; and Theodor Adorno, *The Jargon of Authenticity*, trans. Knut Tarnowski and Frederic Will (Evanston, Ill.: Northwestern University, 1973).
29. Habermas, *The New Conservatism*, p. 265.
30. Adorno and Horkheimer, *Dialektik der Aufklärung*, p. 17.
31. To summarize the Adorno-Horkheimer argument, Habermas in fact quotes from Horkheimer's *Eclipse of Reason*, not *Dialektik der Aufklärung*. See Habermas, *Philosophical Discourse of Modernity*, p. 219.
32. Adorno and Horkheimer, *Dialektik der Aufklärung*, p. 192.
33. Ibid., pp. 198–200, 231.
34. Ibid., p. 211.
35. Frantz Fanon, *Black Skin, White Masks*, trans. Charles Lam Markmann (New York: Grove Press, 1967), p. 129.
36. Edward Said, *Orientalism* (New York: Vintage, 1979), p. 150.
37. James Clifford, *The Predicament of Culture* (Cambridge, Mass.: Harvard University Press, 1988), p. 198n7.
38. Klaus Theweleit, *Male Fantasies*, 2 vols., trans. Erica Carter and Chris Turner (Minneapolis: University of Minnesota Press, 1989).

11. Between Image and Phrase

1. J. F. Lyotard, *Peregrinations: Law, Form, Event* (New York: Columbia University Press, 1988), p. 23.
2. These remarks are drawn from J. F. Lyotard's *The Differend*, trans. G. Van Den Abbeele (Minneapolis: University of Minnesota Press, 1988), p. 169.
3. Martin Broszat and Saul Friedlander, "A Controversy about the Historicization of National Socialism," *New German Critique*, 44 (Spring/Summer 1988), 124.
4. Jürgen Habermas, *The New Conservatism: Cultural Criticism and the Historians' Debate*, ed. and trans. Shierry Nicholsen (Cambridge, Mass.: MIT Press, 1989), pp. 229–230.
5. As Derrida remarks in "White Mythology," the semantic effect of Habermas' phrase "burned into our national history" supposes *the acceptable repression* of the metaphorical sense of that "landing ramp." One is dealing with significations where "language is to be filled, achieved, actual-

ized, to the point of erasing itself, without any possible play, before the (thought) thing which is properly manifested in the truth."

6. Habermas, *The New Conservatism*, p. 252.
7. Ibid.
8. Ibid., p. 233.
9. Peter Sloterdijk, "Cynicism—The Twilight of False Consciousness," *New German Critique* (Fall 1984), 191.
10. Habermas, *The New Conservatism*, p. 235.
11. See the remarks in Habermas' "Modernity—An Incomplete Project" in *The Anti-Aesthetic,* ed. H. Foster (Port Townsend: Bay Press, 1983), p. 11.
12. See G. Deleuze, *Nietzsche and Philosophy* (New York: Columbia University Press, 1983), p. 73.
13. Habermas, *The New Conservatism*, p. 235.
14. See the remarks by J. Habermas, *Communication and the Evolution of Society* (Boston: Beacon Press, 1979), p. 166, and *Theory of Communicative Action* (Boston: Beacon Press, 1984), pp. 307–308.
15. Habermas, *The New Conservatism*, p. 236.
16. Ibid., p. 237.
17. Ibid., pp. 43, 69.
18. Ibid., p. 193.
19. Ibid., p. 54.
20. Ibid., pp. 58–59.
21. See Julia Kristeva, *La révolution du langage poétique* (Paris: Seuil, 1974), "Prolegomenon."
22. Habermas, *The New Conservatism*, p. 62.
23. Ibid., p. 225.
24. Ibid., pp. 64, 69.
25. These remarks are based upon some suggestions by Deleuze and Guattari from their *Thousand Plateaus* (Minnesota: University of Minnesota Press, 1987), pp. 229–232.
26. G. Bennington and R. Young, "Introduction: Posing the Question," in *Post-Structuralism and the Question of History,* ed. D. Attridge, G. Bennington, and R. Young (Cambridge: Cambridge University Press, 1987), p. 9.
27. J. Habermas, *The Theory of Communicative Action*, trans. T. McCarthy (Boston: Beacon Press, 1984), I, 136.
28. J. F. Lyotard, "The Sublime and the Avant-Garde," *Artforum* (April 1984), 37. One might compare this sense of the sublime with Deleuze and Guattari's notion of a "line of flight," in particular the latter's statements that such lines are "deterritorializing," that they are becomings which can both "cross the wall" in "getting out of the black holes" and also be the

potential "microfascism" of "turning to destruction, abolition pure and simple, the passion of abolition." Deleuze and Guattari, *A Thousand Plateaus*, pp. 229ff.

29. An example of this formulation is R. Krauss's rewriting art history according to an uncritical reception of Lacanian psychoanalysis. In asserting that the historicism of Ernst Gombrich relied on the optical and geometral model of an "essentially mimetic account of art's ambitions, of the artist's enduring struggle to replicate for others the optically registered panorama of what he sees," Krauss invokes the Lacanian "counterschema" of modern painting's being about the metaphysical "desiring subject [who] has a horror of seriality, of replication, of substitution, of the copy." It is as if one goes from the smoothing/integration of the sublime in Gombrich to the equally absorptive "negative" of the "seriality of the object," a replacement which does away with painting as an object's capacity to elicit in a viewer an effect which is not "historical." In other words, the "is it happening?" is crushed by the elimination of what Lyotard calls the possible "discrepancy between thought and the real world." See R. Krauss, "The Future of an Illusion," in *The Future of Literary Theory*, ed. R. Cohen (New York: Routledge and Kegan Paul, 1989), p. 288; and Lyotard, "The Sublime and the Avant-Garde," p. 38.

30. Lyotard, "The Sublime and the Avant-Garde," p. 40.

31. See J. F. Lyotard, "Presenting the Unpresentable: The Sublime," *Artforum* (April 1982), 67.

32. J. F. Lyotard, *Des dispositifs pulsionnels* (Paris: Union Generale, 10–18, 1973), p. 88.

33. For a brilliant analysis of this concept, see the essay cited earlier by Charles Levin.

34. Lyotard, *The Differend*, p. 13.

35. Ibid., p. xii. See, in this context, the apocalyptic scenario of Baudrillard, particularly the idea that this nonexistence of affirmative or positive cultural universals has been inverted to the benefit of the negative: "We are in a state of excess . . . which incessantly develops without being measured against its own objectives . . . impacts multiplying as the causes disintegrate." Jean Baudrillard, "The Anorexic Ruins," in *Looking Back on the End of the World* (New York: Semiotexte, 1989), p. 28.

36. Lyotard, *The Differend*, p. 89.

37. Ibid., p. 97; Habermas, *The New Conservatism*, p. 193.

38. Lyotard, *The Differend*, p. 98.

39. Karl Bohrer, "The Three Cultures," in *Observations on "The Spiritual Situation of the Age*," ed. Jürgen Habermas (Cambridge, Mass.: MIT Press, 1985), p. 154.

40. Lyotard, *The Differend*, p. 100.

41. Ibid., p. 101.
42. J. P. Faye's *Langages totalitaires* (Paris: Hermann, 1972) is exemplary on this line of thought.
43. J. F. Lyotard, *Driftworks* (New York: Semiotexte, 1984), p. 36.
44. Lyotard, *The Differend*, p. 101.
45. Ibid.
46. Such judgments continue the practice of inoculation, as Barthes persuasively argued in *Mythologies*, which here amounts to evading what is not reducible to law.

12. Science, Modernity, and the "Final Solution"

Acknowledgments: My thanks to Joel Braslow, Arthur Caplan, Sande Cohen, Saul Friedlander, Wulf Kansteiner, Michael Kater, Tom Laqueur, Kristie Macrakis, Benno Müller-Hill, Robert Proctor, Randy Starn, and Norton Wise for having read and criticized versions of this paper. Special thanks to Nancy Salzer for the many discussions that helped the writing of this piece all along.

1. On the possible reasons for this gap see Michael K. Kater, "The Burden of the Past: Problems of a Modern Historiography of Physicians and Medicine in Nazi Germany," *German Studies Review*, 10 (1987), 31–56; Robert N. Proctor, *Racial Hygiene* (Cambridge, Mass.: Harvard University Press, 1989), pp. 309–310; Benno Müller-Hill, *Murderous Science* (Oxford: Oxford University Press, 1988), p. 98. For a review of recent German literature on the topic see Thomas W. Maretzki, "The Documentation of Nazi Medicine by German Medical Sociologists: A Review Article," *Social Sciences and Medicine*, 29 (1989), 1319–32. On the conference on the use of data from Nazi hypothermia experiments, see Isabel Wilkerson, "Nazi Scientists and Ethics of Today," *New York Times*, Sunday, 21 May 1989, p. 17. The proceedings of the conference will appear as *Monstrous Medicine*, a volume edited by Arthur Caplan for Oxford University Press.

2. Robert K. Merton, "Science in the Social Order," *Philosophy of Science*, 5 (1938), reprinted in *The Sociology of Science: Theoretical and Empirical Investigations* (Chicago: University of Chicago Press, 1973), pp. 254–266. The relationship between science and democratic order and values in Merton's work is at the center of David Hollinger's "The Defense of Democracy and Robert K. Merton's Formulation of the Scientific Ethos," *Knowledge and Society*, 4 (1983), 1–15. On the same topic, see also Everett Mendelsohn, "Robert K. Merton: The Celebration and Defense of Science," *Science in Context*, 3 (1989), 282–291.

3. J. D. Bernal, "Science and Fascism," in *Social Function of Science* (Cambridge, Mass.: MIT Press, 1964), pp. 210–221; Joseph Needham, *The Nazi Attack on International Science* (Cambridge, 1941). Slightly more skeptical views on the relationship between democracy and science are presented by Leo Alexander, "Medical Science under Dictatorship," *New England Journal of Medicine*, 241 (1949), 39–47. See also Proctor, *Racial Hygiene*, pp. 3–6, 338–339, and his "Nazi Biomedical Technologies," in *Lifeworld and Technology*, ed. Timothy Casey and Lester Embree (Washington, D.C.: University Press of America, 1989), pp. 17–19.

4. Bernal, "Science and Fascism," pp. 212–213.

5. A perceptive critique of this view is presented in Peter Weingart, "Science Abused?—Challenging a Legend," paper presented to the Bar-Hillel Colloquium for the History, Philosophy, and Sociology of Science, Tel Aviv, 5 March 1990.

6. Alan D. Beyerchen, *Scientists under Hitler* (New Haven: Yale University Press, 1977). More complex views on the interaction between the physicists and the Nazis are presented in John L. Heilbron, *The Dilemmas of an Upright Man* (Berkeley: University of California Press, 1986), and in Mark Walker, *German National Socialism and the Quest for Nuclear Power, 1939–1949* (Cambridge: Cambridge University Press, 1989).

7. Michael H. Kater, *Doctors under Hitler* (Chapel Hill: University of North Carolina Press, 1989), p. 240.

8. Kater, "The Burden of the Past," pp. 32–33.

9. Kater, *Doctors under Hitler*, pp. 222–240.

10. Kater's review of Müller-Hill, *Murderous Science*, in *Isis*, 80 (1989), 722–723.

11. Müller-Hill, *Murderous Science*, p. 3.

12. Ibid.

13. A homologous strategy can be detected also in a later article by Müller-Hill, "Genetics after Auschwitz," *Holocaust and Genocide Studies*, 2 (1987), 3–20. On p. 5, he describes Eugene Fisher—who was elected president of the International Genetics Congress in 1928—as "transgressing from science into politics."

14. Müller-Hill, "Genetics after Auschwitz," p. 11. Actually, he questions the scientific legitimacy of psychiatry to the point of posing the question: "Is the psychiatric view of mankind possibly a view permeated and obscured by destructive drives?", "Genetics after Auschwitz," p. 12.

15. Müller-Hill, *Murderous Science*, pp. 50, 75.

16. For instance, Müller-Hill links the psychiatrists' success in getting their (in his eyes quite illegitimate) profession recognized as an academic discipline in 1941 to the previous "success" of the euthanasia program. Müller-Hill, "Genetics after Auschwitz," p. 12.

17. Ibid., p. 13.

18. "In much of the scientific output of Weimar biologists, as well as in their social perceptions, genetics was indistinguishable from scientific eugenics. Any demarcation that was to be made was not between genetics and eugenics, but among the different factions of eugenicists." Paul Weindling, "Weimar Eugenics: The Kaiser Wilhelm Institute for Anthropology, Human Heredity and Eugenics in Social Context," *Annals of Science,* 42 (1985), 307.

19. Weindling, "Weimar Eugenics," pp. 304–311. I am referring to Weindling's evidence, not to his argument, which in fact tries to argue that there was a discontinuity between Weimar and Nazi eugenics and that Weimar eugenics should not be seen as a cause of the Final Solution.

20. Robert Jay Lifton, *The Nazi Doctors* (New York: Basic Books, 1986).

21. Lifton re-presents this basic thesis unchanged in *The Genocidal Mentality* (New York: Basic Books, 1990), a book coauthored with Eric Markusen, which proposes a comparative analysis of Nazi and nuclear Holocaust mentalities. See, in particular, pp. 103–106, 161–166.

22. Lifton, *Nazi Doctors,* p. 11.

23. Ibid., p. 345.

24. "At the heart [of Lifton's work] is the transformation of the physician—of the medical enterprise itself—from healer to killer" (ibid., p. 5). The concern for the institutional and psychological dynamics that bring this inversion about are also analyzed in Lifton's *Genocidal Mentality,* esp. pp. 98–191.

25. Lifton, *Nazi Doctors,* pp. 356–359.

26. Bettelheim in Miklos Nyiszli, *Auschwitz: A Doctor's Eyewitness Account* (New York: Fell, 1960), p. xvi.

27. The differences between Bettelheim's and Lifton's views on Nazi science are spelled out in Bettelheim's review of *The Nazi Doctors,* "Their Specialty was Murder," *New York Times Review of Books,* 15 October 1986, p. 62.

28. *Hippocratic Writings,* ed. Geoffrey E. R. Lloyd (Harmondsworth, Middlesex: Penguin, 1978), p. 20.

29. For examples of this problem in contemporary medical research, see Henry K. Beecher, "Ethics and Clinical Research," *New England Journal of Medicine,* 274 (1966), 1354–60.

30. Alexander Mitscherlich and Fred Mielke, *The Death Doctors* (London: Elek, 1962), pp. 322–330. Some of this literature is reproduced in *Nuremberg Military Tribunals, Trials of War Criminals before the Nuremberg Military Tribunals under Control Council Law No. 10* (Washington, D.C.: U.S. Government Printing Office, n.d.) (hereafter referred to as *NT*), II, 95–110.

31. Mitscherlich and Mielke, *The Death Doctors,* pp. 326–327. The cases most frequently cited by the defense were those of eight hundred inmates

of the Illinois State Penitentiary, the New Jersey State Reformatory, and a Georgia penitentiary used as "voluntary" experimental subjects in research programs on malaria (one of them directed by the University of Chicago); and the study on pellagra conducted in 1915 by Dr. Goldberger on twelve "condemned volunteers" of a Mississippi jail (Mitscherlich and Mielke, *The Death Doctors*, pp. 41–47, 346–347; *NT*, II, 95). Beecher's "Ethics and Clinical Research" updates this scenario by presenting a survey of twenty-two recent medical case studies published in American academic journals and based on unethically conducted research.

32. Proctor, *Racial Hygiene*, pp. 3–5, 34–35, 38–39, 284.

33. Ibid., pp. 30, 38, 45, 47, 297.

34. On this process, see also Sheila Faith Weiss, "The Race Hygiene Movement in Germany," *Osiris*, second series, 3 (1987), 193–236.

35. Proctor, *Racial Hygiene*, pp. 292–293.

36. The terms *democracy* and *democratic* are so connoted that some qualification is probably needed in order not to reproduce some of the many mythologies attached to them. I use these terms in a quite narrow sense: to indicate access to arenas where science and policies about science are negotiated. I am not suggesting that a scientific community in which all social constituencies were democratically represented would develop a "rational dialogue" by which "consensus" about what "good" science is and about how it could be produced and used could be established. I am simply suggesting that failure to establish this basic level of access would be likely to lead to dangerous scenarios.

37. Proctor, *Racial Hygiene*, pp. 62–63.

38. Pierre Bourdieu, *Choses dites* (Paris: Minuit, 1987), p. 32.

39. Jack Goody, *The Domesticization of the Savage Mind* (Cambridge: Cambridge University Press, 1977).

40. This is a view of history of science (and of history) which admits that, eventually, the present is the historian's only term of reference. However, this limitation does not imply that the present is either a "fact" or the "necessary" result of historical dynamics. The present (or any other historical scenario) is a problematic artifact—one that has to be interpreted in the process of interpreting the event that happens in it.

41. Ernst Nolte, "Between Myth and Revisionism? The Third Reich in the Perspective of the 1980s," in *Aspects of the Third Reich*, ed. H. W. Koch (London: Macmillan, 1985), pp. 17–38, esp. pp. 36–38.

42. On the problems of the use of analogy in interpreting the Final Solution, see Charles S. Maier, *The Unmasterable Past* (Cambridge, Mass.: Harvard University Press, 1988), pp. 66–99.

43. Jürgen Habermas, *The New Conservatism* (Cambridge, Mass.: MIT Press, 1989), esp. pp. 209–267.

44. On some of the possible links between the discourse of modernity and the Final Solution see Berel Lang, *Act and Idea in the Nazi Genocide* (Chicago: University of Chicago Press, 1990), pp. 165–206.
45. Muller-Hill's strategy is somewhat different from that of Kater and Lifton. Probably because of his being trained in and practicing a "hard" science like molecular biology rather than medicine (the type of science practiced or discussed by Lifton and Kater), Muller-Hill seems to assume that good, pure, "hard" science (like genetics) should not produce values at all.
46. On this debate, see Arthur Caplan, *Monstrous Medicine,* and Isabel Wilkerson, "Nazi Scientists and Ethics of Today," *New York Times,* Sunday, 21 May 1989, p. 17.
47. Nolte, "Between Myth and Revisionism?" pp. 34–36.
48. Ludwik Fleck, *Genesis and Development of a Scientific Fact* (Chicago: University of Chicago Press, 1979). Important similarities between Fleck's and Kuhn's work are acknowledged by Kuhn in the preface to *Structure.* On Fleck's life and publications, see Thomas Schnelle, "Microbiology and Philosophy of Science, Lwow, and the German Holocaust: Stations of a Life—Ludwik Fleck, 1896–1961," in *Cognition and Fact: Materials on Ludwik Fleck,* ed. Robert S. Cohen and Thomas Schnelle (Boston: Reidel, 1986), pp. 3–36.
49. Ludwik Fleck, "Problems of the Science of Science," translated and reprinted in Cohen and Schnelle, *Cognition and Fact,* pp. 113–127. Special thanks to Simon Schaffer for having mentioned, photocopied, and sent me this article.
50. *NT,* I, 508–631; Mitscherlich and Mielke, *The Death Doctors,* pp. 117–164; Eugene Kogon, *The Theory and Practice of Hell* (New York: Farrar, Straus, n.d.), pp. 143–161.
51. Fleck, "Problems of the Science of Science," pp. 118–120; Schnelle, "Microbiology and Philosophy of Science," pp. 26–27.
52. Fleck, "Problems of the Science of Science," pp. 120–121.
53. Ibid., pp. 121–127.
54. The term *discourse of racial hygiene* may seem problematic because historiography on the subject has indicated a range of discontinuities between early twentieth-century German eugenics and the racial hygiene endorsed by the Nazis. However, my concern here is not to evaluate the continuities and discontinuities at the level of the protagonists' statements about the social and human implications of their theories. Rather than looking at statements of intent of the scientists who developed these theories, I am interested in focusing on the conceptual structure of theories of racial hygiene—what Sheila Faith Weiss has called the "logic" of eugenics. Without claiming that there is something intrinsically "evil" about biological theories about race and disease, I want to stress that there was

(and is) something about their conceptual structure that allowed for the interpretation and application of these theories in ways that may have been very different from those of the initial developers. On German eugenics see Sheila Faith Weiss, "The Race Hygiene Movement in Germany"; Peter Weingart, "German Eugenics between Science and Politics," *Osiris*, 5 (1989), 260–282; and Paul Weindling, *Health, Race and German Politics between National Unification and Nazism, 1870–1945* (Cambridge: Cambridge University Press, 1989). The development of eugenics in England and the United States is masterfully traced in Daniel J. Kevles, *In the Name of Eugenics* (New York: Knopf, 1985).

55. Adi Ophir, "On Sanctifying the Holocaust: An Anti-Theological Treatise," *Tikkun*, 2, no. 1 (1987) 64.

56. Ibid., p. 65.

57. *NT*, I, 142–143.

58. Ibid., p. 143.

59. Mitscherlich and Mielke, *The Death Doctors*, pp. 328–329.

60. Nyiszli, *Auschwitz*, p. 31.

61. Ibid., p. 56. Related considerations can be found also at pp. 101–106.

62. For a survey of Nyiszli's conflicting views on Nazi science and on Mengele see Nyiszli, *Auschwitz*, pp. 30–31, 33, 40, 56, 61, 63, 97, 101–102, 104, 109, 171, 181, 221.

63. "I had the bodies of a pair of fifteen-year-old twins before me on the dissection table. I began a parallel and comparative dissection of the two bodies. Nothing particularly noteworthy about the heads. The next phase was the removal of the sternum. Here an extremely interesting phenomenon appeared: a persistent thymus, that is, a thymus gland that continued to subsist . . . The discovery of the thymus gland in the twin brothers was of considerable interest." After having made more findings in the continuation of the dissection, Nyiszli reports, "I committed these curious observations to paper, in a much more precise and scientific manner than I have employed to describe them here, for my dissection report. Later, I spent a long afternoon in deep discussion with Dr. Mengele, trying to clear up a certain number of doubtful points." Nyiszli, *Auschwitz*, pp. 136–137. Nyiszli's finding another "extremely interesting collection of anomalies" is reported at p. 64. Similarly, Mengele's captive radiologist, Dr. Abraham, also referred to his "genuine passion for medical questions." Lifton, *Nazi Doctors*, p. 366.

64. Lifton, *Nazi Doctors*, p. 357.

65. Ibid., p. 365.

66. Besides the evidence cited by Lifton, see Gisella Perl, *I Was a Doctor in Auschwitz* (New York: Arno, 1979), and Olga Lengyel, *Five Chimneys: The Story of Auschwitz* (Chicago: Ziff-Davis, 1947).

67. I do not mean to say that no Nazi scientist was sloppy, incompetent, or

fraudulent. For instance, a recent article by Robert Berger has indicated that Rascher—the young doctor who directed the hypothermia and low-pressure experiments at Dachau—was far from being a conscientious scientist. Robert L. Berger, "Nazi Science—The Dachau Hypothermia Experiments," *New England Journal of Medicine*, 322, no. 20 (1990), 1435–40. This type of judgment does not erase the fact that—despite his sloppy methodology—Rascher developed methods of rescue based on these experiments that, when discovered by the American troops in Germany, were immediately adopted as the treatment for use by all American Air-Sea Rescue Services still fighting in the Pacific (*NT*, II, 66). In short, science does not always need to be canonically produced to be effective. Although Berger's article is well researched and argued, it indicates a somewhat "exorcistic" agenda, that is, an attempt to show that the hypothermia experiments were "bad science" and that therefore there is no need to engage in complex and disturbing debates about the ethical problems connected to the use of these data (p. 1435). The limitations of Berger's "scientific fix" to a debate about ethics are spelled out in an editorial in the same issue of the *New England Journal of Medicine* (Marcia Angell, "The Nazi Hypothermia Experiments and Unethical Research Today," pp. 1462–64).

68. Lifton, *Nazi Doctors*, p. 357.
69. In connection with this issue, I find Primo Levi's discussion of the "gray zone" particularly useful. In fact, it shows that the analysis of the complex and disturbing dynamics between victims and culprits—dynamics that contributed in important ways to the maintenance of the camp system—does not subvert in any way the fundamental distinction between victims and culprits. Primo Levi, *The Drowned and the Saved* (New York: Vintage, 1989), pp. 36–69. I think one could adopt Levi's approach to study victims who, like Nyiszli or Abraham, became reluctantly involved in camp science or—as in the case of Teresa W.—were sympathetic to some of the anthropological theories that were actually implicated in the Final Solution. Also, a study conducted along these lines of Nazi doctors such as Rose or Ernst B., who were at some point reluctant participants in camp management or in experimentations on prisoners, may uncover important aspects of the role of science in the Final Solution without blurring the fundamental distinction between culprits and victims. (On Rose see Mitscherlich and Mielke, *The Death Doctors*, pp. 124–146; on Ernst B. see Lifton, *Nazi Doctors*, pp. 303–336.)

13. Holocaust and the End of History

1. Jacques Derrida, "Of an Apocalyptic Tone Recently Adopted in Philosophy," *Oxford Literary Review*, 6, no. 2 (1984), 20ff.

2. Francis Fukuyama, "The End of History?" *National Interest,* Summer 1989, pp. 3–18; see also the responses to this article, ibid., pp. 19–35.

3. Theodor W. Adorno, *Negative Dialectics* (New York: Continuum, 1983), p. 367.

4. Jean-François Lyotard, *The Differend: Phrases in Dispute,* trans. Georges Van Den Abbeele (Minneapolis: University of Minnesota Press, 1988), p. 56. See also his "Discussion, or Phrasing 'after Auschwitz,'" reprinted in *The Lyotard Reader,* ed. Andrew Benjamin (Oxford: Basil Blackwell, 1989), pp. 360–392.

5. Ibid., pp. 56ff.

6. Maurice Blanchot, *The Writing of the Disaster,* trans. Ann Smock (Lincoln: University of Nebraska Press, 1986). See also George Steiner, "The Long Life of Metaphor: An Approach to 'the Shoah,'" *Encounter* 68 (February 1987), 55: "It may be that the Auschwitz-universe, for it was that, precisely marks that realm of potential—now realized—human bestiality, or rather, abandonment of the human and regression to bestiality, which both precedes language, as it does in the animal, and comes after language as it does in death. Auschwitz would signify on a collective, historical scale the death of man as a rational, 'forward-dreaming' speech-organism . . . The languages we are now speaking on this polluted and suicidal planet are 'post-human.'"

7. See Saul Friedlander, "The 'Final Solution': On the Unease in Historical Interpretation," *History and Memory* 1, no. 2 (1989), 61–73; Arno Mayer, *Why Did the Heavens Not Darken? The "Final Solution" in History* (New York: Pantheon, 1989), p. xv; Istvan Deak, "The Incomprehensible Holocaust," *New York Review of Books,* 28 September 1989; Judith Miller, *One, by One, by One* (New York: Simon and Schuster, 1990), pp. 9–12.

8. Friedlander, p. 66.

9. On the German reception of *Holocaust,* see Anton Kaes, *From 'Hitler' to 'Heimat': The Return of History as Film* (Cambridge, Mass.: Harvard University Press, 1989).

10. For an overview and evaluation of films dealing with the Holocaust, see Ilan Avisar, *Screening the Holocaust: Cinema's Images of the Unimaginable* (Bloomington: Indiana University Press, 1988); Judith E. Doneson, *The Holocaust in American Film* (Philadelphia: Jewish Publication Society, 1987); Annette Insdorf, *Indelible Shadows: Film and the Holocaust* (New York: Random House, 1983).

11. Lyotard, *The Differend,* p. 57.

12. Susan Sontag, "The Eye of the Storm," *New York Review of Books,* 21 February 1980.

13. See Jean-Pierre Faye, "Le troisième Faust," *Le Monde,* 22 July 1987.

14. Philippe Lacoue-Labarthe and Jean-Luc Nancy, "The Nazi Myth," *Critical Inquiry,* 16 (Winter 1990), 291–312; see also Lacoue-Labarthe, "The

Aesthetization of Politics," in *Heidegger, Art and Politics: The Fiction of the Political*, trans. Chris Turner (Oxford: Basil Blackwell, 1990), pp. 61–76.

15. The page numbers in parentheses refer to the filmscript. Hans-Jürgen Syberberg, *Hitler, a Film from Germany*, trans. Joachim Neugroschel (New York: Farrar, Straus and Giroux, 1982). A more detailed analysis of Syberberg's cinema can be found in Kaes, *From Hitler to Heimat*, pp. 37–72; Saul Friedlander, *Reflections of Nazism: An Essay on Kitsch and Death* (New York: Harper & Row, 1984); Eric L. Santner, *Stranded Objects: Mourning, Memory, and Film in Postwar Germany* (Ithaca: Cornell University Press, 1990), pp. 103–149.

16. Christian Zimmer, "Our Hitler," *Telos*, 42 (Winter 1979–80), 150.

17. Quoted in Eva-Suzanne Bayer, "Hitler in uns," *Stuttgarter Zeitung*, 15 April 1977.

18. Ibid.

19. Hans Thies Lehmann, "Robert Wilson, Szenograph," *Merkur*, 437 (July 1985), 554.

20. On the politics of aesthetics and the aesthetics of politics under fascism, see Lacoue-Labarthe, *Heidegger, Art and Politics*, pp. 61–76.

21. Michel Foucault, "Les quatre cavaliers de l'Apocalypse et les vermisseaux quotidiens: Entretien avec Michel Foucault," *Cahiers du cinéma* (February 1980), 95ff. Hannah Arendt's account of the Eichmann trial, *Eichmann in Jerusalem* (New York: Viking, 1963) carries the subtitle "A Report on the Banality of Evil." See also Nathan Rotenstreich, "Can Evil Be Banal?" *Philosophical Forum*, 16, nos. 1–2 (1984–85), 50–62.

22. There are many definitions of postmodernism today. I follow here the account of Linda Hutcheon, *A Poetics of Postmodernism: History, Theory, Fiction* (New York: Routledge, 1988); see also Wolfgang Welsch, *Unsere postmoderne Moderne* (Weinheim: VCH, Acta Humaniora, 1988); Hannes Böhringer, "Die Ruine in Posthistoire," *Merkur*, 406 (April 1982): 367–375. See also Christopher Sharrett's interview with Hans-Jürgen Syberberg, "Sustaining Romanticism in a Postmodernist Cinema," *Cineaste*, 15 (1987) no. 3, 18–20. The interview was held after the New York premiere of Syberberg's new film, *Die Nacht*, a six-hour performance piece with one actress, Edith Clever, dealing with the end of European culture. This film carries on and radicalizes the elegiac tone and antimodernist ideology of his Hitler film.

23. Arnold Gehlen, "Einblicke," in *Gesamtausgabe*, vol. 7 (Frankfurt am Main: Klostermann, 1978), pp. 19, 140. Hendrik de Man, *Vermassung und Kulturverfall: Eine Diagnose unserer Zeit* (Berne: Francke, 1951), pp. 135–136.

24. Arnold Gehlen, Über kulturelle Kristallisation," in *Studien zur Anthropologie und Soziologie* (Darmstadt: Luchterhand, 1963), p. 323; reprinted

in *Wege aus der Moderne: Schlüsseltexte der Postmoderne-Diskussion,* ed. Wolfgang Welsch (Weinheim: VCH, Acta Humaniora, 1988), pp. 133–143. See also Peter Sloterdijk, "Nach der Geschichte," in *Wege aus der Moderne,* pp. 262–273; Lutz Niethammer, "Afterthoughts on Posthistoire," *History and Memory,* 1 (Spring/Summer 1989), 27–53; Niethammer, *Posthistoire: Ist die Geschichte zu Ende?* (Reinbek: Rowohlt, 1989). Gianni Vattimo begins his essay, "The End of (Hi)story," *Chicago Review* 35 (1987) no. 4, pp. 20–30, with the following sentence: "Probably, one of the most important points on which the descriptions of the postmodern condition agree—no matter how different they are from other points of view—is the consideration of postmodernity in terms of 'the end of history.'" See, further, Henry S. Kariel, "The Endgame of Postmodernism within the Momentum of Modernity," *Futures: The Journal of Forecasting, Planning and Policy,* 22 (January–February 1990), 91–99.

25. On the discourse of the apocalypse, see the essays in *Visions of Apocalypse: End or Rebirth?* ed. Saul Friedlander et al. (New York: Holmes & Meier, 1985). See also Ulrich Horstmann's disturbing desire to have all of mankind eradicated in his semi-literary essay *Das Untier: Konturen einer Philosophie der Menschenflucht* (Berlin: Medusa, 1983).

26. Hans-Jürgen Syberberg, *Die freudlose Gesellschaft* (Munich: Hanser, 1981), p. 83.

27. See the published filmscript, Claude Lanzmann, *Shoah: An Oral History of the Holocaust* (New York: Pantheon, 1985). See also Gertrud Koch, "The Aesthetic Transformation of the Image of the Unimaginable: Notes on Claude Lanzmann's *Shoah,*" *October,* 48 (Spring 1989): 15–24; Steven G. Kellman, "Cinema of/as Atrocity: *Shoah's* Guilty Conscience," *Gettysburg Review,* I (Winter 1988): 22–31; Timothy Garton Ash, "The Life of Death," *New York Review of Books,* 19 December 1985.

28. Claude Lanzmann, "From the Holocaust to the *Holocaust,*" *Telos,* 42 (Winter 1979–80), 143.

14. Whose Story Is It, Anyway?

Research for this paper was made possible by an NEH fellowship for the summer of 1989.

1. Alan Berger in *Shofar,* 5, no. 1 (1986), 56.

2. Saul Friedlander, "Roundtable Discussion," in *Writing and the Holocaust,* ed. Berel Lang (New York: Holmes and Meier, 1988), p. 288.

3. No diachrony is intended in this statement. The different paradigms, or "stories" as I call them here, coexist synchronically throughout the different areas of the Israeli cultural system.

4. U. Z. Greenberg, *Rehovot Hanahar: Sefer Ha'iliot Vehakoah* (Streets of

the River: The Book of Dirges and Power), 2nd ed. (Jerusalem: Schocken, 1954). For a description and analysis in English, see Alan Mintz, *Hurban: Responses to Catastrophe in Hebrew Literature* (New York: Columbia University Press, 1984), pp. 163–202. The subsequent development of the topic in Israeli poetry deserves a separate discussion. The present text is devoted to Israeli drama and fiction.

5. They are, however, so viewed in Israel, as evidenced by Ben-Ami Feingold's recent monograph *Hashoah Badrama Ha'ivrit* (*The Theme of the Holocaust in Hebrew Drama*) (Tel Aviv: Hakibbutz Hameuchad, 1989). The plays I refer to are Natan Shaham, *Heshbon Hadash* (*New Reckoning*, 1954); Leah Goldberg, *Malkat Ha'armon* (*The Lady of the Castle*, 1955); Ben-Zion Tomer, *Yaldei Hatzel* (*Children of the Shadow*, 1962); Yehuda Amichai, *Pa'amonim Verakavot* (*Bells and Trains*, 1962); Moshe Shamir, *Hayoresh* (*The Heir*, 1963); Aharon Megged, *Ha'onah Habo'eret* (*The Hot Season*, 1967).

6. Yael S. Feldman, "Deconstructing the Biblical Sources in Israeli Theater: *Yisurei Iyov* by Hanoch Levin," *AJS Review*, 12, no. 2 (1987), 251–277; and "'Identification-with-the-Aggressor' or the 'Victim Complex'?— Holocaust and Ideology in Israeli Theater: *Ghetto* by Joshua Sobol," *Modern Judaism*, 9, no. 2 (1989), 165–178.

7. I develop these ideas in my forthcoming *Freudianism and Its Discontents in Hebrew Literature*. For partial views of the material see my "Back to Vienna: Zionism on the Literary Couch," in *Vision Confronts Reality*, ed. David Sidorsky et al. (Rutherford, N.J.: Fairleigh Dickinson University Press, 1989), pp. 310–335; and "Feminism under Siege: The Vicarious Selves of Israeli Women Writers," *Prooftexts*, 10, no. 3 (1990), 493–514.

8. For other literary works in this vein see, in drama, Yossi Hadar's *Bibof* (1987) and, in fiction, Omer Bartov's *Takrit Gevool* (*Border Patrol*, 1988) and *Karev Yom* (*Surrogate Killers*, 1989).

9. Constraints of space do not allow a full discussion of this group of writers, most of whom began publishing around 1985. The biological and psychological parameters of the creative surge of this group (for instance, the aging of the parents who hitherto kept their reticence, and the maturing into parenthood of the "children" who are now able to better identify with their own parents) deserve a separate discussion. (I wish to thank writer Nava Semel and psychologist Eva Fogelman for generously sharing with me their experience and erudition [as well as publications] in the literature and psychology [respectively] of the second generation. They should not be held responsible for any of my conclusions, which I am not at all sure they share.)

10. See my "The 'Other Within' in Contemporary Israeli Fiction," *Middle East Review*, 22, no. 1 (1989), 47–53.

11. See on this point the debate aroused by Hayden White's metahistorical and historiographical arguments, throughout the present volume.

12. For pertinent statements see Saul Friedlander, *Reflections of Nazism* (New York: Harper and Row, 1984); *Writing and the Holocaust,* ed. Berel Lang (New York: Holmes and Meier, 1988); James E. Young, *Writing and Rewriting the Holocaust* (Bloomington: Indiana University Press, 1988).

13. Irving Howe, "Writing and the Holocaust," in Lang, *Writing and the Holocaust,* p. 186.

14. Gershon Shaked, "Afterword," in *Facing the Holocaust,* p. 287.

15. See Yosef Hayim Yerushalmi, *Zakhor: Jewish History and Jewish Memory* (Seattle: University of Washington Press, 1982); Sidra Dekoven Ezrahi, *By Words Alone: The Holocaust in Literature* (Chicago: University of Chicago Press, 1980); David Roskies, *Against the Apocalypse: Responses to Catastrophe in Modern Jewish Culture* (Cambridge, Mass.: Harvard University Press, 1984); Alan Mintz, *Hurban;* Young, *Writing and Rewriting.*

16. Cf. Hanna Yaoz, *Hashoah Basifroot Ha'ivrit (The Holocaust in Hebrew Literature)* (Tel Aviv: Eked, 1980), p. 61.

17. See for example Hanoch Bartov, *Pitz'ei Bagroot (The Brigade),* trans. David Segal (New York: Holt, Rinehart and Winston, 1968).

18. See especially Naomi Frankel's trilogy *Shaool Veyohanah (Saul and Johanna)* (Merhavia: Sifriyat Poalim, 1956–1967), and Yonat and Alexander Sened's two-volume work *Bein Hahayim Vehametim (Between the Dead and the Living)* (Tel Aviv: Hakibbutz Hameuchad, 1964).

19. See Yehuda Amichai, *Lo Me'achshav, Lo Mikan (Not of This Time, Not of This Place)* (Jerusalem: Schocken, 1963), and Dan Ben-Amotz, *Lizkor Velishkoah (To Remember and to Forget)* (Tel Aviv: Amikam, 1968). We will find no such catharsis in similar narratives that were written later by survivors themselves, for instance Itamar Yaoz-Kest, *Bahalon Habayit Hanosea' (At the Window of the Moving Home)* (Tel Aviv: Eked, 1970); Aharon Appelfeld, *Tor Hapela'ot (Age of Wonders),* trans. Dalya Bilu (Boston: David Godine, 1981); David Schutz, *Ha'esev Vehahol (The Grass and the Sand)* (Tel Aviv: Sifriyat Poalim, 1977).

20. Cf. Gershon Shaked, "We Are Merely Tired," *Gal Hadash Basifroot Ha'ivrit (A New Wave in Hebrew Fiction)* (Tel Aviv: Sifriyat Poalim, 1971), p. 164. The reference is to Appelfeld's early collections of short stories, few of which are familiar to the English reader: *'Ashan (Smoke)* (Tel Aviv: Markus, 1962); *Bagai' Haporeh (In the Fertile Valley)* (Jerusalem: Schocken, 1964); and *Kefor 'al Ha'aretz (Frost on the Land)* (Ramat Gan: Massada, 1965).

21. See Mintz, *Hurban,* p. 238.

22. See Howe, "Writing and the Holocaust," p. 194.

23. This work was published in English translation as two separate novellas, *Tzili: The Story of a Life* (1983) and *The Immortal Bartfus* (1989).

24. Aharon Appelfeld, *To the Land of the Cattails*, trans. Jeffrey M. Green (New York: Weidenfeld and Nicolson, 1986), p. 148.

25. Quoted in Yaoz, *The Holocaust*, p. 192.

26. See Shmuel Shneider's interview with Appelfeld in *Bitzaron*, 4, nos. 13–14 (Winter-Spring 1982), p. 11.

27. Appelfeld's love for the paradoxical and the absurd, as spelled out in his collection *Massot Begoof Rishon* (*Essays in First Person*) (Jerusalem: Zionist Library, 1979), has triggered a crop of paradox-hunting articles; most of them, however, follow his own cues without any attempt to penetrate his literary defenses. See, for example, Nurit Govrin, "To Express the Inexpressible: The Holocaust Literature of Aharon Appelfeld," *Remembering for the Future*, 2 (Oxford: Pergamon Press, 1988), 1580–94.

28. In some sense *Michvat Ha'or* (*Searing Light*) (Tel Aviv: Hakibbutz Hameuchad, 1980) is a sequel to *Tor Hapela'ot* (*The Age of Wonders*), which two years earlier constituted the author's first attempt at "fictional autobiography," an ostensibly first-person memoir of a childhood on the brink of catastrophe. Although in *Searing Light* the confessional voice alternates between first-person plural and first-person singular, it is not difficult to identify the "biographical" details that link the narrators of the two novellas; the latter, however, records the protagonist's *post*-catastrophe memoirs, highlighting the painful confrontation between a group of young refugees and the machinery of Zionist "baptism" in the land of Israel.

29. Appelfeld, *Searing Light*, p. 32 (my translation).

30. Cf. Gershon Shaked, "Transport to Palestine," *Gal 'Ahar Gal Basifroot Ha'ivrit* (*Wave after Wave in Hebrew Narrative Fiction*) (Jerusalem: Keter, 1985), pp. 28–29.

31. Sidra Ezrahi, "Revisioning the Past: The Changing Legacy of the Holocaust in Hebrew Literature," *Salmagundi* (Fall–Winter 1985–86), p. 256.

32. Sidra Ezrahi, "Aharon Appelfeld: The Search for a Language," *Studies in Contemporary Jewry*, 1 (1984), 366–380.

33. Appelfeld, *Essays*, pp. 21, 90, and passim.

34. Appelfeld's forthcoming novel will be the *first* to take place significantly before World War II. The change in setting (around the turn of the century) does not imply a change in theme and authorial position, however. The main character is a Bukovinian apostate, whom the author calls *Timyon*, namely "lost and forgotten" (a personal communication).

35. In her 1980 book Yaoz cites only six reviews of *Adam Ben Kelev* (Tel Aviv: Amikam, 1969), all of them in the literary supplements of the daily press. Later references include Mintz in *Hurban* (1984), Ezrahi in "Revisioning

the Past" (1985–86), and Shaked in the afterword to *Facing the Holocaust* (1985). For the English translation see *Adam Resurrected*, trans. Seymour Simckes (New York: Atheneum, 1971).

36. Terrence Des Pres, "Holocaust Laughter?" in *Writing and the Holocaust*, pp. 216–234.

37. David Grossman, *'Ayen 'Erech 'Ahavah* (*See Under: Love*), trans. Betsy Rosenberg (New York: Farrar, Straus & Giroux, 1989). Only two of the many reviews of the novel mention (although from different perspectives) the ties between Kaniuk and Grossman: Ortzion Bartana, "An Impressive but Limited Achievement," *Davar* (*Massa*), 14, no. 3 (1986), 22; and Stanley Nash, "The Novels by Y. Kaniuk, D. Grossman and Lanzmann's 'Shoah,'" *Bitzaron*, 9, nos. 35–36 (1987), 66–69. Their qualified praise is representative of the reception of the novel by the critical establishment, particularly in Israel. Curiously, it seems that Grossman had anticipated this reception, in the ironic characterization of the "national Hebrew critic," as discussed below.

38. Grossman, *See Under: Love*, p. 102.

39. Ibid.

40. Gershon Shaked, *'Ein Makom 'Aher* (*No Other Place: On Literature and Society*) (Tel Aviv: Hakibbutz Hameuchad, 1988), p. 113.

41. See his critique of Appelfeld's *Searing Light* in "Transport to Palestine," p. 31; and of Saul Friedlander's *When Memory Comes* in *No Other Place*, pp. 56–66.

15. Translating Paul Celan's "Todesfuge"

I am grateful to Adam Goldgeier, Johnny Payne, Claudio Spies, and especially to Mary Lowenthal Felstiner for their help on this text.

1. The poem (in German) appeared first in Paul Celan, *Der Sand aus den Urnen* (Vienna: A. Sexl, 1948); then in Celan, *Mohn und Gedächtnis* (Stuttgart: Deutsche Verlags Anstalt, 1952). It now appears in Celan, *Gesammelte Werke*, ed. Beda Allemann and Stefan Reichert with Rudolf Bücher (Frankfurt: Suhrkamp, 1983), I, 41. This five-volume edition is hereafter referred to as *GW*, and references to it in the text are given by volume and page number.

2. Wolfgang Butzlaff, "Zwei Bemühungen um ein Gedicht, Paul Celans *Todesfuge*" (with Peter Seidensticker), *Der Deutschunterricht*, 3 (1960), 46.

3. Israel Chalfen, *Paul Celan: Eine Biographie seiner Jugend* (Frankfurt: Insel, 1979) remains the only book-length biography; many articles and memoirs augment it. The only book-length critical study is Jerry Glenn,

Paul Celan (New York: Twayne, 1973). See also John Felstiner, "Paul Celan: The Strain of Jewishness," *Commentary* (April 1985), pp. 44–53, and
Felstiner, "Paul Celan's 'Todesfuge,'" *Holocaust and Genocide Studies*, 1,
no. 2 (1986), 249–264.

4. Mark Rosenthal, *Anselm Kiefer* (Philadelphia, 1987), p. 95; *New York
Times Magazine*, 16 October 1988, p. 49.

5. Theodor Adorno, "Kulturkritik und Gesellschaft," written in 1949, pub-
lished singly in 1951, collected in Adorno, *Prismen* (1955), reprinted in
Adorno, *Gesammelte Schriften*, vol. 10¹, ed. Rolf Tiedemann (Frankfurt:
Suhrkamp, 1974), 30.

6. Chalfen, *Paul Celan*, p. 148.

7. The word *fugue* derives from the Latin *fuga*, meaning "flight"; and in psychiatric terms, *fugue* denotes a pathological amnesiac condition. The verb
fugen in German means to "join," "groove," "fit," in carpentry.

8. Bruno Bettelheim, *Surviving and Other Essays* (New York: Knopf, 1979),
pp. 98–99.

9. See John Felstiner, "Paul Celan's 'Todesfuge,'" note 26, pp. 262–263.

10. See Barbara Wiedemann-Wolf, *Antschel Paul—Paul Celan: Studien zum
Frühwerk* (Tübingen: Niemeyer, 1985), pp. 79–87, and Chalfen, *Paul Celan*, p. 133.

11. Paul Celan, "Briefe an Alfred Margul-Sperber," *Neue Literatur*, 7 (1975),
55.

12. Paul Celan's letter of 21 March 1959 in *Deutsche Literatur heute: Eine
Ausstellung, 1968* (Kuratorium unteilbares Deutschland, 1970); letter of
19 May 1961 in Wiedemann-Wolf, *Antschel Paul* p. 85.

13. Jean Amery, *At the Mind's Limits: Contemplations by a Survivor on
Auschwitz and Its Realities*, trans. Sidney Rosenfeld and Stella P. Rosenfeld (Bloomington: Indiana University Press, 1980), p. x.

14. Primo Levi, *If Not Now, When?* trans. William Weaver (New York: Summit, 1985), p. 168; letter Levi to Felstiner, 14 June 1986.

15. Rolf Hochhuth, *The Deputy*, trans. Richard and Clara Winston (New
York: Grove, 1964), p. 223.

16. Roland Penrose, *Picasso: His Life and Work* (Berkeley: University of California Press, 1981), p. 333.

17. Celan's poem first appeared in a Roumanian translation by Petre Solomon
in *Contemporanul* 32 (2 May 1947). See also Solomon, "Paul Celans Bu-
karester Aufenthalt," *Zeitschrift für Kulturaustausch*, 3 (1982), 223.

18. Jewish Black Book Committee, *The Black Book: The Nazi Crime Against
the Jewish People* (New York, 1946), pp. 308–309.

19. Constantine Simonov, *The Lublin Extermination Camp* (Moscow: Foreign Languages Publishing House, 1944), pp. 14, 16.

20. Paul Celan, autobiographical note, in *Die Wandlung*, 4, no. 3 (1949), p. 284.

21. The only recording Celan made of "Todesfuge" is on "Lyrik der Zeit II" (Pfullingen: Neske, n.d.).

22. Friedrich Nietzsche, *Will to Power*, p. 55.

23. Celan, "Briefe," p. 57.

24. Hans Werner Richter, "Wie entstand und was war die Gruppe 47?" in *Hans Werner Richter und die Gruppe 47*, ed. Hans A. Neunzig (Munich: Nymphenburger, 1979), p. 112; Hans Weigel, *In Memoriam* (Vienna: Styria, 1979), p. 36; Reinhard Lettau, ed., *Die Gruppe 47* (Neuwied: Luchterhand, 1967), p. 76; Rolf Schroers, *Meine deutsche Frage* (Stuttgart: Deutsche Verlags Anstalt, 1979), p. 140; Friedhelm Kröll, *Die Gruppe 47* (Stuttgart: Metzler, 1977), p. 67.

25. Helmuth de Haas, in *Die neue literarische Welt* (10 July 1953), 12; rpt. in Dietlind Meinecke, *Über Paul Celan* (Frankfurt: Suhrkamp, 1970).

26. Egon Holthusen, "Fünf junge Lyriker," *Merkur*, 74 (1954), 385–390.

27. Jean Firges, "Sprache und Sein in der Dichtung Paul Celans," *Muttersprache*, 72 (1962), 266–267.

28. Theodor Adorno, "Engagement," in *Noten zur Literatur*, 2 (Frankfurt: Suhrkamp, 1965), 125–127.

29. Reinhard Baumgart, "Unmenschlichkeit beschrieben: Weltkrieg und Faschismus in der Literatur," *Merkur*, 202 (Jan. 1965), 43, 48–49.

30. Letter to Robert Neumann, in *34 x erste Liebe*, ed. Robert Neumann (Frankfurt: Bärmeier & Nikel, 1966), pp. 32–33; Celan, "Briefe," p. 55.

31. Hugo Huppert, *Sinnen und Trachten: Anmerkungen zur Poetologie* (Halle: Mitteldeutscher, 1973), pp. 31–32.

32. Hartmut Lück, "Die Komponisten und die Todesfuge: sieben Vertonungen des Gedichtes von Paul Celan," West German Radio broadcast of 4 February 1983.

33. At this commemorative event, a Bach Society chorus began by singing the first Yiddish Holocaust song, "Undzer Shtetl Brennt," by Mordechai Gebirtig. Then, after Ida Ehre recited "Todesfuge," Philipp Jenninger gave his ill-fated, would-be conciliatory speech on the "Final Solution," which resulted in his having to relinquish his position. Stenographic report of the Bundestag for 10 November 1988; *Die Zeit*, 47 (18 November 1988), Politik, p. 7.

34. Jewish German Dance Theater, "But What about the Holocaust?" During the six-hour television series, broadcast in April and May of 1990, each episode opens with a full-screen image of Celan's face, then pans over death camps and monuments as his voice is heard reciting "Todesfuge" in its entirety.

35. Günter Heintz, "Paul Celans *Todesfuge*," *Blätter für den Deutschlehrer*, 14 (1970), 109–110.

16. "The Grave in the Air"

1. "Und ich finde hier, in dieser äusseren und inneren Landschaft, viel von den Wahrheitszwängen, der Selbstevidenz und der weltoffenen Einmaligkeit grosser Poesie." "Ansprache vor dem hebraïschen schriftstellerverband," Tel Aviv, 14 October 1969, in *Paul Celan: Gesammelte Werke*, III (Frankfurt am Main: Suhrkamp, 1983), p. 203; Eng. trans., Rosmarie Waldrop, *Paul Celan: Collected Prose* (New York: Sheep Meadow Press, 1986), p. 57.
2. Ibid.
3. "Cultural Criticism and Society," in *Prisms*, trans. Samuel and Shierry Weber (London: Neville Spearman, 1967), p. 34.
4. The "most important artists of the age" include such modernists as Kafka, Beckett, and Celan. See Ernst Bloch, Georg Lukács, Bertold Brecht, Walter Benjamin, Theodor Adorno, *Aesthetics and Politics*, trans. and ed. Ronald Taylor, afterword by Fredric Jameson (London: New Left Books, 1977), p. 188; T. W. Adorno, *Aesthetic Theory*, trans. C. Lenhardt (London: Routledge & Kegan Paul, 1970), pp. 352–354, 443–444; T. W. Adorno, *Prisms*, pp. 245–271.
5. See Sylvia Plath's poems in *Ariel*, William Styron's *Sophie's Choice*, D. M. Thomas's *White Hotel*, Fassbinder's *Lili Marlene*, and the controversies, which attended their publication, over the displacement of images or figures relating to the Nazi genocide.
6. "The differend is the unstable state and instant of language wherein something which must be able to be put into phrases cannot yet be . . . The silence that surrounds the phrase, *Auschwitz was the extermination camp* is . . . the sign that something remains to be phrased which is not, something which is not determined . . . The indetermination of meanings left in abeyance [*en souffrance*], the extermination of what would allow them to be determined, the shadow of negation hollowing out reality to the point of making it dissipate, in a word, the wrong done to the victims that condemns them to silence—it is this . . . which calls upon unknown phrases to link onto the name of Auschwitz." Jean-François Lyotard, *The Differend: Phrases in Dispute*, trans. Georges Van Den Abbeele, *Theory and History of Literature*, vol. 46 (Minneapolis: University of Minnesota Press, 1988), pp. 13, 56–57. In suggesting incommensurability, inarticulability, or excess, the "dissipation" that comes of extermination, the diffe-

rend may actually reinforce the idea of the propriety or the limits of symbolic as well as referential language.

7. Leo Bersani, *The Culture of Redemption* (Cambridge, Mass.: Harvard University Press, 1990), pp. 1–2.

8. Quoted by Richard Wolin in "Utopia, Mimesis, and Reconciliation: A Redemptive Critique of Adorno's *Aesthetic Theory*," *Representations* 32 (Fall 1990), 37.

9. T. W. Adorno, *Minima Moralia: Reflections from Damaged Life* (London: New Left Books, 1974), p. 247; for a discussion of utopianism in Adorno's thought, see also Martin Jay, *Adorno* (Cambridge, Mass.: Harvard University Press, 1984), p. 20.

10. Adorno, *Aesthetic Theory*, p. 444.

11. The photograph, taken during the Warsaw Ghetto uprising, is prominently displayed in an enormous blow-up in the museum at Yad Vashem in Jerusalem. (See the "Stroop Report," Nuremberg Documents P.S. 1061.)

12. On this charge and other questions of "literary provenance" see Chapter 15 by John Felstiner in the present volume and Felstiner's "Paul Celan's 'Todesfuge,'" *Holocaust and Genocide Studies*, 1, no. 2 (1986), 262–263.

13. See Felstiner, Chapter 15. Also see "Gedale's Song," by Primo Levi: "Our brothers have risen to the sky / Through the ovens of Sobibor and Treblinka / They have dug themselves a grave in the air." Trans. Ruth Feldman, *Tikkun*, 5, no. 5 (1990), inside cover.

14. Primo Levi, "On Obscure Writing," *Other People's Trades*, trans. Raymond Rosenthal (New York: Summit Books, 1989), pp. 173–174.

15. Ibid., p. 173.

16. Ibid. See Celan's comment on the "obscurity" of poetry in his "Meridian" speech: "This obscurity, if it is not congenital, has been bestowed on poetry by strangeness and distance (perhaps of its own making) and for the sake of an encounter." "The Meridian: Speech on the occasion of receiving the Georg Buchner Prize, Darmstadt, 22 October 1960," in *Paul Celan: Collected Prose*, p. 46.

17. The inherent loneliness of the literary process is embraced by Kafka in the same terms in which it is denied by Levi, withdrawal or separation being equated by both with a presuicidal condition: "What we need are books . . . that make us feel as though we had been banished to the woods, far from any human presence, like a suicide. A book must be the ax for the frozen sea within us." Quoted in Ernst Pawel, *The Nightmare of Reason* (New York: Farrar, Straus, and Giroux), p. 158.

18. See, for example, Levi's admission that the first edition of *Survival in Auschwitz* sold only 2,500 copies, and the somewhat disingenuous remark that after its publication, "I hardly thought about this solitary little book any more," followed by: "even if sometimes I burned to believe that the descent into hell had given me, as to Coleridge's Ancient Mariner, a

'strange power of speech.'" "Beyond Survival," *Prooftexts*, 4, no. 1 (1984), 15. Levi may be the most quoted writer in this volume—see for example Chapter 5 by Carlo Ginzburg. His bid for an objective position as purveyor of the reality of Auschwitz is generally taken at face value, and he is widely regarded as the quintessential "witness." See Irving Howe, introduction to Primo Levi, *If Not Now, When?* trans. William Weaver (New York: Summit Books, 1982), p. 9.

19. An alternative interpretation of both Levi's suicide and his last book is offered by Cynthia Ozick in "The Suicide Note," *The New Republic*, 21 March 1988, pp. 33–35.

20. Celan, "The Meridian," in *Collected Prose*, p. 51.

21. See, for example, Jean-François Lyotard, "Defining the Postmodern," in *Postmodernism: ICA Documents*, ed. Lisa Appignanesi (London: Free Association Books, 1989), pp. 7–10.

22. As one who not only is not a survivor of the Nazi genocide but is far removed from the culture about which he writes, Thomas's "borrowings" are highly conventionalized: he seeks access not to the reports of the atrocities, but to a specific genre of documentary narrative. On the "documentary novel" and the publishing history of *Babi Yar*, see my *By Words Alone: The Holocaust in Literature* (Chicago: University of Chicago Press, 1980), pp. 28–30. For a glimpse at the debate that ensued over the charge that D. M. Thomas plagiarized from *Babi Yar* in sections of *The White Hotel*, see "Letters to the Editor" in the *Times Literary Supplement*, 2 and 9 April 1982, and the symposium on "Plagiarism" vs. literary influence, with the participation of Harold Bloom and others, in the 9 April edition. See also James E. Young, *Writing and Rewriting the Holocaust: Narrative and the Consequences of Interpretation* (Indiana: Indiana University Press, 1988), pp. 53–59.

23. Felstiner, Chapter 15. Felstiner argues elsewhere that Celan himself, in response to aestheticized readings of "Todesfuge," attempted in his later poetry to concretize images that might otherwise be unmoored from their referential base. "Paul Celan's 'Todesfuge,'" p. 254.

24. Felstiner, Chapter 15.

25. See Lyotard, *The Differend*, pp. 97–106. See also Sande Cohen's discussion of his argument in "Between Image and Phrase: Progressive History and the Final Solution as Dispossession," Chapter 11 of this volume.

26. Andreas Huyssen explores the spectrum of responses to these paintings in "Anselm Kiefer: The Terror of History, the Temptation of Myth," *October*, 48 (Spring 1989), 24–45.

27. *The Deputy*, trans. Richard and Clara Winston (New York: Grove, 1964), p. 223. See *By Words Alone*, pp. 42–45.

28. Quoted from a statement made by Celan to his translator Michael Hamburger, in Katharine Washburn's introduction to *Paul Celan: Last Poems*,

ed. and trans. Washburn and Margret Guillemin (San Francisco: North Point Press, 1986), p. vi. Adorno, who described the "hermetic procedure" that allows art to "maintain its integrity only by refusing to go along with communication," was, of course, not the only critic to characterize Celan's poetry as hermetic. T. W. Adorno, *Aesthetic Theory* Appendix I, p. 443. See also Amy Colin, "Paul Celan's Poetics of Destruction," *Argumentum e Silentio: International Paul Celan Symposium*, ed. Amy D. Colin (Berlin: Walter de Gruyter, 1987), pp. 177–178.

29. Paul Celan, *Die Niemandsrose* (1963), from *Sprachgitter; Die Niemandsrose: Gedichte* (Frankfurt am Main: S. Fischer Verlag, 1986), p. 132.

30. Jacques Derrida, "Schibboleth," in *Argumentum e Silentio*, pp. 22, 24.

31. In Derrida's analysis of the poem "In Eins," the incomplete dating (13 February without a specific year) seems to establish historicity not as a limiting fact but as the status and symbolic complexity of reality, past and future. The multiplicity of possible witnesses and the indeterminate nature of this hour or this appointed time which can encapsulate the Spanish Civil War, the French-Algerian War, and of course the unmentioned war make this both an urgent and an open-ended poem. Ibid.

32. Evan Watkin, "Lyric Poetry as Social Language," in *Argumentum e Silentio*, p. 270. Celan's poetic transactions included translations from English, Hebrew, Russian, and German.

33. Hebrew is referred to as the *wahr gebliebene, wahr gewordene,* the language that has remained true, that has therefore become true. Felstiner, "'Ziv, that light': Translation and Tradition in Paul Celan," in *New Literary History,* vol. 18 (1986–1987), 630. See also his "Langue maternelle, langue eternelle: La présence de l'hebreu" in *Contre-Jour: Études sur Paul Celan,* ed. Martine Broda (Les Editions du Cerf), 1986.

34. Celan, "The Meridian," in *Collected Prose*, p. 50.

35. Stéphane Mosès, "Quand le langage se fait voix: Paul Celan: Entretien dans la montagne" in *Contre-Jour,* pp. 125–126.

36. See ibid., p. 126.

37. "Lamb's Lettuce and *Dianthus superbus*, the gillyflower, is not far away. But they, the first cousins, they have (it cries out to heaven) no eyes." *Paul Celan: Last Poems,* p. 208. Blindness to the specific flora, which calls attention parodically to the Jew's insulation from nature, serves also to reinforce the generic, legendary quality of the landscape.

38. "Speech on the Occasion of Receiving the Literature Prize of the Free Hanseatic City of Bremen," in *Paul Celan: Collected Prose,* p. 35.

39. "Conversation in the Mountain," in *Paul Celan: Collected Prose,* p. 17.

40. For a discussion of other poets from Bukovina who continued to write after the war, see Amy Colin, *Paul Celan* (Bloomington: Indiana University Press, 1991), chap. 1.

41. See my "Dan Pagis—Out of Line: A Poetics of Decomposition" in *Proof-*

texts, 10 (1990), 335–363; and "Shattering Memories," *The New Republic,* 25 February 1991, pp. 35–39.

42. See, for example, "How to" in Dan Pagis, *Variable Directions,* trans. Stephen Mitchell (San Francisco: North Point Press, 1989), p. 117.

43. Dan Pagis, *Points of Departure,* trans. Stephen Mitchell with an introduction by Robert Alter (Philadelphia: Jewish Publication Society, 1981), p. 23.

44. Berel Lang, *Act and Idea in the Nazi Genocide* (Chicago: University of Chicago Press, 1990), pp. 138–139.

45. Ibid., p. 139. "Aspen Tree" quoted from Paul Celan, *Poems,* trans. Michael Hamburger (New York: Persea, 1980).

46. Lang, *Act and Idea,* p. 139.

47. Ibid., p. 140.

48. Ibid., p. 139.

49. See Sutzkever's poem "Mother" in which the referent ("bullets") and the metaphor ("roses") both interchange with and undermine each other. *Burnt Pearls: Ghetto Poems,* trans. Seymour Mayne (Oakville: Mosaic Press, 1981), p. 27.

50. For a discussion of the pseudo-documentary status of "The Leaden Plates of Romm's Printing Works," see David Roskies, *After the Apocalypse: Responses to Catastrophe in Modern Jewish Culture* (Cambridge, Mass.: Harvard University Press, 1984), pp. 251–253, and Anita Norich, "Yiddish Poetry: Vilna to Tel Aviv, Lublin to New York," *University of Hartford Studies in Literature,* 18, nos. 2 and 3 (1987), 31.

51. See the poems "For a Comrade," "Mother," "For My Child," in *Burnt Pearls: Ghetto Poems,* pp. 25, 27, 32–33.

52. See Chapter 14 by Yael Feldman, in this volume. Perhaps the most striking example of this phenomenon is the novel *Ayen erekh 'ahava* (See Under: Love) by the Israeli writer David Grossman. At the center of this narrative is a preadolescent child of survivors growing up in Israel in the late 1950s among relatives and friends whose life narratives have been permanently dislocated by what is both unspeakable and irrecoverable. He is propelled by a desperate search for the untold tales that are every child's birthright. Through the public codes of belief and behavior to which he is exposed at school and in the culture at large he encounters a chronicle of reconstruction, heroism, political sovereignty and military prowess. The weight of this coherent ideological and mythical superstructure and the contending vacuum of absent memories are held in tenuous equilibrium by a daring act of synthesis whereby the boy weaves fragments of information into the Zionist ethos and forges a narrative that he can live with, even be proud of and, possibly, use to redeem his parents' ruptured lives: "All his detective work was geared at reordering, as in a puzzle, *That Country* [*eretz sham*] which had eluded them all . . . and he

is the only one who can do that, for only he can save his parents from their terror, from the silences, from the moans [*krechtzens*] and from the curse . . . [Here, then, is his narrative:] 'The Tzar galloped at the head on his trusty steed, and he was very full of glory and shot off his rifle in all directions. Sonder from the Commando covered him from the rear . . . [Later, nine-year-old Mumik] has already prepared a blue and white flag for *That Country*, and between the two blue stripes he has drawn a large *pulke* to which he has attached the rear fuselage of a Supermister [Israeli warplane], and at the bottom he has written: 'if you will it, it is not a dream.'" *Ayen erekh 'ahava*, my translation. See the English translation by Betsy Rosenberg (London: Jonathan Cape, 1990).

This act of literary re-creation is, in the Israeli context, daring not so much for its historical revisionism as for its undermining of the hegemony of the heroic construct in the Israeli narrative of Holocaust and Rebirth. Simultaneously empowering the victims and disempowering the heroes, Grossman, along with Pagis and a number of other contemporary Israeli writers, is rewriting not the history but the constitutive myth that underlies the social ethos.

53. See "Footprints," in Pagis, *Points of Departure*, pp. 28–37.
54. "Brothers," in Pagis, *Points of Departure*, p. 5. The translation I have given here is more literal than Mitchell's.
55. See my "Revisioning the Past: The Changing Legacy of the Holocaust in Hebrew Literature," *Salmagundi*, no. 68–69 (Fall 1985–Winter 1986), 245–270.
56. Steiner, *After Babel: Aspects of Language and Translation* (London: Oxford Press, 1975), p. 389. Quoted in Amy D. Colin, "Paul Celan's Poetics of Destruction" in *Argumentum e Silentio*, p. 172.
57. Ibid.
58. *Paul Celan: Last Poems*, p. xxvi.
59. Ibid., p. xxxv.

17. The Dialectics of Unspeakability

1. The historical text in question is an early version of Saul Friedlander, "The 'Final Solution': Unease in Interpretation," *History and Memory*, 1 (1989), 61–76, presented at a meeting of the UCLA Critical Theory Group in 1988; Himmler's Posen speech is the basis for the discussion of the "representability" of the Holocaust in this chapter.
2. Jacques Derrida, "Comment ne pas parler—Dénégations," in *Psyché* (Paris: Galilée, 1987), pp. 535–596.
3. Theodor Adorno, *Minima moralia*, trans. E. F. N. Jephcott (London: Verso, 1974), p. 152.
4. Gerd Kormen, "The Holocaust in American Historical Writing," in *Holo-*

caust: Religious and Philosophical Implications, ed. John K. Roth and Michael Berenbaum (New York: Paragon, 1989), p. 45, n. 1. Some of the references are to the Book of Job, which is entirely appropriate, since its topic is the (un)justifiability of what humans experience as divinely caused evil.

5. Compare Hilberg's comments in "I Was Not There," in *Writing and the Holocaust*, ed. Berel Lang (New York: Holmes & Meier, 1988), pp. 20–25, with his remarks in the concluding discussion on pp. 273–274.

6. Lucy Dawidowicz, *The War against the Jews, 1939–1945* (New York: Holt, Rinehart & Winston, 1975).

7. Hilberg, *Writing and the Holocaust*, p. 18.

8. The most telling accounts of these phenomena are those by Louis O. Mink and Hayden White. Mink's essays have been collected and published under the title *Historical Understanding* (Ithaca: Cornell University Press, 1987). The major works of Hayden White are *Metahistory* (1973), *Tropics of Discourse* (1978), and *The Content of the Form* (1987), all published by Johns Hopkins Press.

9. Emmanuel Levinas, *Totalité et infini: Essai sur l'extériorité*, 4th ed. (The Hague: Martinus Nijhoff, 1984), p. 10.

10. Emmanuel Levinas, "Signature (Nouvelle Version)," *Difficile liberté*, ed. Emmanuel Levinas, 3rd ed. (Paris: Albin Michel, 1976), p. 406.

11. Serious but amicable criticism of Levinas' treatment of history is to be found at the beginning of "Questions et réponses," *Le Nouveau Commerce*, 36, no. 6 (Spring 1977), 63–86. A greater sensitivity to the presence of history in Levinas is to be found in Jacques Derrida's early essay, "Violence et métaphysique. Essai sur la pensée d'Emmanuel Levinas," *L'écriture et la différence*, ed. Jacques Derrida (Paris: Seuil, 1967), pp. 117–228.

12. "Questions et réponses," p. 85.

13. "la responsabilité *illimitée* pour autrui," ibid., p. 65.

14. Levinas, "Signature (Nouvelle version)," p. 409.

15. Walter Benjamin, "Critique of Violence," *Reflections*, ed. Peter Demetz (New York: Harcourt Brace Jovanovich, 1978); the original text is "Zur Kritik der Gewalt," in volume I of *Gesammelte Schriften* (Frankfurt: Suhrkamp, 1955).

16. Document 1919-PS. The text appears in *Trial of the Major War Criminals before the International Military Tribunal, Nuremberg, 14 November 1945–October 1946* (New York: AMS Press, 1948), pp. 110–173. A partial translation is available in *A Holocaust Reader*, ed. Lucy T. Dawidowicz (New York: Behrman House, 1976), pp. 130–140. I have used this translation where possible, modifying it as necessary.

The text of the speech is one of the documents presented by the American prosecution in the trials of war criminals: it is labeled "Exhibit USA–

170." Although the English heading names it a speech of Himmler's, and although it is always referred to as such, the German-language description considers it a collection of various speeches ("*Sammlung verschiedener Reden*"), perhaps partial. The text is lengthy—more than sixty pages in the fairly small print of the record of the Nuremberg trials.

It is preceded by a brief notice, in English, printed in capital letters, listing the main topics to be discussed in the speech. There is no indication in this notice that the speech contains some of the most extraordinary comments on the Event. The English-language heading, due, presumably, to an American official, repeats, in the elision of its discourse, the extermination which is discussed in the speech, as if to provide a *mise-en-abyme* of literariness, a casting of the topic into the linguistic abyss of silence that parallels the extermination of the Jews in a nonlinguistic reality.

17. I am drawing here on standard concepts in narrative semiotics. Their technical definitions may be found in A. J. Greimas and J. Courtès, *Semiotics and Language: An Analytic Dictionary*, trans. L. Crist, D. Patte, et al. (Bloomington: Indiana University Press, 1982). I have discussed the appropriation of semiotics as a mode of historical interpretation in "Semiotics and History," *Semiotica*, 40 (1982), 187–228, and "Considérations théoriques sur la sémiotique socio-historique," in *Exigences et perspectives de la sémiotique*, ed. Herman Parret and Hans-Georg Ruprecht, 2 vols. (Amsterdam: John Benjamins, 1985), I, 215–228.

18. See the remarks of Lucy Dawidowicz, *Holocaust Reader*, pp. 13–16. Hilberg gives a list of coded terms in his *The Destruction of the European Jews*, student edition (New York: Holmes and Meier, 1985), pp. 133ff. The allegorical quality of the "evacuation" of the Jews as a code for their extermination may be an effect of history upon language. Earlier policy appears to have been, in fact, to rid the German body politic of the Jews considered as a vehicle of social disease by a mass evacuation outside the borders of the German state. What was perhaps originally a "literal" statement became a coded allegory when the name of the policy was retained in spite of a change in its content. See Heinz Höhne, *The Order of the Death's Head*, trans. Richard Barry (New York: Coward-McCann, 1970), pp. 324–353.

19. This rule of morality was doubled by economic interest. Living and dead, the Jews provided the Reich with wealth: "As long as the Jews were allowed to live, their labor was extracted without reward or mercy. After their deportation, the Germans expropriated their remaining goods" (Dawidowicz, *Holocaust Reader*, p. 147). After gassing, gold was extracted from the teeth of the victims. The state, prohibiting pilfering by individual soldiers, had wealth as well as morality at stake.

20. Insofar as other peoples seem to possess these qualities, they are deriva-

tive: the Czechs and Slovaks, for instance, "to whom we gave their sense of Nationality. They themselves were not capable of achieving it; we invented it for them."

21. Arno Mayer, *Why Did the Heavens Not Darken? The "Final Solution" in History* (New York: Pantheon, 1988), p. 90.

22. I am drawing here on the theory of ideology proposed by Louis Althusser in the article "Ideology and Ideological State Apparatuses (Notes towards an Investigation)," in *Lenin and Philosophy*, trans. Ben Brewster (New York: New Left Books, 1971), pp. 127–188. To a remarkable degree, the works of Michel Foucault represent so many transformations and variations on the fundamental notions of Althusser in this and related texts.

23. As such, this propensity is a kind of reaction to the other that has similarities to Levinas' radical ethical injunction, which would thus be seen as having its basis in human nature. Himmler's strategy would then be seen as designed to circumvent a "natural" human propensity, transformable into an ethical imperative and identified as an impediment by his narrative program, in order to achieve his bureaucratic aim.

24. See Friedlander, "The 'Final Solution,'" p. 68.

25. Mayer, *Why Did the Heavens Not Darken?* p. 376.

26. Höhne, *The Order of the Death's Head*, pp. 380–382.

27. Ibid., p. 387.

28. Such a view would allow for a broader historical conclusion of some importance, to the effect that the duality of Nazi power was "the expression, singular up to now, of a flow of ideas, emotions, and phantasms that are kept separate in all other modern Western societies": Saul Friedlander, *Reflections of Nazism: An Essay on Kitsch and Death,* trans. Thomas Weyr (New York: Harper & Row, 1984), p. 134. This answers the question of "relevance" raised by Friedlander elsewhere ("The 'Final Solution'"), by "making sense out of Nazism." The qualification of Nazism has been "singular up to now" in the conjunctions and sutures of semantic elements disjoined by the European tradition. This disregards, however, both the literary tradition of (post)modernism, and its theoretical counterpart, (post)structuralism.

Kenneth Burke, writing before World War II, noted on the basis of a rhetorical analysis of *Mein Kampf* the possible coexistence of sincerity as "the drastic honesty of paranoia" and the deliberation of shrewd, demagogic "*Realpolitik* of the Machiavellian sort": "The Rhetoric of Hitler's Battle," in *The Philosophy of Literary Form: Studies in Symbolic Action* (Baton Rouge: Louisiana State University Press, 1941), pp. 210ff.

29. Höhne, *The Order of the Death's Head*, p. 357; Yehuda Bauer, *The Holocaust in Historical Perspective*, pp. 47ff. Bauer notes that three of the four initial Einsatzgruppen were commanded by members of the intelligentsia, p. 15.

30. Höhne, *The Order of the Death's Head,* pp. 363ff. Their self-pity went as far as to claim that "the real unfortunates were the liquidators themselves." Ibid., p. 364.
31. Höhne, *The Order of the Death's Head,* p. 366.
32. Ibid., pp. 366ff. See also the discussion by Raul Hilberg, *The Destruction of the European Jews,* pp. 274–293.
33. Gitta Sereny, *Into the Darkness* (New York: McGraw-Hill, 1974), p. 101; cited by Terrence Des Pres, "Excremental Assault," in *Holocaust: Religious and Philosophical Implications,* pp. 210ff. An early account of techniques of desubjectification, though not named as such, will be found in Bruno Bettelheim's *Informed Heart* (New York: Free Press, 1960), especially in the chapter "Behavior in Extreme Situations: Coercion," pp. 107–176.
34. Mayer, *Why Did the Heavens Not Darken?*, pp. 16–19.
35. Friedlander, "The 'Final Solution,'" pp. 71–73.
36. Bauer, *The Holocaust in Historical Perspectives,* p. 47f.
37. It was not so much evil itself that was banalized in Auschwitz and the extermination camps, as its agents: the most ordinary persons were capable of the most evil acts.
38. "The 'uncanny' is that class of the terrifying which leads back to something long known to us, once very familiar." Sigmund Freud, "The Uncanny," in *On Creativity and the Unconscious,* ed. Benjamin Nelson (New York: Harper & Row, 1958), pp. 123ff.
39. Ozick, *Writing and the Holocaust,* pp. 280ff.
40. Bauer, *The Holocaust in Historical Perspective,* p. 36.
41. *Hammer on the Rock: A Short Midrash Reader,* ed. Nahum N. Glatzer (New York: Shocken Books, 1962), p. 38.
42. Bauer, *The Holocaust in Historical Perspective,* p. 52.
43. Ibid., p. 60.
44. Ibid., p. 77.

18. The Representation of Limits

1. Mary Douglas, *Purity and Danger* (Harmondsworth: Penguin, 1970), pp. 48, 53.
2. Leonardo da Vinci, *Treatise on Painting,* trans. A. Philip McMahon (Princeton: Princeton University Press, 1956), p. 50.
3. Heinrich Wölfflin, *Principles of Art History,* trans. M. D. Hottinger (New York: Dover, 1950), p. ix.
4. See, for example, Victor Shklovsky, "Art as Technique," in *Russian Formalist Criticism,* ed. Lee T. Lemon and Marion J. Reis (Lincoln: University of Nebraska Press, 1965), pp. 13–16.

5. Aristotle, *Metaphysics*, 1006a–1009a.
6. I. Kant, *Critique of Aesthetic Judgment*, sec. 28.
7. Fernand Braudel, *The Structures of Everyday Life*, vol. 1, trans. Sian Reynolds (New York: Harper & Row, 1982), p. 256.
8. On the role of language in the "Final Solution," see Berel Lang, *Act and Idea in the Nazi Genocide* (Chicago: University of Chicago Press, 1990), chaps. 1 and 4.
9. This proposal draws on Hayden White, "The Value of Narrativity in the Representation of Reality," *Critical Inquiry*, 7 (1980), 5–27—although I alter somewhat the relation White defines between "annals" and "chronicles."
10. On the issues of fact-finding and interpretation between the intentionalists and the functionalists, see, for example, the exchange between Saul Friedlander and Martin Broszat, "A Controversy about the Historicization of National Socialism," *New German Critique*, 44 (1988), pp. 81–126; Eberhard Jäckel, *Hitler in Germany* (Hanover, N.H.: University Press of New England, 1984), pp. 29–46; Christopher R. Browning, "The Decision concerning the Final Solution," in *Unanswered Questions*, ed. François Furet (New York: Schocken, 1989), pp. 96–118; and Charles S. Maier, *The Unmasterable Past* (Cambridge, Mass.: Harvard University Press, 1988).
11. Salman Rushdie, *Is Nothing Sacred?* (New York: Penguin, 1990).
12. The progression here will be evident: if historical representation entails moral limits, then the "imaginative" representation of a historical event will be affected by the limits on *both* historical and artistic representation. To be sure, it is not only in respect to historical subjects that the limits on artistic representation are pertinent. The commonplace that certain stylistic forms or genres are less or better able than others to accommodate certain subjects is a version of the claim made here that art as such may be less or better able than other expressive forms to represent certain subjects.
13. Theodor W. Adorno, "Engagement," in *Gesammelte Schriften* (Frankfurt am Main: Suhrkamp, 1974), p. 422; also in *Negative Dialectics*, trans. E. B. Ashton (New York: Seabury, 1973), p. 362.

19. The Book of the Destruction

1. Claude Lanzmann, in *Nouvelle Révue de Psychanalyse*, 38 (1988), 263. (In Levi's *Survival in Auschwitz* the context of this episode is a guard who snatches an icicle from the newly-arrived and extremely thirsty prisoner.) When Lanzmann, in his film, does ask why of Polish peasants in the scene before the church in Chelmno ("Pourquoi toute cette histoire est arrivée

aux Juifs?") the explanation of deicide surfaces collectively.

2. Jean-François Lyotard, *The Postmodern Condition: A Report on Knowledge* (Minneapolis: University of Minnesota Press, 1984), p. 78. It is interesting that Lyotard cites Diderot's half-fond, half-derogatory phrase, "ma petite technique."

3. Saul Friedlander, in *Writing and the Holocaust*, ed. Berel Lang (New York: Holmes and Meier, 1988), p. 68.

4. Jürgen Habermas, *Eine Art von Schadensabwicklung* (Frankfurt/Main, 1987), p. 163; in English, *The New Conservatism: Cultural Criticism and the Historians' Debate* (Cambridge, Mass., 1989).

5. For an authoritative overview of public opinion in Nazi Europe see Michael R. Marrus, *The Holocaust in History* (New York: New American Library, 1989).

6. For Lyotard's most incisive reflections on the differend in relation to Kant and in terms of reasoning, witnessing, and consensus, reflections in which Auschwitz plays a decisive part, see his work of 1983 translated as *The Differend: Phrases in Dispute* (Minneapolis: University of Minnesota Press, 1988).

7. Lawrence L. Langer, *Holocaust Testimony: The Ruins of Memory* (New Haven: Yale University Press, 1991).

8. In thinking about the testimonies as representations I have been helped by Hayden White's *Content of the Form: Discourse and Historical Representation* (Baltimore: Johns Hopkins University Press, 1987), esp. chap. 1.

9. Aharon Appelfeld, in *Writing and the Holocaust*, p. 86. Primo Levi did not begin to write until two years after his release from the camps, at least in part because of that same sense of unreality.

10. See Isaac Deutscher, "The Jewish Tragedy and the Historian," in *The Non-Jewish Jew and other Essays*, ed. Tamara Deutscher (London: Oxford University Press, 1968).

11. See Terrence Des Pres, "Holocaust Laughter?" in *Writing and the Holocaust*, ed. Berel Lang.

12. The question in this form is most sharply posed by Saul Friedlander, especially in "Historical Writing and the Holocaust" in Lang, *Writing and the Holocaust*, and "The 'Final Solution': Unease in Interpretation," *History and Memory*, 1, no. 2 (Fall/Winter 1989).

13. Terrence Des Pres, *Praises and Dispraises: Poetry and Politics, the Twentieth Century* (New York: Penguin Books, 1988), "Prolog."

14. Fortunoff Video Archive for Holocaust Testimonies (Yale), T-58.

15. See Czeslaw Milosz, *The Collected Poems, 1931–1987* (New York: Ecco Press, 1988). My attention was drawn to this poem by Robert Pinsky's essay in *Testimony: Contemporary Writers Make the Holocaust Personal*, ed. David Rosenberg (New York: Random House, 1989).

Contributors

Perry Anderson, Professor of History, University of California, Los Angeles

Mario Biagioli, Assistant Professor of History, University of California, Los Angeles

Christopher R. Browning, Professor of History, Pacific Lutheran University, Tacoma

Sande Cohen, teaches in the Critical Studies Department, California Institute of the Arts

Dan Diner, Professor of History, Tel-Aviv University and Universität Essen

Sidra DeKoven Ezrahi, Assistant Professor of Comparative Jewish Literature, Hebrew University of Jerusalem

Yael S. Feldman, Associate Professor of Hebrew and Comparative Literature, New York University

John Felstiner, Professor of English, Stanford University

Amos Funkenstein, University Professor, The Koret Chair of Jewish History, University of California, Berkeley

Carlo Ginzburg, Professor of History, University of California, Los Angeles

Peter Haidu, Professor of French, University of California, Los Angeles

Geoffrey H. Hartman, Professor of English and Comparative Literature, Yale University; Revson Project Director, Fortunoff Video Archive for Holocaust Testimonies at Yale

Martin Jay, Professor of History, University of California, Berkeley

Anton Kaes, Professor of German, University of California, Berkeley

Dominick LaCapra, Goldwin Smith Professor of European Intellectual History, Cornell University

Berel Lang, Professor of Philosophy and Humanistic Studies, State University of New York, Albany

Vincent P. Pecora, Associate Professor of English, University of California, Los Angeles

Eric L. Santner, Associate Professor of German, Princeton University

Hayden White, Professor of History of Consciousness, University of California, Santa Cruz

< 399 >

Index

Abel, 275

Abish, Walter: *How German Is It/Wie Deutsch Ist Es?*, 156

Abraham, Dr., 204, 376n63, 377n69

Adenauer, Konrad, 218

Adorno, Theodor W., 2, 4, 178, 228, 242, 250, 251, 259, 262, 267, 316, 322, 323, 359n13, 389–390n28; *Dialektik der Aufklärung* (with Max Horkheimer), 155, 163, 164, 165, 166–167, 168, 169; *Negative Dialectics*, 165, 207

Aeschylus, 328

Althusser, Louis, 156, 395n22

Améry, Jean, 244, 263

Anderson, Perry, 8, 353n35

Antoni, Carlo, 90; *Dallo storicismo alla sociologia*, 87

Apel, Karl-Otto, 105, 106

Appelfeld, Aharon, 17, 19, 229, 230–234, 270, 275, 321, 327, 383nn27,34; *Badenheim 'Ir Hanofesh*, 230, 231; *Be'et Ube 'onah 'Ahat*, 231, 232; *Hakootonet Vehapassim*, 231; *Hametzudah*, 231; *Ha'or Vehakootonet*, 231; *Ke'ishon Ha'ayin*, 230, 231; *Massot Begoof Rishon*, 383n27; *Michvat Ha'or*, 232, 233, 234, 383n28; *Ritzpat Ha'esh*, 231; *Tor Hapela'ot*, 230, 231, 383n28; *To the Land of Cattails*, 231

Arendt, Hannah, 26, 131, 132, 333

Aristotle, 303, 328, 332

Arnold, Gottfried, 73, 74, 79, 80

Auerbach, Erich, 50, 51; *Mimesis: The Representation of Reality in Western Literature*, 50

Augustine, 71, 72, 79, 80; *De Civitate Dei*, 71

B., Ernst, 377n69

Bach, Johann Sebastian, 241

Baeck, Leo, 347n19

Bakhtin, Mikhail, 341n9

Balzac, Honoré de: *Peau de chagrin*, 170

Barth, John: *The Literature of Exhaustion*, 220

Barthes, Roland, 47, 48–49, 51, 90; *Mythologies*, 371n46; "To Write: An Intransitive Verb?" 48, 342n23

Baudouin, François, 85

Baudrillard, Jean, 370n35

Bauer, Yehuda, 292

Beethoven, Ludwig van: "Ode to Joy," 219

Bellow, Saul: *Mr. Sammler's Planet*, 315

Benjamin, Walter, 157, 213, 284

Benn, Gottfried, 218

Bennington, G., 177

Benveniste, Emile, 96

Berger, Alan, 223, 224

Berger, Peter L., 71

Berger, Robert L., 376–377n67

Berlioz, Hector, 247

Bernal, John D., 186

Bersani, Leo, 261

Bettelheim, Bruno, 35, 191, 243

Beyerchen, Alan D., 192; *Scientists under Hitler*, 186–187

Biagioli, Mario, 14

Blake, William: "Shrine of the Imagination," 215

Blanchot, Maurice: *The Writing of the Disaster*, 207

Bloch, Marc, 340n18

Boccioni, Umberto, 94

Bochen, Yaakov, 227

Bohrer, Karl, 180

Bourdieu, Pierre, 195

Bracher, Karl Dietrich, 124

Braudel, Fernand, 305, 306

Brecht, Bertolt, 213, 222

Broszat, Martin, 33, 120, 121, 122–123, 124, 128, 148–149, 358n12

Browning, Christopher R., 4, 7, 8, 323, 364–365n17

Buber, Martin, 248

Bunyan, John, 242

Burckhardt, Jakob, 66

< 401 >